AMERICAN WOMEN
images and realities

AMERICAN WOMEN
Images and Realities

Advisory Editors
ANNETTE K. BAXTER
LEON STEIN

A Note About This Volume

Annie Nathan Meyer was 18 when, in 1885, she enrolled in the Collegiate Course for Women given by Columbia College. Required to read the textbooks and to take the same examinations as the men, she was handicapped by a rule that denied her the right to attend lectures. Her father had often declared that "men hate intelligent wives." But she believed that the vote for women, without equal education for women, was self-defeating. She undertook to raise money for a woman's college and to persuade the Columbia College trustees to approve it. On October 7, 1889 she witnessed the opening of Barnard College. Citing records of feminine achievement, the 18 contributors to this volume assail vestigial obstacles of propriety and patronizing resistance still blocking women's advance into the professions.

WOMAN'S WORK IN AMERICA

EDITED BY

ANNIE NATHAN MEYER

ARNO PRESS
A New York Times Company
New York • 1972

Reprint Edition 1972 by Arno Press Inc.

Reprinted from a copy in The Wesleyan University Library

American Women: Images and Realities
ISBN for complete set: 0-405-04445-3
See last pages of this volume for titles.

Manufactured in the United States of America

- - - - - - - - - - - - - - -

Library of Congress Cataloging in Publication Data

Meyer, Annie (Nathan) 1867-1951, ed.
Woman's work in America.

(American women: images and realities)
Bibliography: p.
1. Woman--Employment--United States. I. Title.
II. Series.
HD6095.M46 1972 331.4'0973 72-2615
ISBN 0-405-04469-0

WOMAN'S WORK IN AMERICA

EDITED BY

ANNIE NATHAN MEYER

WITH AN INTRODUCTION

BY

JULIA WARD HOWE

NEW YORK
HENRY HOLT AND COMPANY
1891

EDITOR'S PREFACE.

To Mr. Theodore Stanton, the editor of "The Woman Question in Europe," I hasten to acknowledge my indebtedness. After reading that interesting book it occurred to me that a volume on the work of women in America could be made equally valuable and interesting.

In the spring of 1888, therefore, I began to collect the necessary material. Naturally it was not possible, nor did it seem desirable, to follow the exact lines of Mr. Stanton's work. In his book, each chapter is devoted to a different country, and the woman question therein is treated by the author of the chapter in all of its aspects.* It seemed best, on the contrary, to divide the American history as nearly as possible into as many chapters as there are phases of woman's work. The task of selecting as collaborators eighteen women, where so many brilliant women abound, was a very difficult one; I need say nothing in defense or explanation of my choice, however, but am satisfied to let the work done speak for itself.

But before the task of selecting the contributors came that of dividing the whole great field of woman's work. Here I can only bow my head before the flood of criticism that is bound to bear down upon me. I suppose it is inevitable that to many it will seem that undue importance has been accorded to one subject, and too little to another. I can but plead that in no case have I allowed myself to be influenced by prejudice, but only by the best judgment I was capable of bringing to bear. On mentioning this book to a well-known editor and poet (a man), I was gravely asked why I had omitted a chapter on "Woman in Marriage," as it would make a very readable and certainly a very prolific subject. My answer was that so far as I knew women had never been denied that privilege, and so it could have no legitimate place in my book. In that

* With the exception of the chapter on England, which is divided into three parts.

reply, although uttered lightly, lies the principle upon which I have worked; the fields of labor described here contain evidences of woman's progress; they are those in which women, if entrance were not absolutely denied them, were at least not welcomed, nor valued. Furthermore, they are phases of woman's work that have some direct bearing on the status of woman in this country.

And now a word on the object of the book, for many will shrug their shoulders and say: "Why separate *work* into *man's* work and *woman's* work? What is gained by this division? Why not be content with the simple word *work?* Is it not sufficient to be a factor in the world's growth, or must the ages keep a constant reckoning of *meum* and *tuum?*"

If the time has come when the word work is a neuter noun, I admit that the value of this book would be reduced; but even then I think it might justly claim a historical value, a value as a history of the struggle on woman's part to have her work accepted just as a "factor in the world's growth," judged on its own merits, not

> Mere woman's work,
> Expressing the comparative respect
> Which means the absolute scorn.

But aside from the value of the book as a record, it claims a value as an inspiration to greater effort; for in our eyes the time has not yet come when all effort should cease. The arguments against the development of woman have been many, and although centuries have passed, the changing years merely ring different tones upon the same theme. We may acknowledge that the day is past when it is necessary seriously to plead the capacity of woman to accomplish certain things; that victory has been won with tears of blood; but the fight still centers about the propriety of it. The large band of ignorant and prejudiced objectors is fast giving place to another of a more kindly, but more dangerous type. More dangerous because instead of employing the weapons of disdain, they use those of homage; instead of goading with scorn, they disarm with the incense of a false and hollow sentimentality. This new wave of feeling divides Life into Intellect and Emotion, the Mind and the Heart, Matter and Soul, etc., the one man, woman the other. These sentimentalists, who certainly include as many women as men, argue that every woman is the natural companion of man, and so is upheld by some strong shoulder. When faced by the awful statistics of unmarried females in the United States, they fall back on some hypothetical father, brother, or cousin. Therefore it is considered highly supererogatory that a woman should be taught to stand upon her own feet, when the adjacent shoulder answers the purpose as well. This belief holds its own with a peculiar tenacity, because there is a certain heroic satisfaction in retaining your sentiment notwithstanding all the arguments that can be brought forward by the low materialists.

This book is nothing else than a history of woman's slow, but sure, training to stand balanced upon her own feet. She has looked about upon the thousands of falling sisters, and has very reasonably reached the conclusion that the only way to make sure of standing is to make use of her own feet.

Women have many so-called champions of their "purity," and "innocence;" champions that are shocked at opening so many new fields of "man's work" to women; but they are strangely ignorant of the very real contamination to which they expose their *protegés* by crowding them into the few already overcrowded channels, and refusing to let in fresh air and sunshine. Men and women both are born into the world helpless and unprotected; it may seem an ugly and bitter truth, but it is so, that in this struggle for existence daily going on about us, men and women do indeed stand "side by side,"—not, as with the poet,

Full summed in all their powers,

but each individually carrying on a struggle against suffering, starvation, crime, and death,—forces that remorselessly attack women, barren of the chivalrous regard of sex with which these sentimentalists seem to grace them.

And if it is true that both sexes fight the same battle for existence, who can honestly deny to women (at present physically the weaker), the best possible equipment that education of all kinds can furnish? I shall not even touch upon the other, and more poetic, argument of the divine rights of genius, which is of no sex; but I am content to employ only the prosaic one of the practical needs of life, an argument which here in America is by far the most potent one.

My own labors on this book have been purely editorial; and after selecting the chapters, and the authors, and laying down certain general principles and suggestions, my responsibility ceased. The principles laid down by me have been:

Facts and history rather than eloquence;

Truth before picturesqueness;

A total absence of railing against the opposite sex.*

The greatest care has been taken to assure accuracy; if mistakes do creep in, notwithstanding this, I must beg the reader not to judge too harshly, as the capacity for making mistakes in a book like this is illimitable. However, I trust the leniency of the reader will not be too severely taxed.

While being an ardent believer in the future progress of woman, it would be impossible to subscribe myself to every theory that may be found in these pages. To say one agrees in every detail with the opinions of eighteen women, all of whom are well known to be "women with opinions," is to boast of a breadth of mind, a roundness of judgment to which I am too modest to lay claim. But I can surely say that every one of the writers has cordially joined hands in the making of the book; the long hours spent in the writing of it, the many annoyances encountered in collecting historical data, all is forgotten in the hope that this book may serve:

1. To set certain plain facts, shorn of all sentiment, before the world in accessible form;

2. To preserve the record of a great, brave, and essentially American struggle;

3. To serve as a stimulus to many women who are working along a very weary road;

4. To hold up before the entire sex in every sphere of life only the highest standard of excellence.

In closing, I want to thank heartily, not only my collaborators, but also those whose names do not appear, but who have, nevertheless, added greatly to the interest and value of the book.

ANNIE NATHAN MEYER.

NEW YORK, *January*, 1891.

* I do not mean for an instant to imply that these principles required emphasizing.

CONTENTS.

I.

INTRODUCTION.

BY

JULIA WARD HOWE.

A COMPREHENSIVE view of the attainments made by American women in this century, and especially during the last fifteen years, cannot but be of great importance and value. The cruel kindness of the old doctrine that women should be worked for, and should not work, that their influence should be felt, but not recognized, that they should hear and see, but neither appear nor speak,—all this belongs now to the record of things which, once measurably true, have become fabulous.

The theory that women should not be workers is a corruption of the old aristocratic system. Slaves and servants, whether male or female, always worked. Women of rank in the old world were not necessarily idle. The eastern monarch who refused an army to a queen, sent her a golden distaff. The extremes of despotism and of luxury, undermining society and state, can alone have introduced the theory that it becomes the highly born and bred to be idle. With this unnatural paralysis of woman's active nature came *ennui*, the bane of the so-called privileged classes. From *ennui* spring morbid passions, fostered by fantastic imaginations. A respect for labor lies at the very foundation of a true democracy.

The changes which our country has seen in this respect, and the great uprising of industries among women, are then not important to women alone, but of momentous import to society at large. The new activities sap the foundation of vicious and degraded life. From the factory to the palace the quickening impulse is felt, and the social level rises. To the larger intellectual outlook is added the growing sympathy of women with each other, which does more than anything else to make united action possible among them. A growing good will and esteem of women toward women makes itself happily felt and will do even more and more to refine away what is harsh and unjust in social and class distinctions and to render all alike heirs of truth, servants of justice.

The initiative is now largely taken by women in departments in which they were formerly, if admitted at all, entirely and often unwillingly under the dictation of men. Philanthropists of both sexes, indeed, work harmoniously together, but in their joint undertakings the women now have their say and, instead of waiting to be told what men would have them think, feel obliged to think for themselves. The result is not discord but a fuller and freer harmony of action and intention. In industrial undertakings they still have far to go, but women will enter more and more into them and with happy results. The professions indeed supply the key-stone to the arch of woman's liberty. Not the intellectual training alone which fits for them, but the practical, technical knowledge which must accompany their exercise puts women in a position of sure defense against fraud and imposition.

In the volume now given to the public the progress of women in all of these departments is presented by persons who have made each of them a special study, and who have done good and helpful work in them, with, moreover, the outlook ahead which is the important element in all labor and service. The world, even the American world, is not yet wholly converted to the doctrine of the new womanhood. Men and women who prize the ease of the *status quo*, and the imaginary importance conferred by exemption from the necessities which prompt to active exertion, often show great ignorance of all that this book is intended to teach. They will aver, men and women of them, that women have never shown any but secondary capacities and qualities. Women who take this ground often secretly flatter themselves that what they thus say of other women does not apply to themselves. A speaker representing this class lately asked at a legislative hearing in Massachusetts why women did not enter the professions? why they did not become healers of the sick, ministers, lawyers? One might ask how he could escape knowing that in all of these fields, so lately opened to them, women are doing laborious work and with excellent results? A book like the present will furnish chapter and verse to substantiate what is claimed for the attainments of women. It will not, indeed, put an end to foolish depreciative argument, based upon erroneous suppositions, but it will furnish evidence to confute calumny, to convince the doubtful.

II.

THE EDUCATION OF WOMAN IN THE EASTERN STATES.

BY

MARY F. EASTMAN.

THE movement in behalf of the education of youth in America followed so closely upon the landing of the colonists on an unsettled and forbidding coast, and was continued so persistently and so successfully, under stress of poverty and peril, that it seizes upon the imagination, and justly stirs a profound sense of gratitude in succeeding generations.

That in its inception, and for a long period, it was but a partial, in fact, but a half movement, after all, appears only in the light of a later day; which, indeed, it had helped to kindle,—when the words, "children," "youth," and "people" began to take a wider significance.

The men who gathered in the cabin of the "Mayflower" in 1620, and framed a compact that every man in the colony should have an equal share in the government, soon assembled to promote the general welfare by encouraging industry in the young.

In 1642, the General Court of Mass. Bay Colony charged itself with "taking account, from time to time, of all parents and masters concerning the calling and employment of their children, especially of their ability to read and understand the principles of religion and the capital laws of this country."

In 1647, says the record, "It being one cheife piect of yt ould deluder Satan to keepe men from the knowledge of ye Scriptures . . . . by psuading them from ye use of tongues, that so at least ye true sense and meaning of ye originall might be clouded . . . . and that learning may not be buried in ye graves of our fathers. . . . . It is therefore ordered tht evry township in this jurisidiction, after ye Lord hath increased ym to ye number of 50 householders, shall therforthwth appoint one to teach all such children as shall resort to him to write and read, whose wages shall be paid eithr by ye parents or mastr, or by ye inhabitants in generall. . . . . It is ordered yt where any towns shall increase to ye number of 100 familis or householders, they shall set up a gramer schoole, ye mr thereof being able to instruct youth so far as they may be fitted for ye university." A penalty of £5 was fixed for violation of this order.

As early as in 1636, the Court "agreed to give £400 toward a school or college," to which, in 1638, John Harvard left, by will, half his property and his library. In 1642, the Court gave to the college "the revenue of the ferry from Charlestown to Boston."

1644, "It is ordered vt ye deputies shall command it to ye severall towns (and ye elders are to be desired to give their furtherance hereto)" . . . . that "Evry family alow one peck of corne, or 12d. in money or other commodity to be sent in to ye Treasurer, for the colledge at Cambridge."

1650, voted that, "Whereas, through the good hand of God, many have been stirred to give for the advancement of all good literature, arts, and sciences in Harvard Colledge—and for all other necessary pvsions that may conduce to the education of ye English and Indian youth of this country in knowledge and godlynes, ordered—tht a corporation be formed, consisting of seauen psons."

Revenues of the college and of the president to the extent of 500 were exempt from taxation, while special exemptions from rates, and military and civil duties, were made to officers, fellows, scholars, and even the servants of the college.

This oldest college of the country was, as thus appears, the child of the State, and while it was the recipient of private benefactions, drew its sustenance, substantially, from the labors of the people.

1683, voted that, "Every towne consisting of more than five hundred families shall set up and maintayne two grammar schools, and two wrighting scholes to instruct youth as the law directs."

So cordial was the interest felt in education among the colonists, that many towns had established free schools before it was required.

Within a year of the founding of Boston, in 1635, the citizens in town meeting assembled, voted to call a schoolmaster, and "Philemon Purmont was engaged to teach the children." Dorchester, Naumkeag (now Salem), Cambridge, Roxbury, and other towns soon took the same course. Salem established a grammar school as early as 1637. Thus, within twenty years from the landing of the Pilgrims at Plymouth, the foundation of the free-school system may be said to have been laid. It was frequently stipulated in the action of town meetings, that the poor should be provided for, and in Boston, at least, Indian children were freely taught. But in the provisions for "free schools," "schools for the people," and the "children," it is not to be understood that girls were included. The broad terms used in the acts of the colonies and the votes of town meetings might mislead, in this respect, if history did not record the periods, long subsequent, when girls were admitted even to the "free schools" under restrictions, usually with great opposition.

This long hiatus, during which girls went, practically, without free-school opportunities, picking up what they might at home, or by aid of the parish minister, was about a century and a half long, though in 1771, Hartford, Conn., opened its common schools to every child, and taught even the girls reading, writing, spelling, and the catechism, and, rarely, how to add. The boys, meantime, studied the first four rules of arithmetic.

The hiatus between the foundation for the college for boys and even the seminary, or the academy, for girls, extended over a long century and a half; and that between colleges for males and those for females was, in Massachusetts, two hundred and thirty-two years long. A prime motive to the encouragement of education in America was that the Scriptures might be properly interpreted. This appears in the preamble to the vote of 1647 establishing schools, which were necessary as tributary to the college, and in the motive which led to the foundation of Harvard and of Yale, "the dread of having an illiterate ministry to the churches when our ministers shall lie in dust."

It has been noted by Charles Francis Adams that "the records of Harvard University show that of all the presiding officers, during the century and a half of colonial days, but two were laymen, and not ministers of the prevailing denomination; and that of all who in the early times availed themselves of such advantages as this institution could offer, nearly half the number did so for the sake of devoting themselves to the service of the gospel. But," he continues, "the prevailing notion of the purpose of education was attended with one remarkable consequence,—the cultivation of the female mind was regarded with utter indifference; as Mrs. Abigail Adams says in one of her letters, 'it was fashionable to ridicule female learning.'"

This discrimination between the intellectual needs of the two sexes should not, perhaps, be matter of surprise, when we consider that the English system of public schools for boys, extending from the "Winchester School" to "Rugby," had been in existence for two centuries, and that of the six hundred who first landed on the coast of Massachusetts, one in thirty was a graduate from the English University of Cambridge, while both the men and the women were heirs to the prevailing sentiment of disrespect for womanly intelligence and education, which marked the demoralization of the reign of the Stuarts in England.

The time of Queen Elizabeth has passed, in which the noble Lady Jane Grey, being asked by Sir Roger Ascham why she lingered to read Plato in Greek while the lords and ladies of the Court were pleasuring in the park, replied, "I wist all their sport in the park is but a shadow to the pleasure I find in Plato. Alas! good folk, they never felt what true pleasure meaneth."

Lady Mary Wortley Montague truly portrayed the time, when she wrote, early in the eighteenth century: "We are permitted no books but such as tend to the weakening and effeminating our minds. We are taught to place all our art in adorning our persons, while our minds are entirely neglected."

It might have been expected that the religious zeal which brought these earnest New England pilgrims to a strange, wild country, would hold in check any tendency to undue display, especially when supplemented by the severe restrictions of their domestic life, which were relieved only by compulsory attendance on protracted services, held in unwarmed churches, to listen to metaphysical sermons on foreordination, reprobation, and infant damnation, and to prayers an hour long.

Yet it appears that while no provision was made for their instruction, they were sometimes arraigned for wearing "wide sleeves, lace tiffany, and such things," while "those given to scolding were condemned to sit publicly, with their tongues held in cleft sticks, or were thrice dipped from a ducking-stool."

It would have been better, perhaps, that their tongues had been trained by instruction to becoming speech, or that they had been permitted to drink at the fountain of learning.

Sentiment in favor of the practical skill of women seems not to have been wanting. They cooked and washed, and the law required them to spin and gather flax, and on one notable occasion women exhibited their skill at the spinning wheel, publicly, on Boston Common. As soon as they could get around to it they no doubt matched the skill of their English kindred whom Hollingshed described a half century earlier. He says, " The females knit or net the nets for sportsmen :

> " 'Fine ferne stitch, finny stitch, new stitch, and chain stitch,
> Brave broad stitch, fischer stitch, Irish stitch, and queen stitch,
> The Spanish stitch, rosemary stitch and mowse stitch;
> All these are good, and these we must allow,
> And these are everywhere in practice now.' "

Aside from their belief in the primary importance of religious training, it may be conceded that the men of colonial times did not lack the sagacity which led Charlemagne in the eighth century to require that the children of those who were to participate in the government should be educated, " in order that intelligence might rule the Empire." The application of this principle in his limited empire opened education to the ruling class ; in America it opened it to the ruling sex.

How small were the opportunities for instruction, outside the free schools, may be known from the fact that the committee for supervising them enjoined upon the selectmen to take care that no person should open a private school except upon their recommendation.

In 1656 a Mr. Jones having opened a private school was visited by the magistrates, who exacted a promise from him to give up the school at the close of the winter term. Apparently he was reluctant in so doing, for it is recorded that the next spring Mr. Jones was sent for by the selectmen " for keeping a Schoole, and required to perform his promise to the Towne in the Winter, to remove himselfe and familye in the Springe, and forbiden to keep Schoole any longer."

The first opportunities for girls in the colonies were in the " Dame-School," in which some woman was hired to gather the little children about her knee to teach them their letters from the New England Primer. They were required to commit to memory the shorter catechism, and sometimes were taught to read enough to decipher it for themselves, from the last pages of their only book, the famous Primer. Training in manners was made of prime importance.

In some cases, as is reported, old women who were a town charge were set to this useful employment. Sometimes these " dames " were housewives, in which case two frequently alternated in caring for the children. In this way, according to the town records of Woburn, in 1635, "Joseph Wright's wife and Allen Converse's wife were able to divide between them £0. 10s. 0d., for a year's work. It is to be inferred that the acquirements of these mistresses were limited, as the next year, October, 1674, the town "agreed with Jonathan Tomson to tech bigger children and Allen Converse's wife to teach leser children."

In the old graveyard in Cambridge, opposite Harvard College, it is recorded that Mrs. Murray died 1707, aged sixty-two years. The title "Mrs." was honorary, as she was unmarried. This betokens the esteem in which she was held, as does the following inscription upon her tombstone:

"This good school dame
No longer school must keep,
Which gives us cause
For children's sake to weep."

Later, especially in the old seaport towns, the children's schools, for girls as well as for boys, were frequently in the hands of women of much refinement. Of such, Miss Hetty Higginson, of Salem, was famous as an instructor about 1782. The record says that, "being asked what she taught, she laughingly replied, 'ethics,' yet to a superficial observer it might seem that she taught nothing. Her manners were courtly, and her conversation was replete with dignity, kind feeling, and sound sense."

Some improvement upon this state of education, or want of education rather, gradually crept in; whether because of the need of teachers for the boys, which had come to be felt, or because in the home there was much early association of the child with the mother, and so some education on her part might prove indirectly advantageous, or whether there was some dawning consideration of her own personal needs, it is impossible to determine. Perhaps there was difficulty in withholding other books from the girl after she could read the catechism, or, later, in drawing a sharp line between the acquisition of the first and the second rule in arithmetic.

Suffice it that by the close of the eighteenth century, most towns in New England had made some slight provisions for educating girls; how slight, almost any early town history will show.

The rate of progress in a thriving Massachusetts town, Newburyport, is given in Smith's History, as follows: ". . . . When speaking of schools we must be understood as referring to boys' schools only." So far as education of females by the town was concerned they were sadly deficient. As late as 1790, a proposition to provide schools for girls was put aside without action, by the town, and deferred for another year, and when they did set about the work it is curious to note of how little consequence they considered it as compared with the provision to be made for boys.

At first three or four schools were suggested for girls between five and nine years of age, which were "to be furnished with dames to learn them good manners and proper decency of behavior." These were the essentials, but in addition they were to be taught "spelling and reading sufficient to read the Bible, and, if the parents desired it, needlework and knitting." . . . . The sessions of the school were to be from April to October. . . . . But a later petition being presented to the town, that some arrangement might be made for the instruction of girls over nine years of age, the town graciously voted, March, 1792, that "during the summer months, when the boys in the school had diminished, the master shall receive girls for instruction in grammar and reading, after the dismission of the boys, for an hour and a half."

Even to this poor privilege there were limitations. No person paying a tax of over three hundred pounds was permitted to send his daughters to these supplementary schools. But the scheme for the larger girls did not work well for the boys, so the masters were directed "not to teach females again."

As late as 1804 we find the female children, over nine years of age, as great a burden on the hands of the school committee of the town as ever. In answer to another petition, of eleven persons, that this class of girls might be taught, by the town, arithmetic and writing, four girls' "schools were established, to be kept six months in the year, from six to eight o'clock in the morning, and on Thursday afternoons." So that, in addition to their other accomplishments, they were in a fair way of being taught early rising.

It was not until 1836 that the school committee decreed "that one female grammar school be kept through the year." This is probably the time of which it is recorded "that, when a school was started for girls in Newburyport, a taxpayer objected to it, and applied for an injunction, bringing out Judge Shaw's celebrated opinion on that point." (Cushing *vs.* Newburyport.)

In 1788 the town of Northampton voted "not to be at any expense for schooling girls." Upon an appeal to the courts the town was indicted and fined for its neglect. In 1792 it voted "to admit girls, between eight and fifteen, to the schools from May 1 to October 31.

Within the memory of a recent resident of Hatfield, an influential citizen, whose children were girls, appealed in town-meeting for the privilege of sending them to the public school, which he helped by his taxes to support. An indignant fellow townsman sprang to his feet and exclaimed, "Hatfield school *shes?* Never!"

The gentleman who narrated this fact lived to witness, also, the foundation and endowment of a college for girls at Northampton by Miss Smith of Hatfield, one of the sex, and probably one of the girls contemptuously forbidden a common-school education.

For a long time after summer schools were provided for girls, in many of the New England towns they were not supported, by a general tax, as were the winter schools for boys, but by tuition fees.

Josiah Quincy, in his "Municipal History of Boston," says "After the peace of 1783, a committee on schools 'laments that so many children should be found in the streets, playing and gaming in school hours.'" There seems as yet to be no search for girls who are losing school advantages.

In 1789 great educational advance was made in Boston. A system was adopted which provided "a 'Latin School' for fitting boys of ten years old and over, by a four years' course, including Greek and Latin, for the University; also three reading and writing schools."

Boys had the right to attend these all the year round; girls from the twentieth of April to the twentieth of October. This was the first admission of girls to the "free schools."

Provision was made this year that "arithmetic, orthography, and the English language shall be taught, in addition to reading and writing." It is to be hoped that this applied to the summer sessions, open to girls, as well as to the all-the-year-round sessions for boys.

When, however, early in the nineteenth century, arithmetic and geography were generally added to the courses of studies in schools, it was only for the winter months, such knowledge being thought quite unnecessary for girls. "All a girl needs to know is enough to reckon how much she will have to spin to buy a peck of potatoes, in case she becomes a widow," was the repulse of a too ambitious girl in the early part of this century.

An old lady, sitting beside the present writer, well remembers that in her youth, having outreached the prescribed limits of the girl's class in arithmetic, she grappled alone with the mysteries of "interest." Meeting some difficulty she appealed to her older brother, who had been duly instructed. His scornful reply was, "I am ashamed of a girl who wants to study 'interest'!"

The need of more teachers led gradually to the employment of women in "those schools where, besides morals, the only requirements were reading, sewing, and writing if contracted for."

In the law of 1789 the expression "master and mistress" makes recognition of women as teachers for the first time. Hitherto women so employed could not legally collect their wages; the receipt of their dues depended upon the honor of their employers.

This act of justice may have been the more appreciated as the wages of female teachers were evidently on a rising scale. Something less than a half century after Mistresses Wright and Converse had shared their year's income of ten shillings, the following vote, passed in the town meeting of Lexington, shows an increased estimate of women's services:

"At a meeting of the inhabitants, July 21, 1717, they agreed that Clerk Lawrence's wife and Ephraim Winship's wife keep school from ye day of ye date hereof until ye last day of October next following; and if they have not scholars sufficient as to numbers to amount to five shillings a week, at three pence a scholar a week, then ye towne to make up what is wanted of ye five shillings out of the treasury thereof; provided ye selectmen do not see cause to demolish sd schole before sd term be expired."

Probably no deductions from the above specified wages were necessary for living expenses, which these mistresses of households may be supposed to have earned in their duties at home. When, in the course of the succeeding century, wages increased to seventy-five cents or even to a dollar a week, the teacher was expected to "board around," though sometimes her board in one place was paid for from public funds. In the latter case, in many New England towns, the privilege of boarding the teacher, like that of boarding town paupers, was put up for public competition, and was struck off to the lowest bidder.

Up to 1828 girls did not go to the public schools in Rhode Island.

Antedating the earliest records here transcribed is the claim made that the first free school in America was made in Virginia in 1621. If so it struck no root, for, in 1671, Bishop Berkely, Governor of Virginia, wrote, "I thank God there are no free schools nor printing; and I hope we shall not have them these hundred years." It was one hundred and seven years later, in 1778, that Thomas Jefferson introduced a bill in the Virginia legislature, designed to establish a system of public schools in that State, arguing that "the greatest sacrifice the people of the republic can make will fail to secure civil liberty to their posterity unless they provide for the education of youth."

In the Dutch settlement of Manhattan a movement for schools was made which proved more successful than in Virginia, as befitted its source in the Netherlands, where, since the sixteenth century, "the fruitfulness of a wise and state-administered system of universal education" had been illustrated.

In 1630, the States-General of Holland issued orders to the Dutch East India Company in Manhattan to maintain a clergyman and a schoolmaster, and in 1633 arrived Adam Roelandsen, and the first school-tax ever levied in America was imposed on each householder and inhabitant. So Brooklyn had the first free public school in the United States. Until 1808, this school was in charge of the local congregation of the Dutch Reformed church; then a board of trustees was appointed. This school still continues.

In 1658, the Burgomasters petitioned for a fit person as Latin schoolmaster. This was granted, and so the first classical school was instituted.

Since it is time that the day of jubilation and self-gratulation should be over in America, and that the day of sober, earnest study of educational work should come in, it is not the part of wisdom to forget that the free school system did not originate in America. In an address to magistrates, in 1524, Luther urged that they should "at least provide the poor suffering youth with a schoolmaster": and what "youth" meant to Luther appears in his plea that "solely with a view to the present, it would be sufficient reason for the best schools, both for boys and girls, that the world, merely to maintain outward prosperity, has need of shrewd and accomplished men and women."

In Manhattan, the successor of Adam Roelandsen found time, outside his duties as teacher, to act as gravedigger, bell-ringer, and precentor"; but if in place of these extra-official duties, the colonists had so profited by the wisdom of Luther as to cause him to take time for the instruction of girls, we may well believe that it would have changed the history of education in America.

Mr. Richard G. Boone reminds us, in his valuable work on "Education in the United States," that "Charles and Gustavus Adolphus did for Sweden and their generations what America, with all her achievements, has failed to do since; they made education so common that in the year 1637, the year of the founding of Harvard, not a single peasant child was unable to read and write."

There is pathetic contrast too, if it be fair to draw it, in the fact that while the colonial fathers were barricading the doors of the little schoolhouses against girls, so that a large part of the wills which women made in that period were signed with a cross, and even many wives of distinguished men could not sign their names, as appears by the registered deeds of the time, an Italian woman, Elena Lucrezia Cornaro, "poet, musician, astronomer, mathematician, and linguist," received a Dr.'s degree at the university of Padua, and Novela d'Andrea, who was both learned and beautiful, occasionally lectured for her father, who was a law professor in the University of Bologna. To be sure, this was in line with a tradition in Italy for which England herself could furnish no parallel.

In that ancient seat of learning, Bologna University, which produced the most famous jurisconsults of the middle ages, women had been for centuries both students and professors.

Bettisia Gozzidini, LL.D., filled the juridical chair from 1239 till her death in 1249; Bettina and Novella Calderini lectured on law a century later; and in succeeding centuries other women became renowned in various departments, including mathematics and anatomical research.

To fill the pages of two centuries, blank, in America, as to female education beyond the merest rudiments of learning, let Abigail, wife of President John Adams, who was descended from the most illustrious colonial families, the Shepards, Nortons, and Quincys, sketch for us the intellectual opportunities for girls of her own rank in her time. Born in 1744, she wrote, in 1817, when past threescore and ten:

"The only chance for much intellectual improvement in the female sex was to be found in the families of the educated class, and in occasional intercourse with the learned of the day. Whatever of useful instruction was received in the practical conduct of life came from maternal lips: and what of farther mental development, depended more upon the eagerness with which the casual teachings of daily conversation were treasured up, than upon any labor expended purposely to promote it. Female education in the best families went no farther than writing and arithmetic, and, in some few and rare instances, music and dancing."

Although at this time the number of post-offices in the country probably did not exceed half a hundred, Mrs. Adams notes a great letter-writing propensity in her circle. "These letters deserve notice," says her biographer, "only as they furnish a general idea of the tastes and pursuits of the day, and show the evident influence upon the writers which study of "The Spectator" and of the poets had exerted." This appears in the train of thought and structure of language, as in trifles of taste for quotation, and for fictitious signatures. "Calliope" and "Myra," "Aspasia" and "Aurelia," have effectually disguised their true names from the eyes of younger generations. Miss Smith's signature appears to have been "Diana," a name which she dropped after her marriage, without losing the fancy that prompted its selection.

Her letters written during the Revolution show clearly enough the tendency of her own thoughts and feelings in the substitute she then adopted of "Portia."

The young ladies of Massachusetts, in the last century, were certainly readers even though only self-taught, and their taste was not for the feeble and nerveless sentiment or the frantic passion of our day, but was derived from the deepest wells of English literature. The superb flowering of native mental gifts in many women of the last part of the eighteenth and the early part of the nineteenth centuries, under so slight stimulus of educational advantage, would almost force upon us the theory of Descartes, that "in order to improve the mind we ought less to learn than to contemplate"; and lead us to accept the dictum of Huxley, that "all the time we are using our plain common sense we are at once scientists and artists."

Rev. William Woodbridge, a descendant of Rev. Jonathan Edwards, and for fifty years an honored educator, wrote, in the latter part of his life, to a correspondent: "You inquire how so many of the females of New-England, during the latter part of the last century, acquired that firmness, and energy, and excellence of character for which they have been so justly distinguished, while the advantages of school education were so limited. The only answer is that it is not the amount of knowledge, but the nature of the knowledge, and, still more, the manner in which it is used to form character. Natural logic, the self-taught art of thinking, was the guard and guide of the female mind. The first of Watts's five methods of internal improvement, 'The attentive notice of every instructive fact and occurrence,' was exemplified in practice. Newspapers were taken in a few families; books were scarce but freely lent; the Scriptures were much read; and, as for time, 'where there is a will there is a way.'"

Since the women of that day left almost no record of their thought in print, the biography of Mrs. Adams, already quoted, may be called upon to illustrate the intellectual and moral characteristics attributed to them. Among the New England women of the early part of this century who are still remembered by the present generation, there was a noteworthy number who, in vigor of intellect and strength of character, might truly be called her peers.

While Mr. Adams was in Europe (from 1780) as Commissioner from the United States, Mrs. Adams was managing the family property, at a time of depreciation of paper money. Speaking of this period Mr. Charles Francis Adams says: "Her letters are remarkable because they display the readiness with which she could devote herself to the most opposite duties, and the cheerful manner in which she could accommodate herself to the difficulties of the times. She is a farmer, cultivating the land and discussing the weather and crops; a merchant, reporting prices current and the rates of exchange, and directing the making up of invoices; a politician, speculating upon the probabilities of peace or war, and a mother, writing the most exalted sentiments to her son. All of these pursuits she adopts together; some from choice, the rest from the necessity of the case; and in all she appears equally well."

The complete sympathy of interest between Mrs. Adams and her distinguished husband in "seeking for political truth in its fundamental principles," as Mr. Adams is said to have done, appears in her letters, and it may be questioned whether, barring the consideration of sex, the term "statesmanlike" might not apply to the views of both.

Just a month before the resolution declaring the independence of the colonies was offered in the Continental Congress by Richard Henry Lee of Virginia and seconded by John Adams of Massachusetts Mrs. Adams wrote to her husband, under date of May 7, 1776.

"I believe 'tis nearly ten days since I wrote you a line. I have not felt in a humor to entertain you. If I had taken up my pen, perhaps some unbecoming invective might have fallen from it. The eyes of our rulers have been closed and a lethargy has seized almost every member. I fear a fatal security has taken possession of them. While the building is in flames they tremble at the expense of water to quench it. In short, two months have elapsed since the evacuation of Boston, and very little has been done in that time to secure it, or the harbor, from future invasion. The people are all in a flame, and no one among us, that I have heard of, even mentions expense. They think, universally, that there has been an amazing neglect somewhere.

"'Tis a maxim of state that 'power and liberty are like heat and moisture; where they are well mixed everything prospers; where they are single they are destructive!'

"A government of more stability is much wanted in this colony, and they are ready to receive it at the hands of Congress.

"And since I have begun with maxims of state, I will add another, namely, that a people may let a king fall yet still remain a people; but if a king let his people slip from him he is no longer a king. And as this is most certainly our case, why not proclaim to the world, in decisive terms, your own importance? Shall we not be despised by foreign powers for hesitating so long at a word?"

To this Mr. Adams replied:

"PHILADELPHIA, *May* 27, 1776.

"I think you shine as a statesman, of late, as well as a farmeress. Pray where do you get your maxims of state? They are very apropos."

All history shows how long the conception of a plan, in some acute mind, precedes the popular impulse toward it. The fertile mind of Daniel De Foe, in an "Essay on Projects," published in 1699, suggests the plan of an Academy of Music, with hints for cheap Sunday concerts, an Academy for Military Science and Practice, and an Academy for Women.

This is the earliest project for a school of this grade, for women, and remained the only one for more than a century in England. In America, from the middle of the eighteenth century, academies were established in many towns where the law requiring instruction to fit boys for the university did not apply. Some of these opened their doors to girls, and, in a few instances, seminaries and academies for young ladies were founded, and, once inaugurated, they multiplied with constantly accelerating speed. A contemporary of these events, writing as "Senex" in "The American Journal of Education," says: "When at length academies were opened for female improvement in the higher branches, a general excitement appeared in parents, and an emulation in daughters to attend them. The love of reading and habits of application became fashionable."

There appear, from the first, to have been no discouragements from lack of mental capacity on the part of girls, even in the academies where they were instructed with boys.

The "Moravian Brethren" have the honor of founding the first private institution in America designed to give girls better advantages than the common schools. A female seminary was opened by them in Bethlehem, Pa., in 1749. Its service went beyond its own work, for Rev. Mr. Woodbridge records that "after the success of the Moravians in female education, the attention of gentlemen of reputation and influence was turned to the subject. Dr. Morgan, Dr. Rush,—the great advocate of education,—with others, instituted an academy for females in Philadelphia. Their attention and influence, and care were successful, and from them sprang all the subsequent and celebrated schools in that city."

It is presumed that it was of the "Philadelphia Female Academy," which held commencement exercises from as early as 1794, that Mr. Woodbridge says, "In 1780, in Philadelphia, for the first time in my life, I heard a class of young ladies parse English."

The "Penn Charter School" has a long and honorable record and has admitted girls for more than a century.

The Penn Charter School was founded in Philadelphia in 1697 as a public school, and has been carried on down to the present day under three charters granted by William Penn in the years 1701, 1708, 1711. These make provision, at the cost of the people called Quakers, for "all Children and Servants, Male and Female . . . . the rich to be instructed at reasonable rates, the poor to be maintained and schooled for nothing." Provision is made in the charters for instruction of both sexes in "reading, writing, work, languages, arts, and sciences."

The foundation laid is broad enough for a university for the people. As a matter of fact the girls and boys have always been educated separately, and the curriculum of the girls' school has always been less advanced than that of the boys. The Latin school has not been opened to them, nor, it is believed, have the ancient languages been taught them.

In 1795, "Poor's Academy for Young Ladies" became "a place of proud distinction to finished females."

The earliest academy for girls in New England was founded in 1763, at Byfield, Mass., by bequest of William Dummer, whose name it took. In 1784, Leicester Academy, open to both sexes, was incorporated.

In the same year the "Friends" established a school which offered the higher education to girls at Providence, R. I. This has been of high repute down to the present day.

In the same city we find, in 1797, the advertisement of a gentleman who "will conduct a morning school for young ladies in reading, writing, and arithmetic," and in 1808 Miss Brenton, at South Kingston, R. I., offers instruction which will include "epistolary style, as well as temple work, paper work, fringing, and netting."

In 1785 Dr. Dwight founded a Young Ladies' Seminary at Greenfield, Conn.

About 1787, Mr. Caleb Brigham, a noted teacher, opened a school for girls in Boston. This has been spoken of as "the most vigorous and systematic experiment hitherto made, and the most systematically antagonized." Upon opening, however, the school was immediately filled. The supply created a demand. More sought admission than could be accommodated. With the selectmen's daughters in school female education was becoming popular.

In 1789 a female academy was opened in Medford, the first establishment of the kind in New England. This was the resort of scholars from all the Eastern States.

We get here and there, proof of the espionage exercised over young women in those days.

Mrs. Rawson was a distinguished teacher who established a boarding-school for girls. The town voted, May 12, 1800, that the second and third seats in the women's side of the gallery of the meeting-house be allowed for Mrs. Rawson, for herself and scholars ; and that she be allowed to put doors and locks on them.

In 1791-92 the Maine Legislature incorporated academies at Berwick, Hallowell, Fryeburg, Westminster, and East Machias.

In 1792 Westford (Mass.) Academy was organized. It offered a very extensive programme. The body of rules and laws for governance provides that "the English, Latin, and Greek languages, together with writing, arithmetic, and the art of speaking shall be taught, and, if desired, practical geometry, logic, geography, and music ; that the said school shall be free to any nation, age, or sex, provided that no one shall be admitted unless able "to read in the Bible readily without spelling."

The impulse which single individuals often give to progress had its exemplification in this awakening period.

Two students of Yale College, during a long vacation after the British troops invaded New Haven, had each a class of young ladies for the term of one quarter. One of these students, well known later as the Rev. William Woodbridge, and before quoted here, during his senior year in college, in 1779, kept a young ladies' school in New Haven, consisting of about twenty-five scholars, in which he taught grammar, geography, composition, and the elements of rhetoric, and the success of this school led to the establishment of others elsewhere.

Mr. Woodbridge, on graduating, took for the subject of his thesis, "Improvement in Female Education." It would be interesting to know whether the school of Mr. Woodbridge led, as seems probable, to the following curious bit of history.

From Yale College, or from as near to it as a girl could get, issued, in 1783, the following attested certificate:

"BE IT KNOWN to you that I have examined Miss Lucinda Foote, twelve years old, and have found that in the learned languages, the Latin and the Greek, she has made commendable progress, giving the true meaning of passages in the Æneid of Virgil, the select orations of Cicero, and in the Greek testament, and that she is fully qualified, except in regard to sex, to be received as a pupil of the Freshman Class of Yale University.

"Given in the College Library, the 22d of December, 1783.

"EZRA STILES, *President.*"

Miss Foote afterwards pursued a full course of college studies and Hebrew, under President Stiles. She then married and had ten children.

Timothy Dwight, President of Yale College, traveled in 1803 through New England and New York, and made careful observation of educational conditions. He reports that "of the higher class of schools, generally styled academies, where pupils are qualified for college, there are twenty in Connecticut and forty-eight in Massachusetts." He adds: "Two of those in Connecticut and three in Massachusetts are exclusively female seminaries. Some others admit children of both sexes." He does not say that any one of the thirteen in New Hampshire or of the twelve in Vermont was open to girls. A third of a century afterwards Massachusetts had 854 academies and private schools. Later, the advance in grade of the public school system so reduced the number of personally supported schools, that in 1886 there were but 74 academies and 348 private schools, about one-half the number of a century before. The rapid growth and as rapid decline of the academy system was due to the fact that, while personal and associated effort had taken up a work for which the people were not prepared, its success proved a rapid educator, especially as to the capacity of girls, and the free school system was steadily pressed to higher levels.

Salem established an English high school for boys in 1827; one for girls eighteen years later, in 1845.

It was in 1836, as has been stated, when the school committee of Newburyport decreed "that one female grammar school be kept though the year"; it was only six years afterwards, in 1842, that the town voted to establish a female high school. This was encouraging, but when, later, the valuable "Putnam Fund" came into use for advanced education, there was much discussion between the special committee, appointed by the town, in conference with the trustees of the fund, as to whether Mr. Putnam designed, by his bequest, to include the instruction of females, and it required a decision of the Supreme Court to sustain the position of the trustees that "*youth*" *might include both sexes.*

The city of Lowell, Mass., which held its first town meeting in 1826, and was not incorporated until 1836, established a high school in 1831, midway between these events, and, to its lasting credit, on a co-educational basis. The first class which it graduated gave to Lowell its first woman principal of a grammar school, and to the country General B. F. Butler. This was one of the earliest high schools, and, so far as the writer can learn, the first that was co-educational.

In connection with the first and ephemeral high school for girls, in Boston, we have unusual opportunities in the "Municipal History of Boston," by Josiah Quincy, to learn the public sentiment of the time among the most intelligent and worthy, and to observe the struggle which it cost the more progressive to persuade those in power that girls had as great need of instruction, and as real claim on the public funds, as their brothers.

In 1825 the school committee of Boston asked an appropriation from the city council for a high school for girls. A few years previous the monitorial, or mutual, system of instruction had been tried in a town school. Some claimed that it had been successful; its cost was certainly less than one-third that of the old system.

Speaking of the formation of the plan for a high school for girls, Mr. Quincy says: "There being at that time a very general desire in the school committee to test the usefulness of monitorial instruction, it was proposed that the school should be conducted on that system; and in respect of expense the report supposed that one large room would be sufficient, at least for one year."

It was objected to the foundation of the school that the best scholars would be drawn away from the grammar schools, to the loss of their influence and of their services as monitors; in spite of this the city council voted an appropriation of $2000 to carry out the plan. "The anticipations of difficulty were, however, so strong and so plausible, that the project was adopted expressly as an experiment, if favorable, to be continued, if adverse, to be dropped, of course."

Difficulties appeared immediately. "Before the examination of candidates occurred, it becomes apparent that the result of a high school for girls would be very different from that of the high school for boys; and that, if continued upon the scale of time and studies which the original project embraced, the expense would be insupportable, and the effect upon the common schools positively injurious.

"Instead of 90 candidates, the highest number that had ever offered in one year for the school for boys, it was ascertained that nearly three hundred would be presented for the high school for girls . . . . and it was evident that either two high schools for girls must be established the first year, or that more than one-half of the candidates must be rejected."

Two hundred and eighty-six candidates presented themselves, and an arbitrary system was adopted to keep all but 130 out. "The girls admitted were the *élite* of the grammar schools, and were among the most ambitious and highly educated of them, and of private schools, from which a majority of those admitted were derived.

"It was impossible that such a school should not be highly advantageous to the few who enjoyed its benefits."

After six months' existence of the school, an alarming report was sent to the school committee to the effect that according to the best calculations, the number of candidates for admission at the next examination would be 427.

Mr. Quincy notes that "the school was chiefly for the advantage of the few and not for the many, and those, also, the prosperous few," and he regards with evident apprehension this large number of girls "to whom a high classical education (though Greek and Latin were excluded) was extremely attractive."

"Again this experiment showed that in the school for boys the number of scholars diminished every year, whereas of all those who entered this high school for girls, not one, during the eighteen months that it was in operation, voluntarily quitted it; and there was no reason for believing that any one admitted to the school would voluntarily quit it for the whole three years, except in case of marriage.

"It was apparent to all who contemplated the subject disinterestedly, that the continuance of this school would involve an amount of expense unprecedented and unnecessary, since the same course of study could be introduced into the grammar schools.

"To meet the exigency many schemes were proposed, the principal being that the age of admission should be fourteen instead of eleven, and no female to be admitted after the age of sixteen; that the requisitions for admission should be raised; and that the school should be only for one year instead of three.

"These modifications, in which the school committee and city council generally concurred, so greatly diminished the advantages which the original plan proposed, that much of the interest which its creation excited was also diminished. The school, however, was permitted to continue, subject to this modification, until November 27, when a committee was raised to consider the expediency of continuing it, which, on December 11, following, reported 'that it was expedient to continue it.'"

Much debate followed, in course of which "the Mayor declared that his opinion was so decidedly adverse to the continuance of the school, that he could not vote in its favor." Largely, no doubt, through the influential opposition of Mr. Quincy, who was then Mayor of the city, and on motion of a Mr. Savage, who said that, though, "as a member of the city council he had voted for the appropriation for the high school for girls, it was merely to make a public experiment of the system of mutual instruction as regards females"; it was voted on June 3, 1826, "that the girls be permitted to remain in the English common school throughout the year." Precisely what was meant by this vote, beyond the abolition of the high school, appears, if we recall that girls were not yet admitted to the grammar school except for half the year.

As Mr. Quincy states it, "The project of the high school was thus abandoned and the scale of instruction in the common schools of the city was gradually elevated and enlarged." As in 1834, eight years later, it was voted "that the school committee be directed so to arrange the town schools that the girls enjoy equal privileges with the boys throughout the year," it is to be presumed that the permission voted in 1826 was inoperative until this date. But the end was gained. The school was abolished, of which Mayor Quincy said in an address to the board of aldermen in 1829: "It may be truly said that its impracticability was proved before it went into operation"; and he again refers to "this high, classical school" with the remark that "no funds of any city could endure the expense."

It may have been that those who were parents of daughters as truly as of sons, saw this action in relation to the fact that the English High School, "for boys only," had been supported for four years, and the Latin School, "for boys only," for almost two centuries, both from the public funds; for, when Mr. Quincy wrote the account from which the above quotations and summary have been made, he recalled the intense opposition to his views of "a body of citizens of great activity and of no inconsiderable influence."

In 1851, speaking of his former opinions with regard to the high school, he wrote: "The soundness of these views and their coincidence with the permanent interests of the city, seem to be sanctioned by the fact that twenty-three years have elapsed, and no effectual attempt during that period has been made for its revival, in the school committee, or in either branch of the city council."

He did not consider that ideas of which the germ is sound have, nevertheless, their periods of incubation; but, if shades are permitted to "revisit the glimpses of the moon," we can imagine the venerable ex-Mayor, ex-President of Harvard, and most worthy man, reflectively regarding the "Girls' High School," established in connection with the Normal School in 1852, almost before his words of self-gratulation had ceased to echo; and, with still more astonishment, contemplating the Girls' Latin School, established in 1878 *to fit girls for college.*

In Massachusetts in 1888, 198 cities and towns supported

high schools, most of them co-educational. The population of the cities and towns in which these schools are maintained is over ninety-five per cent. of the whole population of the State.

It is not to be understood that this marvelous progress had come without resistance at every step, or had been achieved except in the way that a plant with the growing power in it struggles to light from under the pavement.

We have seen that in the lower schools when girls, in process of time, came to be taught at all, it was out of fitting season, sometimes out of due hours, without the best instructors, with limited range of study, and always with deference to the superior claim of boys. In the endeavor of girls toward the higher education, one is too sadly reminded of the struggles of the plebeians against the patricians in Rome, when positions wrung from usurping hands, were yielded, only to be, to the uttermost, shorn of advantage.

As girls have gained successive opportunities for advanced study, the aim of the opponents has always been to keep those only analogous to, not identical with, those of boys. They have, therefore, been steadily weighted with limiting conditions, as the educational history of Boston serves to illustrate.

We have seen that the experimental high school of 1825 was, in its feebleness, hampered by, if, indeed, it was not founded for the trial of the monitorial system, and was moribund from its inception.

When, a quarter of a century later, the demand for better education for girls again took form, those most active thought it discreet to avoid the controversy of the past, and, as a more feasible measure, a Normal School for teachers was projected, and was established in 1852.

It was soon found that girls fresh from the grammar schools were not fit candidates for normal training. To remedy this difficulty a few additional branches of study were introduced, a slight alteration made in the arrangement of the course, and the name changed to the Girls' High and Normal School. Under this name it continued until 1872, when it was found that the normal element had been absorbed by the high school, and had almost lost its independent, distinctive, and professional character. The two courses where then separated and the normal department was restored to its original condition, for the instruction of young women who intended to become teachers in Boston.

Boston had now, at length, a school for girls, devoted, like that for boys, to general culture, though still without opportunity for full classical training, such as had been freely offered Boston boys for almost two and a half centuries. But to taste intellectually, as well as physically, is to stimulate appetite.

In 1877 a society of 200 thoughtful and influential women, incorporated as the "Massachusetts Society for the University Education of Women," supported by men of equal dignity, and prominently associated with educational and kindred movements, petitioned the school committee "that a course of classical instruction may be offered to girls in the Boston Latin School, as is now offered to boys."

This petition was reinforced by a similar one from the "Woman's Educational Association," which, later, instigated and supported the Harvard examination for women. The trustees of "Boston University" officially memorialized the school board in the same interest.

The claim was urged by distinguished divines, physicians, educators, presidents of colleges, a founder of a college, statesmen, and by mothers of girls. They argued a public advantage, a public demand, and a public right. They showed that almost every prominent city and town in the State gave to girls in its public high school,—which was usually co-educational,—a chance to fit for college; while the towns that had been annexed to Boston,—Charlestown, Dorchester, Brighton, and West Roxbury, had thereby lost such advantage, which their girls had previously enjoyed. The presidents of co-educational and female colleges testified that while no Boston high school girl was prepared to enter their institutions, they were receiving well-prepared young women from the more liberal West.

The ladies petitioning, called attention to the fact that the colonial law of 1647 required every township of 100 families "to provide for the instruction of youth so far as to fit them for the University," and that in Massachusetts, from that time, there never has been a law passed concerning any public school which has authorized instruction to one sex not equally open to the other; that nowhere does the word "male" or "boy" occur, but always "children" or "youth."

It appeared that one young woman, daughter of a master, had pursued a three years' course of study in the Latin School, sitting and reciting with the other pupils, and winning the highest esteem for modesty and ability. From this course she had graduated with so solid a foundation of scholarship that at the age of twenty-two she had received the title of "Doctor of Philosophy" from "Boston University," and was the first woman in this country to take such a degree.

The opposition to the granting of the petition was most strongly presented by six distinguished presidents of male colleges and by two Harvard graduates.

President Eliot of Harvard College opposed the admittance of girls to the Latin School, saying, "I resist the proposition for the sake of the boys, the girls, and the schools, and in the general interest of American education."

Hon. Charles F. Adams wrote, "I suppose the experiment of uniting the two sexes in education, at a mature age, is likely to be fully tried. It will go on until some shocking scandals develop the danger."

President Porter of Yale College thought "boys and girls from the ages of fourteen to eighteen should not recite in the same class-room, nor meet in the same study hall. The natural feelings of rightly trained boys and girls are offended by social intercourse of the sort, so frequent, so free, and so unceremonious. The classical culture of boys and girls, even when it takes both through the same curriculum, should not be imparted by precisely the same methods nor with the same controlling aims. I hold that these should differ in some important respects for each."

President Bartlett of Dartmouth College said: "Girls cannot endure the hard, unintermitting, and long-continued strain to which boys are subjected. . . . Were girls admitted to the Latin School I should have no fear that they would not for the time hold their own with the boys, spurred on as they would be by their own native excitableness, their ambition, and the stimulus of public comparison. I should rather fear their success with its penalty of shortened lives or permanently deranged constitutions. You must, in the long run, overtask and injure the girls, or you must sacrifice the present and legitimate standard of a school for boys. . . . It should be added that almost every department of study, including classical studies, inevitably touches upon certain regions of discussion and allusion which must be encountered and which cannot be treated as they ought to be in the presence of both boys and girls."

An eminent classicist, Prof. William Everett, said: "To introduce girls into the Latin School would be a legal and moral wrong to the graduates"; and declared that "Greek literature is not fit for girls"; and, substantially, that what was a mental tonic for boys would be dangerous for girls.

The outcome of the effort was the founding of a "Latin School for Girls," which opened February, 1878, with thirty-one pupils, which number steadily increased to about two hundred.

Its graduates are in all the colleges of the State, at present, to the number of about forty, and they are among the best prepared who enter.

Not only the graduates of the school, but the whole community, must ever hold in grateful memory the names of those who, as representatives of the "Society for the University Education of Women," worked wisely and indefatigably for Boston girls: Mrs. I. Tisdale Talbot, Mrs. James T. Fields, Miss Florence Cushing.

By following the history of high schools down to the present day in one section of the North Atlantic States, taken as a type of progress, we have not paused to note the few helpful agencies which were gradually developed.

Returning to the beginning of the nineteenth century it is easier to discover what women lacked than what they enjoyed in the way of intellectual stimulus. Books and newspapers were few enough to be highly valued by all.

In Boston there was a public library as early as 1637, but women were not considered as patrons. The bold venture, on the part of the sex, of invading the quiet precincts of the reading room of the library of the Boston Athenæum, was made, after a decade or two of the nineteenth century had passed, by a shy woman, grown courageous only through her eagerness for knowledge. This was Hannah Adams, who had learned Greek and Latin from some theological students boarding in her father's house, and who had written books. The innovation shocked Boston people, who declared her out of her sphere. They could not foresee that half a century later there would be more women than men readers in the great public library of the city.

Nor was it considered proper for ladies to attend public lectures, nor to appear in public assemblies except those of a religious character. Either as cause or consequence of this the Lyceum audiences were so rude that it would not have been agreeable for ladies to be present.

In 1828 the Boston Lyceum was started, and after considerable discussion women were allowed to attend lectures. This so quickened the interest and improved the manners that lectures became so popular that the largest halls were required to hold the audiences.

There is something pathetic, as showing how small were the pecuniary resources of women, in the fact that it was customary, at least in the smaller cities, to admit them to lectures at about two-thirds the price of men. "The Lowell Institute," Boston, secured the utmost service to its great benefaction by making no discrimination against women in its free courses of lectures.

Among the English authors who were the resource of this country in way of literature, there began to be known a few women, in whom strong natural impulse had been fostered by exceptional educational opportunity until they ventured to use the pen and even to publish. This was usually done timidly, often protestingly, and one woman, afterwards distinguished, screened her talent behind her father's name.

Lady Anne Barnard, who wrote "Auld Robin Gray," for some reason or other kept the secret of her authorship for fifty years.

Mr. Edgeworth suppressed a translation which his daughter Maria had made, from the French, of a work on education "because his friend, Mr. Day, the author of 'Sanford and Merton,' had such a horror of female authors and their writings," and it was published only after Mr. Day's death.

It is curious to note how large a ratio of the female writers of this time involve, in their essays or novels, some reference to the need of education for their sex. On the contrary, however, Mrs. Barbauld, herself a classical scholar and thinker, and both happy and useful through her acquirements, opposed the establishment of an academy for young ladies. She "approved a college and every motive of emulation for young men," but thought that "young ladies ought only to have *such a general tincture of knowledge* as to make them agreeable companions to a man of sense, and ought to gain these accomplishments in a more quiet and unobserved manner, from intercourse and conversation at home, with a father, brother, or friend. She regarded herself as peculiar, and not a rule for others."

Late in the eighteenth century, Mary Wollstonecraft issued a strong and direct appeal for a recognition of the intellectual needs and capacities of women. She shocked the world into antagonism by her opinions, and by her use of the word "rights," as applied to her sex.

Much interest was felt in the graceful letters of Lady Mary

Wortley Montagu, and society found entertainment in the small talk of the heroines of Frances Burney, "Evelina," "Cecilia," and "Rosa Matilda."

Twenty years after the eloquent appeal had been made for "The Rights of Women," Hannah More, in "Cœlebs in Search of a Wife," introduced to the novel-reading world the subject of female education, with a tact and moderation which the stronger cravings of Mary Wollstonecraft did not permit. Without offensive presumption, and with deference to the superior claim of the other sex to the whole loaves, she meekly, but plainly, suggested the relish of the female mind for intellectual crumbs. The more favorable reception of her milder views, which was said "to have caused more than one dignified clergyman to take down his Eton grammar from the shelf, to initiate his daughters into the hitherto forbidden mysteries of 'hic-hæc-hoc,'" goes to prove, by analogy, the theory of the high potency school of homœopathists, for the smaller the dose administered the greater appear to have been the results.

The tender sentiment and graceful verse of Mrs. Hemans, and the sad domestic experience of Hon. Mrs. Norton, from whose unmasked sorrows her husband could gather pecuniary return, and the sturdy, intellectual vigor of Harriet Martineau, who grappled with the problems of political economy and social ethics, and was the friend and counselor of the first statesmen of her time, could not fail to appeal, on their several lines, to women of corresponding type, if not of equal gifts of expression, on both sides of the Atlantic. So education was going on for women in other ways than in schools, which still furnished them limited supplies, both in quantity and quality.

Among the voices which directly or indirectly were calling women to higher levels of intelligence and of thought, was that of the celebrated wit and divine, Sidney Smith, who proved by his claims for them, what he said of himself, "I have a passionate love for common justice and for common sense." In the *Edinburgh Review*, of which he was one of the founders, he had a way of asking such pointed inquiries as whether the world had hitherto found any advantage in keeping half the people in ignorance, and whether, if women were better educated, men might not become better educated too; and he adds, "Just as though the care and solicitude which a mother feels for her children, depended on her ignorance of Greek and mathematics, and that she would desert her infant for a quadratic equation!"

But so strong are the bonds of prejudice, that, although

this was as early as 1810, abundant cause has been found down to the present day to iterate and reiterate the same arguments, and still to pierce the bubble of conceit of superior right with the arrows of wit and sarcasm.

To show what the best schools open to girls were offering meantime, we quote what "one who had as good advantages in 1808 as New England then afforded," gives as her course of study: "Music, geography, Murray's Grammar, with Pope's Essay on Man for a parsing book, Blair's Rhetoric, Composition, and embroidery on satin. These were my studies and my accomplishments."

"Twenty-five years later than that," says the aged lady once before quoted, "a considerable part of the gain I brought from a private school in Charlestown, Mass., was a knowledge of sixty lace stitches." *

Looking back to this period from the vantage ground of less than a century, most women of nowadays would echo the sentiment of the small boy, one of four brothers, who heard a visitor say to his mother: "What a pity one of your boys had not been a girl!" Dropping his game to take in the full significance of her words, he called out: "I'd like to know who'd 'a benn 'er! I wouldn't 'a benn 'er; Ed wouldn't 'a benn 'er; Joe wouldn't 'a benn 'er, and I'd like to know who would 'a benn 'er!"

The third and fourth decades of the nineteenth century marked an epoch in education through the service done by a few teachers, who seemed to have fresh inspirations as to the capabilities of women, and practical ability to embody them. They helped to verify the forecast of Rev. Joseph Emerson, principal of the Academy at Byfield, Mass.

Mr. Emerson was deeply interested in the theme of the millennium, and regarded woman, in the capacity of educator, as the hope of the world's salvation. Unlike his cotemporaries, he believed in educating young women as thoroughly as young men, and in 1822 predicted "a time when higher institutions for the education of young women would be as needful as colleges for young men." Among his pupils was Mary Lyon.

The pioneer in the new departure was Mrs. Emma Hart Willard, born in 1787, in Connecticut, into a home of liberal thought and tender affection. The clearness of intellect and keen sense of justice which characterized her life, were all in-

* See also accounts of early education of American women authors in chapter on Woman in Literature.—Ed.

dicated, when, as a young woman, on settling her father's straightened estate, she insisted that children have no claim as compared with the mother's superior right to what she has helped to earn. From a child she was noted for interesting herself in the politics of the day. To relieve her husband from financial difficulties, and, as she says, "with the further motive of keeping a better school than those about me," she established a boarding school at Middlebury. This was the beginning of thirty years' service as a teacher, during which she taught 5000 pupils, one in ten of whom became teachers. She aimed to make her pupils comprehend the subject taught, and to give them power to communicate what they knew. Says her biographer, Dr. John Lord, "Her profession was an art. She loved it as Palestrina loved music and as Michael Angelo loved painting, and it was its own reward." There was no flattery to her pupils nor to their parents. Her regular duties, and her never-ending struggle for self-improvement and for better methods of instruction, kept her at her work from ten and sometimes for fifteen hours per day. She keenly felt the disadvantages under which she labored. She wrote: "The Professors of the college attended my examinations, although I was advised by the President that it would not be becoming in me, nor a safe precedent, if I should attend theirs; so, as I had no teacher in learning my new studies, I had no model in teaching or examining them. But I had faith in the clear conclusions of my own mind. I knew that nothing could be truer than truth, and hence I fearlessly brought to examination before the learned the classes to which had been taught the studies I had just acquired. . . . . My neighborhood to Middlebury College made me feel bitterly the disparity in educational facilities between the two sexes, and I hoped if the matter was once set before the men as legislators they would be ready to correct the error."

To this end Mrs. Willard prepared an address to the public, which in 1819, when she resided in New York, she presented to the New York Legislature. As the views set forth mark a distinct departure in educational demands for women, however familiar or antiquated they may now seem, they are quoted and summarized here. She published them only after long and thoughtful deliberation, and said, "I knew that I should be regarded as visionary, almost to insanity, should I utter the expectations that I secretly entertain." She asks that as the State has endowed institutions for its sons it shall do the same for its daughters, and "no longer leave them to become the prey of private adventurers, the result of which has been to make the daughters of the rich frivolous and those of the poor drudges." She laments that "the end of education of one sex has been to please the other . . . . until we have come to be considered the pampered and wayward babies of society, who must have some rattle put into our hands to keep us from doing mischief to ourselves or to others. But reason and religion teach that we, too, are primary existences; that it is for us to move in the orbit of our duty around the Holy Center of Perfection, the companions, not the satellites of men."

Mrs. Willard fears that "should the conclusion be almost admitted that our sex, too, are the legitimate children of the Legislature, and that it is their duty to afford us a share ot their paternal bounty, the phantom of a college-learned ladv would be ready to rise up and destroy every good resolution in our favor."

To show that it is not a masculine education that is here recommended, Mrs. Willard sketches her ideal of a female seminary. She desires it to "to be adapted to the female character and duties, and her first plea is that to which the softer sex should be formed." "To raise the female character will be to raise that of men. . . . . It would be desirable that the young ladies should spend part of their Sabbaths in hearing discussions relative to the peculiar duties of their sex. The difficulty is not that we are at a loss what sciences we ought to learn, but that we have not proper advantages for learning any. . . . . Many writers have given us excellent advice in regard to what we should be taught, but no Legislature has provided us the means of instruction. . . . . In some of the sciences proper to our sex the books written for the other would need alteration, because in some they presuppose more knowledge than female pupils would possess, in others they have parts not particularly interesting to our sex, and omit subjects immediately relating to their pursuits. Domestic instructions should be considered important. Why may not housewifery be reduced to a system as well as other arts?

"If women were properly fitted for instruction they would be likely to teach children better than the other sex; they could afford to do it cheaper; and men might be at liberty to add to the wealth of the nation by any of those thousand occupations from which women are necessarily debarred."

While "coarse men laughed at this proposition to endow a seminary for girls," the plan was so well received by the Legislature that Mrs. Willard's Seminary at Waterford was incorporated, and placed on the list of institutions which received a share of the literary fund. Though this was a small recognition of a large need, to New York belongs the honor of making the first appropriation of public funds for the higher education of women.

The character of the support given to Mrs. Willard is more encouraging than the legislative action. Governor Clinton, a man of great educational foresight, recommended Mrs. Willard's plan in these words, which incidentally indicate common sentiment at the time: "As this is the only attempt ever made to promote the education of the female sex by the patronage of government. . . . . I trust you will not be deterred by commonplace ridicule from extending your munificence to this meritorious work." Distinguished men advocated the plan before the New York Legislature, and John Adams, Thomas Jefferson, and others wrote letters favoring it, all with little success.

A bill passed the Senate granting $2000 to the seminary of Mrs. Willard at Waterford, but failed in the Lower House.

It was at this seminary that in 1820 a young lady was publicly examined in geometry, and "it called forth a storm of ridicule."

The corporation of Troy, N. Y., came to the rescue of Mrs. Willard's project, and raised $4000 by tax, and another fund by subscription, and erected a building of brick, to which Mrs. Willard came in 1821. She was convinced that "young women are capable of applying themselves to the higher branches of knowledge as well as young men," and that the study of domestic economy could be pursued at the same time. Developing these theories she made for the "Troy Female Seminary" and its pupils a distinguished reputation, and gave a decided uplift to the standard of female education.

More than two hundred institutions of the grade of Troy Seminary are now reckoned, extending to South America and to Athens, Greece. Half the number are in the Southern United States, and two-thirds of them confer degrees.

Associated with Mrs. Willard at Troy, in the department of science, was her distinguished sister, Mrs. Almira Lincoln Phelps. Later she was the head of "Patapsco Institute," a female diocesan school of high reputation. She was the second woman elected a member of the "American Association for Advancement of Science," and in 1866 read before that body a paper on "The Religious and Scientific Character and Writings of Edward Hitchcock," and in 1878, one on "The Infidel Tendencies of Modern Science." Her educational works on botany, chemistry, geology, and natural philosophy had a large circulation.

Names which soon rose to high distinction in educational work were those of Miss Grant and Miss Lyon, of Massachusetts, Miss Catherine Fiske of Keene, N. H., Miss Catherine Beecher of Connecticut, and the Misses Longstreth of Philadelphia, Pa.

The work of Miss Fiske was nearly cotemporary with that of Mrs. Willard. For twenty-three years, up to her death in 1836, she carried on a school which received some 2500 pupils to a course of study which embraced botany, chemistry, astronomy, and "Watts on the Mind."

Miss Catherine Beecher, who was endowed with the marked individuality of her family, conducted a seminary at Hartford, Conn., from 1822 to 1832, and later one at Cincinnati, O. Her course of study included Latin, and calisthenic training was a conspicuous feature. She gave prominence in her instruction to the worth of domestic skill.

She wrote text-books on mental and moral philosophy and upon theology, and did not forget to prove by publishing "a domestic receipt book," that, though learned, she had not soared above the true sphere of woman.

To the schools already mentioned came pupils from every State in the Union, either from families of means or to receive the generosity of the principals.

Mary Lyon was born among the Massachusetts hills in 1797, and graduated from the position of teacher in the little schoolhouses, and again as a student from Byfield Academy; then from the charge of Adams Academy at Derry, N. H., and from a like position in Ipswich Academy, Mass., in both which she was associated with Miss Grant. To her was due the conception of "a school which shall put within reach of students of moderate means such opportunities that the wealthy cannot find better ones."

To the execution of her plan the gathering of a few thousand dollars was necessary. The labor involved may be inferred from the fact that in the list of contributions the sum of fifty cents repeatedly appears. The most serious obstacles were found in the antagonism to what seemed to many a needless project. Said Dr. Hitchcock: "Respectable periodicals were charged with sarcasm and enmity to Miss Lyon's plans. She remained unruffled."

When, in 1834, the Massachusetts General Association declined to indorse the enterprise, a Doctor of Divinity made haste to say, "You see that the measure has utterly failed. Let this page of Divine Providence be attentively considered in relation to this matter!"

But in face of all disheartenments, in 1837 Mount Holyoke Seminary was opened in the beautiful Connecticut valley. The mode of living was for a time almost ascetic. The work of the house was mainly done by the pupils, but the cost, lights and fuel excepted, was only sixty dollars per school year of forty weeks, and so continued for sixteen years.

Bible study held a leading place in the curriculum.

It was Miss Lyon's ambition to make the course equal to that required for admission to college, and she planned for steady growth from the small beginnings. Nobly have her expectations been fulfilled!

The hindrances encountered again indicate the slow growth of public sentiment. It was desired that the ancient and some of the modern languages should be studied, but it was necessary to wait ten years before Latin could appear in the course, because "the views of the community would not allow it." As an optional study it was pursued in classes every year after the first. So French, which was taught from the very first year, became a part of the course only in 1877, after the lapse of forty years.

As time has passed, the thorough work done, and the steadily expanding course of study have won to the institution devoted friends, who have added generously to its grounds, its buildings, and its funds. Once the State has been asked for aid, mainly for payment for a gymnasium, and a grant of $40,000 was obtained in 1867.

The triple strain of study, labor, and economy, under the stimulus of lofty aims, might well have given cause, in those early days, for anxiety on the score of health, but statistics were tabulated in 1867 which showed the comparative longevity of graduates of eight institutions, covering a period of thirty years. The colleges noted were "Amherst," "Bowdoin," "Brown," "Dartmouth," "Harvard," "Williams," and "Yale."

Exclusive of mortality in war, the record of "Mount Holyoke Seminary" was more favorable than any other except that of "Williams College," which fell two and one-half per cent. below it in mortality, while "Dartmouth" exceeded it by more than thirty-eight per cent.

It has been the theory of "Mount Holyoke Seminary" that she must have every advantage that the state of education will allow. She must be a college *in fact*, whether or not she take the name.

In this she reversed the theory of many of the 400 institutions in the United States, which easily take the name of college first. Recently her advanced course of study, pursued by 200 pupils, seemed to justify her adding to her powers and to her dignities, and in 1888 the Massachusetts Legislature granted a charter "authorizing Mount Holyoke Seminary and College to confer such degrees and diplomas as are conferred by any university, college or seminary of learning in this Commonwealth."

Educational institutions, which have taken form and gathered impetus from Mount Holyoke Seminary, are to be found not only from ocean to ocean in the United States, including the "Cherokee Seminary," founded by John Ross in the Indian Territory in 1851, but in Turkey, in Spain, in Persia, in Japan, and in Cape Colony, South Africa.

After display of so great administrative ability as appeared in Miss Lyon and her successors, it strikes one as still another mark of the traditional reluctance to recognize true values, that close upon half a century from the founding of the institution had passed before the name of a woman appeared in the list of trustees. Meantime every principal of the seminary had been a woman, every resident physician had been a woman, and every anniversary address had been made by a man.

The debt which the public owes to a few individuals who have used lavishly, for its benefit, their own great endowments, whether of brains or of money, before this same public was conscious of its own highest needs, is distinctly traceable in the kindergarten, kitchen-garden, industrial school, college, and university movements of the present day. Truly, many of these to whom much has been given have read their duty in the light of the scripture, "Of him much shall be required." When values are once demonstrated to the people, they are ever ready to carry on important work with liberality.

While recognizing the importance of the many lines of educational effort, if we sought to learn which has done most to give a solid basis of thoroughness to woman's education, and, secondarily, to general education, during the middle part of the present century, we should find the answer in the Normal Schools. While other institutions have contributed greatly to increase the scope of woman's study, these have added thereto the important consideration of methods.

As a part of the thrifty policy which the States have

shown when dealing with the education of girls, they have furnished Normal School instruction with the especial view to getting skilled labor in return.

Perhaps there is nothing which would insure so great care in instilling first principles. The result has certainly been to make their invaluable influence felt from the cities to the remotest school districts.

The story of the establishment of these schools is another story of personal struggle against more than indifference, and indifference itself may justly be regarded as a solid substance.

The interest in Normal Schools in America, which was aroused by Prof. Denison Ormstead in 1816, and was advocated by De Witt Clinton, by Gallaudet, and by Horace Mann, grew to fervor in the Rev. Charles Brooks of Medford, Mass., who caught his inspiration from Dr. Julius, of Hamburg, who was sent to the United States by the King of Prussia to study our public institutions. In 1865 Mr. Brooks rode in his chaise over two thousand miles to present the subject, at his own cost, to the people. He held conventions and presented the topic in pulpits as "Christian Culture." He says, "My discouragements were legion."

The leading paper in Boston and in New England expressed its sense of the absurdity of the movement by admitting a caustic communication, which ended by representing Rev. Mr. Brooks with a fool's cap on his head, marching up State Street at the head of a crowd of ragamuffin young men and women, who bore a banner, inscribed, "To a Normal School in the clouds." Mr. Brooks was, however, invited to speak on the subject before the House of Representatives, and "some members of the Legislature called the new movement by funny names."

But educators like George B. Emerson, and thinkers like Rev. William Ellery Channing, and statesmen like Horace Mann lent their aid, and, stirred by Mr. Brooks, support was given in public speech by Hon. John Q. Adams and Daniel Webster.

Mr. Mann was Secretary of the Board of Education upon its organization in 1837, and, in his first report, recommended that the Legislature establish Normal Schools. A donation of $10,000 being made by Mr. Dwight to stimulate this interest, a State appropriation was made, and a Normal School for girls was opened at Lexington, Mass., in 1838. Later, others were opened, some of which admitted boys also, but for the first twenty years, eighty-seven per cent. of the graduates were girls. These schools are now widely scattered through the United States. The history of that at Oswego, N. Y., is of especial interest.

The first systematic effort for the physical development of women was made in 1861 in Boston. A "Normal Institute for Physical Culture," was established by Dr. Dio Lewis, aided by the president and some of the professors of Harvard College. At the outset the young women pupils were found lamentably deficient in respect of physical development. Later, Dr. Lewis stated that "in every one of the thirteen classes which were graduated, the best gymnast was a woman. In each class there were from two to six women superior to any of the men." Dr. Walter Channing, one of the professors, often spoke with enthusiasm of the physical superiority of the women to the men. From the graduates of these classes instruction in light gymnastics was widely introduced into schools throughout the country. Now the well-appointed gymnasium is a prominent feature of the leading colleges to which women are admitted, and the erection and endowment of this department is a favorite form of benefaction from the alumnæ.

Prof. Huxley says, "No system of education is worthy the name, unless it creates a great educational ladder, with one end in the gutter and the other in the university." Such was the intuitive feeling of our ancestors, even in the Colonial days, with regard to boys. When, however, in the course of centuries, conviction came to a few that what had been for one sex only was, in fairness, due to the other as well, the atmosphere of the older States did not prove bracing enough to sustain so utopian a theory, and the ambitious daughters of New England were obliged to follow those who, transplanted to the virgin soil of Ohio, had opened Oberlin College, offering such opportunities as it could furnish without distinction of race, and with but limited discrimination against sex.

Something more remarkable than the hungry young mind seeking mental food at disadvantage, was witnessed in 1853, when the full mind and earnest spirit of the leading New England educator, Hon. Horace Mann, eager to inaugurate the best methods of the higher education in a co-educational college, found his only chance by leaving his native New England, to build an institution from its very foundation, in a section remote from literary association. The pathos is deepened that his life was sacrificed in the contest with obstacles.

Following this magnetic leader, again a few New England girls turned westward, and gained at Antioch College, Ohio, what the East still denied them. Twelve years later, and two hundred and forty years after Harvard was established for boys, private beneficence endowed "Boston University" on a co-educational basis, and in 1869 a college in Massachusetts was opened to girls for the first time.

In place of the reply which Harvard College made to girls who asked admission to its vacant seats, "We have no such custom," was heard the cheering, "Welcome to all we have to offer!" and the old habit of keeping something of the best in reserve for the male sex, which has been so persistent in State, and municipal, and institutional economy, and which made the restricted sex feel an unwelcome pensioner on somebody's bounty, has never characterized Boston University. As a result, the report of the University for the year 1879–80, shows that already over thirty-seven per cent. of the regular classes in the College of Liberal Arts were women, and, in encouraging contrast to many colleges from which women are excluded, it adds, "no rowdyism or scandal has brought discredit on the institution."

In a few cases institutions for the higher education of women have been established in university towns or cities, and have availed themselves of the opportunity afforded for instruction by professors of the neighboring university, and have been granted, under restrictions, use of the libaries, museums, etc., connected with it. Each of these differs from the other in respect of its relationship to the university. The first established was that at Cambridge, Mass., in 1879, under the direction of "The Society for the Collegiate Instruction for Women," which has, unfortunately, come to be known by the misleading title of "The Harvard Annex." Applicants for admission to the most advanced work of the institution are required to pass the same examinations which admit young men to Harvard College, and these examinations are conducted in different parts of the country by local committees, under the auspices of The Society for the Collegiate Instruction for Women. Certificates of proficiency thus gained admit the student to classical and scientific courses at the collegiate institution, corresponding to those given to young men at Harvard College.*

* The graduates of the Harvard Annex are given a certificate issued by The Society for the Collegiate Instruction of Women. Although the work of the "Annex" students is acknowledged to be the same as that of the students of the University, and the instruction is given by the University professors, the degrees that are bestowed on the graduates of the University are refused to the graduates of the "Annex." It would certainly seem a more

EVELYN COLLEGE.

Evelyn College, Princeton, N. J., founded under similar circumstances in 1888, differs from the institution at Cambridge, having been formally authorized to confer degrees and to exercise all the functions of a college for the higher education of women.*

It offers classical and scientific courses corresponding to those of the neighboring university ; also elective and post graduate courses.

By resolution of the Board of Trustees of Princeton College any help may be given to Evelyn College by the Princeton Faculty which does not interfere with their duties in the University, and the use of the libraries, museums, etc., is granted.

---

consistent position on the part of that august institution if it disclaimed all belief in the collegiate education of women. But Harvard smiles upon its Annex to the extent, at least, of permitting its professors to give their valuable time to instructing "the gentle sex." Harvard apparently acknowledges the capacity of the female mind to attain to the heights of Harvard culture, but strangely enough it withholds the only proper recognition which surely is due, and fitting.

The following certificate issued by The Society for the Collegiate Instruction of Women will some day, let us hope, be preserved only as a curious relic of an archaic past :

> THE SOCIETY FOR THE COLLEGIATE INSTRUCTION OF WOMEN.
> CAMBRIDGE, MASSACHUSETTS.
>
> WE HEREBY CERTIFY *that under the supervision of this Society, has pursued a course of study equivalent in amount and quality to that for which the* DEGREE OF BACHELOR OF ARTS *is conferred in Harvard College, and has passed in a satisfactory manner examinations on that course, corresponding to the College examinations.*
>
> IN TESTIMONY WHEREOF *we have caused these presents to be signed by our President and Seeretary and by the Chairman of the Academic Board, this day of in the year of our Lord, one thousand eight hundred and*
>
> *President.*
> *Secretary.*
>
> *Chairman of the Academic Board.*

It may be added as a commentary that the Sargent prize for 1890–91 was won by a student of the "Annex." This prize is offered to "Undergraduates of Harvard College and students pursuing courses of instruction in Cambridge, under the direction of The Society for the Collegiate Instruction of Women," and was awarded for, "The best metrical version of the ninth ode of the fourth Book of Horace."—ED.

* The Society for the Collegiate Instruction of Women, being duly incorporated, could also be authorized to confer degrees. But it wisely prefers to await the time when Harvard College will bestow the University degree ; meanwhile doing what lies in its power to establish the identity of the work done in the two colleges. In the same way as Evelyn, Barnard College is

COLUMBIA COLLEGE IN RELATION TO THE HIGHER EDUCATION OF WOMEN.

The first college for women to confer degrees upon graduates of an affiliated college is Columbia College, New York City. As the aim of this paper is rather to trace the growth of educational opportunity than to tabulate results, the various steps which led to the opening of Barnard College, New York City, in 1889 are given, as typical of the progressive nature of movements for opening the doors of established colleges to women. While many still regard it as wise to discriminate between the sexes in respect of opportunities, while others would instruct them equally but separately, there is apparently an increasing

---

duly incorporated and is authorized by the Regents of New York State to confer upon its graduates a degree of its own. But Barnard prefers to waive its right and to accept the degree from the parent University, Columbia College.

There is too much pluming of one's self in this country, on the right to confer a college degree, a right granted by State Legislatures in a lamentably superficial manner. I have received many communications gravely announcing that the degrees conferred by certain colleges are every way equal to those of the greatest and oldest institutions of learning in the country—as the State Legislature—by a special act—has made them so" (!) I have always failed to see the connection between acts of legislative bodies, and the true greatness of universities.

The trustees of Evelyn College decided to give a separate degree not because Princeton College refused to officially recognize the work of the students of Evelyn, but because thus far (December, 1890) no candidate has been received for a college course answering in every way to that for which the Princeton degree is given. The trustees of Evelyn College gives its graduates a degree which is granted for less work than is demanded by Princeton: (Music and Art are made regular electives, and Greek is not demanded even for entrance examinations).

Even at the risk of repetition, I will here state the relative standing of the three American affiliated colleges. I include the following colleges in the term Affiliated College, because each seeks in some way to extend to women the advantages that are offered to men by another (neighboring) college. Some one has given the *raison d'être* of the affiliated college to be "the economy which applies to a new purpose resources already organized and tested."

Harvard Annex, founded in 1879, instruction received from Faculty of Harvard College, admits special students in all departments, gives no degree to its own graduates, prefers to await official recognition from Harvard College.

Evelyn College, founded in 1888, instructions received from Faculty of Princeton College, admits special students, gives its own degree, has never asked for the Princeton degree.

Barnard College, founded in 1889, instruction received from Faculty of Columbia College, no special students admitted except in Laboratory work and Graduate department, degrees conferred by Columbia College. The only affiliated college in the world, so far as I can learn, that has received *full official sanction* and recognition from the University with which it is affiliated.—ED.

number of these who would apply to colleges, in general, what the late far-sighted President Barnard of Columbia said of that under his charge. "I regard the establishment of an annex as desirable only considered as a step toward what I think must, sooner or later, come to pass, and that is the opening of the College proper to both sexes equally."*

Efforts to gain for young women the advantages of Columbia College, New York City, have been made at intervals since 1873, when several qualified young women applied for admission to the college, and one, a graduate of Michigan University, for admission to the medical school. A plea in their behalf was made before the faculty by Mrs. Lillie Devereux Blake, on the ground that the charter of the College declared that it was "founded for the education of the youth of the city," and "youth" includes both sexes. President Barnard and several of the faculty favored the admission of women as students, but the committee on education decided that any action was inexpedient.

In December, 1876, a memorial was presented to the Board of Trustees of Columbia College by "Sorosis," a well-known woman's club, of the city, asking that young women should be admitted to the college classes. The memorial was laid on the table by a unanimous vote.

Up to 1879 women were informally admitted to the lectures of certain professors, during regular class hours. This was forbidden in 1879, not from any harm resulting, but because it was discovered that the statutes forbade any but regularly matriculated students to attend lectures. This law had no reference to women, but the trustees declined to change the letter of the law and women were banished. Three years later a motion made in the board that the statutes should be so

---

* Although this remark was made by the late President Barnard, it did not voice the sentiment of those who inaugurated the movement to establish Barnard College. The affiliated college is not always a mere "step toward co-education"; there are many that believe that institutions such as the affiliated colleges, Girton and Newnham (were their graduates entitled to the University degree), best solve the problem of the collegiate education of women to-day. Instruction in undergraduate work is given at the women's colleges, and is obtained not only from university professors, but also from some able women instructors. But in graduate work, which is the real work of the University, men and women are most properly allowed to attend the lectures together at the University. The vexed problem of co-education becomes a different question as it deals with the undergraduate work of young men and women, or with the university and professional studies of men and women of mature age.—ED.

changed as not to prohibit the attendance of women, conditionally, on certain courses of lectures was lost. But from 1886 women have been admitted to lectures given on Saturday mornings, and two hundred ladies have listened weekly, and many more have desired admittance.

In 1883 an association was formed in New York to promote the higher education of women. A petition signed by 1400 persons, many of them of highest distinction in public and private life, and indorsed by President Barnard of Columbia, asked that the benefits of education at Columbia College be extended to qualified women with as little delay as possible, by admitting them to lectures and examinations. In June of that year, 1883, the trustees of Columbia College resolved that a course of collegiate study, equivalent to the course given to young men, should be offered to such women as may desire it, to be pursued under the general direction of the faculty of the College.

This resolve was, however, restricted by regulations which seemed to contradict both its spirit and its letter, since it narrowed the opportunity of women to that of getting the required instruction where they might, except at Columbia, which would, however, admit them to examinations to prove whether or not they had done so. As these examinations were not limited to the subjects as treated in the courses of lectures, as were the corresponding examinations of matriculated students of the University, they were more difficult. In spite of the great difficulties to be encountered, and the very limited advantage to result, many young women were attracted by the offer. In 1888 twenty-eight girls were availing themselves of this opportunity for examination tests of proficiency. In 1885 the trustees of Columbia resolved to grant the degree of Bachelor of Arts to women who had pursued for four years a course of study fully equivalent to that for which the same degree is conferred in the school of arts. Those who had secured this degree, or its equivalent (elsewhere), might study for higher degrees under the direction of the faculty of the College.*

---

* These courses of examinations were offered by Columbia College for the laudable purpose of "raising the standard of female education." [Extract from the minutes of the Board of Trustees; Report of the Select Committee, March 5, 1883.] Notwithstanding the criticism and eloquent expostulation of some women aimed at the "conservative" Board of Trustees of Columbia College, we must not forget that Columbia has never refused *equal recognition for equal work.* It saw no logical pause between the acknowl-

BARNARD COLLEGE.

So manifest became the public demand for collegiate and post collegiate instruction,—from graduates of the city Normal School (which had 1600 pupils), from the pupils of the best class of private schools, where, sometimes, not less than one fourth were preparing for admission to some college,* and from graduates of other colleges,—that a movement was made, in which the efforts of leading men and women in New York City were conspicuous both for their unflagging zeal and for their judicious methods, to secure necessary funds to found and, at the outset, to maintain a college for women whose professors and instructors should be those of Columbia, and upon whose graduates Columbia College should confer the same degrees as upon her own. The woman who first approached the Trustees of Columbia College with a plan to found an affiliated college for women was Mrs. Annie Nathan Meyer, who had been one of the first young women to take advantage of the course of examinations offered by Columbia College. After the appeal for an affiliated college was made it was discovered that had such a plan, supported by the proper persons, and bearing likelihood of success, been brought before the Board, it would have met with approval some years before. The former petitions had, however, asked for co-education, and at first there was considerable opposition to the "annex movement," as it was called, on the part of those whose battle-cry might have been almost said to have been "Co-education or no education."

But the wiser policy prevailed, and it was acknowledged by the majority that "those co-educationalists who ignore the annex project are butting their heads against a stone wall when a nicely swarded path lies before them." † Barnard College received official sanction from the Trustees of Columbia College, March, 1889, was chartered by the Regents of New York State, July, 1889, and formally opened October, 1889.

---

edgement that women could follow the collegiate course and the conferring of official sanction upon such a course.

The same Report goes on to say: "and offering suitable academic honors and distinctions to any who, on examination, shall be found to have pursued such courses of study with success.—Ed.

* See article by Mrs. Annie Nathan Meyer in *The Nation*, January 21, 1888. The petition to the Columbia Board for official sanction to open Barnard College was largely based on this article.

† See article by Annie Nathan Meyer, in *University*, February 22, 1888.

Barnard College was appropriately named in grateful tribute to the late President Barnard of Columbia College.

The great void that it was to fill appeared in many ways,—among others in the fact that the botanical and chemical laboratories which it established were the only ones in the city open to women.

The trustees of Barnard, one half of whom are women, hope to find much of its usefulness in the encouragement and provision for graduate work which it will offer to the hundreds of women who are gathered in New York, in the pursuance of some profession.

VASSAR COLLEGE.

The late Matthew Vassar, "recognizing in woman the same intellectual constitution as in man," resolved to give a fair chance to girls for a liberal education, under conditions in every way favorable to health. To this end he erected college and dormitory buildings in the midst of a lawn of two hundred acres, at Poughkeepsie, N. Y., with careful provision for pure air, good water, abundant sunshine, and good sewerage. He provided a gymnasium and provided for out of door sports. He instituted a professorship of physiology and hygiene, and made its incumbent "resident physician" and supervisor of sanitary arrangements.

In September, 1865, the institution received, upon examination, about 350 young women as students to a course of study and mode of life determined by the trustees, who believed that "the larger the stock of knowledge, and the more thorough the mental discipline a woman attains, the better she is fitted for any womanly position, and to perform any womanly duty of home and in society," a position which the subsequent experience of this and kindred institutions has abundantly illustrated.

Up to 1890, Vassar College has conferred the degree of A.B. upon between 800 and 900 graduates.

It has included in its corps of professors several women of distinguished ability—of whom we may name the late Prof. Braislin of the department of mathematics, and the late Prof. Maria Mitchell, who had not only a national, but a European reputation, as an astronomer. From the opening of the institution till near the time of her death, in 1889, she was the head of the department of astronomy and in charge of the excellent observatory. Three women are serving on the Vassar board of trustees, and three on standing committees.

SMITH COLLEGE.

Smith College was founded in Northampton, Mass., by Miss Sophia Smith, of the neighboring town of Hatfield. Finding herself in possession of a large fortune to dispose of she took counsel with her pastor, Dr. John M. Green, as to the best use to make of it. He conferred, in her behalf, with the leading representatives of education, and the general opinion of the time was voiced by Dr. Edward Hitchcock. When Dr. Green asked him, in 1861, "Would you dare to endow a college for women?" he said, "No! The matter of woman's higher education is still an experiment." Prudence seemed to compel further deliberation. Strong efforts were made to secure the fund for established colleges, and other schemes of beneficence were considered, but by 1868 Miss Smith and Dr. Green, to whom she had continuously turned for counsel, had come to the conviction that in no other way could the money be so well invested for the benefit of human kind, as in founding a college which should give young women opportunities for education equal to those which established colleges offered to young men. The plan was at once developed, and the college at Northampton is to-day Miss Smith's noble monument.

Its high aim has been well sustained, and more than five hundred students are named in the Annual Report of 1889.

Two thirds of the faculty are women, to whom, however, the title of professor is not accorded. This is not thought to imply lack of competency to fill the positions usually so designated. Neither can the current report be credited, that the President does not consider it altogether womanly to bear such title, since Smith College conferred upon Dr. Amelia B. Edwards, the English Egyptologist, the honorary degree of LL.D., and only the highest courtesy could be intended.

WELLESLEY COLLEGE.

Wellesley College, Wellesley, Mass., fifteen miles from Boston, was founded in 1875 by the benefaction of Henry F. Durant. The purpose of the trustees was "the establishment of a college in which girls should have as good opportunities for higher education as the best institutions afforded to young men, and to do so with due regard to health." They held that "it is not hard study but violation of law that injures health."

The college is beautiful for situation, with extensive grounds, like an English park, varied by oak woods and elm-shaded avenues, and including Lake Waban, which furnishes ample facilities for rowing and skating. Thousands of rhododendrons and other flowering shrubs have been set to brighten the grounds, and the spring turf blossoms in crocuses and snow-drops.

Amid all this seductive beauty, suggestive of dreaming, rise noble structures, of solid and elegant proportions, dedicated to successful work. Within them the practical and the æsthetic are charmingly combined. Music has its temple, art has its ministry, science its every facility, and the air of a happy home life broods over all.

Thoroughness and system are manifest everywhere. This is not a college of yesterday. Nowhere are the latest methods and the best facilities more promptly welcomed. One wanders charmed and glad through its fine library, its extensive laboratories, its dining-roon, where a special grace of living comes with the refined service of the students themselves, its dainty parlors and reception-rooms, and, seeking some flaw to prove it real, finds it, at last, in the fact that only half the youth of the land—only girls are admitted to it.

From the opening of the college it has been under the presidency of women. Miss Ada Howard, a graduate of Mount Holyoke Seminary, was succeeded by Miss Alice Freeman, who received the degree of "Doctor of Philosophy," from her alma mater, the University of Michigan, and that of Doctor of Literature from Columbia College. In 1887 Miss Palmer resigned the presidency of Wellesley College, but as Mrs. Alice Freeman Palmer continues to serve it as a member of the board of trustees, which out of twenty-five members has one third women members. Miss Freeman was succeeded by the present President, Miss Helen A. Schafer, a graduate of Oberlin College.

CORNELL UNIVERSITY.

Cornell University is one of the national colleges founded upon the land-grant of 1862. The share of New York was nearly a million acres, and, by act of the Legislature of New York, passed in 1865, the university was incorporated, and the income from the sale of this land was given it for its maintenance. There were certain conditions, the principal one being the donation of $500,000 to the university by Ezra Cornell. This was made, together with 200 acres of land. In simple and comprehensive phrase, Mr. Cornell said: "I would found an institution where any person can find instruction in any study."

The act of incorporation provides for instruction "in order to promote the liberal and practical education of the industrial classes in the several pursuits and professions of life." Thus thrice bound to the general service, by employment of the people's resources, by acceptance at once of the gift and of the intent of the broad-minded donor, and again by provision of its own act, it would seem to go without saying that the State should see to it that there should be no discrimination against any class.

The university was opened, October, 1868, and, happily, it goes with saying, that by act of the trustees, passed in April, 1872, "Women are admitted to the university on the same terms as men, except that they must be at least seventeen years old."

On the authority of the Dean of the faculty, Mr. H. S. White, August, 1890: "As to the status of young women at Cornell, they enjoy all the advantages which are open to young men, including the university scholarship and fellowships. We have eight fellowships which are open to graduate students, awarded by vote of the faculty, not only to our own graduates, but to graduates of other institutions. In 1888–89, three of these fellowships were secured by young women: one in botany; one in architecture; and one in mathematics. The present year the Fellows happen to be all young men; but this is a mere accident, and the question of sex cannot be said to be considered in the award. There were established, a few years ago, three Sage scholarships, set apart exclusively for the young women who attended the university; they were also eligible for the six university scholarships; so that at times four or five out of the nine scholarships might be held by young women. These Sage scholarships have recently been converted into university scholarships, open to all applicants without distinction of sex. Sage College was built and endowed by Hon. Henry W. Sage, in 1875, at a cost of $250,000, and was given to Cornell University as a place of residence for young women students. The gift had but one condition, that "instruction shall be afforded to young women by Cornell University, as broad and thorough as that afforded to young men."

Up to the present time no professorship or offices of instruction in this university have been held by women.

SYRACUSE UNIVERSITY.

Syracuse University, Syracuse, N. Y., embraces a college of liberal arts, a college of medicine, and a college of fine arts. Said the Chancellor, Dr. Sims, "Syracuse throws open the doors of all its colleges for the admission of women on the same terms as men. No especial rules are made because of the presence of both sexes in the university, the young women having every right that is accorded to young men. We have never had difficulty growing out of the presence of both sexes in the institution. The young ladies are as scholarly in every department as the young men."

It is not strange that women's benefactions set to such an institution. In addition to its general library of about 35,000 volumes, and a valuable professional library in connection with the college of medicine, in 1887, Mrs. Dr. G. M. Reid made a gift to the college of the great historical library of Leopold von Ranke. In 1889, Mrs. Harriet Leavenworth, of Syracuse, presented to the college of fine arts the Wolff collection of engravings, containing 12,000 sheets of rare and costly etchings of engravings from the great masters of art in all ages. The "John Crouse Memorial College for Women" was presented to Syracuse University in 1889. It is said to be the finest college building in the world.

BRYN MAWR COLLEGE.

Bryn Mawr College, situated at Bryn Mawr, ten miles from Philadelphia, Pa., was endowed by Dr. Joseph W. Taylor of Burlington, N. J., of the society of Friends, to afford to women opportunities for study equal to those given in the best men's colleges. It was opened in 1885, and admits to lectures and class work three grades of students,—viz., graduates, undergraduates, and hearers. The entrance examinations are strict, and graduate students have from the first formed a large proportion of the students,—from one sixth to one fifth of the whole number. The time of graduation is determined only by the completion of the prescribed course.

The students at Bryn Mawr College enjoy exceptional opportunity for development of character through the important habit of self-direction. Notably wanting here are the customary restrictions on freedom of movement. For example, the student may choose her rising, retiring, and study hours; she may go in and out of Philadelphia at her discretion. This recognition of the student as personally responsible has been attended, it is said, with the happiest results.

Five fellowships are annually awarded: one in Greek, one in English, one in mathematics, one in history, and one in biology. The Bryn Mawr European fellowship is awarded annually to a member of the graduating class for excellence in scholarship. The holder receives $500, applicable to the expenses of one year's residence at some foreign university.

The whole number of students enrolled during the year 1888–89 was 116. At the close of the scholastic year the degree of B.A. was conferred upon twenty-four candidates. All but two had been for four years in attendance at the college, and the president's report says: "All of them left the college in their best state of health."

No person is appointed a member of the faculty who is not, in every way, qualified to direct graduate as well as undergraduate study. There is absolutely no difference made in the salaries paid to the men and women employed in instruction; there is no difference made in academic rank.

The present Board of Trustees, twelve in number, are all men, appointed by the founder of the college. Should a vacancy occur it might be filled by a woman.

SWARTHMORE COLLEGE.

Swarthmore College, ten miles from Philadelphia, Pa., was founded in 1864 by members of the religious society of Friends, for the higher education of both sexes. The two sexes are about equally represented, not only among the pupils, but in the officers of the corporation and in the officers and committees of the board; in this latter respect differing from the record of any other college.

The number of female students in the collegiate department for the scholastic year 1888–89, was 80.

The college confers the degrees of Bachelor of Arts, of Letters, and of Science, on completion of the corresponding courses, and, conditionally, the Masters' degrees, A.M., M.L., M.S., and also the degree of C.E., in the engineering department.

UNIVERSITY OF PENNSYLVANIA.

The first admission of women to special courses in the University of Pennsylvania was in 1876 when, on application, two young women of Philadelphia were granted, after examination and payment of a fee, the full privileges of the analytical laboratory, and during that year were regular students, passing the final examinations with the junior class. The next year, 1877–78, they were admitted to lectures, laboratory work, recitations, and final examinations by the department of organic chemistry. In the years directly following, the physical laboratory received two young women, and upon lectures on modern history, opened to all fitted by previous study to appreciate them, from twenty-four to thirty ladies were regular attendants. In all departments the ladies received the highest courtesy and appreciation. One of the number writing of it says: "You have *carte blanche* to say all you will in this respect,—you could not say too much."

Through the favor of the dean of the college department the following very complete statement is presented of the progress toward giving to women the advantages of this venerable university, which has been gathering its rich resources since its foundation in 1746.

In 1876 a department of music was established, in which advanced instruction in the theory of music was given, and from the beginning women were admitted to the classes. While a degree was attainable, under certain conditions of post graduate work, none have been awarded.

In 1878 Mrs. Bloomfield Moore presented $10,000, the income of which was to pay the tuition fees of women who sought to qualify themselves for teaching, in any of the courses open to them. Certain special courses of lectures and laboratory work, e. g., English history, chemistry, mineralogy, were open to the public on a fee, and of course women were included, a few availing themselves of the opportunity; but these were not matriculated, nor entered upon the roll of students.

In 1880 Miss Alice Bennett, M.D., received the degree Ph.D. in the Auxiliary Faculty of Medicine,—a two years' course in certain sciences open to graduates in medicine.

In 1888 Mrs. Carrie B. Kilgore received the degree LL.B., on completing the full two years' course in the law department.

In neither of these cases was there any formal action opening the courses specified to women. They were simply accepted as students by the several deans, and when they had complied with the terms were, without demur, admitted to their degrees.

The School of Biology, organized in 1884,—a two years' course, no degree,—has from the first been freely open to women, has always had a fair proportion among its students, and some of them have proved to be of superior ability. Its force and material are used in the new four years' course in natural history, one of the college courses, but to this women are not yet admitted.

Applications were often made for the admission of women to the medical department, but trustees and faculty concurred in always refusing it. This was the more unanimously done since the establishment of the admirable Women's Medical College, which would have been fatally injured by the opening of our doors to women.

Requests to open the college department to women have been periodically made for many years. At first the faculty positively declined to recommend this, but gradually opposition to the proposal weakened, until last year (1889–90) a bare majority voted the other way.

Before the trustees had taken action upon the matter, Col. Joseph M. Bennett came forward and presented two valuable houses, adjacent to the university, and a sum of $10,000 for establishing a college for women as a department of the university. The trustees accepted the offer, and after careful consideration and consultation with prominent women educators, decided, with Col. Bennett's full approval, to make this a post graduate department of the highest grade.

Its organization and government are entrusted to a board of managers, one half women. By the autumn of 1891 the department will be open ; ranking with the Faculty of Philosophy, giving the degree Ph.D. (which is no longer given by the Auxiliary Faculty of Medicine), and having special courses not leading to a degree. It is hoped that an ample number of free scholarships will be provided. The Faculty of Philosophy is freely open to women, and prepared to give Ph.D. degrees. Of course, when the department for women is opened it will practically be in this faculty.

In 1889–90 there were the following women students : College, Department of Music, 11, not candidates for a degree ; Biology, 12, not candidates for a degree ; Auxiliary Department of Medicine, 1, candidate for Sc.B. Total, 24.

MASSACHUSETTS INSTITUTE OF TECHNOLOGY.

The Massachussetts Institute of Technology was chartered in 1861. By a special vote of the Corporation in December, 1870, a graduate of Vassar College was admitted as a special student in chemistry. In June, 1873, the lady took the final examinations, covering two years of professional work. As no tuition fee was charged no precedent was established by this action. In 1873, at the request of the Woman's Educational Association, and with its co-operation, the woman's laboratory for chemistry and botany was established, to which women came as special students. Although they had not been recognized during their course as regular students, two women received the Institute Degree in 1881–82.

In 1883 final action was taken, opening all the courses to women on precisely the same terms as to men. Women now go into the laboratories with the regular classes.

The foregoing sketch of woman's educational progress, while extended beyond due limit, leaves out the most encouraging record,—as it is the latest,—the story of what women are doing for themselves, and, no less, for humanity. No one can fairly estimate the educational forces of the coming decades who does not take into consideration the varied means of growth outside of both school and college ; means which do not displace the need of these, but rather emphasize it. We may not even touch upon these here, but from a moment's comprehensive glance backward we may dimly conceive the forward outlook.

It is not yet a century from the time when New England towns were voting "not to be at any expense to school girls," and lo ! as a type of to-day, Wellesley College, with a million and a half dollars wisely invested to entice girls from the remotest islands of the sea, to love and to get learning. For the unlettered housekeeper, filching time from her heavy labors to gather the children about her knee in the "Dame school," we have the young but learned president of the college of nearly 700 students; or the woman directing, as its head, the orderly movement of a thousand or more pupils in the great city grammar school, which may represent a half score of nationalities. For the girl accustomed to denial, and deprecatingly asking for a little instruction when the boys shall have had their fill, we have the bright-faced, trustful young woman who expects and will get ere long the best the world has to offer.

In a country which finds its safety in the intelligence of its people and its peril in their ignorance, it behooves its thinkers to consider whether it is not too great a risk to leave four fifths of the instruction of youth in the hands of a sex of inferior education. The distinguished president of Harvard College, called attention some two years since, in an article in *The Atlantic Monthly*, to the condition of inferiority of our secondary schools, and he proposed remedying it by displacing a part of the female teachers. It would seem more in accordance with the spirit of the time, and certainly more practicable, to open to them the closed doors of opportunity and fit them to meet the demand made upon them.

The terror of the learned woman which, in one form or another, has had its many victims, has well nigh passed. Even the more timid and conservative are learning that it is the ignorant, not the instructed woman, that confuses affairs and works disaster. "A little knowledge is," beyond doubt, "a dangerous thing"; but only because it is little.

It is told of Saint Avila that she gained her renown by this marvel. At one time, when frying fish in the convent, she was seized with a religious ecstacy, yet so great were her powers of self-control that she did not drop the gridiron, nor let the fish burn!

So the educated woman of the nineteenth century has quieted many grave apprehensions as to the consequences of much learning to her sex. After the manner of Saint Avila, she does not permit her intellectual ecstacy to blind her to her simple duties. She has abundantly proved that she can carry the triple responsibility of loving and serving and knowing.

III.

THE EDUCATION OF WOMAN IN THE WESTERN STATES.

BY

MAY WRIGHT SEWALL.

No formal history of the movement in the West on behalf of the higher education of women has been published. The materials for this paper have been derived from the reports issued under the auspices of the Bureau of Education; from the catalogues of institutions open to women; from various monographs, some of which recite the history of a single college (like "Oberlin, its Origin, Progress, and Results," by Pres. J. H. Fairchild), others of which present the educational history of a State (like "Higher Education in Wisconsin," by Professors Allen and Spencer); from a miscellaneous collection of baccalaureate sermons and congratulatory addresses delivered before the graduating classes and the alumnæ associations of many colleges; from old files of newspapers, and from scrap books which for a series of years have been collecting the records of contemporary effort along the lines of higher education; from the biographies of distinguished educators in our country; and from scores of letters, many of which have been written by college presidents and professors in response to my own inquiries, while others have been placed at my disposal by Dr. Carroll Cutler, formerly President of Adelbert College. No stronger evidence of the interest felt in the higher education of women could be found than the cordial, generous answers to my inquiries, which have come from the officials of scores of institutions extending from the Ohio to the Pacific. I am withheld from naming gentlemen to whom I am so deeply indebted only by the fact that a list of those who have courteously replied to my appeals for information would occupy more space than I can afford to give out of the limited number of pages allotted me in this volume.

The Western States and Territories in the order of their admission into the Union under their present names, include Ohio, Indiana, Illinois, Missouri, Michigan, Iowa, Wisconsin, California, Minnesota, Oregon, Kansas, Nevada, Nebraska, Colorado, North Dakota, South Dakota, Montana, and Washington—eighteen States; and Utah, Idaho, and Wyoming—three Territories. The changes undergone and the relations sustained by each of the above in its progress toward its present independent condition are exhibited in Table I. given in Appendix B. In this vast territorial expanse, embracing communities just being born into statehood, together with others which have enjoyed that dignity for periods varying from ten to eighty-seven years, one has an opportunity to witness almost every phase of the struggle for the higher education of women.

Conditions that ceased to exist in one State so long ago that they had almost passed from the memories of their victims, arose at a later period to vex other States. Questions long settled in one community became living issues in another; and such is the reluctance of the human being to learn from the experience of others, that these questions are still discussed with as much vivacity, not to say acrimony, as if they had never been settled.

Higher education in the West has been fostered by the national government, by the governments of the separate States, by many different denominations of the Christian church, and by individual enterprise and devotion.

As a large number of the strongest institutions in the West, open to women, owe their origin to provisions made by the general government, it is fitting to direct our first inquiry to the relations of that government to education in the West. On May 25, 1785, the Continental Congress passed an ordinance disposing of lands in the Northwestern Territory, by which it was decreed that: "There shall be reserved Lot No. 16 of every township for the maintenance of public schools within said township." On July 13, 1787, the famous Ordinance relating to the government of the territory northwest of the Ohio River was passed; in it occurs the passage which is so frequently cited in proof that the United States government stands pledged to aid the higher as well as the lower education: viz., "Religion, Morality, and Knowledge being necessary to good government and the happiness of mankind, schools and the means of education shall forever be encouraged." Ten days later, Congress passed another ordinance fixing the terms of sale for the tract of land purchased by the Ohio

Company. This ordinance stipulated not only that section 16 of every township should be reserved for the maintenance of schools, but also "that two complete townships shall be given perpetually for the purposes of an university, to be laid off by the purchaser or purchasers as near the center as may be, so that the same shall be good land, to be applied to the intended object by the Legislature of the State."

In these ordinances of 1787, we find the germ of all our State Universities in the West.

Owing to the grant secured by Congress in its contract with the Ohio Company, the Ohio University at Athens, O., was founded. It was first chartered as the "American Western University." The name implies that its friends expected it to supply the educational needs of the then vague "West"; but only a year after the admission of Ohio as a State, i.e., in 1804, the University received a new charter from the State Legislature, under its present name. This precedent of Congressional grants for the endowment of institutions of higher education has been followed by the government to the present time.

Sometimes the two townships of land have been given *en bloc*, and some times they have been so given as to permit the the location of university lands in different portions of the State; sometimes they have been kept as an endowment of the State University; sometimes they have been in part devoted to the founding of the university. But in every State and Territory in the above list, a university exists which owes its origin and its maintenance in part to the government of the United States.

A study of the history of the State Universities shows that in many States a strange hostility existed toward them. A feeling that by appropriating lands for their endowment, the general government was encouraging the growth of an aristocratic class of learned men, seems not to have been uncommon in the early days. This appears to be one valid explanation of the reluctance of State Legislatures to make generous or permanent appropriations for the support of such universities.

The truth is, however, that the State Universites are the most democratic of all the institutions of higher learning; this truth is now generally perceived, and the institutions are growing proportionally popular. It is due to their necessarily democratic nature that they are now without exception open to women. Their chief feeders are the public high schools, with which they must maintain direct and constant communication. Their chief financial support comes directly and equally from all property-holding citizens; either by appropriation from the public treasury, varying in amount with each Legislature, or by a fixed, special tax, of a certain percentum of all assessed property. Finding their students in the public high schools, which in the West are almost universally co-educational, and their support in the public treasury, into which flow taxes upon the property of women and girls as well as upon that of men and boys, the wonder is that the State Universities did not from their origin admit women as students.

The following table will show when each State University was chartered, opened, and opened to women. The list of States in this table is presented as above in the chronological order of their admission to the Union.

	CHARTERED.	OPENED.	ADMITTED WOMEN.
Ohio { Athens	1804	1809	1871
Ohio { Columbus	1870	1873	1873
Indiana	1820	1824	1867
Illinois	1867	1868	1871
Missouri	1839	1843	1870
Michigan	1837	1841	1870
Iowa	1847	1860	1860
Wisconsin	1848	1849	1860, 1863, 1868, 1871, 1875
California	1868	1869	1870
Minnesota	1868	1869	1869
Oregon	1876	1876	1876
Kansas	1861	1866	1866
Nevada	1864	1874	1874
Nebraska	1869	1871	1871
Colorado	1861	1877	1877
North Dakota	1883	1884	1884
South Dakota	1862	1885	1885
Montana	1884	1883	1883
Washington	1861	1862	
Utah, Deseret	1850	1850	1850

A glance at the table will show that the periods of time during which these universities received men only, vary from two to sixty-two years, that but one of those opened prior to 1861 has been from the outset co-educational; that all opened prior to 1861 became co-educational between 1861 and 1871: and that all organized since 1871 started as co-educational institutions.

National government made additional provision for higher education by an act usually referred to as "The Agricultural College Act of 1862." By this act each State received 30,000 acres of land for each Senator and Representative to whom it was entitled in the United States Congress, "the proceeds to be applied to the maintenance of at least one college in each State," "without excluding other scientific and classical studies, and including military tactics, to teach such branches as are related to agriculture and the mechanic arts." Under this act there have been established in the territory discussed in this chapter, since 1862, fourteen colleges of the character indicated.

In Ohio, Wisconsin, California, Minnesota, Oregon, Nevada, and Nebraska such institutions exist as Departments of the State University, and, like all its other departments, admit women.

In Indiana, Illinois, Missouri, Michigan, Iowa, Kansas, and Colorado, such institutions, under various names, as "Agricultural College," "Industrial and Mechanical College," "College of Applied Science," etc., enjoy an independent organization, in some States loosely connected with, in others entirely separate from, the State University.

These institutions are authorized to give degrees appropriate to the courses of study pursued in them, and they are likewise open to women. The act of 1862 gave a distinct impulse to the higher education of women in the West, for reasons to be hereafter mentioned.

Although the germ of a State University was secured by the national government to each of the twenty-one States and Territories in our list at or prior to the time of its admission, in many instances the State action relative to these institutions, upon which the government aid had been conditioned, was postponed for a long series of years. In the mean time the desire for the higher education was stimulated, and opportunities for obtaining it were provided by the churches.

Appendix B, Table II., to this article, gives a list of 165 institutions, within my prescribed territory, open to women, which are of sufficient importance to be included in the tables of "Colleges of Liberal Arts," published by the United States Commissioner of Education, in his Report for 1888–89 (taken from the advance sheets). Of these, 45 are non-sectarian. The remaining 120 are distributed among the various denominations as follows:

Methodist Episcopal, 31; Baptist, 16; Presbyterian, 14; Congregational, 13; Christian, 10; United Brethren, 7; Lutheran, 6; United Presbyterian, 4; Reformed, 3; Friends, 3; Cumberland Presbyterian, 2; M. E. South, 2; Universalist, 2; Seventh Day Baptist, 1; Methodist Protestant, 1; Evangelical

Association, 1 ; Brethren, 1 ; Church of God, 1 ; New Church, 1 ; Protestant Episcopal, 1.

At the present time one frequently hears people deprecate the effort to maintain so large a number of colleges. It is asserted truly that the distribution of patronage among so many, necessarily prevents any from attaining commanding influence. Especially do the advocates of non-sectarian education recommend that the weaker institutions be closed, that their properties be sold, and that effort be concentrated upon the few stronger ones. The arguments by which this recommendation is sustained are sound.

If the financial support, the love, the loyalty, the ambition, and the students that are distributed among the thirty-one colleges of Liberal Arts in the State of Ohio, could be united in the support of any one of the number, the fortunate recipient might soon rank with the great universities of our country, nay, of the world. But however desirable such a concentration of patronage ultimately may be, one cannot read the history of the educational work of the churches, without feeling that " Wisdom is justified of her children."

It is true that many of these colleges were founded in the interests of sectarian theology, rather than of liberal culture; that they were all in some degree, some of them in very large degree, regarded and used by their supporters as the most available instruments in the labor of securing proselytes to the particular school of Christian faith in whose name they were planted. In the degree to which these institutions have nurtured sectarian zeal, emphasized distinctions in minor points of doctrine, and strengthened the barriers between denominations, it must be conceded that their influence has been benumbing and narrowing ; and in this degree they have tended from instead of toward culture, whose mission is to broaden and quicken instead of to narrow and benumb.

In spite of this limitation upon the work of denominational colleges, they merit the profoundest respect and gratitude of the public. A large proportion of these institutions were established when the wilderness was being cleared and settled.

It is related by its historian that the site of Ripon College was chosen by two enthusiasts in the cause of higher education, in the year 1850, when the State of Wisconsin was but two years old, when "there were but fourteen rude buildings in the village of Ripon," and when but a single year had elapsed since the first clearing on the village site had been made. At once these brave men applied for a charter for a college ; and the purpose of the corporation was declared to be, "To found, establish, and maintain at Ripon, in the county of Fond du Lac, an institution of learning of the highest order, embracing also a department for preparatory instruction."

This is hardly an exceptional, but a typical instance.

The people were few, scattered, and poor. Communication between places remote from each other was slow and uncertain. Means of travel and transportation were limited to the pack horse, the private wagon, the stage coach, and the flat-boat. If poverty had not rendered it impossible for the pioneers to incur the expense of sending their children on long and slow journeys, to distant colleges, the time consumed in such journeys, and the anxiety incident to separation, in the absence of any means of frequent and speedy communication, would have prohibited it.

Forty years ago, in all of the territory covered by the twenty-one States and Territories under consideration, twenty-five years ago in most of it, and so lately as ten years ago in much of it, the time, fatigue, and expense which a dweller in a remote corner of a county incurred in traveling to its county seat, was more than he will now expend to reach the State capital. Under such conditions the question with the pioneer was not whether he should send his children to a near or to a distant college, but whether he should send them to the near college or to none.

The influence of these 165 colleges upon the life of the Western States cannot be measured by the number of their graduates, nor by adding to this number those who have attended the colleges one or more terms.

The presence of a college, with its educated faculty, in any community, modifies the tone of its intellectual and social life. The colleges have been centers of leavening influence in the new States. While recognizing this with gratitude, one can also see that the conditions which justified and demanded the multiplication of these small colleges have ceased to exist, and that the different conditions which now prevail counsel denominations to consolidate their weak institutions, and to concentrate their dissipated forces upon a few strong ones. The present means of speedy and certain communication and transit enable a strong college, with high standards and an able faculty, to bring its influence to bear upon all parts of a State and to command the patronage of its remotest corner.

That the tendency is toward concentration of effort is indicated by the Year Books of the denominations for 1888–89.

In studying the educational work of the churches, one cannot fail to discern the results of creeds and habits of worship. In a sketch of this character it would be unjust to withhold the fact that the colleges under Methodist control have been generally first and most generous in opening their opportunities to women; and that they are also conspicuous among the colleges that include women in their faculties and in their boards of trustees.

The progressiveness of Methodists in regard to the education of women is evinced not only in their co-educational colleges, but also in institutions founded by them for the exclusive education of women.

The latest report of the United States Commissioner of Education contains over two hundred institutions for the superior education of women. The list includes colleges and seminaries entitled to confer degrees, and a few seminaries, whose work is of equal merit, which do not give degrees. Of these more than two hundred institutions for the education of women exclusively, only 47 are situated within the territory here discussed. Of these 47, but 30 are chartered with authority to confer degrees. Of these 30, 7 are non-sectarian; the remainder are distributed among the denominations as follows:

Presbyterian, 7; Methodist Episcopal, 5; Baptist, 3; Christian, 2; Protestant Episcopal, 1; Congregational, 1.

The religious affiliations of the remaining four have not been ascertained.

The extent to which the higher education of women is in the West identified with co-education, can be seen by comparing the two statements above given. Of the total 212 higher institutions receiving women, and of the total 195 such institutions which confer the regular degrees in arts, science, and letters, upon their graduates, 165 are co-educational. Almost necessarily, therefore, the most important discussion in this article will be that of co-education.

Before approaching it, however, some space must be devoted to women's colleges in the West. Almost without exception they include preparatory departments; very generally the attendance in the preparatory department exceeds that in the collegiate; frequently members of the faculty divide their attention between preparatory and collegiate classes; generally the courses of study offered are less numerous and less complete than those offered in colleges of liberal arts for men; most of these institutions have paltry or no endowments. With all these limitations, some of them do much creditable work; but, at present, they occupy a rather vague, indefinite position between "the ladies' seminary" of thirty years ago and the modern college. Quoting from the United States Commissioner of Education (Report for 1887-88): "The adjustment of studies is evidence of a double purpose in these institutions. On the one hand they have endeavored to meet the general demand with respect to woman's education. On the other they have sought to maintain that higher ideal which would appropriate for women as well as for men the advantages of the kind of instruction and training approved, by wise effort and long experience, as the best for mental discipline and culture."

A double purpose, when its parts are, as in this instance, to a degree contradictory, imposes impossible tasks. A process of sifting is now going on among these institutions. Some of the weaker will doubtless be absorbed by stronger ones having the same denominational support. Some, whose strength is chiefly in their preparatory departments, will find their ultimate place in the lists of secondary schools; and, ceasing to compete with colleges, will do an important and much needed work in preparing students to enter college. Others, already strongest in their collegiate departments, pledged by a noble past to achieve a corresponding future, will persist in emphasizing their real collegiate side until at last they secure an absolute separation between their preparatory and their collegiate work, and can take rank with genuine colleges of liberal arts.

In this sketch it is impossible to give the history of all these institutions; but among colleges characterized from birth by a liberal and progressive spirit may be mentioned "The Cincinnati Wesleyan Woman's College." This institution was chartered in 1842, and claims to be "the first liberal collegiate institution in the world for the exclusive education of women." This claim sounds somewhat boastful, but a perusal of the discussions which were called forth by the establishment of this college, will convince one that its undertaking was novel and quite foreign to the thought of its public, if not, indeed, quite unprecedented in the world's history. Dr. Charles Eliot, the editor of the *Western Christian Advocate*, heroically defended the project against the attacks of both the secular and the religious press. Rev. P. B. Wilber was elected president, and his wife, Mary Cole Wilber, was made principal.

The broad claim made by these enthusiastic educators was "that women need equal culture of mind and heart with men, in their homes, in the church, and in the state." The enterprise was accused of "being counter to delicacy and to custom, as it was to orthodoxy." Mrs. Wilber, who is still living (in 1890), writes that those who had upheld the college "were convinced that a higher intellectual and moral education for women was indispensable to the continued prosperity and existence of civilization, especially under our form of government. They believed it would be a powerful influence for good in the home, in social life, and in all benevolences and philanthropies. They believed in the elevation of women through education, which is development; through labor, which is salvation; and through legal rights, which should give freedom to serve and to save." These sentiments do not seem antiquated in 1890, and must have seemed not merely advanced but dangerous in 1842.

Violations of precedent continued to keep the watchful eye of the public on the college. The college professed to give to women the same instruction which secured for young men the degree of A.B., and it obtained from the Legislature authority "to confer the degrees of A.B. and B.S." The college held public commencement exercises, at which the graduates read their own productions, a performance that was the occasion of much scandal.

September 25, 1844, "The Young Ladies' Lyceum" was organized in the college. This was a literary society, at the meetings of which debates upon current public questions were conducted and essays were read. Cuttings from contemporary newspapers show that this lyceum created no small stir.

In 1852 the graduates of the college organized an alumnæ association, which is claimed to be the first organization of the kind in this country. The preamble to the constitution adopted by this body begins thus:

"The undersigned, graduates of the Wesleyan Female College of Cincinnati, believing that as educated American women, society and the world at large have peculiar claims upon them, which they can neither gainsay nor resist," etc.

The association at once decided to publish an annual which should contain only original articles from the pens of its members; and Article VII. of the constitution says: "The immediate object of this publication shall be to afford an opportunity for continued mental effort and improvement to members; and its ultimate aim shall be the elevation of woman." Rachel L. Bodley, so long dean of the Woman's

Medical College in Philadelphia, was one of the original members of this association.

The professions, claims, and efforts above indicated, probably show the high-water mark of educational aspiration of women in the West in and before the middle of this century.

The college drew students from all parts of the country, and from Canada; and, at one time, according to one of its historians, there were in attendance upon it "representatives from every State in the Union, excepting New Hampshire, Delaware, North Carolina, and Florida."

At one time this college enrolled nearly five hundred students; but, as seminaries and colleges for women have multiplied throughout the region from which it drew its patronage, and especially as more richly endowed colleges which were established for men have opened their doors to women, its numbers have diminished and its influence has waned. But such a past should compel its alumnæ and its friends to give it an endowment, a course of study, and a corps of instructors that shall make it the peer of its strongest young sisters.*

There is a function for the true woman's college which the co-educational college does not and as yet cannot perform.

---

* As the Cincinnati Wesleyan College is an example of the best that Methodism has done for the separate education of women, so Albert Lea College in Minnesota, founded and controlled by the synod of that State, would appear to be the most ambitious attempt of the Presbyterian Church to aid the separate higher education of women in the West. This college was founded in 1882, and opened to students in 1885. Its president makes for it, with relation to the country west of the Alleghanies, the same claim that the president of the Wesleyan made in its behalf with relation to the entire country, forty-eight years ago. Its president, Dr. R. B. Abbott, writes: "This is the only real college for women west of the Allegheny Mountains. There are female seminaries in abundance, some of which are named college, but are without a full college curriculum and without authority to confer the degrees of Bachelor and Master of Arts. Albert Lea is a college in fact as well as in name."

Albert Lea is now in only its fifth year. I have not been able to obtain its latest catalogue. The above quotation from its president's letter indicates its promise. Should it redeem this promise in its spirit and word, it would be a great blessing to the West; not so much young because women in this part of the country need another college within their easy reach, but because the entire community needs to have the difference between the nominal and the real college continually emphasized.

If Albert Lea draws sharp and visible lines between its standards and tests of scholarship, between its quality and methods of instruction and those of the majority of institutions in the above list, its influence will be potent in securing greater harmony between names and things in matters pertaining to education.

To get one's college education in an institution which admits only women, and to enjoy some years of post-graduate work in a co-educational university, is the ideal of opportunity now cherished by some most careful and intelligent parents and by some ambitious young women. It is possible that provision for satisfying the first half of this ideal is held in germ by some or all of the thirty colleges for women only, now existing in the West.

CO-EDUCATION IN THE WEST.

That in the Western States and Territories, the higher education of women is generally identical with co-education is indicated, as has been previously suggested, by the following facts:

1. Of 212 institutions in the West, exclusive of colleges of agriculture and the mechanic arts, which afford the higher culture to women, 165 are co-educational.

2. Of the 5563 women reported to the Bureau of Education in 1887-88 as students in the collegiate courses of these institutions, 4392 were in the co-educational colleges.

3. In the twenty-one States and Territories which boast 165 co-educational colleges and 47 colleges for the separate education of women, 30 of which are authorized to confer regular degrees, there are but 25 colleges devoted to the exclusive education of men.

4. Of these 25 (devoted to the exclusive education of men,) not one is non-sectarian, and they are all supported by the Roman Catholic, the Protestant Episcopal, the Lutheran, or the Presbyterian denomination. In several of the States most conspicuous for zeal in the cause of the higher education, as in Michigan, Iowa, and Kansas, not one college for the exclusive education of men exists.

These facts support the statement that the West is committed to co-education, excepting only the Roman Catholic, the Lutheran, and the Protestant Episcopal sects,—which are not yet, as sects, committed to the collegiate education of women at all,—and the Presbyterian sect, whose support, in the West, of 14 co-educational colleges against 4 for the separate education of young men, almost commits it to the co-educational idea.

How has this triumph of the higher co-education been achieved? How is the system regarded by the community in which it is established? What are its social effects and tendencies? What are its defects and limitations? These are the inquiries which next present themselves.

Of the 165 co-educational colleges under consideration, a few, like Ripon College, Wisconsin, were founded for women and subsequently admitted young men; a larger number have admitted both men and women from the date of their opening; these, with a few notable exceptions, like Oberlin College in Ohio, and Lawrence University in Wisconsin, are of recent origin, with charters dating from periods since 1860. The great proportion of the entire number were founded for the exclusive education of men, and have, one after another, yielded a participation in their benefits to women since 1860.*

To tell in detail the story of the struggles which have ended in the admission of women into each of these institutions would be quite impossible; if possible, it would, for general purposes, be quite unprofitable, since the principles involved have in all cases been the same. The same arguments, pro and con, have been advanced in every contest, the illustrations and modes of application being modified in each by local conditions and circumstances. Local history should preserve a record of such modifications of the argument and its application, together with the names of those persons who were conspicuous in the contest; but the purposes of general history do not require this, and the discrepancy between the extent of territory and the number of pages assigned to this chapter does not permit it.

In Ohio, the oldest of the Western States, the higher education of women first became a question; and in connection with its various institutions every aspect of the question has been exhibited. Moreover, as the oldest of the group, the example of Ohio has exerted a marked influence upon the other Western States. These facts justify the discussion of co-education in connection with Ohio colleges.

No institution has been more frequently cited in discussions of co-education than Oberlin; and perhaps the attitude of no other has been so persistently misunderstood. In reading numerous discussions incident to opening men's colleges in other States to women, one finds it implied and asserted that "Oberlin was founded to give to women the same educational advantages enjoyed by men."

Sketches and histories of Oberlin College, sermons, addresses, and letters, explanatory of its aims and policy, are numerous and accessible; and if these authoritative documents agree upon any one point it is in showing that Oberlin was not

---

* Appendix B, Table II., gives a table by which is shown when each of these colleges was founded, when opened, and when opened to women.

"founded to give to women the same educational advantages enjoyed by men"; that at the outset the intention to do this was not entertained by her founders; that such form of collegiate co-education as Oberlin now offers has been developed gradually; and, finally, that co-education at Oberlin to-day differs in many essential respects from the co-education to be found in our State Universities.

Let the following facts sustain these statements:

1. It was as "Oberlin Collegiate Institute" that Oberlin began its work in 1833, and the name of "Oberlin College" was not taken until 1850.

2. The original plan included a "female department," under the supervision of a lady, where "instruction in the useful branches taught in the best female seminaries" could be obtained; the circular setting forth the plan also says: "The higher classes of the female department will also be permitted to enjoy the privileges of such professorships in the teachers', collegiate and theological departments as shall best suit their sex and prospective employment."

3. This "female department" contemplated a separate building, and separate classes in which women should pursue merely academic studies. But this department was never formed, according to the original plan, because at first poverty prevented the erection of a separate school building; and because, in the beginning, there were only high school classes, into which, for economy and convenience, young men and women were together admitted with no thought whatever of their ultimately entering collegiate classes together.

4. In lieu of the anticipated "female department," a "ladies' course," was provided and maintained until 1875. This course demanded no Greek and but two years of Latin, and, according to its present president, required only "a year more time than is devoted to study in the best female seminaries."

5. Separate classes were organized for ladies in essay-writing until the commencement of the junior year, when they were admitted to the regular college class; their work was still limited to writing and reading, none of the ladies having any practice in speaking.

6. At the present time the "literary course," under the department of philosophy and arts, takes the place of the former "ladies' course."

7. In 1837, four ladies, having prepared themselves to enter the freshman class of the collegiate department, were admitted

on their own petition; since then ladies have been received into all the college classes excepting those of the theological department, which has never been open to ladies as regular members, though at one time two ladies "attended all the exercises of this department through a three years' course, and were entered upon the annual catalogue as resident graduates pursuing the 'theological course.'" So long as the "ladies' course" continued, the apparent expectation of the college was that a majority of ladies would take that course. The influence of the college was apparently exerted in that direction, and with such effect that the number of ladies graduating from the "ladies' course" was, to the number graduating from the "college course," nearly as five to one.

8. That the present "literary course" in the department of philosophy and arts is practically the same as the original "ladies' course," will be seen by comparing the lists of subjects upon which candidates for entrance into each must be examined, and also by considering the scheme of study followed in the "literary course," as presented in the catalogue, for 1888–89. This view is further sustained by the fact that in 1888–89, 175 ladies and 3 gentlemen were registered in this course.

9. The latest catalogue states that: "Young women in all the departments of study are under the supervision of the principal of the ladies' department and the care of the ladies' board. They are required to be in their rooms after eight o'clock in the evening during the spring and summer months, and after half past seven during the fall and winter months.

"Every young woman is required to present, once in two weeks, a written report of her observance and her failure in the observance of the regulations of the department, signed by the matron of the family in which she boards."

The catalogue in another connection says: "In addition to lectures announced in the course of study, practical lectures on general habits, methods of study, and other important subjects, are delivered once in two weeks to the young women by the principal of the ladies' department, and *to the young men of the preparatory schools* (the italics are my own), by the principals of these schools."

The regulations here cited may be admirable, and highly advantageous to those whom they affect. It may be matter of regret that the young men are not given similar supervision, and that the "practical lectures on general habits," etc., to which women in all departments are required to listen, are, in the case of young men, limited to those of the preparatory schools. The propriety and value of these requirements is, however, not the subject of discussion. They are referred to here only because they illustrate the difference between the methods of Oberlin and the methods of what is popularly understood by the term "co-educational college." Because, indeed, taken in connection with the preceding eight points, they show that while Oberlin is largely co-instructional, it is also largely not, in the current sense of the term, co-educational at all.

The history and method of co-education at Oberlin, as summed up above, proves the truth of what the presidents and professors of Oberlin have said in one and another form again and again : viz., that co-education there did not originate in any radically new idea of the sphere and work of women ; nor in any conscious purpose to do justice to woman as an individual.

Oberlin originated in religious zeal. As a high school, it admitted women because of the great need of educated women who could serve their own country as teachers, or foreign countries as missionaries or missionaries' wives ; women were, upon their own petition, suffered to enter the college course by men too just and too logical to deny a request grounded in justice and reason ; but they were not welcomed by men who saw in this petition the realization of any theory of the mental equality of the sexes.

The present Oberlin system has been molded slowly by poverty and resulting economy, by local needs and, partially, too, though resistingly, by the progressive spirit of the times. It is curious and interesting that so conservative a college (independently of her own intention or desire) should have been appealed to as their inspiration, and cited as their model, by colleges between whom and Oberlin great dissimilarity exists ; but it is true that Oberlin has done more for the cause of co-education than she could possibly have done had she taken the attitude of a propagandist. Probably no college for men has opened its doors to women in the last thirty years without first consulting Oberlin's experience. The Oberlin authorities have always unhesitatingly testified to the success of the Oberlin plan ; almost always the testimony of these witnesses has indicated their conviction that the Oberlin plan, being the outgrowth of peculiar conditions, would not be certain to flourish if transplanted ; and this moderation, this abatement of enthusiastic advocacy, has given the testimony of

Oberlin men incomparable weight during this controversy in the West.

In 1853, Antioch College was opened at Yellow Springs, O. It was the first endeavor in the West to found a college under Christian but non-sectarian auspices. Its president, Horace Mann, wrote of it: "Antioch is now the only first-class college in all the West that is really an unsectarian institution. There are, it is true, some State institutions which profess to be free from proselyting instrumentalities; but I believe without exception they are all under control of men who hold as truth something which they have prejudged to be true."

This fact has a distinct bearing on co-education, and it is curious to observe that even this most non-sectarian of colleges provided by charter that two thirds of the trustees and two thirds of the faculty should belong to the "Christian Connection"; a body of people who, by separating themselves from the sects, had really become a new sect.

The opening of this college under so distinguished an educator as Mr. Mann, gave a new *impulse* to higher education throughout the West. Antioch was from the first avowedly co-educational; this was demanded by the liberality of the Christian thought by which it was supported. But the best friends of the higher education of women, even Mr. Mann himself, regarded this feature of the new college with suspicion, if not with aversion. How serious the objection that marriages might grow out of the intimacies of college life was considered, may be inferred from the fact that Mr. Mann discussed it in his inaugural address; and from the passage of a by-law providing that marriages should not take place between students while retaining their connection with the college. At one time Mr. Mann advised against co-education on this ground.

The effect that his experience with a co-educational institution produced upon Mr. Mann's own opinion has been frequently urged as a strong argument in the behalf of co-education.

In view of the probable necessity of closing the college, Mr. Mann wrote: "One of the most grievous of my regrets at this sad prospect is the apprehension that the experiment (as the world will still call it) of educating the sexes together will be suddenly interrupted, to be revived only in some indefinite future."

In his baccalaureate address of 1859, there occurs a passionate paragraph expressing Mr. Mann's longing to do more and better than he had done for the higher education of women, which shows that he had found women at Antioch worthy of their opportunities.

Women were not only received as students at Antioch, but also, in the beginning, were included in the faculty. These facts, especially the latter, excited marked attention, and, notwithstanding the disasters which interrupted the work of Antioch, and the poverty which has kept it a small college, the fame of Horace Mann, inseparably connected with its history, has made its influence in behalf of co-education potent.

OPENING WEDGES.

The conditions of pioneer life are favorable to co-education. The exigencies incident to life in a new country destroy certain barriers between men and women which are fixed in old and settled communities. The women in a pioneer settlement not infrequently join in labors in which, under more settled conditions, they would never be called to participate. Many women in the West have assisted their husbands and fathers in the field, the office, and the shop, simply because hired male labor was unattainable. On the other hand, men in pioneer homes assist their wives in household labors, because domestic help cannot be found. In the organization of churches, schools, and Sunday-schools, the sparseness of the population compels men to divide the work with women. Thus, without intention on the part of either men or women, they become used to working together in many unaccustomed ways; and the idea of going to college together does not seem so unnatural as in older communities, where traditions of long standing have separated men and women in their occupations.

The almost universal connection of preparatory departments with colleges in the West is properly deplored; but the "preparatory" has been a stepping-stone to co-education. In their origin the Western colleges found it necessary to maintain preparatory schools in order to obtain any college classes. This is illustrated by the experience of Antioch. Out of 150 students who applied for admission to that college in 1853, but 8 were able to pass the examinations for admission to the freshman class, meager as were the requirements. These 8 included men and women, married and single. The older colleges in this new country have a similar chapter in their history. There were few high schools, and the course of study of those was narrow. To have students, each college was compelled to prepare them. The preparatory department in a college town did the work of the present high school; it was very natural that the residents of those towns should desire to send both their sons and daughters to the " preparatory," which was usually, perhaps always, the best school accessible to them. This desire, however, gave no forecast of a desire to send both to the college later on. Sometimes the "preparatory" was not provided with a separate building, but its work was done in some room or rooms of the college building proper. The preparatory course finished, some bright girl would wish to go forward with her class into college work; she could not enter the class formally, but "if the professor was willing" she could attend lectures in this or the other subject; in many college towns there are middle-aged and elderly women who, as young girls, with the tacit consent of parents and college instructors, thus obtained the larger part of a college education. They had no formal recognition from any one; their names appeared in no catalogues, but they acquired substantial benefits. The present permitted but unacknowledged presence of women at Leipzig and other universities on the Continent, was thus antedated in the West.

Occasionally one of these students, spurred by what she considered the demands of her self-respect, made formal application for regular admission to the college; and not a few of our Western colleges became co-educational by these natural, easy, and noiseless approaches.

The manner in which the desire of one woman for a college education has transformed a men's into a co-educational college, is illustrated in the history of the State University of Indiana. Miss Sarah P. Morrison wished to enter college, and began agitating the question of opening the State University to women. Mr. Isaac Jenkinson of Richmond, Ind., tells the whole pregnant story thus briefly. He writes me:

"I was a member of the board of trustees in 1866, when Miss Morrison's appeal was made to the trustees. (Miss Morrison had for several years been agitating the question among her friends.) I at once offered a resolution admitting young women on equal terms with young men, but I had no support whatever in the board at that time; at a following session the same year, my resolution was adopted by a vote of 4 in favor, to 3 against it."

Many colleges in the West had from the beginning a "female course" much like the "ladies' course" at Oberlin. This course was, like the preparatory department, a way of approach for the more ambitious. The story of one is, with a change of names, the story of many such colleges. The following from

"A Report on the Position of Women in Industries and Education in the State of Indiana," * illustrates the function of the "ladies course" in facilitating co-education.

"Butler University at Irvington, Ind., founded in 1855, admitted women as students from the outset, but at first only into what was denominated its female course. In its laudable endeavor to adapt its requirements to an intermediate class of beings, the university, in its 'female course' substituted music for mathematics and French for Greek. Few young women availed themselves of this 'course' and it was utterly repudiated by Demia Butler, a daughter of Ovid Butler, the founder of the university, and a gentleman of most enlightened views concerning woman's place in life. Miss Butler, upon her own petition, indorsed by her father, entered the university in 1858, and graduated from what was then known as the 'male course' in 1862. From that time the 'female course' became less popular, and in 1864 was formally discontinued."

The normal class was another of the steps toward co-education. In the middle of this century it was not uncommon for special short terms of instruction for teachers to be held during the fall or spring vacations of the common schools. To secure the advantage of good lecture rooms and appliances, and also to secure the aid of distinguished professors, the State Superintendent of Public Instruction would obtain permission to hold his normal class at the State university; or for similar reasons a county Superintendent would hold such a school for the teachers within his jurisdiction, in a college town. In these "normal schools," having no formal or permanent relation with the college at which they were held, one sees the origin in many colleges of their present "departments of the theory and practice of elementary instruction."

From the earliest settlement of the West women taught the district schools in the summer, and the work of elementary instruction fell naturally more and more into their hands, until it was, during the war of 1861–5, almost monopolized by them. Necessarily, when the "normal classes" were organized, women entered and sometimes exclusively composed them. After the normal class had transcended its original limits of four or six weeks, and had developed into a "normal department," women still, in part or in whole, constituted it. Lec-

---

* Prepared by May Wright Sewall at the request of the commissioners for Indiana, for the Indiana Department of the New Orleans Exposition.—Ed.

tures were always being delivered in other departments of the college which would be beneficial to the students in the normal department, whose members were, therefore, gradually admitted to one privilege after another, until at last the college awakened to a consciousness that it had no reserves.

More State universities than denominational colleges have been entered by women *viâ* the "normal class," though many of the latter have been opened by the same insidious influence. So far as the State university was concerned, the end must have been seen from the beginning by all clear-sighted people.

The State university, like the common school, is supported at public expense, and free to the children of the State, who pass into it from the common school. What more natural indeed, more necessary, than that the teachers who are to prepare the boys for the university shall know, by their own experience in it as students, what the requirements of the university are? In illustration of this view, the steps by which co-education was attained in the universities of Wisconsin and Missouri are briefly indicated.

In the spring of 1860 a ten weeks' course of lectures was given at the University of Wisconsin, to a "normal class" of fifty-nine, of whom thirty were ladies. In the spring of 1863 a "normal department" was opened, which was at once entered by seventy-six ladies. At this time the Regents announced that the lectures in the university proper upon chemistry, geology, botany, mechanical philosophy, and English literature would be free to the "normal" students.

Conditions at the close of the war demanded a reorganization of the university. This was effected in 1866, and Section Fourth of the Act under which the university was reconstructed, says: "The university in all its departments and colleges shall be open alike to male and female students."

However, the Regents were obliged to ask the State to recede from this broad statement of co-education, and the next year the Legislature amended the charter upon this point as follows: "The university shall be open to female as well as to male students under such regulations and restrictions as the Board of Regents may deem proper." The charter was thus amended because Dr. Chadbourne, to whom the presidency had been offered, had refused it on the ground that he feared that this innovation would lose to the university the confidence and support of the public.

Up to 1868 the ladies pursued the course which had been

laid down for the "normal department." This course, limited to three years, was now enlarged to four.

Until 1871 the recitations of the young women were separate from those of the young men. In that year, the number of professors and instructors being insufficient to carry on separate classes, the young women were permitted at their option to enter the regular college classes. In 1875 the president reported that "for the first time women have been put, in all respects, on precisely the same footing, in the university, with young men."

The year 1875 does not date the end of the contest in Wisconsin, but it dates the last incident pertinent to this part of the discussion, the object of which is to show the relation between the "normal class" and co-education.

In Missouri, State university co-education was reached by similar steps. A "normal class" was organized for women, who were next invited into the "normal department," which was originally open to men only. Then the women were admitted to such lectures in the university proper as were thought to have a special value for them as teachers. They were next invited to attend chapel, but at first only as silent witnesses to the worship of the male students; later they were solicited to join in the services of song and prayer; and finally, in 1870, they were admitted to the university on the same conditions with young men.

In the early years, denominational effort was on double lines; wherever it founded a college for men, soon, in its nearer or more remote vicinity, it established a "female seminary" or "ladies' institute." Generally the ladies' school was unsupplied with books, apparatus, or cabinets; it often happened that an ambitious instructor sought and obtained occasional permission to use the laboratory and the museum of the college for the benefit of her pupils, and to draw books for them from the college library. Sometimes, when a college professor was about to perform experiments of especial interest before his classes, the young ladies of the neighboring "seminary" would be invited, under escort of their instructors, to witness them.

Usually the college maintained a lecture course, the benefits of which were open to the seminary students. Unless the frivolous conduct of some college youth and seminary maiden excited a scandal which terminated such neighborly offices (a calamity that alone still withholds two or three colleges from becoming co-educational), these friendly relations were strengthened from year to year, and in many instances have resulted in a reorganization by which the seminary has become a woman's college and an equal component part of the university which has been formed by its union with the college for men.

This process of building up a co-educational institution is illustrated in the history of the Northwestern University, at Evanston, Ill.

In reading current college history as presented in catalogues, college papers, and the general press, it is very interesting to observe how certain departures from ancient standards of college study have aided co-education. The cry for the "practical" and the answer which colleges have made to this cry, by offering their scientific courses, may be named as one of these. The average person thinks of practical as a synonym for *useful.* One opinion in which all men agree (the most conservative with the most radical) is, that women should be useful. In connection with education the average man thinks that "scientific" is also a synonym for "practical." The conviction that such a scientific, practical course of study will enlarge a woman's capacity for daily usefulness has sent many a young woman to a college where such courses of study were offered, who would not have been permitted to go to the college which offered only the inflexible course of classics and mathematics. The modern classical course, which permits the substitution of French and German for Greek is, on similar grounds, favorable to co-education.

The elective system has silenced a host of objectors to co-education. All people who entertain vague notions that women are intuitional creatures, that their perceptions are quicker, but their reflective powers less developed than those of men, and who hold the consequent conviction that women cannot so well conform to prescribed lines of study, all of this class are reconciled to co-education by the elective system. The following quotation supports this view. A father writes: "My daughter has entered Michigan University. Under the old régime I should not have permitted it, for I do not believe in a woman's undertaking a man's work; but under the elective system she can take what she likes, can take just what she would in a woman's college, in short; and as all of the professors are men, the subjects will be much better taught." This letter is written by an intelligent but rather old-fashioned gentleman, and the sentiments here expressed and implied concerning the elective system are entertained by a still numerous class.

The influence of the introduction of co-education at State universities upon the policy of smaller colleges has been irresistible.

Although, as has been shown, State universities did not take the initiative in co-education, the influence of the admission of women into such universities as those of Michigan and Wisconsin, has secured a similar change of policy in a large number of denominational and smaller non-sectarian colleges, founded for men only.

Appendix B., Table II., will show the relative number of colleges opened to women prior and subsequent to 1870, the year of the admission of women into Michigan University.

GENERAL ARGUMENT.

On the appearance of Dr. Clarke's book, "Sex in Education," in 1873, the controversy, which up to that time had been limited to the localities where co-education was being introduced, at once became general. For the next ten years this subject was discussed in the press, in the pulpit, in meetings of medical societies, and on the platform. In a large collection of old programs there is proof that every phase of the question was considered by all kinds of organizations of teachers, from national conventions to township institutes. Young teachers advanced their opinions, old teachers recited their experience, and the press everywhere gave the widest publicity to these discussions. At the end of a decade the public mind had fully expressed, and, through expressing, had gradually formed its opinion, which was in general favorable to co-education. In 1883 the whole question was opened in a new form by the attempt to exclude women from Adelbert College of Western Reserve University, which had already been open to them for twelve years.

Every reason which had formerly been urged against the admission of women was now offered for their exclusion. The peculiar origin of the discussion and the able and gallant defense of the rights of the women already enrolled in its classes which was made by Dr. Carroll Cutler, the president of Adelbert, attracted wide notice, and the arguments, pro and con, were reviewed by the press of the country.

Dr. Cutler wrote to the authorities of all the principal co-educational colleges, for the results of their experience. The courtesy of Dr. Cutler makes this voluminous correspondence available for this chapter.

Stated briefly and in the chronological order of their development, the arguments against co-education are as follows:

a. Women are mentally inferior to men, and therefore their presence in a college will inevitably lower the standard of its scholarship.

b. The physical constitution of women makes it impossible for them to endure the strain of severe mental effort. If admitted to college they will maintain their position and keep pace with men only at the sacrifice of their health.

c. The presence of women in college will result in vitiating the manners, if not the morals, of both men and women; the men will become effeminate and weak, the women coarse and masculine.

d. If women are admitted to college, their presence will arouse the emotional natures of the men, will distract the minds of the latter from college work, and will give opportunity for scandal.

e. The intimacies of college life will result in premature marriages.

f. Young men do not approve of the collegiate education of women; they dislike to enter into competition with women, and if the latter are admitted to our colleges it will result in the loss of male students, who will seek in colleges limited to their own sex, the social life which cannot be furnished by a co-educational institution.

g. A collegiate education not only does not prepare a woman for the domestic relations and duties for which she is designed, but actually unfits her for them.

h. Colleges were originally intended for men only, and the wills of their founders and benefactors will be violated by the admission of women.

i. Whatever the real mental capacity or physical ability of women, so fixed is the world's conviction of their inferiority, that colleges admitting them will inevitably forfeit the world's confidence and respect.

This chapter affords no space for the *à priori* arguments which answer these objections; and indeed the best answer to all objections against co-education is found in its result. Let the following letters testify to the fruits of experience. Extract from a letter from James B. Angell, president of the University of Michigan, dated September 2, 1884:

"Women were admitted here (Michigan University) under

the pressure of public sentiment, against the wishes of most of the professors; but I think no professor now regrets it, or would favor their exclusion. The way had been well prepared. Denominational colleges had for years admitted women; and in the high schools, which are our preparatory schools, it was the universal custom to teach both sexes. Most of the evils feared by those who opposed the admission of women have not been encountered.

"We made no solitary modification of our rules or requirements. The women did not become hoydenish; they did not fail in their studies; they did not break down in health; they have graduated in all departments; they have not been inferior in scholarship to the men; the careers of our women graduates have been, on the whole, very satisfactory. They are teachers in many of our best high schools; six or seven are in the Wellesley College faculty." *

Extract from a letter from Moses Coit Tyler, dated at Cornell University, September 30, 1884:

"I was connected with the University of Michigan before the advent of women there; was present during the process of their introduction; for several years afterward watched the results; and am now entering on my fourth year here at a co-educational university. And now, after all these years, upon my word, I cannot recall a fact which furnishes a single valid objection to the system; while the real utility, convenience, and wholesomeness of it have so long been before my eyes, that I am startled by your letter as implying that anybody still has any doubt about it. . . . . I do not know a member of the faculty either at Michigan or here who would favor a return to the old plan, although, before the adoption of the new one, many were anxiously opposed to it. My observation has been that under the joint system the tone of college life has grown more earnest, more courteous and refined, less flippant and cynical. The women are usually among the very best scholars, and lead instead of drag; and their lapses from good health are rather (yes, decidedly) less numerous than those alleged by men. There is a sort of young man who thinks it is not quite the thing, you know, to be in college where women are, and he goes away, if he can, and I am glad to have him do so. The

* It is only fair to add that one of its graduates became a college president—Miss Alice Freeman, president of Wellesley College during six years, now Mrs. Alice F. Palmer, member of the Massachusetts State Board of Education.—ED.

vacuum he causes by his departure is not a large one, and is more than made up by the arrival, in his stead, of a more robust and a manlier sort."

Extracts from two letters written by the Hon. Andrew D. White while president of Cornell University, and bearing dates respectively of August 5, 1884, and October 25, 1884:

"My own opinion is that all the good results we anticipated, and some we did not anticipate, have followed the admission of young women; on the other hand, not one of the prophesied evils, unless possibly some young men may have imbibed a prejudice against the university from the presence of young women, and so have gone elsewhere. This, of course, we can hardly determine. I have never thought the admission of women injured us to any appreciable extent, even in this matter. Scholarship has certainly not been injured in the slightest degree, while order has been improved. . . . There have been no scandals. Hardly any attachments have ever grown up between the students of the two sexes. . . . The best scholars are, almost without exception, men; but there is a far larger proportion of young women than of young men who become good scholars. Having now gone through one more year, making twelve in all since women were admitted, I do not hesitate to say that I believe their presence here good for us in every respect. There has not been a particle of scandal of any sort. As to the relations between the sexes, they give us no uneasiness."

Extract from a letter written by John Bascom, then president of the University of Wisconsin, dated August 20, 1884:

"Co-education is with us wholly successful. There is no difference of opinion concerning it, either in our faculty or our board. We find no additional difficulty in discipline; our young women do good work, and the progress of our young men is in no way impeded. It does not seem to us to be any longer an open question.

"I believe the character of both young men and women is helped, though the results in this particular are difficult of proof. The advantages of the system are manifold; the evils are none. We have ceased to think about its fitness save as questions from abroad redirect our attention to it."

Extract from a letter by Joseph Cummings, president of Northwestern University:

"The effect of co-education in this institution, upon the manners and morals of both men and women, is only good. The history of co-education shows that men and women trained under its influence are less open to temptations of the passions than are those trained in separate institutions.

"Women are less inclined to pursue long courses of study, but the average scholarship of those who do persevere and graduate is higher than that of the men ; and women here do not retard the progress of men."

In more than 200 letters from presidents and professors in co-educational colleges, a part of which were written during the Adelbert College controversy, and a larger part of which have been received by the writer of this chapter within the last three months, there is not one which does not give testimony to the value of the system, similar to that above quoted.

I have chosen to quote from letters written in 1884 because the controversy then pending impelled the writers to a fuller and more specific statement of their experience than would be elicited by a series of questions propounded at this date. It is only necessary to add that in every instance letters dated in 1889 or 1890 fully accord with those written in 1883 and 1884.

Presidents Angell, White, Bascom, and Cummings, and Professor Tyler are quoted because of their distinguished reputation as educators, because their experience has been in institutions universally acknowledged to rank among the highest in our country, and because, as no one of them has ever taken the position of an apostle of co-education, their words will be received as the testimony of witnesses, and not as the pleadings of advocates.

THE SOCIAL EFFECTS AND TENDENCIES OF CO-EDUCATION.

But few of all the 165 colleges in the West now open to men and women have compiled statistics which present the records of their graduates, prior or subsequent to the admission of women, in reference to health, domestic state, occupation, social position, official place, financial or other form of success. Perhaps the most important and successful attempt to obtain such statistics is that made by the Association of Collegiate Alumnæ, whose inquiries were limited to the women who had graduated from the small number of institutions for either separate or joint education, admitted to that association.

These statistics, of course, relate to women only ; and, moreover, they are too incomplete to establish any general law ; but they do permit the inference that college life confirms and improves the health of women ; and that it does not disincline them to matrimony, or render them averse to or incapable of maternity and its consequent duties. In the absence of statistical data one can only consider the probabilities.

That a general impression that women were intellectually inferior to men formerly prevailed cannot be disputed.

If their work in co-educational colleges has (as, according to the testimony of their instructors, is the case) been, on an average, better than that of their male classmates, the young men who for four years have witnessed daily this exhibition of an intellectual vigor and interest equal to their own, will not be likely to entertain the doctrine of women's natural and therefore necessary inferiority. The minds of the women in these colleges will be correspondingly affected; they will acquire a respect for themselves and for their sex greater than was formerly characteristic of women.

The intellectual association of men and women on a plane of accepted equality, begun in college, will continue after leaving it, and will modify the social life of every circle into which graduates of co-educational colleges enter.

These inferred effects of co-education are already visible in Western communities. Visitors from the Eastern States, and from over the sea, comment upon the relative absence of prudery among women and of false gallantry among men; they notice that sentimentality and condescension on the one hand, and affectation and soft flatteries on the other, are, to a degree, superseded by a mutual good understanding and respect.

Literary clubs, associations for the promotion of art and science, and committees engaged in philanthropy, are frequently composed of men and women; and the offices in these organizations are distributed between the two sexes in proportion to their respective representation in the membership. In communities where there are many graduates from co-educational colleges, one finds that societies of the kind above referred to have passed that transition state of mixed clubs, in which men always held the offices of president, secretary, and treasurer, while women held those of vice-president and corresponding secretary.

Men who have studied with women in college, almost invariably favor their admission to county and State, medical, legal, and editorial associations; and thus we already see that co-education prepares society to give women welcome and patronage in business and professional life.

The growth of this cordial recognition of equality, this *bonhomie*, has not, as it was feared would be the case, been accompanied by the decadence of man's reverence for womanhood and woman's admiration for manliness. Shrewd observers testify that both these sentiments apparently survive intellectual acquaintance, competition, and partnership; and that the former is expressed with more simplicity and the latter with more frankness than formerly, or than is still usual in sections of the country where co-education does not so generally exist.

But it is too soon for the final word on this subject to be spoken. Statisticians, sociologists, and novelists have much new work to do in recording the social consequences of co-education.

DEFECTS AND LIMITATIONS IN THE SYSTEM OF HIGHER EDUCATION FOR WOMEN IN THE WEST.

The ideal of higher education in the West suffers from an habitual exaggeration of speech. Nothing is more conducive to clear and accurate thinking than a strictly accurate vocabulary. The custom of calling institutions which do only secondary work—some of which offer a limited course of even this work—colleges, and of naming colleges universities, tends to mislead and confuse the public mind as to the distinctions between the different kinds of institutions and as to the essential character of each. The inhabitants of the West find their defense for this custom of giving things disproportionate names in the general vastness of their surroundings and in the consequent vastness of their plans and hopes. One of the simplest and surest remedies for the vague and contradictory notions now suggested in the phrase higher education, may be found in giving to every institution of learning a name that frankly implies the limit of its work; and every institution would gain in dignity through this nomenclature.

Nominal honors are too easy in Western institutions; and the conditions upon which different institutions confer them are so various that they have ceased to convey any fixed notion of the kind and amount of intellectual discipline which those bearing them have received.

The remedies for this are to be found in some concerted action among the colleges by which they will agree upon minimum requirements for admission to any one of them. The minimum adopted by the Association of Collegiate Alumnæ might answer this purpose. This would tend, not only to unify but also to raise the average requirements for admission to college, and this in turn would enable secondary schools to maintain a higher standard than is at present common.

As almost all colleges arrange their courses of study to occupy four years, unifying and raising the conditions of entrance would result in unifying and raising the requirements for graduation in the various courses; and this would tend to give to B.A., B.S., and B.L. an intelligible and honorable significance, long since lost. Legislative action could be taken in the different States, at least with reference to new colleges as they shall be founded, limiting the authority to confer degrees to those institutions adopting these improved minimum requirements; this would elevate the public ideal of the higher education and tend to save our young people from being betrayed by words and alphabetical combinations.

The defects above indicated should be frankly admitted to exist, but they are less universal and less disastrous than people living in the Eastern States are disposed to consider them.

A large number of the professorships in Western colleges are filled by men educated in Eastern institutions, who, after graduating from Harvard, Yale, Princeton or some other college which receives only young men, taught in Eastern colleges for either men or women separately before entering into their present connection with some one of our co-educational colleges. The experience of such men and their natural prejudice in behalf of early associations makes their favorable testimony to the merit of Western colleges particularly valuable.

The following extract from a letter from J. W. Bashford, of the Ohio Wesleyan University, is a very moderate statement of views expressed by many of my correspondents. He says: "Four women came to our university during the last two weeks of the term last spring, and afterward visited the leading colleges for women in New England. After personally inspecting the advantages for education for their daughters in the East and in the West, each of the four women decided in favor of co-education and of our university; each came with her daughter and entered her among our students at the opening of our university this year. Belonging to the East myself, I have a very high idea of the work done in our Eastern colleges, and personally do not hold that we can give students superior scholastic advantages, or in some respects equal scholastic advantages to those enjoyed in our best Eastern colleges. There is, however, a greater spirit of earnestness, and possibly a more strongly developed type of manhood and womanhood among our Western students than can be found in our Eastern colleges."

The cause of higher education for women suffers from the

fact that life offers fewer incentives to young women than to young men.

Dr. Smart, the President of Purdue University, and Dr. Jordan, the President of the Indiana State University, men of distinction in their profession, and well acquainted with educational questions, both say that the need of the young women in their respective institutions is that of sufficient incentive. The highest of all incentives, self-development and the possession of culture, appeals as directly to young women as to young men, and not less strongly; but this highest of incentives is sufficient for only the highest order of minds; and in the case of the average young person of either sex, must be reinforced by incentives more immediate and tangible. In this connection the need of improving the normal schools may be legitimately discussed. The normal school has done much to lift the occupation of teaching into the rank of the professions; but teaching can never be accounted one of the learned professions until the learning which is generally considered requisite in the doctor, the lawyer, and the clergyman is demanded in the teacher. It is quite true that the education implied by a full college course is not made a condition of entrance to schools of medicine, law, and theology; but if such preliminary culture is not demanded by these schools, it is expected by them. On the contrary, it is not only not demanded, but not expected, that applicants for admission to a normal school shall present a degree from some reputable college of liberal arts.

The professions which a majority of ambitious young men with intellectual tastes expect to enter, offer incentives to do preliminary college work; the one profession into which young women may enter with undisputed propriety not only does not offer incentives for taking a preliminary college course, but by its entrance requirements and its curriculum implies that such a course is not requisite.

Now that State universities are the direct continuance of the high schools, it would seem desirable that at least those teachers who expect to engage in high school work should have taken the courses of study implied by a college degree. Could the standard of normal school instruction and of high school preparation be thus lifted, it would act as a powerful incentive to young women.

The growth of progressive thought in the West, concerning the social and civil position and the industrial and professional freedom of woman, tends to supply women with incentives to obtain the best education: and the defects in their education hitherto caused by the absence of incentive, promise to be remedied with increasing rapidity.

The colleges, particularly the State universities of the West, are charged with being defective in their provisions for the development and culture of the social qualities of their students. Many of them have no dormitories, and the students upon entering them, women and men alike, go into boarding-houses or private families, or form co-operative boarding clubs, according to their own tastes and under conditions of their own making.

If in these universities students were received for post graduate work only, no criticism could attach to this custom of leaving every student to regulate his or her own domestic and social affairs, for such students are usually mature men and women. But this custom is open to criticism in institutions, in all of which the majority, and in most of which all the students, are under-graduates of immature age.

A study of their latest catalogues shows that, excluding the State universities, most of these institutions which enjoy more than a local patronage have erected or are contemplating the erection of dormitories for the accommodation of the young women in attendance upon them. Although some colleges, as, for example, the Ohio Wesleyan University, continue to build dormitories large enough to accommodate one or two hundred young women, there is a tendency favorable to the erection of less pretentious buildings under the name of hall or cottage, each of which shall accommodate from twenty to sixty young women. The refinement both of college life and of subsequent social life would be enhanced by the multiplication of these homes for moderate numbers of college women—if each were put under the charge of a woman whose intellectual culture, stability, and nobleness of character, and experience of life and the world, made her the evident and acknowledged peer of every member of the college faculty. But, if these college homes for women students are placed under the charge of matrons who are expected to combine motherly kindness and housewifely skill with devout piety, but in whom no other qualities or attainments are demanded, and if the matrons are the only women, besides the students, connected with the institution, the influence of the college home will tend to lower the ideal of woman's function in society; to rob the ideal of domestic life of all intellectual quality; and in general to diminish for young women the incentives to study.

Every one knows that the strongest stimulus to exertion that young men experience in college is afforded by their contact with men whose cultivated talents, whose sound learning, whose successful experience, and whose rich characters they admire, venerate, and emulate.

The almost universal absence of women from college faculties is a grave defect in co-educational institutions; and negatively, at least, their absence has as injurious an influence upon young men as upon young women.

Under the most favorable conditions, the college home, in which a large number of young women are brought into a common life under one roof and one guidance, is abnormal in its organization. If, in the university town where young women find homes in boarding-houses or in private families, there could be a local board of ladies authorized to exercise some supervision over the young women, the arrangement might secure the aims of a college home under more natural conditions than the latter now provides.

But women in the faculty, women on the board of visitors, women on the board of trustees, holding these positions, not because of their family connections, not because they are wives or sisters of the men in the faculty and on the boards, but because of their individual abilities, are the great present need of co-educational colleges. Only the presence of women in these places can relieve the young men who are students in these institutions from an arrogant sense of superiority arising from their sex, and the young women from a corresponding sense of subordination.

In a statement of the "Theory of Education in the United States of America," prepared by the Hon. Duane Doty and Dr. Wm. T. Harris, the present Commisioner of Education, we read the following:

"The general participation of all the people in the primary political functions of election, together with the almost complete localization of self-government by local administration, renders necessary the education of all, without distinction of sex, social rank, wealth, or natural abilities." Farther: "The national government and the State government regard education as a proper subject for legislation, on the ground of the necessity of educated intelligence among a people that is to furnish *law-abiding* citizens, well versed in the laws they are to obey, and likewise *law-making* citizens, well versed in the social, historic, and political conditions which give occasion to new laws and shape their provisions."

These statements are in perfect accord with the following words of Washington, quoted from his "Farewell Address to the American People": "In proportion as the structure of a government gives force to public opinion, it is essential that public opinion should be enlightened."

Here is the whole argument for the existence of State universities. In the West, these are destined to be the strongest, richest, and best equipped institutions for the higher learning; and are likewise clearly destined to have a determining influence upon the policy of other colleges in respect to co-education.

The "West" remains an indefinite term; and in that part of it which the word accurately describes, a people will be born who know nothing of distinctions in opportunity between men and women.

A people reared under such conditions will ultimately exhibit the influence of the "Higher Education of Women in the West."

IV.

THE EDUCATION OF WOMAN IN THE SOUTHERN STATES.

BY

CHRISTINE LADD FRANKLIN.

THE education of women in the South has suffered from the same cause which has kept back the education of women all over the world. Woman was looked upon as merely an adjunct to the real human being, man, and it was not considered desirable to give her any other education than what sufficed to make her a good housewife and an agreeable, but not too critical, companion for her husband. When Dr. Pierce traveled through Georgia, in 1836–37, to collect funds for establishing the Georgia Female College, he was met by such blunt refusals as these, from gentlemen of large means and liberal views as to the education of their sons: "No, I will not give you a dollar; all that a woman needs to know is how to read the New Testament, and to spin and weave clothing for her family"; "I would not have one of your graduates for a wife, and I will not give you a cent for any such object." In an address delivered before the graduating class of the Greenboro Female College of North Carolina in 1856, the speaker said: "I would have you shun the one [too little learning] as the plague, and the other [too much] as the leprosy; I would have you intelligent, useful women . . . . yet never evincing a consciousness of superiority, never playing Sir Oracle, never showing that you supposed yourself born for any other destiny than to be a 'helpmeet for man.'" An intelligent lady who was educated in the best schools in Richmond, just before the war, writes me: "If the principal of the school to which I went had any high views, or any views at all, about the education of women, I never heard her express them; and I fancy that, consciously or unconsciously, her object was to make the girls under her care charming women as far as possible, sufficiently well read to be responsive and appreciative companions to men." And this view of the matter has not yet entirely disappeared, for, in the catalogue for 1889 of the Norfolk College for Young Ladies, the aims of the school are said to be molded in accordance with the principle that "a woman's province in life is to throw herself heartily into the pursuits of others rather than to have pursuits of her own." It is plain that so long as this view of the function of women prevails they will have little incentive and little opportunity for undertaking the severe labors which are the necessary condition of a solid education. The lighter graces which are supposed to result from a little training in French and music and from some study of English literature, have for a long time been accessible to Southern girls, both in schools of their own and in the numerous private and fashionable schools of Baltimore, Philadelphia, and New York. When a girl was a member of a thoroughly cultivated family, she naturally became a cultivated woman; there was usually a tutor for her brothers, whose instruction she was allowed to share (the mother of Chancellor Wythe of Virginia taught her son Greek); and there was usually, either in her own house or in the parsonage, a large and carefully selected library of English books. If by the right kind of family influence a girl has been thoroughly penetrated with a love of books, something has been done for her which, of course, the regular means of education often fail to produce. The women of New Orleans, and Charleston, and Richmond were often cultivated women in the best sense of the word, but of the higher education, as the modern woman understands it, very little has hitherto existed in the Southern States.

In a long and exhaustive paper on "Colonial Education in South Carolina,"* by Edward McCrady, Jr., absolutely the only mention made of women is in the following sentences: "An education they prized beyond all price in their leaders and teachers, and craved its possession for their husbands and brothers and sons," and, "These mothers gloried in the knowledge. . . . of their husbands and children, and would forego comforts and endure toil that their sons might be well instructed, enterprising men."† But in this respect South

* Read before the Historical Society of South Carolina, August 6, 1883, and reprinted by the Bureau of Education, Circular of Information No. 3, 1888.

† Mention is made of a charitable school for girls, which they were not allowed to attend after the age of twelve, and of a school, apparently for boys, kept open by Mrs. Gaston, the wife of Justice John Gaston, at Fishing Creek.

Carolina was not behind Massachusetts. The public schools of Boston, established in 1642, were not open to girls until 1789, and then only to teach them spelling, reading, and composition for one half the year. The Boston High School for girls was only opened in 1852.*

The beginnings of the secondary education for girls throughout so large a territory as the entire South we have not room to trace here, and we shall confine ourselves chiefly to a description of the existing condition of things. But it may be mentioned that Mrs. Lincoln-Phelps (born Almira Hart), the sister of the Mrs. Emma Willard † who revolutionized the education of girls in the North, was one of the first to introduce a better state of things in the South. In 1841 she took charge of the Patapsco Institute, near Baltimore, and she transformed it at once into a school of the same grade as the Troy Female Seminary, where she had been for eight years teacher and vice-principal. She writes :‡ "The course of instruction, besides the preparatory studies, embraced three years : the class of rhetoric, the class of philosophy, and the class of mathematics and natural sciences ; and distributed through each, with studies appropriate to the advancement of the members, were the ancient and modern languages. . . . . Besides the twelve resident teachers, there were special teachers who came from Baltimore, in the Italian, Spanish, German and French languages and in elocution and general literature. To the regular classes should be added the class of normal pupils, varying from twelve to twenty, which contributed many accomplished governesses and teachers to the families and schools of the South." The natural sciences she taught herself, using her own well-known text books in botany, geology, chemistry, and natural philosophy.§ "It was not easy at first to render mathematics popular among girls, who were disposed to consider accomplishments as the great requisite in education ; but by establishing a regular course of studies and by awarding diplomas to those only who had honorably completed this course, ambition was awakened which led to efforts that often surprised the pupils themselves no less than their friends. Thus the study of algebra, geometry, and trigonometry, as well as mental and moral philosophy, up

---

* See chapter "Education in the East."—ED.

† See chapter "Education in the East."—ED.

‡ Quoted in the *Am. Jour. of Education*, September, 1868, p. 622.

§ Mrs. Phelps, Mrs. Willard, and Maria Mitchell were the first three women members of the American Association for the Advancement of Science.

to this time deemed by many repulsive, by degrees became not only tolerable, but in some cases fascinating."

A year and a half before this, namely, in January, 1839, the Georgia Female College (now the Wesleyan Female College) was opened at Macon, Ga. It had from the beginning the power of conferring degrees, and eleven young women took the degree of A.B. in 1840. It is commonly said that this is the first college for women that ever existed. That it was called a college was doubtless merely owing to the politeness of the Georgia Legislature. I have not been able to find out what the course of study consisted in at that time, but at present Harkness' First Year in Latin is the only preparation in languages required for entering the freshman class, and plane geometry is studied during the sophomore year. It is not likely that the course was better than this in 1840, and hence it is plain that then as now it was a college only in name,* and not in any way superior to Mrs. Lincoln Phelps's more modest Patapsco Institute.

The years about 1840 seem to have been a period of general awakening in the South in regard to the importance of the education of women. The Judson Institute was founded by the Baptist State Convention of Alabama in 1839; the "first incorporated college for women in North Carolina," the Greensborough Female College (Methodist), obtained its charter in 1838, but was not opened for the reception of students until 1846; in Maryland, the Frederick Female Seminary was incorporated in 1840 and opened in 1843. St. Mary's School, at Raleigh, N. C., was opened in 1842.

But it is the Moravians in the South, as well as in the North, who have been foremost among the religious denominations in the establishing of schools for girls of a thorough, if of an elementary, type. The devotion of Moravian parents to missionary enterprises made it necessary for them to have schools in which their children might find a substitute for family life, together with such teaching as they were thought to require. "Parental training, thorough instruction in useful knowledge, and scrupulous attention to religious culture were the characteristics of their early schools," and are the main features of the five institutions of higher learning which are still carried on by that Church. The Salem Female Academy, in the northwestern part of the State of North Carolina, among the

* The first college to grant real degrees to women was Oberlin. See chapter "Education in the West."—Ed.

foot-hills of the Blue Ridge, was opened in 1804. The curriculum consisted of reading, grammar, writing, arithmetic, history, geography, German, plain needlework, music, drawing, and ornamental needlework. Between six and seven thousand pupils have been educated in this school. The course is still very low; the requirements for admission into the junior class are arithmetic to the end of simple interest, geometry to quadrilaterals, and one book of Cæsar. But the instruction seems to be thorough, and the catalogue exhibits a freedom from pretense which is very refreshing. The author of the "History of Education in North Carolina,"* says: "The influence of the Salem Academy has been widespread. For many years it was the only institution of repute in the South for female education. . . . . A great many of its alumnæ have become teachers and heads of seminaries and academies, carrying the thorough and painstaking methods of this school into their own institutions. It is probably owing to the influence of the Salem Academy that preparatory institutions for the education of girls are more numerous in the South and, as a rule, better equipped than are similar institutions for boys."

The war was the occasion of a serious break in the education of woman in the South and of a serious loss in the small amount of funds that had been accumulated for their schools. The Georgia Female College, however, went on with its work without interruption, with the exception of two or three weeks; the Confederate authorities were at one time on the point of seizing it for a hospital, but were restrained by an injunction from the civil courts, on the ground that the college was the residence of several private families, and that many of the boarding pupils were unable to return to their homes, or even to communicate with their parents, on account of the general disruption of the railroads.† The Salem Academy, also, was overcrowded with students during the war, sent as much for shelter and protection as for education. After the war, most of the existing schools for girls were reopened, and a large number of new ones have been established since that time.

COLLEGIATE EDUCATION OF WOMEN IN THE SOUTH.

Most people would probably be ready to say that except for the newly founded Woman's College in Baltimore and Tulane University, the collegiate education of women does not exist

* Bureau of Education, 1888.

† Historical Sketch in the catologue for 1888–9.

in the South. But as matter of fact, there are no less than one hundred and fifty institutions in the South which are authorized by the Legislatures of their respective States to confer the regular college degrees upon women. Of these, forty-one are co-educational, eighty-eight are for women alone, and twenty-one are for colored persons of both sexes. The bureau of education makes no attempt to go behind the verdict of the State Legislatures, but on looking over the catalogues of all these institutions * it is, as might have been expected, easy to see that the great majority of them are not in any degree colleges, in the ordinary sense of the word. Not a single one of the so-called female colleges presents a real college course, and many of the co-educational colleges are colleges only in name. The female colleges, however, easily fall into two distinct classes ; not a few of them offer a course such that the students who are entering upon the junior year are, in a general way, as well fitted as those who are just admitted to the freshman year of a regular college. This kind of college there will be such constant occasion to speak about that it is necessary to coin a new word for it, and I propose to call them *semi-colleges.* The course is such that two years of the work of a regular college is done instead of four, and by a regular college I mean one which comes up to the standard set by the Association of Collegiate Alumnæ for admission into its ranks.

As there will be several references to the standard of scholarship set by the Association of Collegiate Alumnæ, I add here the requirements for admission into the freshman class of any college the graduates of which are recognized as eligible for membership.

In Latin - - -	Cæsar (four books). Æneid (six books). Cicero (seven orations).
In Greek † - -	Anabasis (three books). Iliad (three books).
In Mathematics	Arithemetic. Algebra through quadratics. Plane geometry.

The Southern colleges which attain the rank of a semi-college I shall speak of with more detail farther on. The real colleges

* The Bureau of Education has been extremely kind in placing its collections at my disposal, and in making extracts for me from its manuscript statistics for 1889–90, which will not be published for two years to come.

† An equivalent amount of French or German may be substituted for Greek.

for women in the South consist of the Woman's College of Baltimore and the co-educational colleges (including in that term those in which the management and the degrees are the same for the men and the women, though the recitations may be conducted separately). Of these, the University of Texas, the Tulane University (which is the State university of Louisiana), the University of Mississippi, and the Columbian University in Washington are the important ones. The admission of women into all of these universities is of very recent date, and may be taken as an indication of a general movement in favor of a greater degree of generosity toward women, which may, in time, sweep over the entire South. The geographical distribution of these entering wedges is worthy of note. Baltimore and Washington on the north, the University of Missouri on the west, the State Universities of the three States of the extreme southwest,—add to this the fact that the State of Florida has every one of its four colleges for men open to women, and that it has not a single girls' seminary of the old-fashioned type, and it may well be believed that the modern idea of what a woman requires in the way of education is destined to close in upon the entire Southern country, and that the contentment which Southern women have hitherto shown with the unsubstantial parts of learning will eventually be replaced by more far-reaching claims. The University of Virginia is the very mold and glass of form for all the other schools and colleges of the South, and if that were to throw down the barriers which it now keeps up against the unobtrusive sex, it might be considered that the battle was already won. But the University of Virginia is far from being unimpregnable; the chairman of its faculty writes me:

"In reply to your interesting * letter of November 25, '89, I would say that opinion is much divided both in our faculty and in our board of visitors on the question of opening this university to women." There is at this moment no way in which any one who wished to benefit women could do so more effectively than by offering this university a handsome endowment on condition of its terminating this state of indecision in the right way. The Johns Hopkins University has lately accepted a gift of a hundred thousand dollars from a woman; it remains to be seen whether it will show its appreciation of this act of generosity on the part of the self-forgetful sex by opening its doors to women. Whatever the result of the next few years may be upon the

---

* Interesting on account of an extract from a letter from a Virginia girl.

history of the education of women in the South, there can be no doubt that the situation at the present moment is far more hopeful than it was ten or even five years ago, and far more hopeful than any one would have believed who has not recently looked into the matter.

For the present, the Woman's College of Baltimore is the only representative in the South of separate education for women of a collegiate grade. This college was established by the Methodist Church (aided by liberal endowments from a number of enthusiastic advocates of the higher education,—first among them the Rev. John F. Goucher) for the purpose of providing women with the best attainable facilities for securing liberal culture. It is the intention to increase the endowment to two millions of dollars, exclusive of the value of the buildings,—this is stated to be necessary in order to meet the objects which the incorporators have in view. There are at present nine professors and associate professors, together with other instructors; there are laboratories and lecture-rooms, a spacious and carefully planned boarding-hall, and a gymnasium which contains a swimming pool and running track, and which is fitted with the best imported appliances for both general and special gymnastic movements. The wealth of the South is becoming so great that there is no reason why thoroughly equipped colleges like this should not spring up in various quarters.

I have received the most emphatic testimony as to the good standing of the women in the best of the men's colleges to which they have been admitted. Professor Fristoe, of Columbian University, writes me:

"In 1884 women were admitted to the medical and scientific departments of this university, and in 1887 to the academic, except to the preparatory school. We have eleven ladies in the academic department, seven in the medical, and seven in the scientific. We admitted them simply because there seemed to be a demand for it, and because we could find no objection. The girls admitted have been, *without exception*, superior students. They have had no injurious effect, but the reverse, and we find no inconvenience from our course. We have had so far only two who finished the course in the Corcoran Scientific School, but they were very fine scholars. One of them excelled especially in mathematics, the other in mental philosophy and such subjects. I am rather proud of the girls."

The italics are not mine. Professor Adison Hogue, of the University of Mississippi, writes me:

"Women are admitted here because the board of trustees gave them the privilege some years ago. I know of no other reason than that. Not many avail themselves of the opportunity, especially as the State for some years past has had, at Columbus, an industrial institute and college solely for women. This year we have eleven in attendance here; in each of my previous three years the number was five. Their standing averages above that of the boys, I think. In '85 and '87 the first honor was taken by young ladies; and in our present sophomore class a slender girl is spoken of as the 'first honor man.' Their social standing is in no way impaired by their coming here, although the plan of mixed education is not greatly in favor, as the small number shows."

Professor Halsted, of the University of Texas, says, in his report to the Superintendent of Public Instruction: "Several young ladies have shown marked ability in the acquirement of the newer and more abstruse developments of mathematics, for example, quaternions."

The president of the H. Sophie Newcomb College, which is a department of the Tulane University of Louisiana, has a larger number of students upon which to base his conclusions. He writes:

"When the college was inaugurated two years ago, it was discovered that very few of the applicants for admission were qualified to undertake a regular college course. The schools of this city (mostly private), which they had previously attended, had not hitherto arranged their courses of study with reference to advanced or college work, and had not therefore adopted any fixed standard of acquirement. . . . . The grade of the present freshman class is fully a year and a half in advance of that which entered two years ago, and at the same time there has been a steady increase in numbers. The greatest gain has been shown in mathematics, science, and Latin. Our advanced classes are doing excellent work in calculus and analytical geometry, laboratory work in chemistry and biology, etc. . . . . . While I can testify from experience to the equal ability of the Louisiana young women with those in the East or elsewhere in mathematical, scientific, or other studies, yet on account of the social pressure, and long established customs which demand early graduations, we must be content to see our institution develop more slowly than it would otherwise do."

I give in Appendix C, Table I., a list of the co-educational colleges in the Southern States, prepared for me by the Bureau of Education from the manuscript statistics for 1889–90. The following so-called colleges have in no sense a proper equipment nor a proper course of study for enabling them to deserve the name of college: Eminence, Classical and Business, South Kentucky, (Ky.); Keachie, (La.); Florida Conference and St. John's River (Fla.); Western Maryland, (Md.); Kavanagh, (Miss.); Salado, Hope, (Tex.) That leaves the following number of students who are in the collegiate departments of real, white, co-educational colleges in the South:

State	Students	State	Students
Alabama	1	South Carolina	10
Arkansas	3 22	Tennessee	34 16 28 10
District of Columbia	3. 25		
Florida	1 4	Texas	40 20 70 40 175
Georgia	30		
Kentucky	24		
Louisiana	77		
Maryland	25	West Virginia	32 1
Mississippi	11		
North Carolina	53		

Texas	345
Louisiana	77
Other States	328
Total	750

This table discloses the remarkable fact that there are 750 women studying in such men's colleges in the South as have a decent claim to the name of college, and also that Virginia is the only State in the South that has not got at least some kind of a co-educational college.

The testimony in favor of co-education, by all those colleges which have tried it, is very emphatic. The president of Rutherford College (N.C.), says: "This school [established in 1853] is the first experiment in the South, of which we have any information, in which an attempt has been made to train the two sexes together in the course of a college education. Its results prove the experiment to be a *complete success*." The president of Bethel College (Tenn.), says: "The mutual refining influences of co-education, socially, mentally, and morally, upon the sexes, is unquestionably good."

The president of Vanderbilt University, which is the most important university in the South after the University of Virginia, writes me that, although co-education has not been formally adopted there, yet women have never been refused admission into classes, that degrees would always be conferred upon those who had taken the proper examinations, and that one young woman had actually completed the course and received the degree of A.M. What more can the women of the central Southern States desire? It is not necessary that every male college should be open to them; there may be parents who think that the conventual life is best suited to the moral and social development of their sons, and such parents should have an opportunity for carrying out the plan which commends itself to them. All that women ask is that they should have freedom of access to the *best* men's colleges. In that way a standard for a woman's education will be fixed, and every woman will be able to reach that standard if she desires it; the second best colleges may then be allowed to be as exclusive as they please.

There is one more bright spot in the educational outlook for Southern women: it is announced that in the new Methodist university, which is about to be founded in Washington, on a large scale, every department will be open to women on exactly the same terms as to men.

It lies with Southern women to decide whether they shall accept the large privileges which are now open to them. It is hard for mothers who did not go to college themselves, and who have still lived what seemed to them to be happy lives, to feel that something different is desirable for their daughters; but may there not be fathers who, having tasted the pleasures of intellectual activity for themselves, will be minded to lead their daughters into the same fields which they have found to be attractive?

THE SEMI-COLLEGES.

I give in Appendix C, Table II., the list of semi-colleges, as determined from their catalogues. Of course, it cannot be inferred from the fact that the course is a good one that it is well carried out: but if the course is very limited, if the text-books used are poor, if there is no indication that the school has any library nor any scientific apparatus, it can be inferred that the school is not of a high grade; the above list may therefore be taken as a superior limit of the semi-colleges in the South. On the other hand, it may happen that the teachers of the classics and of English literature are persons of culture and of wide learning, and that a greater number of authors are read than the course laid down demands.

In the Mary Sharp College (Winchester, Tenn.), in 1887–88,

four young ladies completed the following post graduate course in the first half year*: Seneca's Essays, Œdipus Tyrannus, Dindorf's Metres, Colloquia in Latin, etc.; in the second half year two of them read Lycias' Orations,—against Eratosthenes, concerning the sacred olive, and the funeral oration,—the Panegyric of Isoscrates, Xenophon's Symposium, Lucian's Charon, and Plutarch's Delay of the Deity; and one of them, Miss Ada Slaughter, read, in addition, the Ajax of Sophocles, Plato's Apology and Crito, Iliad (three books), Lucian's Dream, Seneca's Epigrammatica, Seneca's Letters, Ovid's Metamorphoses (nine books), Cicero de Officiis, Pliny's Letters, Sallust's Jugurtha, and Eutropius. This college was founded in 1850, and for many years "it maintained a course of study, a method of instruction, and plan of government far in advance of any college in America for women."† From the beginning it has required both Latin and Greek for graduation, and a very respectable amount of both; it thus deserves, more than the Georgia Female College, the name of the first college exclusively for women in the country. It has over three hundred graduates, and in 1887–88 it had 182 pupils.

The Nashville College for Young Ladies seems to be one of the most important of the colleges of this grade in the South. It has frequent lectures from the professors of Vanderbilt University, and students in the scientific department attend lectures in the laboratories and cabinets of that university. A teacher of the school is present, and examines the class afterward. The professor quizzes in the daily lecture course, but is not responsible for the examinations. The president of the school writes me:

"Until I began here in 1880, the thought of arresting the graduation of a girl was not entertained. If she went through the curriculum without preliminary tests or without any intermediate or final examinations, the diploma followed as a matter of implied contract. Pupils were received to be graduated within a specified time. This sounds incredible, I know, and yet I have the best proof of the fact. When I announced that no pupil would be graduated in my institution without sufficient tests of her scholarship, it was freely predicted that such an innovation would destroy the patronage of the school. I

---

* Catalogue.

† Vassar was not opened until 1865. See chapter on Education in East.—ED.

am glad to say that the vaticination was false, but I allude to to the facts to throw light upon the status among us."

THE OTHER FEMALE COLLEGES.

The schools for women which are of a higher grade than the ordinary high school, but not so high as the college, the Bureau of Education classifies under the head of Superior Instruction. It will be seen from Appendix C, Table III., that the State of Kentucky has nineteen of these female colleges, and that six of the Southern States have an average of fourteen each. They are of all possible degrees of excellence. Such schools as the Hollins Institute and the Norfolk College for Young Ladies in Virginia, and Caldwell College at Danville, Ky., have every mark of being thoroughly good schools. The difficulty with nearly all these schools is, of course, that they are private and money-making enterprises, and do not care to incur large expenses for teachers or for the proper appliances for instruction, nor to make the course of study so rigid as to drive away pupils. It is remarkable to see how soon the character of the course, and especially the character of the textbooks, is changed as soon as the majority of the teachers are graduates of Northern colleges. On the other hand, it is the lack of intelligence and care on the part of parents that permits the poorest of these schools to continue to exist. If the worst half of these schools could be starved out of existence, and if their patronage could be transferred to the better half, the quality of the instruction which women receive in the South would be completely changed. It is a duty which parents owe to the public, no less than to their daughters, to discriminate carefully against the thoroughly worthless schools.*

In one of these so-called colleges no foreign language is taught; in another, the senior class takes a whole year to complete plane geometry; in very many of them Steele's textbooks in the sciences are used. In the Chickasaw Female College, Latin is optional, no other language and very little mathematics is taught, and the president says: "An experience of very many years proves to me that this course is not too far extended." In many of these small colleges the subjects of study constitute separate schools, following the plan of

---

* A Kentucky mother who had taken the trouble to send her daughter to Helmuth College in Canada, found that she was carrying on sixteen studies at the same time, and that she gave one half hour a week to geometry, during which the teacher gave the demonstrations and did not permit the class to ask any questions.

the University of Virginia. In the Marion Female Seminary, "the schools being distinct, the student may become a candidate for graduation in one or all of them at once." There are sometimes thirteen distinct schools; in the Huntsville Female Seminary there are ten, all carried out, as far as appears from the catalogue, by a single instructor, the president.

The rules and regulations in many of these colleges are extremely minute and harassing; they are largely copied from one catalogue to another; in several instances the pupils are not allowed to read any book nor any newspaper without the express permission of the president; in nearly all, the discipline will be "mild, but, if necessary, firm." In one catalogue only, it is said that "there are no rules and but few regulations; ladylike conduct is the one thing required."

A uniform dress must be worn in many of these colleges. The Sunday suit is frequently "of navy blue, made fashionably, but with no trimmings of either silk or satin, no ruffles, and no beads." In one of these schools, a uniform dress was at first required only for Sundays, but the week day dressing was found to be so extravagant that it became necessary to restrict the material worn to a black and white check gingham. In the catalogue of the Suffolk Female Institute, it is stated that "the uniform dress usually prescribed by other institutions is not required here"; and, in that of another school, that "uniformity is not needful or wise."

The cost of board and tuition in these schools (exclusive of music and painting and fancy work) is most frequently about two hundred dollars. Parents who can afford it usually send their daughters North, or at least as far North as to Virginia or Tennessee, as it is considered that a few years passed in a colder climate have a good effect in establishing their health. Only a small number have as yet taken the college courses that are offered in the North. The following table gives the results of my inquiries:

SOUTHERN GRADUATES OF NORTHERN COLLEGES.

Vassar College	42
Wellesley College	16
Smith College	10
Swarthmore College	5
Boston University	5
Bryn Mawr College	2
Cornell University	1
Syracuse University	0
Kansas University	0
Massachusetts Institute of Technology	0
Total	81

The president of Michigan University is able to recall from six to ten women graduates from Southern States, and the number from the University of Wisconsin has been "not large."

SECONDARY INSTRUCTION.

From the statistics for secondary instruction in the Southern States, it may be discovered that there are more than twice as many girls as boys in attendance upon public high schools. There are three times as many girls as boys throughout the whole country, it will be remembered, who complete the high school course. I do not find that a single Southern city provides a high school for boys without providing one for girls also, and usually it is the same school for both (though the recitation-rooms may be separate). Where the schools are distinct, the girls' school is usually much inferior to the boys'. This is notably the case in Baltimore, where the boys' high school (it is called the City College) fits admirably for the Johns Hopkins University, and where the two girls' high schools are of an extremely low grade. Throughout the entire South there are only forty-one high schools, while there are seventy-six in Massachusetts alone, but it must be remembered that any system of public schools has hardly existed in the South previous to the war.

An important feature in secondary education in the South is the establishment of the Bryn Mawr Preparatory School in Baltimore. In 1884 five ladies formed themselves into a committee and appointed a secretary and six teachers (science, classics, mathematics, history, French, and German), all college graduates, and a drawing teacher. The school opened with forty pupils, and in the third year it met all its expenses. A very handsome building, containing a thoroughly well-equipped gymnasium, is now (1889) being erected by Miss Mary Garrett (one of the directors) for the future accommodation of the school. For this building the directors expect to pay a fair rent—if not on the actual cost, yet on the price of a building that would have met the needs of the school. They are anxious to prove that a school of this grade can be made to pay.* They intend, out of the earnings of the school, to pay the college expenses for four years of the two best students of each year's graduating class. The distinguishing mark of the school is that it requires each child who enters to take the subjects required for entrance to college (the Bryn Mawr College

* The tuition is $150 a year.

entrance examinations are given in the sixth and seventh years) and at the same time a continuous course in drawing, science, and history, in order that a satisfactory course of study may be offered to girls who do not intend to go to college. The number of pupils is limited to 150.

NORMAL SCHOOLS AND INDUSTRIAL EDUCATION.

In the great advance which has been made in the South since the war in the establishment of systems of public schools, the managers of the Peabody Fund have played a very important part. It has been said, and without exaggeration, that no two millions of dollars ever did so much good to the cause of education. Normal schools, in particular, have been the object of their special care. In accordance with the express wishes of the founder, the fund has offered aid proportionate to what a State might do in order to secure the establishment of such schools ; and the initiative steps in every State included in its administration have been taken under the suggestion and stimulus of its managers. There are now thirty-two normal schools in the South ; Alabama has seven, Georgia and North Carolina have none. The Normal College at Nashville is not only a normal school for Tennessee, but for the whole South as well ; the trustees of the Peabody Fund distribute 114 free scholarships annually among ten Southern States. They have also established recently the Winthrop Training School for white girls in South Carolina, and that State has for the first time made an appropriation especially for the higher education of girls.*

Industrial training on any important scale has existed throughout the country only since 1862. In that year Congress granted large bodies of public lands to each of the States for the establishment of agricultural and mechanical colleges. The law permitted the introduction of a moderate college curriculum into these institutions. Gradually the returning Southern States accepted this gift, and all of them have made some endeavor to utilize it, either by attaching a department to the existing State university, or, as in Virginia, Texas, Mississippi, Kentucky, and Alabama, by maintaining a separate agricultural and mechanical college.

Women ought, of course, to have had a share in these government grants, and the statistics for the whole country show that of the thirty-two colleges to which they have been given,

---

* Report of the Peabody Education Fund, 1889.

no less than twenty report students of both sexes.* But in the Southern States, with the exception of Arkansas and Kentucky, none but colored women have received any benefit from these grants. The Arkansas Industrial University is an admirably administered institution; the literary course, which forms the ground-work for the industrial training, is only a year behind a good college course. The first class was graduated in 1875, and consisted of seven women and one man. The Kentucky Agricultural and Mechanical College has at present twenty-four women in the college course.

The Legislature of Georgia passed a bill last year (1889) appropriating $200,000 for the establishment of an industrial school for girls. In Mississippi an admirable industrial school for girls has been in existence since 1885,—the Industrial Institute and College, at Columbus. The entire income of this school is derived from State appropriations; tuition is free to all girls of Mississippi, and board is also free to 300 girls apportioned among the several counties of the State. Other pupils are furnished board at cost, usually about nine dollars a month, including washing. The industrial subjects taught are phonography, telegraphy, type-writing, decorative and industrial art, répoussé and art needle-work, printing, dress-making, designing, engraving, modeling, cooking, laundry-work, housekeeping (in a separate cottage), and book-keeping. There are 113 students in the collegiate course and 275 in the business course. The collegiate course shows a "marked advance upon the usual course of study in girl's colleges, especially in the elements of a solid education, in the mathematical and scientific studies. Analytical geometry, Juvenal, Livy, and Horace, Hamilton's metaphysics, and political economy, are among the required studies, and the calculus, descriptive geometry, quantitative analysis, and Ueberweg's History of Philosophy are among the subjects offered in post graduate courses. The standard of scholarship is high: 75 per cent. must be obtained in examinations in order to advance from one class to another. The laboratories are fitted up with the best modern appliances. The students in turn do the work of the dining-room and the sleeping apartments. Many of the former pupils are already earning good salaries in telegraphy, phonography, book-keeping, etc. It is plain that this industrial school of Mississippi presents a model which other States, both North and South, would do extremely well to copy.

* Bureau of Education Report, 1887–88.

CONCLUSION.

On the whole, the outlook for the education of women in the Southern States is not discouraging. The difficult first step has been taken,—there are women college graduates here and there, and it is no longer necessary to look upon them as monstrosities. In many a Southern family, the question whether a girl shall go to college or not has become, at least, a question to be discussed. It rests largely with existing college graduates to determine whether a sentiment in favor of the higher education for women shall grow rapidly or slowly, and whether schools for "superior instruction" shall be or shall not be improved in quality. It is not necessary that every girl should go to college, but it is necessary that some should go, for there is absolutely no other way of keeping up the standard of the lower schools except by making sure that they give such instruction as will stand the test of the college entrance examinations. No more important work could be done for women than to establish a dozen preparatory schools throughout the South, similar to the Bryn Mawr school in Baltimore, for the purpose of giving Southern mothers a standard of comparison, and enabling them to exterminate, by loss of patronage, those girls' schools which are thoroughly unfitted for the performance of their work.

V.

WOMAN IN LITERATURE.

BY

HELEN GRAY CONE.

> " I am obnoxious to each carping tongue
> That says my hand a needle better fits.
> * * * * *
> Men can do best, and women know it well.
> Pre-eminence in each and all is yours,
> Yet grant some small acknowledgment of ours."
> —ANNE BRADSTREET, 1640.

> " Let us be wise, and not impede the soul. Let her work as she will. Let us have one creative energy, one incessant revelation. Let it take what form it will, and let us not bind it by the past to man or woman."
> —MARGARET FULLER, 1844.

IT is difficult to disengage a single thread from the living web of a nation's literature. The interplay of influences is such, that the product spun from the heart and brain of woman alone must, when thus disengaged, lose something of its significance. In criticism, a classification based upon sex is necessarily misleading and inexact. As far as difference between the literary work of women and that of men is created by difference of environment and training, it may be regarded as accidental; while the really essential difference, resulting from the general law that the work of woman shall somehow, subtly, express womanhood, not only varies widely in degree with the individual worker, but is, in certain lines of production, almost ungraspable by criticism. We cannot rear walls which shall separate literature into departments, upon a principle elusive as the air. "It is no more the order of nature that the especially feminine element should be incarnated pure in any form, than that the masculine energy should exist unmingled with it in any form." The experiment which, Lowell tells us, Nature tried in shaping the genius of Hawthorne, she repeats and reverses at will.

In practice, the evil effects which have followed the separate consideration of woman's work in literature are sufficiently plain. The debasement of the coin of criticism is a fatal measure. The dearest foe of the woman artist in the past has been the suave and chivalrous critic, who, judging all "female writers" by a special standard, has easily bestowed the unearned wreath.

The present paper is grounded, it will be seen, upon no preference for the Shaker-meeting arrangement which prevailed so long in our American Temple of the Muses. It has seemed desirable, in a historical review of the work of women in this country, to follow the course of their effort in the field of literature; to note the occasional impediments of the stream, its sudden accessions of force, its general tendency, and its gradual widening.

The colonial period has of course little to give us. The professional literary woman was then unknown. The verses of Mrs. Anne Bradstreet, called in flattery "the tenth Muse," were "the fruit but of some few hours, curtailed from her sleep and other refreshments." The negro girl, Phillis Wheatley, whose poetical efforts had been published under aristocratic patronage in England, when robbed of her mistress by death "resorted to marriage"—not to literature—"as the only alternative of destitution." Mrs. Mercy Warren was never obliged to seek support from that sharp-pointed pen which copied so cleverly the satiric style of Pope, and which has left voluminous records of the Revolution. She too wrote her tragedies "for amusement, in the solitary hours when her friends were abroad."

Miss Hannah Adams, born in Massachusetts in 1755, may be accepted as the first American woman who made literature her profession. Her appearance as a pioneer in this country corresponds closely in time with that of Mary Wollstonecraft in England. She wrote, at seventy-seven, the story of her life. Her account sets forth clearly the difficulties which, in her youth, had to be dealt with by a woman seriously undertaking authorship. Ill-health, which forbade her attending school, was an individual disadvantage; but she remarks incidentally on the defectiveness of the country school, where girls learned only to write and cipher, and were, in summer, "instructed by females in reading, sewing, and other kinds of work. . . . I remember that my first idea of the happiness of heaven was of a place where we should find our thirst for knowledge fully gratified." How pathetically the old woman recalls the longing of the eager girl! All her life she labored against odds;

learning, however, the rudiments of Latin, Greek, geography, and logic, "with indescribable pleasure and avidity," from some gentlemen boarding at her father's house. Becoming interested in religious controversy, she formed the plan of compiling a "View of Religions"; not at first hoping to derive what she calls "emolument" from the work. To win bread she relied at this time upon spinning, sewing, or knitting, and, during the Revolutionary War, on the weaving of bobbin lace; afterward falling back on her scant classical resources to teach young gentlemen Latin and Greek. Meanwhile the compilation went on. "Reading much religious controversy," observes Miss Adams, "must be extremely trying to a female, whose mind, instead of being strengthened by those studies which exercise the judgment, and give stability to the character, is debilitated by reading romances and novels." This sense of disadvantage, of the meekly accepted burden of sex, pervades the autobiography; it seems the story of a patient cripple. When the long task was done, her inexperience made her the dupe of a dishonest printer, and although the book sold well, her only compensation was fifty copies, for which she was obliged herself to find purchasers, having previously procured four hundred subscribers. Fortunately she had the copyright; and before the publication of a second edition, she chanced to make the acquaintance of a clerical good Samaritan, who transacted the business for her. The "emolument" derived from this second edition at last enabled her to pay her debts, and to put out a small sum upon interest. Her "History of New England," in the preparation of which her eyesight was nearly sacrificed, met with a good sale; but an abridgment of it brought her nothing, on account of the failure of the printer. She sold the copyright of her "Evidences of Christianity" for one hundred dollars in books.

This, then, is our starting-point: evident character and ability, at a disadvantage both in production and in the disposal of the product; imperfect educational equipment; and a hopeless consciousness of inferiority, almost amounting to an inability to stand upright mentally.

Susanna Rowson, who wrote the popular "Charlotte Temple," may be classed as an American novelist, although not born in this country. She appears also as a writer of patriotic songs, an actress, a teacher, and the compiler of a dictionary and other school-books. "The Coquette, or the History of Eliza Wharton," by Hannah Webster Foster, was another prime favorite among the formal novels of the day.

Kind Miss Hannah Adams, in her old age, chanced to praise a certain metrical effort,—unpromisingly labeled "Jephthah's Rash Vow,"—put forth by a girl of sixteen, Miss Caroline Howard. Here occurs an indicative touch. "When I learned," says this commended Miss Caroline, "that my verses had been surreptitiously printed in a newspaper, I wept bitterly, and was as alarmed as if I had been detected in man's apparel." Such was the feeling with which the singing-robes were donned by a maiden in 1810—a state of affairs soon to be replaced by a general fashion of feminine singing-robes, of rather cheap material. For during the second quarter of the present century conditions somewhat improved, and production greatly increased. "There was a wide manifestation of that which bears to pure ideality an inferior relationship," writes Mr. Stedman of the general body of our literature at this period. In 1848 Dr. Griswold reports that "women among us are taking a leading part"; that "the proportion of female writers at this moment in America, far exceeds that which the present or any other age in England exhibits." Awful moment in America! one is led to exclaim by a survey of the poetic field. Alas, the verse of those "Tokens," and "Keepsakes," and "Forget-me-nots," and "Magnolias," and all the rest of the annuals, all glorious without in their red or white Turkey morocco and gilding! Alas, the flocks of quasi swan-singers! They have sailed away down the river of Time, chanting with a monotonous mournfulness. We need not speak of them at length. One of them early wrote about the Genius of Oblivion; most of them wrote for it. It was not their fault that their toil increased the sum of the "Literature suited to Desolate Islands." The time was out of joint. Sentimentalism infected both continents. It was natural enough that the infection should seize most strongly upon those who were weakened by an intellectual best-parlor atmosphere, with small chance of free out-of-door currents. They had their reward. Their crude constituencies were proud of them; and not all wrought without "emolument," though it need hardly be said that verse-making was not and is not, as a rule, a remunerative occupation. Some names survive; held in the memory of the public by a few small, sweet songs on simple themes, probably undervalued by their authors, but floating now like flowers above the tide that has swallowed so many pretentious, sand-based structures.

Mrs. Lydia H. Sigourney, the most prolific poetess of the period, was hailed as "the American Mrs. Hemans." A gentle and pious womanhood shone through her verse; but her books are undisturbed and dusty in the libraries now, and likely to remain so. Maria Gowen Brooks,—"Maria del Occidente,"—was, on the other hand, not popular at home, but put forth a far stronger claim than Mrs. Sigourney, and won indeed somewhat disproportionate praises abroad. "Southey says 'Zophiel, or the Bride of Seven,' is by some Yankee woman," writes Charles Lamb; "as if there had ever been a woman capable of anything so great!" One is glad that we need not now consider as the acme of woman's poetic achievement this metrical narrative of the loves of the angels; nevertheless, it is on the whole a remarkably sustained work, with a gorgeousness of coloring which might perhaps be traced to its author's Celtic strain.

As Mrs. Samuel Gilman, Caroline Howard, of whom we have already spoken, carried the New England spirit into a Southern home, and there wrote not only verses, but sketches and tales, much in the manner of her sisters, who never left the Puritan nest; though dealing at times with material strange to them, as in her "Recollections of a Southern Matron." With the women of New England lies our chief concern, until a date comparatively recent. A strong, thinking, working race,—all know the type; granite rock, out of its crevices the unexpected harebells trembling here and there. As writers they have a general resemblance; in one case a little more mica and glitter, in another more harebells than usual. Mrs. Sigourney, for instance, presents an azure predominance of the flowery, on a basis of the practical. Think of her fifty-seven volumes—copious verse, religious and sentimental; sketches of travel; didactic "Letters" to mothers, to young ladies; the charmingly garrulous "Letters of Life," published after her death. Quantity, dilution, diffusiveness, the dispersion of energy in a variety of aims,—these were the order of the day. Lydia Maria Child wrote more than thirty-five books and pamphlets, beginning with the apotheosis of the aboriginal American in romance, ending in the good fight with slavery, and taking in by the way domestic economy, the progress of religious ideas, and the Athens of Pericles, somewhat romanticized. Firm granite here, not without ferns of tenderest grace. It is very curious and impressive, the self-reliant dignity with which these noble matrons circumambulate the whole field of literature, with errant feet, but with a character central and composed. They are "something better than their verse," and also than their prose. Why was it that the dispersive tendency of the time showed itself especially in the literary effort of women? Perhaps the scattering, haphazard kind of education then commonly bestowed upon girls helped to bring about such a condition of things. Efficient work, in literature as in other professions, is dependent, in a degree, upon preparation; not indeed upon the actual amount of knowledge possessed, but upon the training of the mind to sure action, and the vitality of the spark of intellectual life communicated in early days. To the desultory and aimless education of girls at this period, and their continual servitude to the sampler, all will testify. "My education," says Mrs. Gilman, "was exceedingly irregular, a perpetual passing from school to school. . . . I drew a very little and worked 'The Babes in the Wood' on white satin, with floss silk." By and by, however, she "was initiated into Latin," studied Watts's Logic by herself, and joined a private class in French. Lydia Huntley (Mrs. Sigourney), fared somewhat better; pursuing mathematics, though she admits that too little time was accorded to the subject; and being instructed in "the belles-lettres studies" by competent teachers. Her day-school education ceased at thirteen; she afterward worked alone over history and mental philosophy, had tutors in Latin and French, and even dipped into Hebrew, under clerical guidance. This has a deceptively advanced sound; we are to learn presently that she was sent away to boarding-school, where she applied herself to—"embroidery of historical scenes, filigree, and other finger-works." (May we not find a connection between this kind of training, and the production of dramatic characters as lifelike as those figures in floss silk? Was it not a natural result, that corresponding "embroidery of historical scenes" performed by the feminine pen?) Lydia Maria Francis (Mrs. Child) "apart from her brother's companionship, had, as usual, a very unequal share of educational opportunities; attending only the public schools"—the public schools of the century in its teens—"with one year at a private seminary." She writes to the Rev. Convers Francis in 1838, "If I possessed your knowledge, it seems to me as if I could move the whole world. I am often amused and surprised to think how many things I have attempted to do with my scanty stock of learning." Catherine Sedgwick, "reared in an atmosphere of high intelligence," still confesses, "I have all my life felt the want of more systematic training."

Another cause of the scattering, unmethodical supply may have been the vagueness of the demand. America was not quite sure what it was proper to expect of "the female writer";

and perhaps that lady herself had a lingering feudal idea that she could hold literary territory only on condition of stout pen-service in the cause of the domestic virtues and pudding. "In those days," says Thomas Wentworth Higginson, "it seemed to be held necessary for American women to work their passage into literature by first compiling a cookery-book." Thus we have Mrs. Child's "Frugal Housewife"; and we find clever Eliza Leslie of Philadelphia, putting forth "Seventy-five Receipts," before she ventures upon her humorous and satirical "Pencil Sketches." The culinary tradition was carried on, somewhat later, by Catherine Beecher, with her "Domestic Receipt Book"; and we have indeed most modern instances, in the excellent "Common Sense Series" of the novelist "Marion Harland," and in Mrs. Whitney's "Just How." Perhaps, however, it is not fancy that these wear the kitchen apron with a difference.

In addition to lack of training, and to the vague nature of the public demand, a third cause operated against symmetrical artistic development among the women of those electric days preceding the Civil War. That struggle between the art-instinct and the desire for reform, which is not likely to cease entirely until the coming of the Golden Year, was then at its height. Both men and women were drawn into the maelstrom of the antislavery conflict; yet to a few men the artist's single aim seemed still possible: to Longfellow, to Hawthorne. Similar examples are lacking among contemporary women. Essential womanhood, "das Ewigweibliche," seems at this point unusually clear in the work of women; the passion for conduct, the enthusiasm for abstract justice, not less than the potential motherhood that yearns over all suffering.

The strong Hebraic element in the spiritual life of New England women, in particular, tended to withdraw them from the service of pure art at this period. "My natural inclinations," wrote Lydia Maria Child, "drew me much more strongly toward literature and the arts than toward reform, and the weight of conscience was needed to turn the scale."

Mrs. Child and Miss Sedgwick, chosen favorites of the public, stand forth as typical figures. Both have the art-instinct, both the desire for reform; in Mrs. Child the latter decidedly triumphs, in spite of her romances; in Miss Sedgwick, the former, though less decidedly, in spite of her incidental preachments. She wrote "without any purpose or hope to slay giants," aiming merely "to supply mediocre readers with small moral hints on various subjects that come up in daily life." It is interesting to note just what public favor meant, materially, to the most popular women writers of those days. Miss Sedgwick, at a time when she had reached high-water mark, wrote in reply to one who expected her to acquire a fortune, that she found it impossible to make much out of novel-writing while cheap editions of English novels filled the market. "I may go on," she says, "earning a few hundred dollars a year, and precious few too." One could not even earn the "precious few" without observing certain laws of silence. The "Appeal in Behalf of that class of Americans called Africans" seriously lessened the income of Mrs. Child. That dubious America of 1833 was decided on one point: this was not what she expected of "the female writer." She was willing to be instructed by a woman—about the polishing of furniture and the education of daughters.

And now there arises before us another figure, of striking singularity and power. Margaret Fuller never appeared as a candidate for popular favor. On the polishing of furniture she was absolutely silent; nor, though she professed "high respect for those who 'cook something good,' and create and preserve fair order in houses," did she ever fulfill the understood duty of woman by publishing a cookery-book. On the education of daughters she had, however, a vital word to say; demanding for them "a far wider and more generous culture." Her own education had been of an exceptional character; she was fortunate in its depth and solidity, though unfortunate in the forcing process that had made her a hard student at six years old. Her equipment was superior to that of any American woman who had previously entered the field of literature; and hers was a powerful genius, but, by the irony of fate, a genius not prompt to clothe itself in the written word. As to the inspiration of her speech, all seem to agree; but one who knew her well has spoken of the "singular embarrassment and hesitation induced by the attempt to commit her thoughts to paper." The reader of the Sibylline leaves she scattered about her in her strange career receives the constant impression of hampered power, of force that has never found its proper outlet. In "Woman in the Nineteenth Century," there is certainly something of that "shoreless Asiatic dreaminess" complained of by Carlyle; but there are also to be found rich words, fit, like those of Emerson, for "gold nails in temples to hang trophies on." The critical Scotchman himself subsequently owned that "some of her Papers are the undeniable utterances of a true heroic mind; altogether unique, so far as I know, among the Writing Women of this generation; rare enough, too, God knows, among the

Writing Men." She accomplished comparatively little that can be shown or reckoned. Her mission was "to free, arouse, dilate." Those who immediately responded were few; and as the circle of her influence has widened through their lives, the source of the original impulse has been unnamed and forgotten. But if we are disposed to rank a fragmentary greatness above a narrow perfection, to value loftiness of aim more than the complete attainment of an inferior object, we must set Margaret Fuller, despite all errors of judgment, all faults of style, very high among the "Writing Women" of America. It is time that, ceasing to discuss her personal traits, we dwelt only upon the permanent and essential, in her whose mind was fixed upon the permanent, the essential. Her place in our literature is her own; it has not been filled, nor does it seem likely to be. The particular kind of force which she exhibited—in so far as it was not individual—stands a chance in our own day of being drawn into the educational field, now that the "wider and more generous culture" which she claimed has been accorded to women.

We may trace from the early publications of Lydia Maria Francis and Catherine Sedgwick the special line along which women have worked most successfully. It is in fiction that they have wrought with the greatest vigor and freedom; and in that important class of fiction which reflects faithfully the national life, broadly or in sectional phases. In 1821 Miss Francis, a girl of nineteen, wrote "Hobomok," a rather crude novel of colonial Massachusetts, with an Indian hero. Those were the times of the pseudo-American school, the heyday of what Mr. Stedman has called the "supposititious Indian." To the sanguine, "Hobomok" seemed to foreshadow a feminine Cooper; and its author put forth in the following year "The Rebels," a novel of Boston before the Revolution. A more effective worker on this line, however, was Miss Sedgwick; whose "New England Tale"—a simple little story, originally intended as a tract—was published in 1822, and at once drew attention, in spite of a certain thinness, by its recognizable home flavor. The plain presentation of New England life in "Redwood," her succeeding book, interests and convinces the reader of to-day. Some worthless elements of plot, now out of date, are introduced; but age cannot wither nor custom stale the fresh reality of the most memorable figure,—that manly soul Miss Deborah, a character as distinct as Scott himself could have made her. "Hope Leslie," "Clarence," and "The Linwoods" followed; then the briefer tales supplying "small moral hints," such as the "Poor Rich Man and Rich Poor Man." All are genuine, wholesome, deserving of the hearty welcome they received. "Wise, clear, and kindly,"—one must echo the verdict of Margaret Fuller on our gentle pioneer in native fiction; we may look back with pride on her "speech moderate and sane, but never palsied by fear or skeptical caution"; on herself, "a fine example of the independent and beneficent existence that intellect and character can give to woman." The least studied among her pathetic scenes are admirable; and she displays some healthy humor, though not as much as her charming letters indicate that she possessed. A recent writer has ranked her work in one respect above that of Cooper, considering it more calculated to effect "the emancipation of the American mind from foreign types."

Miss Sedgwick, past three-score, was still in the literary harness, when the woman who was destined to bring the novel of New England to a fuller development reached fame at a bound with "Uncle Tom's Cabin." At last the artist's instinct and the purpose of the reformer were fused, as far as they are capable of fusion, in a story that still holds its reader, whether passive or protesting, with the grip of the master-hand. The inborn powers of Mrs. Stowe were fortunately developed in a home atmosphere that supplied deficiencies in training. Fate was kind in providing occasional stimulants for the feminine mind, though an adequate and regular supply was customarily withheld. Miss Sedgwick attributes an especial quickening force to the valuable selections read aloud by her father to his family; Miss Francis, as we have seen, owed much to the conversation of her brother. To Harriet Beecher was granted, outside her inspiring home circle, an extra stimulus, in the early influence of the enthusiastic teacher whose portrait she has given us in the Jonathan Rossiter of "Oldtown Folks." A close knowledge of Scott's novels from her girlhood had its effect in shaping her methods of narration. She knew her Bible—perpetual fountain feeding the noblest streams of English literature—as Ruskin knew his. Residence for years near the Ohio border had familiarized her with some of the darkest aspects of slavery; so that when the passage of the Fugitive Slave Law roused her to the task of exhibiting the system in operation, she was as fully prepared to execute that task as a woman of New England birth and traditions well could be. Since the war, Southern writers, producing with the ease of intimacy works steeped in the spirit of the South, have taught us much concerning negro character and manners, and have accustomed us to an accurate reproduction of dialect. The sublimity of Uncle Tom has been tried by the reality of the not less lovable Uncle Remus. But whatever blemishes or extravagances may appear to a critical eye in the great anti-slavery novel, it still beats with that intense life which nearly forty years ago awoke a deep responsive thrill in the repressed heart of the North. We are at present chiefly concerned with its immense practical success. It was a "shot heard round the world." Ten thousand copies were sold in a few days; over three hundred thousand in a year; eight power-presses were kept running day and night to supply the continual demand. The British Museum now contains thirty-five complete editions in English; and translations exist in at least twenty different languages. "Never did any American work have such success!" exclaims Mrs. Child, in one of her enthusiastic letters. . . . "It has done much to command respect for the faculties of woman." The influences are, indeed, broad and general, which have since that day removed all restrictions tending to impress inferiority on the woman writer, so that the distinction of sex is lost in the distinction of schools. Yet a special influence may be attributed to this single marked manifestation of force, to this imposing popular triumph. In the face of the fact that the one American book which had stormed Europe was the work of a woman, the old tone of patronage became ridiculous, the old sense of ordained and inevitable weakness on the part of "the female writer" became obsolete. Women henceforth, whatever their personal feelings in regard to the much-discussed book, were enabled, consciously or unconsciously, to hold the pen more firmly, to move it more freely.

In New England fiction, what a leap from the work of Miss Sedgwick, worthy as it is, to that of Mrs. Stowe! The field whence a few hardy growths were peeping, seems to have been overflowed by a fertilizing river, so rich is its new yield. It is the "soul of Down-East" that we find in "The Minister's Wooing" and "Oldtown Folks." Things spiritual are grasped with the insight of kinship, externals are drawn with the certainty of life-long acquaintance. If we glance at the humorous side of the picture, surely no hand that ever wrought could have bettered one smile-provoking line in the familiar figure of Sam Lawson, the village do-nothing. There is a free-handedness in the treatment of this character, not often found in more recent conscientious studies of local types. It is a painting beside photographs. A certain inequality, it may be admitted, appears in the range of Mrs. Stowe's productions. They form links, more or less shining, between a time of confused and groping effort on the part of women and a time of definitely directed aims, of a concentration that has, inevitably, its own drawbacks.

The encouragement of the great magazines, from the first friendly to women writers, is an important factor in their development. *Harper's* dates from 1850; the *Atlantic Monthly*, in 1857, opened a new outlet for literary work of a high grade. Here appeared many of the short stories of Rose Terry, depicting the life of New England; unsurpassable in their fidelity to nature, their spontaneous flow, their grim humor, pathos, tragedy. In the pages of the *Atlantic*, too, suddenly flashed into sight the brilliant exotics of Harriet Prescott, who holds among American women a position as singular as that of Poe among men. Her characters have their being in some remote, gorgeous sunset-land; we feel that the Boston Common of "Azarian" is based upon a cloud rather than solid Yankee earth, and the author can scarce pluck a Mayflower but it turns at her touch to something rich and strange. Native flavor there is in some of her shorter stories, such as "The South Breaker," and "Knitting Sale-Socks"; but a sudden waft of foreign spices is sure to mingle with the sea-wind or the inland lilac-scents. "The Amber Gods" and "A Thief in the Night" skillfully involve the reader in a dazzling web of deceptive strength.

In "Temple House," "Two Men," and "The Morgesons," the peculiarly powerful works of Mrs. Stoddard, the central figures do not seem necessarily of any particular time or country. Their local habitation, however, is impressively painted; with a few swift vigorous strokes, the old coast towns spring up before us; the very savor of the air is imparted. Minor characters strongly smack of the soil; old Cuth, in "Two Men," dying "silently and firmly, like a wolf"; Elsa, in the same book. There are scenes of a superb, fierce power,—that of the wreck in "Temple House," for instance. The curt and repressed style, the ironic humor of Mrs. Stoddard, serve to grapple her work to the memory as with hooks of steel; it is as remote as possible from the conventional notion of woman's writing.

The old conflict between the reformer's passion and the art-instinct is renewed in the novels and stories of Elizabeth Stuart Phelps; who possesses the artist's responsiveness in a high degree, with but little of the artist's restraint. Exquisitely sensitive to the significant beauty of the world, she is no less sensitive to the appeal of human pain. In "Hedged In" and "The Silent Partner," in her stories of the squalid tenement and the storm-beaten coast, her literary work reflects, point for point, her personal work for the fallen, the toiling and the tempted. Her passionate sympathy gives her a power of thrilling, of commanding the tribute of tears, which is all her own. An enthusiast for womanhood, she has given us in "The Story of Avis," and "Dr. Zay" striking studies of complementary themes; "Avis," despite certain flaws of style to which objection is trite, remaining the greater, as it is the sadder, book. All Miss Phelps's stories strike root into New England, though it is not precisely Mrs. Cooke's New England of iron farmers and stony farms; and none strikes deeper root than "Avis," a natural product of the intellectual region whence "Woman in the Nineteenth Century" sprang thirty years before. No other woman, among writers who have arisen since the war, has received in such fullness the spiritual inheritance of New England's past.

The changes brought about by the influx of foreigners into the factory towns of the East, are reflected in the pages of Miss Phelps, particularly in "The Silent Partner." A recent worker of the same vein is Lillie Chace Wyman, whose short stories, collected under the symbolic title "Poverty Grass," are marked by sincerity and simple power. Sarah Orne Jewett roams the old pastures, gathering many pungent handfuls of the familiar flowers and herbs that retain for us their homely preciousness. She is attracted also by the life of the coast. Without vigorous movement, her sketches and stories have always an individual, delicate picturesqueness, the quality of a small, clear water-color. "A Country Doctor" is to be noted for its very quiet and true presentation of a symmetrical womanhood, naturally drawn toward the large helpfulness of professional life.

A novel which has lately aroused much discussion, the "John Ward, Preacher," of Margaret Deland, is, although its scene is laid in Pennsylvania, a legitimate growth of New England in its problem and its central character. The orthodox idea of eternal future punishment receives a treatment somewhat similar to that applied by Miss Phelps, in "The Gates Ajar," to the conventional heaven. The hero seems a revisitant Thomas Shepard, or other stern yet tender Puritan of the past, miraculously set down in a modern environment. The incisiveness of portions of "John Ward," as well as the grace of its side scenes, gives promise of even more valuable coming contributions to American fiction, by the poet of the charming "Old Garden." A still more recent New England production is the book of stories by Mary E. Wilkins, "A Humble Romance"; vigorous work, brimful of human nature.

We need not now enter into the circumstances, tending to the misdirection of intellectual effort, which so affected the work of Southern women in literature that for some time they produced little of enduring value. These causes have been of late fully set forth by a writer of the New South, Thomas Nelson Page; who, in naming the women of Southern birth or residence most prominent as novelists before the Civil War, places Mrs. Terhune in a class by herself. "Like the others, she has used the Southern life as material, but has exhibited a literary sense of far higher order, and an artistic touch." Mrs. Rebecca Harding Davis, a native of West Virginia, has chosen a Pennsylvanian background for some of her best work; producing, perhaps, nothing stronger than "Life in the Iron Mills," published long since in the *Atlantic;* a story distantly akin to those of Miss Phelps and the author of "Poverty Grass." The hopeless heart-hunger of the poor has seldom been so passionately pictured. A distinguishing characteristic of the work of Mrs. Davis is her Browning-like insistence on the rare test-moments of life. If, as in the complicated wartime novel "Waiting for the Verdict,"—a work of high intention,—the characters come out startlingly well in the sudden lights flashed upon them, the writer's idealism is tonic and uplifting.

It was a woman of the North who pictured, in a series of brief tales and sketches full of insight, the desolate South at the close of the Civil War: Constance Fenimore Woolson, the most broadly national of our women novelists. Her feeling for local color is quick and true; and though she has especially identified herself with the Lake country and with Florida, one is left with the impression that her assimilative powers would enable her to reproduce as successfully the traits of any other quarter of the Union. Few American writers of fiction have given evidence of such breadth, so full a sense of the possibilities of the varied and complex life of our wide land. Robust, capable, mature,—these seem fitting words to apply to the author of "Anne," of "East Angels," of the excellent short stories in "Rodman the Keeper." Women have reason for pride in a representative novelist whose genius is trained and controlled, without being tamed or dispirited.

Similar surefootedness and mastery of means are displayed by Mary Hallock Foote in her picturesque western stories, such as "The Led Horse Claim: A Romance of the Silver Mines," and "John Bodewin's Testimony"; in which a certain gracefulness takes the place of the fuller warmth of Miss Woolson. One is apt to name the two writers together, since they represent the most supple and practiced talent just now exercised by women in the department of fiction. Mrs. Frances Hodgson Burnett, English by birth and education, and influenced by the Dickens tradition, though reflecting the tone of her environment wherever fate may lead her, touches American literature chiefly on the Southern side, through "Louisiana" and "Esmeralda." Despite the ambitious character of her novel of Washington society, "Through One Administration," her most durable work is either thoroughly English, or belongs to the international school. This particular branch of fiction we cannot now pause to note, though conscious that such books as the beautiful "Guenn" of Blanche Willis Howard have their own distinct value.

A truly native flower, though gathered in a field so unfamiliar as to wear a seemingly foreign charm, is Mrs. Jackson's poetic "Ramona." A book instinct with passionate purpose, intensely alive, and involving the reader in its movement, it yet contains an idyl of singular loveliness, the perfection of which lends the force of contrast to the pathetic close. A novel of reform, into which a great and generous soul poured its gathered strength, it none the less possesses artistic distinction. Something is, of course, due to the charm of atmosphere, the beauty of the background against which the plot naturally placed itself; more, to the trained hand, the pen pliant with long and free exercise; most, to the poet-heart. "Ramona" stands as the most finished, though not the most striking example, that what American women have done notably in literature they have done nobly.

The magazine-reading world has hardly recovered yet from its shock of surprise, on discovering the author of "In the Tennessee Mountains," a book of short stories, projecting the lines on which the writer has since advanced in "The Prophet of the Great Smoky Mountain" and "The Despot of Broomsedge Cove." Why did Miss Murfree prefer to begin her literary career under the masculine name of "Charles Egbert Craddock"? Probably for the same reason as George Sand, George Eliot, Currer Bell; a reason stated by a stanch advocate of woman, in words that form a convenient answer to the common sneer. "Not because they wished to be men, but because they wished for an unbiassed judgment as artists." The world has grown so much more enlightened on this point, that the biassed critic is now the exception, and the biassed editor is a myth. The precaution of disguise cannot much longer remain a necessity, if, indeed, it was necessary in the case of Miss Murfree.

From whatever cause adopted, the mask was a completely deceptive one. Mr. Craddock's vivid portrayal of life among the Tennessee Mountains was fairly discussed, and welcomed as a valuable and characteristic contribution from the South; and nobody hinted then that the subtle poetic element, and the tendency to subordinate human interest to scenery, were indications of the writer's sex. The few cherishers of the fading superstition that women are without humor, laughed heartily and unsuspiciously over the droll situations, the quaint sayings of the mountaineers. Once more the *reductio ad absurdum* has been applied to the notion of ordained, invariable, and discernible difference between the literary work of men and that of women. The method certainly defers to dullness; but it also affords food for amusement to the ironically inclined.

This review, cursory and incomplete as it is, of the chief accomplishment of American women in native fiction, serves to bring out the fact that they have, during the last forty years, supplied to our literature an element of great and genuine value; and that while their productions have of course varied in power and richness they have steadily gained in art. How wide the gap between "Hobomok" and "Ramona"! During the latter half of the period, the product gives no general evidence of limitation; and the writers would certainly be placed, except for the purposes of this article, among their brother authors, in classes determined by method, local background, or any other basis of arrangement which is artistic rather than personal.

In exceptional cases, a reviewer perhaps exclaims upon certain faults as "womanish"; but the cry is too hasty; the faults are those of individuals, in either sex. It is possible to match them from the work of men, and to adduce examples of women's work entirely free from them. Colonel Higginson has pointed out that the ivory-miniature method in favor with some of our masculine artists is that of Jane Austen. Wherein do Miss Sprague's "Earnest Trifler," or "The Daughter of Henry Sage Rittenhouse," display more salient indications of sex than works of similar scope by Mr. Henry James?

"The almost entire disappearance of the distinctively woman's novel,"—that is, the novel designed expressly for feminine readers, such as "The Wide, Wide World," and "The Lamplighter,"—has lately been commented upon. It is to be observed that this species—chiefly produced in the past by women, as the Warner sisters, Maria S. Cummins, Elizabeth Payson Prentiss, the excellent Miss McIntosh—has become nearly extinct at the very time when women are supplying a larger proportion of fiction than ever before; and, further, that the comparatively few "domestic semi-pious" novels very popular in late years have been of masculine production. The original and suggestive, though perhaps at times over-subtle, work of Mrs. Whitney, thoroughly impregnated with the New England spirit, and portraying, with insight, various phases of girlhood, takes another rank. Whatever may be concluded from the decadence of fiction written of women, for women, by women, it is certainly probable that women will remain, as a rule, the best writers for girls. In connection with this subject must be mentioned the widely known and appreciated stories of Louisa M. Alcott, "Little Women," and its successors,—which "have not only been reprinted and largely sold in England, but also translated into several foreign languages, and thus published with persistent success." We are told that when "Little Men" was issued, "its publication had to be delayed until the publishers were prepared to fill advanced orders for fifty thousand copies."

A like popularity is to be noted of the spirited and artistic "Hans Brinker, or the Silver Skates," of Mrs. Mary Mapes Dodge; which "has had a very large circulation in America; has passed through several editions in England; and has been published in French at Paris, in German at Leipsic, in Russian at St. Petersburg, and in Italian at Rome. . . . The crowning tribute to its excellence is its perennial sale in Holland in a Dutch edition." No name in our juvenile literature so "brings a perfume in the mention" as that of Mrs. Dodge, who for years has been as "the very pulse of the machine" in the production of that ideal magazine for children, which is not only an ever-new delight but a genuine educational power.

In poetry, the abundant work of women during the last half-century shows a development corresponding to that traced in the field of fiction. As the flood of sentimentalism slowly receded, hopeful signs began to appear; the rather vague tints of a bow of poetical promise. The varying verse of Mrs. Oakes Smith, Mrs. Kinney, Elizabeth Lloyd Howell, and Harriet Winslow

Sewall, represents, in different degrees, a general advance. The "little vagrant pen" of Frances Sargent Osgood, as she confessed, "wandered lightly down the paper," but its fanciful turns had now and then a swift, capricious grace. The poems of Sarah Helen Whitman, belonging to the landscape school of Bryant, are of marked value, as are also the deeply earnest productions of Mrs. Anna Lynch Botta; which display a new distinctness of motive, possibly attributable to the influence of Longfellow. The same influence is felt in some of the early work of Alice Cary; whose individual strain of melancholy melody clings to remembrance, its charm stubbornly outliving our critical recognition of defects due, in great measure, to over-production. Emily Judson sometimes touched finely the familiar chords, as in the well-known poem of motherhood, "My Bird." The tender "Morning Glory" of Maria White Lowell, whose poems are characterized by a delicate and child-like simplicity, will be remembered.

In 1873 a critic not generally deemed too favorable to growths of the present day, recorded the opinion that there was "more force and originality,—in other words more genius,—in the living female poets of America than in all their predecessors, from Mistress Anne Bradstreet down. At any rate there is a wider range of thought in their verse, and infinitely more art." For the change first noted by Mr. Stoddard there is no accounting; the tides of genius are incalculable. The other gains, like those in fiction, are to be accounted for partly by the law of evolution working through our whole literature, by the influence of sounder models and of a truer criticism, and by the winnowing processes of the magazines; partly also, by the altered position and improved education of women in general—not necessarily of the individual, since change in the atmosphere may have important results in cases where other conditions remain unchanged.

The poems of Mrs. Howe express true womanly aspiration, and a high scorn of unworthiness, but their strongest characteristic is the fervent patriotism which breathes through the famous "Battle-Hymn of the Republic." The clear hopeful "orchard notes" of Lucy Larcom—it is impossible to refrain from quoting Mr. Stedman's perfect phrase—first heard long since, have grown more mellow with advancing years.

The dramatic lyric took new force and naturalness in the hands of Rose Terry Cooke, and turned fiery in those of Mrs. Stoddard; whose contemplative poems also have an eminent sad dignity of style. The fine-spun subjective verse of Mrs. Piatt flashes at times with felicities as a web with dew-drops. Many names appear upon the honorable roll: Mrs. Fields, Mrs. Spofford,—whose rich nature reveals itself in verse as in the novel,—Mrs. Margaret J. Preston, Mrs. Mary Ashley Townsend; Elizabeth Akers Allen, Julia C. R. Dorr, Mrs. Stowe, Mrs. Whitney, Mrs. Dodge, Mrs. Moulton; Mrs. Thaxter, the sea's true lover, who has devoted herself to the faithful expression of a single phase of natural beauty; Mrs. Mary E. Bradley, Kate Putnam Osgood, Nora Perry, Mary N. Prescott, and Harriet McEwen Kimball; Mary Clemmer Hudson, Margaret Sangster, Miss Bushnell, "Susan Coolidge," "Howard Glyndon," "Stuart Sterne," Charlotte Fiske Bates, May Riley Smith, Ella Dietz, Mary Ainge De Vere, Edna Dean Proctor, the Goodale sisters, Miss Coolbrith, Miss Shinn, "Owen Innsley," Elizabeth Stuart Phelps, and Alice Wellington Rollins. There is a kind of white fire in the best of the subtle verses of "H. H."—a diamond light, enhanced by careful cutting. Generally impersonal, the author's individuality yet lives in them to an unusual degree. We may recognize, also, in the Jewish poems of Emma Lazarus, especially in "By the Waters of Babylon" and the powerful fourteenth-century tragedy, "The Dance to Death," "the precious life-blood of a master spirit, embalmed and treasured up on purpose to a life beyond life." The poems of Edith M. Thomas, with their exquisite workmanship, mark the high attainment of woman in the mastery of poetic forms, and exhale some breath of that fragrance which clings to the work of the young Keats. Miss Hutchinson's "Songs and Lyrics" have also rare quality. The graceful verse of Mrs. Deland has been quick to win the ear of the public. Louise Imogen Guiney, sometimes straining the voice, has nevertheless contributed to the general chorus notes of unusual fullness and strength. In other branches of literature, to which comparatively few women have chosen to devote themselves, an increasing thoroughness is apparent, a growing tendency to specialism. The irresponsible feminine free-lance, with her gay dash at all subjects, and her alliterative pen-name dancing in every melée like a brilliant pennon, has gone over into the more appropriate field of journalism. The calmly adequate literary matron-of-all-work is an admirable type of the past, no longer developed by the new conditions. The articles of Lucy M. Mitchell on sculpture and of Mrs. Schuyler van Renssalaer on art and architecture; the historical work of Martha J. Lamb and of Mary L. Booth, the latter also an indefatigable translator; the studies of Helen Campbell in social science; the translations of Harriet Waters Preston—these few examples, given at random, are typical of the determination and concentration of woman's work at the present day. We notice in each new issue of a magazine the well-known specialists. Miss Thomas has given herself to the interpretation of nature in prose as in verse; "Olive Thorne" Miller to the loving study of bird-life. Mrs. Jackson, the most versatile of later writers, possessed the rare combination of versatility and thoroughness in such measure that we might almost copy Hartley Coleridge's saying of Harriet Martineau, and call her a specialist in everything; but her name will ever be associated with the earnest presentation of the wrongs of the Indian, as that of Emma Lazarus with the impassioned defense of the rights of the Jew.

The just and genial Colonel Higginson expresses disappointment that woman's advance in literature has not been more marked since the establishment of the women's colleges. "It is," he says, "considerable and substantial; yet in view of the completeness with which literary work is now thrown open to women, and their equality as to pay, there is room for some surprise that it is not greater."

The proper fruit of the women's colleges in literature has, in fact, not yet ripened. It may at first seem strangely delayed, yet reflection will suggest the reasons. An unavoidable self-consciousness hampers the first workers under a new dispensation. It might appear at a casual glance that those released from the burden of a retarding tradition were ready at once for the race; but in truth the weight has only been exchanged for the lighter burden of the unfamiliar. College-bred women of the highest type have accepted, with grave conscientiousness, new social responsibilities as the concomitant of their new opportunities.

> "Pealing, the clock of Time
> Has struck the Woman's hour;
> We hear it on our knees,"

wrote Miss Phelps for the graduates of Smith College ten years ago. That the summons has indeed been reverently heard and faithfully obeyed, those who have followed the work of the Association of Collegiate Alumnæ can testify. The deed, and not the word, engages the energy of the college woman of to-day; but as these institutions grow into the life of our land, that life will be everywhere enriched; and the word must follow in happy time. Individual genius for literature is sure sooner or later to appear within the constantly widening circle of those fairly equipped for its exercise. It would be idle to expect that the cases in which native power and an adequate preparation go hand in hand, will be frequent; since they are infrequent among men. The desirable thing was, that this rare development should be made a possibility among women. It is possible to-day; some golden morrow will make it a reality.

VI.

WOMAN IN JOURNALISM.

BY

SUSAN E. DICKINSON.

THE pioneer woman in American journalism was Mrs. Margaret Craper, of the *Massachusetts Gazette and News Letter*, in the years of the Revolutionary War. After her to the year 1837 must be referred the first entrance of any American woman into the field of active journalism. At that time Mrs. Ann S. Stephens accepted the duties of editorial writer and literary critic in the columns of the *New York Evening Express*. Her connection with that paper continued for thirty years, but after 1857 it was limited to the editorial pages by the press of exacting duties elsewhere. In the last named year Mrs. Elizabeth F. Ellet succeeded her as literary editor of the *Express*, sustaining well the reputation which Mrs. Stephens had gained for it of a just and high standard of criticism. But in the intervening twenty years other women had followed Mrs. Stephens's lead, and made their mark in journalism with a freshness, a vigor, and a brilliance unsurpassed by any of the numerous later comers. During the thirties Mrs. Sarah Josepha Hale and the once famous Grimke sisters, Sarah and Angelina, availed themselves of the opportunities offered for special writing by New York and Philadelphia papers. In 1841 Mrs. Lydia Maria Child, one of the most widely known authors of the day, made her appearance in the arena of New York journalism as editor of the *Anti-Slavery Standard*, a weekly newspaper published by the American Anti-Slavery Society. Mrs. Child had already demonstrated her editorial ability in the establishment and conduct, for eight years, of the *Juvenile Miscellany*, the pioneer children's magazine of America. For two years Mrs. Child conducted the *Standard* alone; then, for six years more, in conjunction with her husband. But her best work during these years was done in 1842–'3–'4 as special New York correspondent for the *Boston Courier*, then edited by Joseph T. Buckingham. These weekly letters of hers, original, sparkling, thoughtful, vigorous, depicting the social, literary, musical, and dramatic life of the metropolis, were afterwards republished in two volumes, which hold a wonderful fascination still, when read after the lapse of more than a generation.

It was while Mrs. Child's letters were forming one of the greatest attractions of the *Boston Courier*, in 1843, that Miss Cornelia Wells Walter took charge of the editorial columns of the *Boston Transcript*, doing her work as ably and faithfully as any of her masculine fellow journalists. And in the next year, 1844, Margaret Fuller, who in 1840 had founded, and for two years edited, that famous quarterly, the *Dial*, came from Boston to New York at the request of Horace Greeley to fill the position of literary editor of the *Tribune.* Here she set the standard of criticism at high-water mark, and made its literary notices famed for a discrimination, sincerity, justness, and fearlessness of judgment and utterance which contributed largely to the influence of the paper. In the summer of 1846, when she sailed for Europe, its review columns had in her hands attained a reputation which in after years the scholarly editing of Dr. Ripley did but sustain.

In the same year that saw the beginning of Mrs. Child's brilliant letters from New York, the readers of the *Louisville Journal* greeted the advent of another woman, Mrs. Jane G. Swisshelm, in letters and editorial contributions bearing the strong stamp of an earnest, aggressive, deeply thoughtful but vivacious mind, intense in its sympathies, ready to do battle against every form of wrong-doing, and gifted with a bright humor which winged the shafts she sent abroad with unfailing vigor. It was but a little while until she became also special correspondent for the *Spirit of Liberty*, issued at Pittsburgh. She speedily proved herself a worthy compeer of her Eastern sisters in the journalistic field. In 1848 she removed to Pittsburgh and established there the *Saturday Visitor*, a paper which grew rapidly into wide circulation and influence.

But before she had reached this point in her career, while in fact the fame of this Western worker was just beginning to be heard of in the seaboard cities, the reading public of those cities was startled into a fever of enthusiasm by the letters of a Western girl in Eastern papers, the *Home Journal*, the *Saturday Gazette*, the *Saturday Evening Post*, the *National Press.* It was in 1845 and '46 that "Grace Greenwood" first took her place, while still a girl in her teens, as one of the most brilliant, clear-headed, and versatile of newspaper correspondents, in which special province, so far as journalistic work is concerned, she has elected to remain, with the exception of the few years, beginning with 1853, during which she published and edited the *Little Pilgrim*. Mrs. Swisshelm's ambitions, on the contrary, led her always to prefer the active duties of editor and publisher. The *Saturday Visitor* under her management was a power in the fields of political and social reform, of home duties and graces. She enlisted the services of other women for its departments. Chief among these helpers was Mrs. Frances D. Gage of Ohio, who became afterwards widely known as a charming writer for children, an earnest woman's rights speaker, and contributor to the *New York Independent*. In 1856, after her connection with the *Visitor* ceased, Mrs. Gage led the van of women journalists in her own State by becoming associate editor of an agricultural paper in Columbus, conducting its Home department with marked success. Mrs. Swisshelm, attracted in 1856 by what seemed a wider sphere for work in the new Northwest, sold her Pittsburgh paper and soon afterwards started, in Minnesota, the *St. Cloud Visitor*. In this she of course continued her advocacy of Free Soil and antislavery doctrines, and within a year her office was raided and her press destroyed by a mob. Fearlessly she gathered her resources together, and began the publication of the *St. Cloud Democrat*, in which she afresh demonstrated her ability, and in the campaign of 1860 supported Mr. Lincoln for the Presidency. After the close of the war she returned to the duties of active journalism; having, during the years of conflict, laid them aside to perform efficient service as a nurse "at the front." Her vigorous pen until nearly the close of her life failed not to serve every cause in whose truth and justice she believed.

Near the same time at which Mrs. Swisshelm founded the *Pittsburgh Visitor*, Mrs. C. I. H. Nichols became the editor of the *Windham County Democrat*, a Whig paper published at Brattleboro, Vermont. This she conducted for many years with admirable success, her editorials being often widely copied. In 1851 "Gail Hamilton" made a brilliant dash into journalism as special contributor to the *National Era*, Dr. Bailey's paper at Washington, for which Mrs. Stowe wrote "Uncle Tom's Cabin," and Grace Greenwood did some of her best work. In 1854 the woman's rights agitation, which had taken form several years before at the Seneca Falls Convention, and received a new impulse at the Worcester Convention of 1851, was reinforced by the appearance at Boston of a new paper, the

Una, published and edited by Mrs. Paulina Wright Davis and Mrs. Caroline H. Dall. This failed of long life for want of pecuniary support, but it was energetically conducted while it lived, and is well worthy of remembrance as the pioneer woman suffrage paper of America. In 1855 Miss Antoinette Brown, afterwards Mrs. Blackwell, became for a time one of the special contributors to the *New York Tribune*. She devoted her writing to social and reformatory subjects, giving chief place therein to the bearing upon women of the vices and defects of our social system.

In any notice of American women in journalism it is needful to give thus, in somewhat broad detail, an account of the workers during those first twenty years, because of the wide influence which they wielded in behalf of noble living and high thinking, and the practical stimulus which they gave to work in the various lines of social reform.

After those twenty years were over, as the country became more widely and thickly settled, as newspapers multiplied and enlarged their departments, and called for an increasing staff of writers of varying abilities, women journalists also became more numerous, and began to take up special lines of correspondence and reportorial work. In 1856 Miss Cunningham, who soon after became Mrs. D. G. Croly, still better known as "Jennie June," entered upon her journalistic career as a fashion writer, first on the *Sunday Despatch*, then on various other New York papers. In 1857 she invented the manifold or syndicate system of correspondence, supplying fashion items, gossip, and news of social topics and occurrences, simultaneously to newspapers all over the country. In this department of work her followers have multiplied until it would be hopeless to name or to count them. In 1860 she suggested the founding of *Demorest's Illustrated Magazine of Fashions*, and edited it for twenty-seven years, during which time she not only maintained her syndicate work, but proved herself a good "all round" writer for the press, having held at different times a position on the staff of nearly all of the leading New York dailies. In the autumn of 1889 Mrs. Croly issued the first number of a weekly paper, *The Woman's Cycle*, the aim and purpose of which are amply indicated by its title.

During the period of the Civil War and the few years immediately succeeding, the larger city papers began to avail themselves of the work of women as special writers, as correspondents, and reporters. The *New York Tribune* numbered upon its editorial staff Mrs. Rebecca Harding Davis and Mrs. Lucia

Gilbert Calhoun; Mrs. Louise Chandler Moulton supplied it weekly with the literary, dramatic, and art news of Boston, and Miss Ellen Mackay Hutchinson began her work upon it as assistant to Dr. Ripley in its book review department. Miss Middie Morgan on the *Times* has shown among journalists as thoroughly as Mlle. Rosa Bonheur has done among painters, that a woman may fill admirably any unusual place to which she is adapted by inclination and circumstance. Quite recently Miss A. L. Wilson has won a kindred success as manager and assistant editor of the San Francisco *Breeder and Sportsman.*

Of correspondents in this period, Mary Clemmer (then Mrs. Ames) was the first to become widely known. Her Washington letters to the *New York Independent*, and other papers, continued for a series of years to stand in the front rank of journalistic correspondence. Succeeding her come a long line whose names and work have become famed. Mrs. Burnham, afterward Mrs. Fiske, in the *Republican* of St. Louis, later in various Chicago, Washington, and New York papers; Miss Anna M. H. Brewster, Mrs. Lucy H. Hooper, Mrs. John Sherwood, Miss Kate Field, are among those whose unmistakable gifts and conscientious work have won high place for themselves and opened the way for others.

The religious press, weekly and monthly, was not far behind its secular contemporaries in securing the aid of women as conductors of special departments. For the last thirty years there have been few or none of these that have not steadily numbered one or more women among their regular contributors.

No woman in New York had taken the editorial control of a paper after 1849, when Mrs. Child relinquished her place upon the *Standard*, until 1867 Miss Mary L. Booth took the charge, from its initial number, of *Harper's Bazar*. Her reputation, earned as historian of New York and as a translator, had become a national one when in 1861, in a week's time, she rendered accurately into brilliant English Gasparin's famous "Uprising of a Great People." It aided in drawing immediate popular attention to the new journal. How faithfully and admirably her editorial work was done for the remaining twenty-two years of her life has but recently been borne witness to over her grave.

In 1868, one year after the *Bazar* was started, the lively agitation in favor of woman suffrage gave birth to the *Revolution*, of which Miss Susan B. Anthony was the publisher and Mrs. Elizabeth Cady Stanton editor-in-chief. Two years later the *Woman's Journal* was started in Boston, with Mrs. Lucy Stone, Mrs. Julia Ward Howe, and Mrs. Mary Livermore upon its editorial staff. If these two papers, and the by no means insignificant number which have arisen to follow their footsteps, have not as yet seen the accomplishment of their especial aim, they have served as potent factors in woman's educational, industrial and social advancement, in helping to secure the repeal of unjust laws, and, if last named, by no means least, in awakening women to a sense of their solidarity as a sex—to the truth that "where one of the members suffers all the members suffer with it."

In the mean time there were, both in the West and South, women who had demonstrated their ability and fitness for the profession of journalism. In New Orleans Mrs E. J. Nicholson, first as coadjutor and then as successor to her husband, has for thirty years or more held editorial control of the *Picayune*, of which she is the chief owner. On her paper and on the *Times-Democrat*, also owned by a woman, women have for many years held responsible positions. In Assumption, the *Pioneer* has, for a term second only to that of Mrs. Nicholson's career, been owned and edited by Mrs. Susan Dupaty. Mrs. S. V. Kentzel has for fourteen years made her paper, the *St. Tammany Farmer*, of eminent practical value and importance to the agricultural and material interests of a large part of the State. Of later years there have been quite a number of additions to the list of women journalists of Louisiana, foremost among these being Miss Addie McGrath of the *Baton Rouge Truth*, who is one of the chief officers of the Press Association, and Mrs. M. L. Garner, owner and editor of the *Carroll Banner* at Lake Providence; Mme. Marie Roussel is the editor of *Le Propagateur Catholique* of New Orleans. A Woman's National Press Association was formed at New Orleans in May, 1885. Two years later the addition of foreign members caused a change of name to the Woman's International Press Association. Mrs. Nicholson is its President. Near the same time that Miss Booth assumed charge of *Harper's Bazar*, Mrs. Mary E. Bryan entered upon the literary management of the *Sunny South* at Atlanta, Georgia. She had served her apprenticeship to journalism as assistant editor upon an Atlanta paper, and had afterwards edited a political journal in Natchitoches. After ten years management of the *Sunny South* she joined the corps of women editors in New York, taking charge of the *Fashion Bazar* a dozen years ago. After Mrs. Bryan's departure from Atlanta there seems to have been no other woman in that part of the South inspired with an ambition for newspaper work until Miss Andrews recently took a place upon the *Atlanta*

Constitution. Texas has a number of women journalists, most of whom are new-comers in their profession; but one of them, Mrs. S. L. McPherson, in 1877, established and still edits and publishes at Sherman the *Daily Democrat.* For the two or three previous years her home had been in Caddo, Indian Territory, where she had aided her husband in publishing the *Oklahoma Star.* These ladies are all welcome members of the Texas Press Association. There are a number of recent indications that journalism is likely to become a favorite profession among Southern women.

In the West, while Mrs. Swisshelm was still making herself felt as a power in Minnesota, Mrs. Susan C. Vogl, of late years the successful business manager of the *Boston Woman's Journal*, began journalistic work upon the *Western Spy* of Sumner, Kansas. Afterwards she wrote for St. Louis and New England papers for some years before her removal to Boston. In 1868 Mrs. Myra Bradwell founded the *Chicago Legal News*, of which she has been ever since the editor and business manager. In 1871 the Illinois Legislature passed special acts making the columns of the *News* evidence in the courts; and after the burning of all records in the Chicago fire, Mrs. Bradwell's paper was selected by the circuit and supreme court judges as the publication to have exclusive right to publish notices in regard to their cases. Mrs. Agnes Leonard Hill's journalistic work began as early as 1869 in Kentucky, was carried on in Chicago papers, and for the last eight years she has been engaged in editorial labors in Colorado.

In 1876 Miss Margaret F. Buchanan, now Mrs. Sullivan, entered upon the journalistic career, in which she speedily gained an enviable reputation, showing herself as thoroughly equipped as any brother of the press among them all to meet the serious questions and vexed problems of political and social science, and equally ready for brilliant descriptive work or discriminating criticism. Near the same time Miss Emily S. Bouton took the position upon the *Toledo Blade* which, in its varied demands upon her, not only as the head of its literary and household departments, but as leader writer and special contributor, has served to show the wide range of her accomplishments and her ability in every line of journalistic labor. The editorial and dramatic columns of the *Blade* have been indebted to her for some of their strongest work. It was to the *Blade* also that "Shirley Dare" gave much of the best of her early versatile achievements in the journalistic field. Somewhat earlier Mrs. Kate Brownlee Sherwood had filled a responsible position upon another Toledo paper. The *Indianapolis Journal* has for many years given a fair field to women journalists, and in its columns Miss Anna Nicholas, Mrs. Florence Adkinson, Mrs. May Wright Sewall, and others have achieved success. In 1878 Mrs. Belle Ball entered on a very different line of newspaper works as traveling correspondent of the *Albuquerque* (New Mexico) *Journal*, and of two Kansas papers, her especial duty being to report the progress of the Atlantic and Pacific Railroad, with all its incidental accompaniments—one of these being for months together the peril to life from Indian foes. After two years of this arduous experience she became an associate editor on a Kansas paper. For the last two years she has been the literary editor of the *Kansas City Times*.

After 1876 women journalists multiplied in the West as rapidly as in New England. The Illinois Woman's Press Association, formed in 1886, at the close of 1888, numbered 66 members, of whom 45 are either business managers of important journals, editors, or editorial assistants. Investigation shows a large number of newspaper women in the State who have not enrolled themselves in this or any association. The Western Association of Writers, organized in July, 1885, has may women editors, correspondents, and reporters among its members. The Ohio Woman's Press Association has in its Cincinnati branch over thirty members, nearly all of whom are journalists. The Cleveland branch numbers between forty and fifty, about one-half of whom are authors and one-half journalists.

Earlier than any of these was the Woman's National Press Association, organized at Washington, D.C., in July, 1882. This has a large membership, and, like all of the others, is in a prosperous condition. Since 1887 a special press gallery for its members has been set apart in each of the houses of Congress. The New England Woman's Press Association was organized in Boston in November, 1885. At present it numbers nearly 100 members, all journalists or magazine editors. When the *Woman's Journal* was established it found no woman journalist in Boston save Miss Sallie Joy, now Mrs. White, who was then doing more or less desultory work upon the *Boston Post*. In 1869 she was enrolled as one of the regular staff of that paper. After her marriage in 1874 she transferred her services to the *Advertiser*, and later to the *Herald*, and to-day she is duly honored by the numerous sisterhood of Boston newspaper women as their pioneer and leader.

Since New York saw the establishment of *Harper's Bazar* in the interests of women in one direction, and of the *Revolution* in another, women's publications in both of the lines thus indicated have multiplied until it is quite out of the question to give a list of them outside of the pages of a newspaper directory. The most widely known follower in the path of the *Bazar* is the *Ladies' Home Journal* of Philadelphia, of which Mrs. Louisa Knapp was from the beginning until January, 1890, the editor, with a salary of ten thousand dollars a year, and with Mrs. Emma Hewitt and Mrs. Mary Lambert as assistants. There are probably not many more such pecuniary prizes as yet in the grasp of women journalists; but, on the whole, there are not many such open for any one. It may as well be said here that Philadelphia, which was the first city in the United States to set wide open many doors for woman's work, as yet numbers fewer women journalists than any other large Northern city. Mrs. Hollowell, for many years past editor of the Household department of the *Ledger*, and more recently Mrs. Kate Upson Clark of the *Press*, have broadened their departmental work and made it of great value in educational and divers other lines.

Following the lead of the *Revolution* and the *Woman's Journal* there are many others; some as out-and-out suffrage papers, and others covering more broadly the circle of woman's industrial and social interests. In the East, the van among these is led by the *Woman's Magazine*, published by Mrs. Esther T. Housh at Brattleboro, Vermont. Mrs. Housh began its publication originally at Lexington, Kentucky, under the title of *Woman at Work*. In the south is the *Woman's Chronicle* of Little Rock, Arkansas. In the far West are the *Queen Bee* of Denver, Colorado, the *Woman's Tribune* of Beatrice, Nebraska, and the *New Northwest* of Portland, Oregon,—all owned and edited by women. Those in the nearer West are too many to specify. With these, widely differing yet in one sense kindred to them, should be named *The Woman's Exponent*, the official organ of the Woman's Association of Utah. It is edited by Emmeline B. Wells, and carries the motto "The Rights of the Women of Zion, and the Rights of the Women of all Nations." The association which publishes it claims a membership of 22,000 women, "thoroughly organized for the relief of the poor, and for medical, philosophical, historical, and religious study."

The Pacific slope has had comparatively few women journalists, but the names of several appear upon the roll of membership of the lately formed Central and Northern California Press Association.

The Woman's Christian Temperance Union has within the last four or five years multiplied greatly the number of women engaged in the practical work of journalism. Beginning with the *Union Signal*, founded by Mrs. Matilda B. Carse in Chicago, they have started up in almost every State of the Union, and many local papers have W. C. T. U. departments, all edited by women.

The vital interest of working women in the vexed problems of the relation beween capital and labor has called into existence at least one paper, the *Working Woman*. This is the organ of the Woman's National Industrial League. It is published in Washington, D. C., by Mrs. Charlotte Smith, who long ago proved her editorial ability in St. Louis. Miss Mary F. Seymour has, more recently, established in New York the *Business Woman's Journal*, which from its initial number has carried the prestige of success in its chosen field. Miss Fanny M. Earl, of the *Hartford Insurance Journal* has made her name widely known in business circles all over the country, and aided in conquering their respect for woman's practical abilities.

Our Anglo-African sisters are awakening to a comprehension of the use of the press as an instrument of value to themselves and their race. The names of half a dozen who have been or are now in editorial charge of race papers are well known, and at least a score of others who are actively engaged in journalism. A few of them have been employed as reporters or as special contributors on some of the leading dailies in our great seaboard cities.

Having noted the rapid increase in the number of newspaper women who in other parts of the country are doing faithful and worthy work in this their chosen profession, it remains to say that New York City has not fallen behind in this respect. The evidence of their capacity and fitness for the work is before the public in almost every daily, weekly, and monthly publication issued in the metropolis. Besides these are many whose work goes, through the syndicate system, all over the country. Their work, usually signed, serves even more widely to attract ambitious and intelligent young women to the same profession than does the exceptional reputation of such editors as Miss Booth, Mrs. M. M. Dodge, Mrs. Martha J. Lamb, and Miss Miss Jeanette Gilder. There are two Amateur Press Associations of these youthful intending journalists in New England.

There may be others in other parts of the country. And the number of those who are being inducted into the practical work of journalism, on rural and county papers, owned by their relatives or friends, grows greater every year.

From the very first there have been for women in journalism an open door and a fair field. The earliest comers went into it because their services were sought for. Themselves and those whom their success led to embrace the same profession met with a warm welcome from the public; in not a few instances even an enthusiastic one.

In each and every department of journalism—whether in office work, i.e. as editors, editorial assistants, or reporters; or in outside work, as correspondents, special contributors, or syndicate writers—the wages paid to women are the same as those paid to men of similar capacity, doing the same work. The prices paid vary according to the financial status of the papers themselves. In the larger cities writers "on space" receive on some journals payment at the rate of five dollars per column; some other papers pay as much as ten dollars per column. With all these writers, except where special articles have been ordered by the chief, and the length thereof specified, it is a matter of uncertainty how much space will be given them. The exigencies of the case often cut down what, under other circumstances, would be a welcome column article to two or three paragraphs, sometimes to as many lines. Office salaries in large cities vary from ten or even only eight dollars per week to as much as fifty or sixty dollars per week. A fair average for syndicate correspondence is probably about ten dollars per column. On country and county papers wages are of course much lower, often running down to a figure which makes outside labor needful for even plain country living. But whether in city or country women who can do the needful work as well as men may be sure of as good pay as men, and of fair and just treatment at the hands of their journalistic brethren.

VII.

WOMAN IN MEDICINE.

BY

MARY PUTNAM JACOBI, M.D.

"Fifty years hence, it will be difficult to gain credit for the assertion that American women acquiesced throughout the former half of the 19th century, in the complete monopoly of the medical profession by men, even including midwifery, and the diseases peculiar to women. The current usage in this respect is monstrous."—*New York Tribune*, Editorial, 1853.

THE history of the movement for introducing women into the full practice of the medical profession is one of the most interesting of modern times. This movement has already achieved much, and far more than is often supposed. Yet the interest lies even less in what has been so far achieved, than in the opposition which has been encountered: in the nature of this opposition; in the pretexts on which it has been sustained, and in the reasonings, more or less disingenuous, by which it has claimed its justification. The history, therefore, is a record not more of fact, than of opinion. And the opinions expressed have often been so grave and solid in appearance, yet proved so frivolous and empty in view of the subsequent event, that their history is not unworthy careful consideration among that of other solemn follies of mankind.

In Europe, the admission of women to the profession of medicine has been widely opposed because of disbelief in their intellectual capacity.* In America it is less often permitted to doubt—out loud—the intellectual capacity of women. The controversy has therefore been shifted to the entirely different ground of decorum.

At the very outset, however, two rival decorums confronted

* See the arguments interchanged in open letters,—learned essays, between Prof. Bischoff attacking, and Prof. Hermann defending, the admission of women to the University of Zurich. See also the address made last year by Prof. Waldeyer, before the Society of German Physicians and Naturalists.

each other. The same centuries of tradition which had, officially, reserved the practice of medicine for men, had assigned to women the exclusive control of the practice of midwifery. It was assumed that midwifery did not require the assistance of medical art,—that the woman in labor traversed a purely physiological crisis, and required only the attendance of kindness, patience, and native sagacity,—all obtainable without scientific knowledge, from her own sex. This being taken for granted, the propriety of limiting such attendance to women appeared so self-evident, that, from the beginning of the world till the eighteenth century A.D , the custom was not seriously questioned. There is an exact parallelism between the relations of men to midwifery and of women to medicine. The limitation of sex in each case was decided by a tradition so immense, as to be mistaken for a divinely implanted instinct, intended by Providence as one of the fundamental safeguards of society and of morals. In each case the invasion by one sex of a "sphere" hitherto monopolized by the other, aroused the coarsest antagonism of offended delicacy. In each case finally, a real basis existed for the traditional etiquette: there *was* some reason for protesting against the introduction of the male accoucheur into the lying-in room, or of the ardent young girl into the medical school. But in each case, whatever reasons for protest existed, were outnumbered and outweighed by others, to whose greater importance they were finally compelled to give way. Other things being equal, it *was* unpleasant for a woman to be attended in the crisis of her confinement by a man. But when the necessity for knowledge was recognized, when men became skilled while midwives remained ignorant,—the choice was no longer possible; the greater decorum of female midwifery was obliged to yield to the greater safety of enlightened masculine practice. Similarly, it *was* occasionally unpleasant for young women students to find themselves engaged in certain subjects of medical study together with classes of young men. But in proportion as midwifery became enlarged by the new province of gynæcology, did occasions multiply on which it was extremely unpleasant for non-medical women to be medically treated by men. The difficulties of educating a relatively few women in medicine were compelled to be accepted, in order to avert the far greater difficulties of medical treatment for a very large number of women.

The history of medical women in the United States, to which these pages exclusively apply, may be divided into seven periods, as follows:

First, the colonial period of exclusively female midwifery,* many of whose practitioners, according to their epitaphs, are reported to have brought into the world one, two, or even three thousand babies apiece. The Mrs. Thomas Whitmore of Marlboro, mentioned in the note, is especially described as being "possessed of a vigorous constitution, and frequently traveling through the woods on snow-shoes from one part of the town to another by night and by day, to relieve the distressed."†

During this period of female midwifery, the medical profession proper of the colonies remained entirely unorganized and inarticulate.‡ Without making especial inquiry, a superficial observer could have almost overlooked the existence of doctors, as a special class, in the community.

There followed, however, a second period, that, namely, of the Revolution, and the years immediately preceding and following it. During the former, physicians began to travel to Europe for instruction. During the Revolutionary war their public services in the military hospitals, though apparently not very useful to the sick,§ yet served to bring the profession, for the first time, out of obscurity; and the

---

* "It is scarcely more than half a century, since among us, females were almost the only accoucheurs."—"Remarks on the employment of Females as Practitioners in Midwifery," by a Physician. Boston, 1820. See also collections Maine Historical Society; Proceedings General Court held at Wells, July 6, 1646, to "present" Frances Rayns for presuming to act the part of midwife. Also, Blake's Annals of the town of Dorchester. Record of death, in 1705, of Mrs. Wiat, aged 94 years, having as midwife assisted at the births of 1100 and odd children. Also Thomson's History of Vermont, sketching the career of Mrs. Thomas Whitmore in town of Marlboro, 1765. In the town records of Rehoboth is mentioned the arrival, on July 3, 1663, of Dr. Sam Fuller and his mother, he to practice medicine,—she as midwife, "to answer to the town's necessity, which was great." So also Mrs. Elizabeth Phillips settled in Charleston in 1718. Anne Hutchinson began her career as a midwife. It will be remembered that the mother of William Lloyd Garrison practiced midwifery in Baltimore, and thereby supported herself and two children, after she had been mysteriously deserted by her husband.

† This sturdy woman lived to be eighty-seven years of age; an ironical comment on the theory of necessarily deficiency of endurance in the female sex.

‡ "More than 150 years elapsed after the first settlement, before a single effort was made either by public authority or by the enterprise of individuals, for the education of physicians, or for improving the practice of medicine. . . . . No medical journal was published in America, until toward the close of the 18th century. . . . . The first anatomical dissection was made in New York, in 1750.—Thacher, *Am. Med. Biog.* 1828, p. 16.

§ "It would be shocking to humanity to relate the history of our general hospital in the years 1777 and 1778, when it swallowed up at least one half

opportunities afforded for the collective observation of disease on a large scale, first breathed the spirit of medical science into the American profession. The first achievement of the new-born interest in medical art and education was the expulsion of "females," from even the outlying provinces of the profession, and from their world-old traditional privileges as accoucheurs.* It was a harsh return to make for the services rendered to the infant settlements by these valiant midwives, who had been tramping through the snow by night and by day to bring into a very cold world the citizens of the future republic!†

Third. After this, however, came a period of reaction. In 1848, a Boston gentleman, Mr. Samuel Gregory, began to vehemently protest against the innovation of "male midwives," and, opened a crusade on behalf of the women, with something of the pathetic ardor of the Emperor Julian for a lost cause.‡ To judge by the comments of the public press, Mr. Gregory's protest against "man-midwifery" awoke sympathetic echoes in many quarters. At the present day the interest in the movement thus roused, at once progressive and reactionary, lies chiefly in the remarkable similarity between the arguments which were then advanced against the intrusion of men into

---

our army, ... by crowding and consequent infection." . . . . "At Bethlehem, out of 40 men who came sick from one regiment,—not three returned alive.—Tilton on Military Hospitals (quoted by Tower, "Medical Men of the Revolution." Address 1876, p. 77.)

* "It was one of the first and happiest fruits of improved medical education in America, that females were excluded from practice; and this has only been effected by the united and persevering efforts of some of the most distinguished individuals of the profession."—Remarks of a Boston physician, cited *ut supra*.

† The suppression of midwives was more immediately due to the development of obstetrical science in England, whither the more ambitious among the colonial physicians were beginning to travel for instruction, and where their intellects were quickened by direct contact with the minds of men of genius. In 1752 Dr. James Lloyd, returning after two years' study in England, began to practice obstetrics in Boston: In 1762, Dr. Shippen, similarly prepared, began to lecture on obstetrics in Philadelphia. ("Hist. of Art of Midwifery," Lecture by Dr. Augustus Gardner, 1851). These actions sounded the professional death-knell of the poor midwives. Organized knowledge must invariably triumph over unorganized ignorance, even though tradition, decorum, and religion be all on the losing side.

‡ "Man-midwifery Espoused and Corrected; or, The Employment of Men to attend Women in Childbirth, shown to be a modern innovation, unnecessary, unnatural, and injurious to the physical welfare of the Community, and pernicious in its influence on Professional and public Morality." By Samuel Gregory, A.M., Lecturer on Physiology. Boston, 1848.

midwifery, and those which were subsequently urged against the admission of women to medicine. Thus:

"The employment of men in midwifery practice is always grossly indelicate, often immoral, and always constitutes a serious temptation to immorality." — *Summary of Mr. Gregory's argument in "Man-Midwifery Exposed,"* 1848.

"I view the present practice of calling on men in ordinary births, ... as a means of sacrificing delicacy and consequently virtue.— *Thomas Ewell, M.D., of Virginia.*

"The practice (of male midwifery) is unnecessary, unnatural, and wrong,—it has an immoral tendency."— *W. Beach, M.D., New York.*

"There are many cases of practice among women . . . . in which the sense of propriety would decide that the presence of a female practitioner is more desirable than that of a man.—*New York Observer,* 1850.

"There are a few self-evident propositions which it would be questioning the common sense of mankind to doubt. One is that women are by nature better fitted than men to take care of the sick and the suffering."—*Godey's Lady's Book,* 1850.

"The especial propriety of qualifying women to practice among

"To attend medical clinics in company with men, women must lay aside their modesty. There are still enough *gentlemen* who would blush to expose their mothers or sisters or wives to what, before women, would be improper and indecent."—*Letter to editor N. Y. Med. Record,* 1884, *by M. K. Blackwood.*

"History, physiology, and the general judgment of society unite in the negative of woman's fitness for the medical office."—"*Woman and her Physician.*" *Lecture, Theoph. Parvin, Prof. Dis. Women,* 1870.

"If I were to plan with malicious hate the greatest curse I could conceive for women, if I would estrange them from the protection of women, and make them as far as possible loathsome and disgusting to man, I would favor the so-called reform which proposed to make doctors of them." — *Editorial Buffalo Med. Journal,* 1869, p. 191.

"There are free-thinkers in the medical profession as there are free-lovers in social life. . . . . The opposition of medical men arises because this movement outrages all their enlightened estimate of what a woman should be. It shocks their refined appreciation of woman to see her assume to follow a profession with repulsive details at every step, after the disgusting preliminaries have been passed."—*Sherry, Med. and Surg. Reporter, July* 6, 1867.

"It is obvious that we cannot instruct women as we do men in the science of medicine ; we cannot carry them into the dissecting room and hospital ; many of *our* more delicate feelings, much of *our* refined sensibility must be subdued before we can study medicine ; in females they must be destroyed "—*Remarks on Employment of Females as Practitioners, Boston,* 1820.

"The ceremonies of graduating Miss Blackwell at Geneva may well

children and their own sex, will be admitted I hope by all."—*Rt. Rev. Bishop Potter*, 1850.

"We have long been persuaded that both morality and decency require female practitioners of medicine. Nature suggests it; reason approves it; religion demands it."—*Northern Christian Advocate*, 1850.

"This is one of the most important projects of the day for the improvement of the condition of women."—*Zion's Herald*, 1850.

"The employment of men as 'midwives' is a modern custom, and one not to be commended."—*Phil. Saturday Post*, 1850.

be called a farce. I am sorry that Geneva should be the first to commence the nefarious process of amalgamation. The profession was quite too full before."—*Letter by D. K. to Boston Journal, Feb.* 1849.

"The bare thought of married females engaging in the medical profession is palpably absurd. It carries with it a sense of shame, vulgarity, and disgust. Nature is responsible for my unqualified opposition to educating females for the medical profession." —*Dissert. on Female Phys. by N. Williams, M.D., read before a N. Y. Med. Soc.*, June 6, 1850.

"Females are ambitious to dabble in medicine as in other matters, with a view to reorganizing society."—*Edit. Boston Med. and Surg. Jour.*, 1852, p. 106.

"The serious inroads made by female physicians in obstetrical business, *one of the essential branches of income to a majority of well established practitioners*, make it natural enough to inquire what course to pursue."—*Ibid.*, Feb. 1853.

These parallel columns might be extended much further, did our space permit. We cannot, however, pass by the following gem of eloquence from an English source, but quoted in the Cincinnati *Lancet and Clinic* for 1881. It is from the address at the British Medical Association by the President of that year:

"I am not over-squeamish, nor am I over-sensitive, but I almost shudder when I hear of things that ladies now do or attempt to do. One can but blush, and feel that modesty, once inherent in the fairest of God's creation, is fast fading away. You gentlemen, who know the delicacy of women's organization,—you must know that constitutionally they are unfit for many of the duties of either doctor or nurse.

"May not habit so change that fine organization, that sensitive nature of women, as to render her dead to those higher feelings of love and sympathy which now make our homes so happy, so blessed?

"Will not England's glory fade without its modest sympathizing women, and its race of stalwart youths and blooming maidens?

"You now, gentlemen, know my views as to the propriety of ladies *becoming doctors or nurses.*" *

The Fourth period of woman's medical history was initiated when Mr. Gregory, supported by the popular enthusiasm he had aroused, succeeded in opening a School of Medicine (so called) for women, in Nov. 1848.† The first term lasted three months: a second term began the following April, 1849;—and with the announcement for the second year it was declared that the twenty pioneer pupils had not only followed the lectures, but "had attended above 300 midwifery cases with the most satisfactory success."

In the prospectus issued for the second year of the school, Mr. Gregory brought forward a new set of arguments in its support, in addition to those previously adduced. There was then (1849) in New England, a surplus female population of 20,000 persons,—and "hundreds of these would be willing to devote any necessary length of time to qualify themselves for a useful, honorable, and remunerative occupation." They could afford, moreover, to give their services at a much cheaper rate than men, charging about a third the ordinary fees,—thus $5 instead of $15 for attendance on a confinement case.

Thus not only would the morals of the community be preserved, but the burdens on its purse be considerably lightened by the employment of educated women as obstetricians. As the medical profession had just become keenly alive to the peculiarly lucrative character of obstetrical and gynæcological practice, this suggestion that it might now profitably be undersold naturally aroused the keenest resentment. It was soon retorted that the cheaper practitioners were to be prepared by a system of education so cheap as to be absolutely worthless; and unfortunately the early history of the first medical schools for women entirely justified this accusation.

To support Mr. Gregory's school, a Female Medical Education Society was formed in Boston, and incorporated with a state charter. Nothing seemed at the outset fairer than the promises of the new college,—but it had one fatal defect. There was no one connected with it who either knew or cared what a medical education should be. It followed that, under

* Is it possible not to seem to hear, from some quiet corner of dispassionate observation, the echo of the immortal "Fudge!" which so disturbed the complacency of the innocent Vicar of Wakefield?

† "To Massachusetts is due the credit of establishing the first medical school for women in the world."—Chadwick, "The Study and Practice of Medicine by Women," *International Review*, October, 1879.

the name of medical education, was offered a curriculum of instruction, so ludicrously inadequate for the purpose, as to constitute a gross usurpation of the name,—in a word, to be an essentially dishonest affair. And still more unfortunately, the same inadequacy, naïvely or deliberately unconscious of itself, continued in greater or less degree, to characterize all efforts for the isolated medical education of women for the next twenty years. This, the fourth period of their medical history,—deserves therefore to be considered by women rather as a pre-medical or preliminary epoch; where purposes were enunciated that were only to be fulfilled many years later.

The Gregory Medical School maintained a precarious existence until 1874, when, by an enabling act of the Legislature, the funds were handed over to the Boston University, just founded,—upon condition that women should be admitted to the medical department of the latter. This condition was punctually fulfilled; women students were rendered eligible to all departments of the new university. But as the medical school, for some reason, became exclusively homœpathic,—the fortunes of medical women in the regular profession were not thereby greatly advanced.*

Now, however, the movement for women had widened and reached Philadelphia, where two schools were started. One of these, the Penn Medical School, ran a permanently unenviable career of unfitness, and was finally extinguished. The other, the Woman's Medical College of Pennsylvania, was founded in 1850, and after a long and precarious period of struggle, finally touched upon a solid basis of medical realities, and thence began its prosperous modern career. In the mean time, and fortunately for the cause, a new departure had been taken in several other directions. The Gregory School had been founded with the avowed intention of educating women for

* On two other occasions did these fortunes become associated with those of homœopaths. When in 1869 the State University of Michigan opened its medical department to women, the Legislature simultaneously ruled that two professors of homœopathic medicine must be appointed in the school. And when in 1886 the trustees of the Boston City Hospital inquired into the propriety of admitting female medical students, they reported at the same time upon the application of homœopathic physicians, to be appointed in the medical service of the wards. At this point, however, the fortunes of the two classes of applicants diverged: the first request was granted; the second refused.

The class of 1890 of the Boston University School only contains nine women.

midwives; and it did not succeed even in this limited aim, because it was either ignorant of or indifferent to the rigid system of education imposed, wherever, as in Europe, midwives are recognized and educated. In America, where hostility to class distinctions is so profound as to interfere with the recognition of even the intellectual distinctions which are alone just,—it was probably a foregone conclusion that the various ranks in medicine which exist in European countries would never here become officially established.* But a startlingly long step was taken at a stride, when, thirty years after the pæan of victory had been sounded over the complete suppression of female midwifes, so that not even this corner of possible medicine might remain in possession of women,—that then, half a dozen women, unknown to each other, and widely separated in this immense country, should appear almost simultaneously upon the scene, and demand the opportunity to be educated as full physicians. Their history marks a fifth period in the movement.

The first of this remarkable group of women was Harriet K. Hunt of Boston.

This lady had for several years assumed the responsibility of practicing medicine, while yet unprovided with a medical diploma. This was reprehensible, but from a practical standpoint, the course seems to have been justified by subsequent events. For when, in 1847, Miss Hunt requested permission to attend lectures at the Harvard Medical School, her request was promptly refused. After the graduation of Elizabeth Blackwell at Geneva in 1849, Miss Hunt thought that the times might have become more favorable, and, in 1850, repeated her application at Harvard. In mobile America, three years may sometimes effect such a change in sentiment as would require three centuries in the Old World. On this occasion, five out of the seven members of the Faculty voted "That Miss Hunt be admitted to the lectures on the usual terms, provided that her

---

* Thus in France,—docteur en médecine, officier de santé, sage femme; In England,—physician, surgeon, apothecary. The midwife in England, was, until recently, assumed not to exist; but as she existed nevertheless, she became all the more dangerous because uncontrolled. "At present date, 60 per cent. of poor women are attended in their confinements by midwives, uninstructed and uncultivated,—probably 10,000 in number. The fatal results to both mothers and children arising from the ignorance of these midwives is notorious. They must either be annihilated or instructed."—Dr. Aveling, writing to Gen. Med. Council, 1873.

The Obstetrical Society of London now undertakes to instruct and examine midwives.

admission be not deemed inconsistent with the statutes." * A week later, the President and Fellows of the University announced that the statutes of the Medical School offered no obstacle to the admission of female students to their lectures. But, on the eve of success, Miss Hunt's cause was shipwrecked, by collision and entanglement with that of another of the unenfranchised to privileges. At the beginning of the session, two, and later a third, colored man, had appeared among the students, and created by their appearance intense dissatisfaction. When, as if to crown this outrage to gentlemanly feeling, it was announced that a *woman* was also about to be admitted, the students felt that their cup of humiliation was full, and popular indignation boiled over in a general meeting. Here resolutions were adopted, remonstrating against the "amalgamation of sexes and races." The compliant Faculty bowed their heads to the storm, yielded to the students, who, though young and inexperienced, were in the majority, and might possibly withdraw in a body to Yale,—and, to avoid the obloquy of rejecting, under pressure, a perfectly reasonable request, advised the "female student" to withdraw her petition. This she did ; the storm subsided, and the majesty of Harvard, already endangered by the presence of the negro, was saved from the further peril of the woman. Miss Hunt returned to her private medical practice, which, though unsanctioned by law and condemned by learning, was so successful that, in 1872, she celebrated her silver wedding to it.†

Thus, on this first occasion, it was not a sentiment of delicacy that forbade the Harvard students to share their privileges with a woman ; but a sense of offended dignity of sex, which distinctly allied itself with the other and equally touchy dignity of race. The odd idea was advanced on this, as on so many other occasions, that whenever a woman should prove herself capable of an intellectual achievement, this latter would cease to constitute an honor for the men who had previously prized it. Hence the urgent necessity of excluding women from all opportunity of trying.‡

---

* Drs. Jacob Bigelow and James Jackson voted in the negative. The latter had been the physician to introduce into Boston the midwife, Mrs. Janet Alexander. So it would seem that his objection was not to women, but to *educated* women, who might aspire to rank among regularly educated men physicians.

† The details of Miss Hunt's application to Harvard are dispassionately related by Dr. Chadwick, *loc. cit.*

‡ When, in 1872, the London University, after a two years' bitter contro-

In 1849, "Diplomas and advanced courses of study were things entirely outside the intellectual life of women." * The pioneer female colleges, the Troy Seminary and the Mt. Holyoke school, had scarcely been founded,† and women everywhere received only the most rudimentary education. On the other hand, the medical education of men, was, as compared with the objects to be attained by it,—in about an equally rudimentary condition. The intrinsic tests were so shifting and unreliable, the standard of attainments so low, that it was proportionately necessary to protect the dignity of the profession by external, superficial, and arbitrary safeguards. Of these the easiest to apply was the distinction of sex. It was often difficult to decide, in the absence of intrinsic tests, whether a given individual were or were not a competent physician : but it was of course always easy to recognize that he was a man. This simple principle of distinction was adopted, therefore, as the guiding rule in future controversies. All men, however or wherever educated, were to be considered competent physicians, if only they chose to say so themselves. And all women were correlatively to be declared incompetent, no matter what care they had taken to prepare themselves. The principle was well suited to crude and uncultured societies, and became proportionately popular.

Elizabeth and Emily Blackwell were led to the study of medicine in a different manner than Harriet Hunt, their immediate predecessor. While still quite young girls, they were, by the sudden death of their father, unexpectedly confronted with the necessity of supporting not only themselves, but their mother, and a large family of younger brothers and sisters. "Then we realized the infinite narrowness and pettiness of the avenues open to women, and the crowds of competitors who kept each other down in the struggle. We determined that we would endeavor to open a new door, and tread a fresh path,—rather than push for a footing in one already filled to overflowing." ‡

In this determination a new key-note was sounded. The

---

versy, declared women eligible to its degrees, the journals were flooded with letters from indignant physicians, who declared that by this action their own diplomas, previously obtained, had been lowered in value, their contracts violated, and their most sacred property rights invaded.

* Address at Chickering Hall, New York, March 18, 1888, by Dr. Emily Blackwell.

† Mt. Holyoke was founded by Mary Lyon in 1837.

‡ Address of Emily Blackwell, *cit. ut supra*.

Blackwells, and especially Elizabeth, were less the associates of Harriet Hunt, and of their own immediate successors, than the spiritual daughters of Mary Wollstonecraft, whose courageous demand for a wider field for her sex had remained hitherto almost alone, like a voice crying in the wilderness. They did not seek wider opportunities in order to study medicine, but they studied medicine in order to secure wider opportunities for all women.*

It was by sheer force of intellect, and of the sympathetic imagination born of intellectual perception, that Elizabeth Blackwell divined for women the suitableness of an occupation whose practical details were, to herself, intrinsically distasteful. Among all the pioneer group of women physicians, hers chiefly deserves to be called the Record of an Heroic Life. For with her, the struggle with bitter and brutal prejudices in the world was not sustained by the keen and instinctive enthusiasm for medicine, which has since carried hundreds of women over impossibilities. Rather was the arduousness of the struggle intensified by a passionate sensitiveness of temperament, which, under a cold exterior, rendered her intensely alive to the hardships of the social obloquy and ostracism which she was destined to encounter in such abundance.

Those accustomed to value ideas according to their intrinsive power, as shown by their originality and their fruitful result, should admit that there was real grandeur in this thought : the thought that the entire sex might be lifted upon a higher intellectual plane, by means of a practical work, for which, at the moment, not half a dozen people in America discerned the opportunity. "The thorough education of a class of women in medicine will exert an important influence upon the life and interests of women in general." "Medicine is so broad a field, so closely interwoven with general interests, and yet of so personal a character in its individual applications, that the coöperation of men and women is needed to fulfill all its requirements." "It is not possible or desirable to sanction the establishment of an intermediate class" [of midwives.]†

---

* Elizabeth Blackwell, like Tennyson's Princess,

"Shuddered but to dream that maids should ape
Those monstrous males that carve the living hound,"

And also like the Princess, it was

"through many a weary moon
She learned the craft of healing."

† "Medicine as a Profession for Women." Address by Elizabeth and Emily Blackwell, delivered Dec. 2, 1859.

So much more broad and sound were the views of this self-taught Cincinnati school-teacher,* than of the kind-hearted but short-sighted men, who in Boston were then trying to establish the Female Medical Education Society!

It was in 1845 that the plan of studying medicine became with Elizabeth Blackwell a settled resolution; and she was thus the first person on the American continent to whom such an idea did come.

It is worthy of note, that the originality of the main idea was sustained by an almost equal originality of view in regard to the true nature of a medical education.

Only a few years ago an eminent New York professor† showed that it was both practicable, and a common thing to do, for men to graduate, even from New York schools, after only ten months attendance upon lectures, of which the second five months was a mere repetition of the first: and without ever having seen a sick person. If this were true of New York,—where, after all, it is possible to do otherwise,—it may be imagined what would be true of the multitude of small schools scattered through the country, where the resources for either clinical or didactic instruction were confessedly inadequate. And if this were true in 1880 the status of 1850 may be divined.

It was at this time that Elizabeth Blackwell recognized that preparation for medical practice demanded the sanction of test examinations at a respectable school; not a few months, but years of study; and above all abundant clinical experience. Rather than accept as final the indorsement of little schools established *ad hoc*, or exclusively for women, she applied to be admitted as student at twelve medical schools throughout the country, and among these found one, the school at Geneva, N. Y., to grant her request. The faculty referred the matter to the students, and they decided to invite the courageous applicant. Poor, dependent entirely upon her own exertions, and with others more or less dependent upon her, she nevertheless found means to devote five years to the study of her profession, of which two were spent in Europe, at that time a rare extravagance.‡ Uninstructed or informed by the laws and cus-

---

* Miss Blackwell was of English birth and family, but had come to Cincinnati at the age of twelve.

† Dr. Robert Weir.

‡ Miss Blackwell earned money by several years' work at school teaching, the great resource of American girls.

toms of the entire country that attendance on didactic lectures was sufficient to justify a medical diploma, and hospital training was superfluous,—her native common sense perceived the absurdity of this theory, and left no stone unturned to secure such fragments of hospital training as were obtainable for her in either hemisphere. During the term of study at Geneva, she utilized a vacation to seek admittance to the hospital of the Blockley almshouse at Philadelphia, and obtained it by skillful manipulation of the opposing political influences which prevailed among the managers of the institution.* After graduating at Geneva in 1849, the first woman in America or of modern times to receive a medical diploma, Miss Blackwell immediately went to Europe, and by exceptional favor succeeded in visiting some of the hospitals of both London † and Paris. In Paris, moreover, she submitted for several months to the severe imprisonment of the great school for midwives, La Maternité.

Emily Blackwell was refused admission to the Hobart College at Geneva, which had graduated her sister; but was allowed, for one year, to study at the Rush College of Chicago. For this permission, however, the college was censured by the State Medical Society, and the second term was therefore refused to the solitary female student. She was, however, enabled to complete her studies at Cleveland, Ohio, and graduated thence in 1852. During one of her vacations, she obtained permission to visit in Bellevue Hospital, where Dr. James Wood was just initiating the system of regular clinical lectures. After graduation, Emily Blackwell also went to Europe, and had the good fortune to become the private pupil of the celebrated Sir James Simpson of Edinburgh. She remained with him for a year, and when she left he warmly testified to her proficiency and competence for the work she had undertaken. The testimonial is worth quoting entire:

"My Dear Miss Blackwell:

"I do think that you have assumed a position for which you are excellently qualified, and where you may, as a teacher, do a great amount of good.

"As this movement progresses, it is evidently a matter of the utmost importance that female physicians should be most fully

* "It was the first time that a unanimous vote was ever cast in the board."—*Personal letter from Dr. Blackwell.*

† Especially St. Bartholomew, through the influence of Dr., afterwards Sir James, Paget.

and perfectly educated; and I firmly believe that it would be difficult or impossible to find for that purpose any one better qualified than yourself.

"I have had the fairest and best opportunity of testing the extent of your medical acquirements during the period of eight months, when you studied here with me, and I can have no hesitation in stating to you—what I have often stated to others—that I have rarely met with a young physician who was better acquainted with the ancient and modern languages, or more learned in the literature, science, and practical details of his profession. Permit me to add that in your relation to patients, and in your kindly care and treatment of them, I ever found you a 'most womanly woman.' Believe me, with very kindest wishes for your success,

"Yours very respectfully,

"JAMES G. SIMPSON." *

Miss Blackwell received similar testimonials from several distinguished physicians in London and Paris, in whose hospital wards she faithfully studied. Thus equipped, she returned to New York in 1855 to join her sister, with a fair hope of success in the arduous undertaking before them.

Dr. Elizabeth Blackwell, with the aid of a few generous friends, had opened a little dispensary for women and children,—which after three years' existence, and one year of suspension, developed into the New York Infirmary. This was first chartered in 1854. But when Emily Blackwell returned from Europe, no opportunities existed for either of the sisters to secure the hospital medical work, whose continued training is justly regarded of such inestimable advantage to every practicing physician. This was recognized even at a time that hospitals were regarded as superfluous in undergraduate education.

In 1850, Dr. Marion Sims, arriving as an exiled invalid from Alabama, with a brilliantly original surgical operation as his "stock in trade,"—succeeded, with the aid of some generous New York women, in founding the first Woman's Hospital in the world. It was just seven years since the first imperfect medical school for women had been opened

* The "ancient and modern languages," comprised Latin, Greek, French, German, and Italian,—an unusual list of accomplishments for a self-taught, Western bred girl of those days. Miss Blackwell particularly charmed Dr. Simpson by translating for him into English (or Scotch) some Latin versions of old Arabic medical treatises.

in Boston: six years since the first woman physician had graduated at Geneva: five years since a permanent school for women had been founded in Philadelphia. The coincidence of these dates is not fortuitous. There is a close correlation between the rise of modern gynæcology, and the rise of the movement for readmitting women to the medical profession, where they once held a place, and whence they had been forcibly extruded. While it is far from true that women physicians are intended only for obstetrics and gynæcology, it is unquestionably true that these two great branches of medicine peculiar to their sex constitute the great opportunity, the main portal, through which women have passed, and are destined to pass, to general medicine. It would have been well if those who conducted the one movement had frankly allied themselves with the leaders of the other. Unfortunately, the more important, and especially the more lucrative, the new medical spheres * seemed likely to be,—the more eager were those who engaged in them to keep out women.

Dr. Sims thus describes the circumstances of the founding of the Woman's Hospital:

"As soon as they (the New York surgeons) had learned how to perform these operations successfully" (those that Sims had invented), "they had no further use for me. My thunder had been stolen, and I was left without any resources whatever. I said to myself, 'I am a lost man unless I can get somebody to create a place in which I can show the world what I am capable of doing. *This was the inception of the idea of a woman's hospital.*"—"Story of My Life."

When the New York women organized the hospital they framed a by-law,—which has since passed into oblivion,—to the effect that the assistant surgeon should be a woman. Emily Blackwell was the woman who should have been chosen. She had had an education far superior to that of the average American doctor of the day, a special training under the most distinguished gynæcologists of the time,—Simpson and Huginer—and had received abundant testimonials to capacity; while there was really not another person in New York possessed of either such opportunities or of such special testimonials. At her return, informal inquiries were made to ascertain whether the second woman physician in New York would be allowed a footing where she so justly belonged, in New York's first Woman's Hospital. The overtures were

* For modern obstetrics is almost as new a sphere as gynæcology.

rejected : Dr. Sims passed by these just claims to recognition, and evaded the mandatory by-law of his generous friends, in a way that is most clearly shown in his own words : " One clause of the by-laws provided that the assistant surgeon should be a woman. I appointed Mrs. Brown's friend Henri L. Stuart, who had been so efficient in organizing the hospital. *She was matron and general superintendent.*"*

Having thus evaded the distinct and far-sighted intention of the founders of the hospital, Dr. Sims proceeded to select his medical assistant upon grounds extraordinarily frivolous.

" The hospital had been opened about six months, when I told the board of lady managers that I must have an assistant. They told me to select the man. I offered the appointment to Dr. F. N. Johnson, Jr., *who had just graduated.*† He was about to be married, and was going to locate in the country near Cooperstown. I then offered the place to Dr. George F. Shrady. He too was about to be married, and for some cause or other he did not see fit to accept it. Soon after this, a young friend of mine at the South, was married to Dr. Thomas Addis Emmett, of New York. As I was looking for an assistant, I did not know that I could more handsomely recognize the friendship of former days, than to appoint the husband of Mrs. Emmett assistant. So to the accident of good fortune in marrying a beautiful Southern young woman, Dr. Emmett owes his appointment."

Suffering womanhood undoubtedly owes much to Marion Sim's inventive genius. But, on the other hand, Sim's fame and fortune may be said to have been all made by women, from the poor slaves in Alabama who, unnarcotized, surrendered their patient bodies to his experiments,‡ to the New York ladies whose alert sympathies and open purses had enabled him to realize his dream, and establish his personal fortunes. It would have been an act both graceful and just on his part, at this crisis, to have shared his opportunities with the two

---

* "Story of My Life," by Marion Sims, p. 299.
It must be said that Dr. Sims was subsequently president of the American Medical Association, at the meeting which received its first woman delegate ; and doubtless his influence contributed toward her favorable reception.

† It will be remembered what were the conditions of graduation in New York in 1855.

‡ " This was the thirtieth operation performed on Anarcha." (1849.—Sims, *loc. cit.* p. 246.) 1849, foundation date of American gynæcology, was the date of the year when Elizabeth Blackwell received her diploma.

women who, like himself, had been well buffeted in an opposing world,* and whose work and aspirations were so closely identified with his own. But this he failed to do; and the lost opportunity made all the difference to the pioneer women physicians, between brilliant and modest, between immediate and tardy professional success.

Unable elsewhere to obtain hospital opportunities, the Blackwells resolved to found a hospital that should be conducted not only for, but by women. The New York Infirmary, chartered in 1854, preceded the Woman's Hospital by a year, and, like it, was the first institution of the kind in the world. For three years it consisted exclusively of a dispensary; then was added a tiny lying-in ward of twelve beds. At this moment the advance guard of women physicians received their fourth recruit, Marie Zakzrewska, a young midwife from Germany. She had been a favorite pupil of Dr. Schmidt, one of the state examiners of the school for midwives in Berlin, and chief director of the Charity Hospital. He had been so impressed by the talents of his pupil, as to entrust her with the responsibility of teaching his own classes, when ill-health compelled him to resign his work. Discouraged, however, by some intrigues which sprang up after the death of her powerful friend, Fräulein Zakzrewska decided to abandon the home where a career seemed ready marked out for her, and to seek a wider horizon and larger fortunes in America. Here she arrived in 1853. Her pluck and courage carried her safely through the first difficult year of an almost penniless exile; then the generous kindness of Elizabeth Blackwell secured her a place among the advance guard of women physicians, taught her English, and procured her admission to the Medical School at Cleveland. She assisted the Blackwells in the task of collecting from an indifferent or hostile community the first few hundred dollars with which to found the New York Infirmary, and in this served as physician for a year; was thence invited to lecture on midwifery at the Female Medical School at Boston; was finally summoned to build up the New England Hospital, which for many years was almost identified with her name and

* Dr. Sims, in his autobiography, complains that he was denounced as a quack by the "conservative" surgeons of New York, some of whom did not hesitate to secretly try to dissuade the ladies from doing anything about the Woman's Hospital, and urging that the New York Hospital already accomplished every purpose.

Thus whatever *is*, invariably seeks to strangle in the birth that which is about to be!

with that of Dr. Lucy Sewall,* and of Dr. Helen Morton. This, the second hospital to be conducted by women physicians, was founded in 1862.

The fifth pioneer was Ann Preston, a Quaker lady of Philadelphia, an ardent abolitionist, as it was the inherited privilege of the Friends to be.† Miss Preston had become early habituated to interest herself in the cause of minorities. Small and fragile in body, she possessed an indomitable little soul; and when the suggestion had once been thrown out, that a medical college for women might be opened in Philadelphia, Ann Preston never ceased working until had been collected the meagre funds considered sufficient for its establishment. This was in 1850; and the sixth annual announcement of the school mentions Dr. Preston as already installed as professor of physiology. This position she held till the day of her death.

At the outset, the new medical school was scarcely an improvement upon its Boston predecessor. Four months lectures,—composed of compilations from three or four text-books,—the same repeated the following year, constituted the curriculum. There was much zeal, but little knowledge. Dr. Preston herself, philanthropist and excellent woman as she was, was necessarily ignorant of her subject, because she had never had any opportunity to learn anything about it. The other professors were not more qualified, although without the same excuse of necessity. Ten years after the opening of the college, the Philadelphia County Medical Society found an apparently plausible pretext for refusing recognition to the school, in the fact that the lecturer on therapeutics was not a physician but a druggist,—who moreover presumed to practice medicine over his counter, and "irregular" and advertised medicine at that. Even more to the purpose than these accumulated crimes was the fact that his lectures consisted almost exclusively of strings of prescriptions, and had no real claim to be accepted as exponents of the modern science of therapeutics.

The first adequate teacher to appear in the school was Emmeline Cleveland, who, having graduated under its meagre instructions, was sent to Europe through the generosity of two

* Dr. Zakzrewska's life has been sketched in outline down to the above date, in a little volume entitled "Practical Illustration of Woman's Right to Labor," by Caroline Dall.

† A petition for the emancipation of negro slaves was presented to Congress by a group of Quaker gentlemen, within a few years after the framing of the Constitution.—Van Holst, *Constitutional History of America.*

Quaker ladies,* to fit herself at the Paris Maternité to lecture upon obstetrics. Dr. Cleveland thus repeated the career of Dr. Shippen in 1762,† and like him found in Europe the instructions and inspiration her native city would not afford. Dr. Cleveland was a woman of real ability, and would have done justice to a much larger sphere than that to which fate condemned her. Compelled by the slender resources of the college to unite the duties of housekeeper and superintendent to those of professor, she not unfrequently passed from the lecture room to the kitchen to make the bread for the students who boarded at the institution. Possessed of much personal beauty, and grace of manner, she had married young; but her husband had been stricken with hemiplegia early in their married life, and it was the necessity of supporting him as well as herself, which led the wife, childless and practically widowed, to enter the profession of medicine.

Of the remaining typical members of the pioneer groups of woman physicians, all were married, either already when they began their studies, or immediately after graduation. The latter was the fortune of Sarah Adamson, the second woman in the United States to receive a medical diploma, and who a year later married Dr. Dolley, of Rochester, where she at once settled and has been in successful practice for thirty-eight years. Miss Adamson was a niece of the Dr. Hiram Corson, who, in Montgomery County of Pennsylvania, was destined to wage a forty years' chivalrous warfare in defense of women physicians. At the age of eighteen, having come across a copy of Wistar's Anatomy, she devoted a winter to its engrossing study, and became fired with enthusiasm for the medical art, to which anatomy formed such a grand portal.‡ At that time, 1849, the Philadelphia Medical School had not yet opened; but the Eclectic School at Rochester had announced its willingness to receive woman students, and to this Miss Adamson persuaded her parents to allow her to go. She graduated in 1851.

Besides Miss Adamson, four other ladies availed themselves of the liberality of the "irregular" eclectic school at Rochester, but of these only one graduated. Even more than her Quaker colleagues, did this lady represent a distinctive type

* Hannah Richardson and Rebecca White.

† See *ut supra*, p. 13, note.

‡ *Galaxy*, 1868. The innocent young Quaker girl did not find this "a disgusting preliminary!"

among women physicians, for she was already married when she began her studies. Mrs. Gleason was the wife of a young Vermont doctor, who opened an infirmary in the country for chronic invalids, shortly after acquiring his own diploma. In the management of his lady patients, the young doctor often found it an advantage to be assisted "by his wife as an intermediary, on the one side to relate the symptoms, on the other to prescribe the directions." Thus the wife became gradually associated with the husband's work, while he on his part remained generously alive to her interests. He it was, who, in order to secure an opportunity for his wife for some kind of systematic medical education, persuaded the eclectics, assembled in council, to open the doors of their new school to women. "In his opinion, the admission of women was the reform most needed in the medical profession." "I remember vividly," writes Mrs. Gleason, "the day of his return, when he exclaimed, with enthusiasm, 'Now, wife, you can go to medical lectures.'"* The husband and wife have practiced medicine in harmonious partnership ever since this early epoch. Their sanitarium at Elmira still exists to sustain its old and honorable reputation.†

There is something idyllic in this episode. Here in western New York was realized, simply and naturally, the ideal life of a married pair, as was once described by Michelet, where the common interests and activities should embrace not only the home circle, but also professional life. It is the secret ideal of many a sweet-natured woman, hitherto attained more often when the husband is a clergyman than when he is a physician, but in America is by no means unknown in the latter case. By Mrs. Gleason's happy career, the complex experiment in life which was being made by the first group of women physicians was enriched by a special and, on some accounts, peculiarly interesting type.

The two remaining women of the group were also married, and the husband of one, Mrs. Thomas, was also a physician.‡ She and her sister, Mrs. Longshore, both graduated in the first class sent out from the Woman's Medical College of Phila-

---

* Personal letter.

† To them were born two children, a son who died in early childhood; a daughter who lived to grow up and became educated as a physician.

‡ Out of 189 graduates of the Philadelphia College whose status was reported in 1881, 56 were married women. The total number of graduates at that time was 276. (Rachel Bodley, "The College Story," Commencement address, 1881.

delphia.* Dr. Longshore was the first woman to settle in practice in this city, and her sign was regarded as a monstrous curiosity, collecting street idlers for its perusal. On one, and perhaps more than one, occasion, a druggist refused to fill a prescription signed by the "female doctor," and took it upon himself to order her home "to look after her house and darn her husband's stockings."† But Dr. Longshore ultimately established herself in a lucrative practice. Mrs. Thomas, the sister, first began to study medicine privately, with her husband, a practitioner in Indiana. For four years, while caring for a family of young children, Mrs. Thomas "read medicine" at all odd minutes; and at last, upon hearing that a medical college had been opened for women in Philadelphia, she made a grand final effort to secure its advantages. She sewed steadily until she had provided her family with clothes for six months in advance, and then started for the East. Returning with her coveted diploma, Mrs. Thomas began to practice medicine with her husband at Fort Wayne, and continued to do so until her death about a year ago (1889). During eight years she held the position of city physician, and for twelve years was physician to a home for friendless girls.

The married women physicians of the West, with protection and sympathy at home, and encountering abroad only a good-natured laxity of prejudice, were in a favored position compared with their colleagues in Philadelphia, Boston, and New York. At the time that the tiny New York infirmary was opened (1857) the name of "woman physician" had become a by-word of reproach, from its usurpation by a notorious abortionist, "Madame" Restell. So wide a stain could be diffused over innocent persons by a single evil reputation, that it was difficult for Drs. Blackwell and Zakzrewska to obtain lodgings or office room; their applications were refused on the ground that their business must be disreputable. Scarcely more than fifty years had elapsed since the practice of obstetrics at least was entirely in the hands of women: yet the recollection of this had so completely faded away, that the women who now renewed the ancient claim to minister to the the physical necessities of their sex, were treated as repro-

* There were eight graduates. The first medical class that ever graduated in Philadelphia about a century before consisted of a single number.

† Quite a group of bystanders collected to hear the discussion, which was animated by opposing cheers and hisses.

bates.* The little group of women who nevertheless dared to face this opprobrium, contained collectively nearly all the elements necessary for success, although in no one member of the group were these united. Instinctive enthusiasm for the science of life, instinctive predilection for medical practice, enlightened resolve to elevate the intellectual capacity and enlarge the practical opportunities of women,—the habit of progressive philanthropy,—personal interest in the pursuits of the nearest friend, the husband; literary training, exceptional among the uncultivated physicians of the day,—the tradition of centuries in the discipline of the practical European midwife,—all these were representative, and certainly none could have been spared. What was most conspicuously lacking was systematic education, which might have enabled the medical students to judge more critically of the medical education which was offered them. However, even without adequate intellectual preparation, there was a complex representation of interests which sufficiently showed that the enterprise was no isolated eccentricity, but sprang from roots widely ramifying in the permanent nature of things, and in the changing circumstances of the day.

This fourth period in the history of women physicians, to which belong the early careers of the pioneers in the movement, must nevertheless be considered as a sort of pre-medical episode, analogous in many respects to that of the entire American profession before the Revolutionary War. And this notwithstanding, and indeed a good deal because during this epoch some women were admitted to inferior or "irregular" schools, already established, and because other medical schools were founded exclusively for them. The Philadelphia school owed its foundation to the most generous impulses: but knowledge and pecuniary resources were both inadequate, and the active and bitter opposition of the medical profession of the city was an almost insuperable obstacle in the way of securing efficient assistance for instruction. The idea of the school seems to have originated with Dr. Bartholomew Fussell, a poor schoolmaster, who had been educated by an elder sister

* "To be addressed in public as doctor," writes Dr. Zakzrewrka, "was painful, for all heads would turn to look at the woman thus stigmatized." (Personal letter.) "Women," said Dr. Blackwell at this time, "occupy an anomalous position, standing alone in medicine,—often opposed or ignored by the profession, not acknowledged by society, and separated from the usual pursuits and interests of women."—("An Appeal in behalf of the Medical Education of Women." New York: 1856).

"to whom he looked up with veneration ; and he thought that such as she ought to have a chance of studying medicine, if they desired." *

A few friends were collected, the plan was matured, the charter secured, and the school opened for the reception of students in 1850. During the first four years the yearly sessions did not last more than four months ; but in the fifth annual catalogue the trustees announced with pride an extension of the course to five and a half months, and claimed that this was the longest course of instruction adopted by any medical college in the United States. They further, and with evident sincerity, declared that the curriculum of study was fully equal to that of any other medical college.

The instruction consisted of rambling lectures, given by gentlemen of good intentions but imperfect fitness, to women whose previous education left them utterly unprepared to enter a learned profession, and many of whom were really, and in the ordinary sense, illiterate. As fast as possible the brightest students were chosen, after graduation, to fill places in the Faculty, and among these one, Emmeline Cleveland, having received a real education, at least for obstetrics, in Europe, returned to Philadelphia to become a really effective teacher. For twelve years scarcely any opportunity existed for the students of the college to see sick people, an anomaly which would at the time have been considered more outrageous in any other country than the United States. As late as 1859, nine years after the foundation of the college, the Philadelphia County Medical Society passed resolutions of excommunication against every physician who should teach in the school, every woman who should graduate from it, and everybody else who should even consult with such teachers.

Had the tiny college been a virulent pest-house, the *cordon sanitaire* could not have been more rigidly drawn around it. Nevertheless, the trustees claimed that their graduates rapidly secured medical practice, at least to the extent of a thousand dollars a year ; and that applications were frequently received from communities in different parts of the country, requesting that women physicians be sent to settle among them.† In 1857 115 students had matriculated at the college.

In 1859 Elizabeth Blackwell estimated that about 300 women had managed to " graduate " somewhere in medicine, supposing

* Personal letter of niece.—*R. L. Fussell.*

† Annual Catalogue, 1854.

that their studies had really "qualified them to begin practice, and that by gaining experience in practice itself, they would gradually work their way to success." "It is not until they leave college, and attempt their work alone and unaided, that they realize how utterly insufficient their education is to enable them to acquire and support the standing of a physician. Many of them, discouraged, having spent all their money, abandon the profession ; a few gain a little practical knowledge, and struggle into a second-rate position."

This view of the realities of the situation is in curious contrast with the cheerful optimism of the leaders of the Philadelphia School. These did indeed walk by faith,—and the numerous addresses of Ann Preston, who for many years was its guiding spirit, breathe a spirit of moral enthusiasm which, as the final result proved, really did manage to compensate for the intellectual inadequacy. Dr. Preston seems to have been thoroughly convinced, that if the moral behavior of the new physicians were kept irreproachable, intellectual difficulties would take care of themselves, or be solved by an over-ruling Providence.*

The fifth period for women physicians began with the founding of hospitals, where they could obtain clinical training, and

---

* "Every woman will be narrowly watched and severely criticised because she is a woman. If she bear not herself wisely and well, many will suffer for her sake. Gentleness of manner, the adornment of a quiet spirit, are as important to the physician as the woman. . . . . I too have felt the hopes and the aspirations after a fuller and more satisfying life, which have arisen in the souls of some of you. . . . . The office of healing is Christlike. . . . . Your business is, not to war with words, but to make good your position by deeds of healing. . . . . Probity, simplicity, modesty, hope, patience, benevolence, prudence,—are needed alike by the woman and the physician. All the brave, struggling women, who, in various walks of life, are laboring for small compensations, will be benefited by a movement which opens to women another department of remunerative and honorable activity."

Contrast with these modest statements of the gentle Philadelphia Quakeress the aggressive self-consciousness of the emancipated French woman, who rushes into the arena, with a little red flag waving in every sentence: "À nos lectrices, à nos lecteurs, à nos collaborateurs, à nos amis connus et inconnus, à tous ceux qui s'interessent à notre entreprise. Salut ! . . . . . Nous voyons tous les jours des professeurs qui ont étudié dans leurs moindres détails, tous les êtres organises qui forment la série zoologique, et qui semblent ignorer absolument ce qu'est cet être qui tient tant de place dans l'humanité, la femme. Faisons-nous connaître, et quand ils sauront ce que nous valons, ils nous apprecieront comme nous le meritons."—Mme. C. Renooz, *Revue Scientifique des femmes*. Paris, Mai, 1888.

The *Revue* is already extinguished after a year's existence. The college survives and prospers after forty years of struggle.

thus give some substance to the medical education they had received in mere outline. The oldest of these institutions is the New York Infirmary, chartered, as has been said, in 1854 as a dispensary,—opened with an indoor department in 1857, with the Drs. Blackwell and Zakzrewska as attending physicians. The Infirmary was fortunate in securing several eminent New York physicians as consultants, Dr. Willard Parker, Dr. Kissam, Dr. James B. Wood, Dr. Stephen Smith, Dr. Elisha Harris. The medical profession in New York never took the trouble to organize opposition and pronounce the decrees of ostracism that thundered in Philadelphia; its attitude was rather that of indifference than active hostility.

From 1857 until 1865, the indoor department of the Infirmary was limited to a single ward for poor lying-in women, and which contained but twelve beds. But in the dispensary, several thousand patients a year were treated, and the young physicians living in the hospital also visited the sick poor at their own homes. The persevering efforts of the Blackwells, moreover, finally succeeded in opening one medical institution of the city to their students, the great Demilt dispensary. As early as 1862, the succession of women students who annually pressed forward to fill the two vacancies at the Infirmary patiently waited in the clinic rooms of Demilt, and there gleaned many crumbs of experience and information.* These, together with the practical experience gained in the obstetrical ward and the out-practice of the Infirmary, afforded the first and for a long time the only opportunity for clinical instruction open to women students in America.

In 1865, a medical college was added to the Infirmary; a new building was purchased for the hospital, which became enlarged to the capacity of 35 beds. For the first time it then began to receive private patients, chiefly from among self-supporting women of limited income, to hundreds of whom the resources of the Infirmary has proved invaluable. Their pay, though modest, has contributed materially to the resources of the hospital for the treatment of entirely indigent patients.†

The report for 1869 shows a hospital staff of: Resident

* The celebrated Dr. Camman, who for many years held a clinic for heart and lung diseases at the Demilt, gave valuable instruction to the women students.

† This innovation (for it was one) was effected during the residentship of Dr. Elizabeth Cushier, who has contributed immensely to the building up of the hospital.

physician, 1; internes, 3; visiting physicians, 3; associate physicians, 3; out-visiting physician, 1.

Total number in-patients, 342; Total number dispensary patients, 4825; Total number patients treated at home, 768.

The Woman's Hospital at Philadelphia was founded in 1862 during the excitements of the great Civil War. It was the outgrowth of a singularly brutal incident. In 1861 the resources of the college became entirely exhausted; there was not enough money in the treasury to hire lecture rooms, and it was reluctantly decided that the lecture course must be suspended. Permission, however, had been obtained for the students to visit the wards at the Blockley almshouse, and thither they went under the tiny escort of Dr. Ann Preston. On one occasion, in order to effectually disconcert the women students, one of the young men suddenly introduced into the room a male patient perfectly nude. The insult stung the friends of the college to renewed exertions, which were not relaxed until funds were collected sufficient to purchase a house in which might be opened a hospital where women could obtain clinical instruction by themselves. A lecture room was rented in this house, and lectures were resumed in the fall of 1862. From this date, the obstetrical chair of the college, at least, was fairly supplied with clinical material. The double institution, college and hospital, was first lifted out of its period of depressing struggle, when, at the death of its generous president, the Hon. Wm. S. Pierce, it received a bequest of $100,000. With this, a really beautiful building was erected for the use of the college.

Adjoining the college, soon sprang up a separate building for a general hospital, which has, however, always been predominantly gynæcological. Later was added a special maternity pavilion. The report of 1889 reads as follows:

Hospital staff: Resident physicians, 1; internes, 6; visiting physicians, 6; district physicians, 12; in-patients, 583;* dispensary patients, 6365; patients treated at home, 695.

The woman's hospital in Boston, the New England Hospital for Women and Children, was also founded during the war, and incorporated in 1862. The women who engaged in it were all heavily burdened by the great public anxieties of the time. But the very nature of these anxieties, the keen interest aroused in hospital work and in nursing organizations, helped to direct attention to the women's hospitals. In New York, the first meeting to consider the organization of nursing for the army

* This is an increase of 100 patients over the preceding year.

was held in the parlors of the Infirmary, and at the suggestion of Elizabeth Blackwell. This little meeting was the germ from which subsequently developed the splendid organization of the Sanitary Commission.

Dr. Zakzrewska was invited by the founders of the New England Hospital to preside over its organization;* and to do this, she left the Female Medical School, with which great dissatisfaction was beginning to be felt. Dr. Zakzrewska received powerful assistance for the work from one of the graduates of the school, Lucy Sewall, descendant of a long line of Puritan ancestors. This young lady seemed to have been the first girl of fortune and family to study medicine in the United States. Her romantic and enthusiastic friendship formed for Dr. Zakzrewska, while yet her pupil, led the young Boston girl to devote her life, her fortune, and the influence she could command from a wide circle of friends, to building up the hospital, where she might have the privilege of working with her.

This element of ardent personal friendship and discipleship is rarely lacking in woman's work, from the day—or before it—that Fabiola followed St. Jerome to the desert, there to build the first hospital of the Roman Empire.

Other pupils of the rudimentary Gregory school also felt the magnetism of Dr. Zakzrewska's personal influence, and entered a charmed circle, banded together for life, for the defense of the hospital,—Anita Tyng, Helen Morton, Susan Dimock, the lovely and brilliant girl whose tragic death in the shipwreck of the *Schiller*, in 1875, deprived the women physicians of America of their first surgeon. Dr. Morton spent several arduous years in the Paris Maternity, where she became chief assistant in order to fit herself for the medical practice at home in which she has so well succeeded. Dr. Dimock went to Zurich, and was the first American girl to graduate from its medical school. In the three brief years that she was resident physician at the New England Hospital, she exhibited a degree of surgical ability that promised a brilliant professional career. The three surgical cases published by her in the New York *Medical Record* (see Bibliographical List) are of real importance and originality.†

---

* In the chapter on "Women in Hospitals," in this volume, Mrs. Ednah Cheney gives the details of the early formation of the New England Hospital.—Ed.

† "She was as fresh and girlish as if such qualities had never been pronounced incompatible with medical attainments. She had, indeed, a certain

The New England Hospital, like its sister institutions at New York and Philadelphia, outgrew, and more rapidly than they, its early narrow limits in Pleasant Street, and in 1872 the present beautiful little building was erected in the suburbs of Boston. The work was steadily enlarged, year by year. The report for 1889 shows:

Hospital staff: Resident physician, 1; advisory physicians, 3; visiting physicians, 3; visiting surgeons, 3; internes, 6. In-patients for year, 376; Dispensary patients, 3175.

In 1865, a fourth hospital for women and children was organized in Chicago, "at the request and by the earnest efforts of Dr. Mary H. Thompson, the pioneer woman physician in the city. Opened just at the close of the war, many of those to whom it afforded shelter, nursing, and medical attendance were soldiers' wives, widows, and children, and women whose husbands had deserted them in hours of greatest need. There came from the South refugees both white and colored." * Thus in the West as in the East, we find repeated for the women physicians of the nineteenth century the experience of the men of the eighteenth; it was amidst the exigencies of a great war that their opportunities opened, their sphere enlarged, and they "emerged from obscurity" into the responsibilities of recognized public function.

In 1871, just as money had been collected to purchase a better house and lot for the small hospital, the great fire occurred; and when after it, "the remnants were gathered together, they were found to consist of one or two helpless patients, two housemaids, a nurse, a pair of blankets, two pil-

---

flower-like beauty, a peculiar softness and elegance of appearance and manner. I have wondered whether she did not resemble Angelica Kaufman. Underneath this softness, however, lay a decision of purpose, a Puritan austerity of character that made itself felt, though unseen. "She ruled the hospital like a little Napoleon," said a lady who had been there. . . . . Both the surgical talents and surgical training of Dr. Dimock are certainly at the present date (1875), exceptional among women. It is on this account that our loss is irreparable, for at this moment there seems to be no one to take her place. Many battles have been lost from such a cause. But although ours be ultimately won, we would not, if we could, grieve less loyally for this girl, so brilliant and so gentle, so single of purpose and so wide of aim, whose life had been thus ruthlessly uprooted and thrown upon the waves at the very moment it touched upon fruition."—M. P. Jacobi in *New York Medical Record*, 1875.

Dr. Dimock, like so many of the early gynæcological surgeons of America, was a Southerner, born in North Carolina.

* Nineteenth Annual Report Chicago Hospital for Women and Children, 1884.

lows, and a bit of carpet." * The hospital "remnant," however, profited with others by the outburst of energy which so rapidly repaired misfortune and rebuilt the city. In 1871, a building was purchased by the Relief and Aid Society, for $25,000, and given to the hospital, on conditions, one of which was that it should annually care for twenty-five patients free of charge.

During the first nineteen years of its existence, up to 1854, over 15,000 patients had been cared for by the hospital, of which 4774 were house patients, 9157 were treated in the dispensary, and 1404 attended at home. The report of the hospital for 1888 gives a summary for four years.† There is a hospital staff, comprising attending physicians, 5; pathologist, 1; internes, 3. Annual average from four years summary: In-patients, 334; dispensary, 806; visited at home, 138.

The fifth woman's hospital was opened in San Francisco in 1875, under the name of the Pacific Dispensary, by Dr. Charlotte Blake Brown and Dr. Annette Buckle, both graduates of the Philadelphia school. During the first year, it contained but six beds. To-day, after fifteen years' untiring work, the enlisted sympathies of generous friends have developed it to a hospital for 110 beds, to which sick children are admitted gratuitously, and adult female patients on payment of a small charge. It is under the care of six attending physicians, who serve in rotation.

Finally, in distant Minneapolis, a sixth hospital has spurng up in 1882. At its latest report, only 193 patients had been received during the year. But the history of its predecessors, and the irresistible Western energy of its friends, predict for this a growth perhaps even more rapid than that possible in cities in the East.

It is worth while to summarize the actual condition of these six hospitals in a tabulated form :

---

* Report, *loc. cit.*

† "To the fixedness and honesty of purpose of Dr. Mary H. Thompson, may be credited these satisfactory results of nineteen years' work. They mean a devotion and self-sacrifice on her part that few can estimate."—*Report of results from* 1884 *to* 1888.

NAME.	DATE OF ORIGIN.	CAPACITY.	NO. ON STAFF.	ANNUAL NO. IN-PATIENTS.	ANNUAL NO. DISPENSARY.	ANNUAL NO. OUT-PATIENTS.
New York Infirmary.	1857	35 beds	3 visiting physicians. 3 internes, 3 associates. 1 resident. 1 out physician.	342 (report for 1889)	4,825	768
Woman's Hospital, Philadelphia.	1862	47 beds	6 visiting. 6 internes. 1 resident. 12 district.	583 (report for 1889)	6,365	695
New England Hospital.	1863	58 beds	6 visiting. 6 advisory. 6 internes.	376 (report for 1889)	3,175	
Woman's Hospital, Chicago.	1865	80 beds	5 visiting. 3 internes. 1 pathological.	354 (average of collective report for 4 years)	806	138
Hospital for Sick Children and Women, San Francisco.	1875	110 beds	6 attending. 2 specialists. 2 internes.			
Northwestern Hospital, Minneapolis.	1882		4 visiting.	193 (report for 1889)		

Thus, total number of women physicians engaged in six hospitals, 94; number renewed annually, 32; annual number indoor patients, 1828; annual number of dispensary patients, 15,171; annual number patients treated at home, 1601; total number patients, 18,600.

This represents the growth since 1857, when the only hospital conducted by women, in this country, was the lying-in ward of the New York Infirmary, containing twelve beds.

The foundation of these hospitals effected the transition for women physicians from the pre-medical period, when medical education was something attempted but not effected, to a truly medical epoch, when women could really have an opportunity to engage in actual medical work. Correlatively the theoretic education began to improve. In Boston, the Female Medical College was happily extinguished as an independent institution. In Philadelphia, the Faculty gradually struggled free of its inefficient or objectionable members, utilized its legacy of $100,000 to fully equip its beautiful college building, with amphitheatres, lecture rooms, and even embryo laboratories, museums, and libraries,—enlarged its corps of instructors until they numbered twenty-three, instead of the original and meagre seven,—and even, though more timidly, began to enforce something like a rigid discipline among its students, in regard to conditions of admission, examination, graduation, and terms of study. In 1885, Lawson Tait, the famous English surgeon, described the college building as "being very large and splendidly appointed. Last year twenty-six degrees of doctor of medicine were granted by the Faculty, and from the perusal of the curriculum, as well as from conversation with some of the graduates, and from discussion with both the friends and opponents of the school, I am quite satisfied that its graduates are quite as carefully trained as those in any other medical school. When I tell you that last winter 132 students matriculated in this school, that the amphitheatre in the hospital is large enough to seat 300 persons, and that every year about 4000 patients pass through this amphitheatre in the college clinics, I shall have said enough to prove to you that in the United States the practice of medicine by women has become an accomplished fact." *

In New York, after much hesitation, a charter was obtained in 1865 for the establishment of a medical college in connection with the Infirmary. "This step was taken reluctantly, because the desire of the trustees of the Infirmary, of Drs. Elizabeth and Emily Blackwell, was not to found another medical school, but to secure the admission of women to the classes for instruction already organized in connection with the medical charities of the city, and to one at least of the New York medical colleges. . . . The demand of women for a medical education had resulted in the founding of small colleges in different places, all, with the exception of the Philadelphia School, limited to the narrow and cheap standard of legal requirements, and producing equally cheap and narrow results in the petty standard of medical education they were establishing among women students.† Application was made to the College of Physicians and Surgeons for advice, and the case was laid before the Faculty. It was stated that a sufficient number of women were studying medicine to show that there was a demand for instruction that must be satisfied; that the

* *Medical News*, 1885. Reprint of address at Birmingham by Lawson Tait.

† The establishment of such schools, professing to further the education of women, has continued to be the greatest bane to the movement for their effective education. So late as the current year (1890), a lady writes from Cincinnati: "The college already in existence is one of the unpardonable sins against a confiding public."

standard of education was so low that incompetent women were in possession of degrees, while competent women could not obtain the thorough instruction they desired, and those who were fitted to do good work had to contend, not only against popular and unjustified prejudice, but against the justified prejudices of those who saw the slipshod work of ignorant graduates from women's medical colleges."* The trustees proposed to the College of Physicians and Surgeons, the oldest and most reputable in New York, that they receive a limited number of female students on scholarships established by the Infirmary, to the amount of $2000 a year. This proposition was rejected, and the opinion expressed, in no unfriendly spirit, that the ends proposed were only to be obtained by establishing an independent school for women in connection with the Infirmary.

The establishment of such a school called for money,—but the money was forthcoming. A new building was purchased for the hospital ; the old one, which had done such modest but effective work, was surrendered to the use of the college, and a prospectus issued announcing the requirements of the lattter. In this prospectus a bold attempt was made to outline a scheme of education, which should not only satisfy the conventional existing standard, but improve upon this. It was realized, and, oddly enough, for the first time, that the best way to compensate the enormous disadvantages under which women physicians must enter upon their work, was to prepare them for it with peculiar thoroughness. Women students were almost universally deficient in preliminary intellectual training : their lesser physical strength rendered a cramming system more often dangerous to health, and more ineffective as a means of preparation ; and the prejudices to be encountered in their medical career would subject them not only to just, but also to abundant unfair criticism. Instead, therefore, of the senseless official system which then everywhere prevailed, it was proposed to establish a three years graded course, with detailed laboratory work during the first years, and detailed clinical work during the last. A chair of hygiene was established for the first time in America, and an independent board of examiners was appointed consisting of professors from the different city schools. By this means the college voluntarily submitted itself to the external criticism of the highest local authori-

* Memorial of Trustees of Women's Medical College of N. Y. Infirmary, 1887.

ties. When the Infirmary put forth this prospectus, drawn up by the Drs. Blackwell, no college in the country required such a course: it was deemed Quixotic by many medical friends, and several of its features were for a time postponed. The independent board of examiners, however, was established from the beginning, and, little by little, the other parts of the scheme were realized. In 1876, the three years graded course, at first optional, was made obligatory. At this time no college but Harvard had taken this step. The next year the class fell off one-third,—a curious commentary on the character or circumstances of the students.* In 1881, the college year was lengthened to eight months, thus abandoning the time-honored division of a winter and spring course, the latter comparable to the Catholic works of supererogation, and equally neglected. At the same time entrance examinations were established. These moderate improvements upon the naïve barbarism of existing customs again reduced the classes one-half. When people first began to think of educating women in medicine, a general dread seemed to exist that, if any tests of capacity were applied, all women would be excluded. The profound skepticism felt about women's abilities, was thus as much manifest in the action of the friends to their education as in that of its opponents. But by 1882, the friends dared to "call upon those who believe in the higher education of women, to help to set the highest possible standard for their medical education; and upon those who do not believe in such higher education to help in making such requirements as shall turn aside the incompetent,—not by an exercise of arbitrary power, but by a demonstration of incapacity, which is the only logical, manly reason for refusing to allow women to pursue an honorable calling in an honorable way." †

"A career is open to women in the medical profession, a career in which they may earn a livelihood; a career in which they may do missionary work among the poor of our own country, and among their own sex in foreign lands; a career that is practical, that is useful, that is scientific." ‡

Even when a theoretic demand is not entirely realized in the actual facts of the case, its distinct enunciation remains a great achievement; and, in an almost mysterious way, constantly

---

* The same thing had happened at Harvard, when it raised its standard of requirements.

† Memorial Trustees, *loc. cit.*

‡ *Ibid.*

tends to effect its own ultimate realization. And so it has been here.

During the current year, the college has emerged from its original chrysalis condition within the inconvenient precincts of a private house building, and entered upon a new phase of existence in a suitable building especially erected for its needs. The money for this building was collected from private subscriptions, by the indefatigable exertions of the friends of the college, and may be said to some extent to measure the growth of interest in the medical education of women, which had become diffused through the community.

In the West, two medical schools for women were opened in the same year, 1869; in Chicago a separate women's school; in Michigan the medical department of the State University.

The State University was founded and controlled by the State Legislature. On this account, in accordance with a principle generally recognized in the West, the youth of both sexes are equally eligible to its schools, as being equally children of the citizens who support the schools by means of taxation.* The application of this simple principle to the medical school at once solved the question of "medical co-education of the sexes," which had been such a bugbear in the East. The difficulties which had elsewhere been considered so insolvable, were arranged in the simplest manner. In regard to all subjects liable to create embarrassment, if discussed before a mixed audience of young students, the lectures were duplicated, and delivered to the male and female students separately. These was thus a double course for obstetrics, gynæcology, and some sections of internal medicine and surgery. The lectures, lecturers, and subsequent examinations of the students were, however, identical, and the clinics are held in common.

The value to women of this State recognition, and of opportunity to study at a university school, was immense. There were numerous disadvantages due to the youth and undeveloped character of the school, and still more to its control by a popular legislature, unversed in the requirements of learned professions. Yet there was promise of indefinite growth in the future, and in all the development of the future, women might hope to share.

At first the course of instruction was limited to two years; it has lately been extended to three; though it still has the serious defect of demanding no thesis from students as a con-

* See history of the founding of the University of Michigan, chapter Education in the Western States.—ED.

dition of graduation. Clinical instruction has been necessarily inadequate in a small country town. It has been lately proposed to transfer this part of the curriculum to Detroit, where large hospitals furnish clinical material in abundance.

In Chicago, application to admit women was made in 1865 to the Rush College, where Emily Blackwell had studied during the winter of 1851. The appeal was refused.

In 1868, application was made at a rival school, the Chicago Medical College, and was accepted. For a year female students attended the lectures and clinics in company with young men. "The women," observes a Chicago writer, "were all right; but the men students were at first embarrassed and afterwards rude. The mixed classes were therefore abandoned, but the woman's movement, being essentially just and correct," * was not abandoned, but led to the founding of a special school for women in 1869.

The pioneer woman physician in Chicago was Dr. Mary H. Thompson, who, having graduated at Philadelphia, and spent a year as interne at the New York Infirmary, settled in the West in 1863. At this period she was often introduced as a curiosity. Western curiosity, however, is rarely ill-natured, and in this case was soon exchanged for respect and a substantial sympathy, which enabled Dr. Thompson to establish the Hospital for Women and Children. In 1869, when the medical school was opened for women, its students found in this little hospital their first opportunities for clinical instruction. From 1869 till 1877, the collegiate course was conducted in a "small two-story building containing a dissecting room and one little lecture room furnished with two dozen chairs, a table, a portable blackboard, and a skeleton. There were scarcely any means for practical demonstration in the lectures, there was no money to procure them." † Worse than all, several among those who had consented to teach the students seemed, strangely enough, to have done all they could to discourage them. "One lecturer only delivered two lectures in the entire term, and then took up part of the time in dwelling upon the 'utter uselessness of teaching women.' The professor of surgery went on the staff with great reluctance, and remarked in his introductory lecture that he did not believe in female

---

* Letter from Chicago in *Boston Med. and Surg. Journal,* July, 1878.

† "History of Competitive Examinations for the Woman's Medical College of Chicago." Read before its Alumnæ Association, April 1, 1889, by Dr. Marie Mergler.

doctors, and that the students were greatly mistaken if they imagined the world was waiting for them. His lectures chiefly consisted of trifling anecdotes."* The class which graduated in 1871 under these discouraging circumstances consisted of three students. No one would study more than two years, "because it was found that in that time could easily be mastered all the college had to teach." But in 1881, the graduating class rose to 17, and in 1889, to 24. There is now a Faculty of twenty members, with eight lecturers and assistants. There were 90 students in the current year, and it was announced that in twenty years had been graduated 242 pupils.

In 1863, the same year in which Dr. Thompson settled in Chicago, another graduate of the Philadelphia school penetrated still further west, and tried to establish herself in San Francisco. But this pioneer enterprise failed. In 1872, Mrs. Charlotte Blake Brown applied to be admitted to the medical colleges of San Francisco, but being refused, went to Philadelphia to study. In 1874 Mrs. Lucy Wanzer applied at the Toland Medical School. This had been founded by a generous millionaire, who presented it to the State University,—and as the State laws provide for the admission of both men and women to the State schools, the regents were compelled to receive Mrs. Wanzer, who thus was the first woman to graduate in medicine on the Pacific Coast. In 1875 the rival school, the Cooper Medical College, also opened its doors to women, Mrs. Alice Higgins being the first candidate. Both colleges now freely admit women, and there are about half a dozen in each class.

Three of the ladies at present practicing in San Francisco are, however, graduates of Paris.†

Two other medical schools, both in Western New York, have for several years admitted women: the school of the Syracuse University, and the school at Buffalo.

Finally, in 1882, a fourth woman's school was opened in Baltimore, and has connected with it a hospital, which is not, however, managed by women. The total number of students annually attending the various institutions which have now been enumerated may be approximately tabulated as follows:

---

* These early experiences were, as has already been hinted, common to all the schools ever established independently for women. Until very recently, the gentlemen who have professed to teach surgery have never persuaded themselves to take their subject seriously.

† Dr. Sutro Merritt, daughter of the famous engineer, and who married a fellow student from the University of California; and the twin sisters, Agnes and Isabel Lowry.

Woman's Medical College of Pennsylvania, report in 1890, 181 students.

Woman's Medical College, N. Y. Infirmary, report in 1890, 90 students.

Woman's Medical College, Chicago, report in 1890, 90 students.

University of California, report in 1890, 8 female students out of total of 27.

Cooper College, San Francisco, report in 1890, 18 women out of total of 167.

From Ann Arbor I have only obtained the list of female graduates, which is 88.

The total number of graduates from the Philadelphia School, who have been enrolled among the alumnæ, is 560.

The total number of graduates of the New York School is 135.

During the current year, a movement has been inaugurated to obtain admission for women to the medical school of the Johns Hopkins University for the purpose of advanced study.*

Future advance for the education of women in medicine must be in the line of their admission to the schools where the highest standard of education is maintained; and to such affiliation of their own schools with universities, as may bring them under the influence of university discipline. There is no manner of doubt that, with a few unimportant restrictions, co-education in medicine is essential to the real and permanent success of women in medicine. Isolated groups of women cannot maintain the same intellectual standards as are established and maintained by men. The claim of ability to learn, to follow, to apply knowledge, to even do honest original work among the innumerable details of modern science, does not imply a

---

* "The education of the college is a conquered standpoint: what remains is to make the post-collegiate education equally easy of access to women. To duplicate the great laboratories and the great professorships of the two or three colleges which give adequate post-graduate instruction, would be foolish in the extreme. It is little less than silly to suppose that seriously minded men and women could not brave the associations of the lecture room without danger of impropriety. What possible reason can Columbia College, or Clark University, or the Johns Hopkins urge for not throwing open their post-graduate courses to women? What more graceful act could be imagined with which to mark this memorable year, when Vassar College celebrates her first quarter of a century and when Phillipa Fawcett is four hundred marks ahead of the senior wrangler, than for these universities, without further wheedling or coaxing or bribing, to open to women the opportunities for hard work which women covet, and which the sense of justice of men, tardy though it be, will not permit them much longer to refuse.—Editorial in *New York Evening Post*, June 17, 1890.

claim to be able to originate, or to maintain by themselves the robust, massive intellectual enterprises, which, in the highest places, are now carried on by masculine strength and energy.

Whether, as has been asserted,* the tendency to quackery among women is really more widespread than among men, may well be doubted. It is true that their lesser average strength peculiarly inclines women to follow the lines of the least resistance. On that very account, it is singularly unfortunate that the greatest, indeed in this country an invincible, resistance has been offered to woman's entrance at the best schools, while inferior and "irregular" colleges have shown an odd readiness to admit them. It would seem that co-educational anatomy is more easily swallowed when administered in homœopathic doses! Evidently, however, for the maintenance of these irregular schools,† the women are not responsible: and they only have two of their own.

Because women require the intellectual companionship of man, to be able to recognize the highest intellectual standards, or to attain them in some cases, and to submit to their influence in others,—it does not follow that they have no special contributions of their own to offer to the work of medicine.

The special capacities of women as a class for dealing with sick persons are so great, that in virtue of them alone hundreds have succeeded in medical practice, though most insufficiently endowed with intellectual or educational qualifications. When these are added, when the tact, acuteness, and sympathetic insight natural to women become properly infused with the strength more often found among men, success may be said to be assured.

The sixth period is that of the struggle to obtain for women physicians official recognition in the profession. In the prolonged debate which followed, the women's cause was defended by many distinguished men, with as much warmth as it was opposed by others. This debate began long before the close of the period which has just been described. It was the Philadelphia County Medical Society, which assumed the responsibility of being the first to check the alarming innovation of women's schools and female doctors. In 1859, was introduced the resolution which has already been mentioned,‡ declaring

---

* *New York Medical Record*, June 24, 1885.

† Of which sixteen admit women. There are altogether thirty-five co-educational medical schools. See *Record*, *loc. cit.*

‡ *Ut supra*, p. 106.

that any member who should consult with women should forfeit his membership. Upon this resolution the censors declined to express an opinion. Endorsement was, however, obtained from a committee of the State Medical Society. The recommendations of this society were supposed to be mandatory on all the county societies throughout the State. But one of these, that of Montgomery County, under the chivalrous inspiration of Dr. Hiram Corson, early distinguished itself by a revolutionary independence in this matter. It passed a resolution "that females, if properly educated, should receive the same treatment as males, and that it was not just to deny women admission to male colleges, and then, after they had with great perseverance established one for themselves, to refuse it recognition." This resolution being brought before the State Medical Society in 1860, a new resolution was passed, which reaffirmed the decree of excommunication. In 1866, the State Society met at Wilkesbarre, and Dr. Corson, who then entered the lists as a champion for women, moved that this motion be rescinded. Dr. Mowry offered a resolution declaring that the resolution in question was not intended to prevent members from consulting with "regularly" educated female physicians, who observe the code of ethics. This latter resolution was finally referred for discussion to the different county societies, and in 1867, was the subject of an elaborate report from a special committee, of which Dr. Condie was the chairman.*

Dr. Condie opposed the repeal of the resolution of 1860, because (he claimed) "the present condition of female colleges is rather worse than it was when the resolution was adopted." He strongly "objected to women having schools of their own, where any physician, of any kind of notoriety, no matter what his moral or professional standing, might be admitted to teach. We will have female practitioners. We must decide whether they shall be properly educated. It cannot be doubted that there are women well qualified by nature and who could be thoroughly instructed as practitioners in medicine. To such women should be freely extended the advantages of the leading medical colleges,—and they should graduate, if at all, at the same schools and under the same conditions as men." To this recommendation, Dr. Bell objected that there were no means at present existing where the women could be instructed. Dr. Coates said he had no doubt but that women were perfectly competent under favorable circumstances to make good prac-

---

* *Phil. Med. and Surg. Reporter*, 1867, vol. 16.

titioners, but it seems to be very rarely the case that they do. He did not believe it possible at that date to give women a proper medical education. "The tendency of female medical schools seems to be of the cheapening kind."

Dr. Condie remarked that the report [which, however closed with a resolution not to "recognize" the woman's college], begins by stating that females are competent, if properly educated, to practice medicine. History instructs us that the female mind is competent to anything the male mind has accomplished. Nevertheless females ought not to be encouraged to become physicians. God never intended them to be physicians. Dr. Atlee * urged that the policy of non-recognition, if persisted in, should be placed absolutely on the ground of the status of the female colleges. "Have not women applied year after year at our doors and begged to be received, yet been rejected? In self-defense they had to organize their own college, which had now been in existence seventeen years." Dr. Atlee then warmly defended the college on the basis of its published curriculum and on the reputation of such of the gentlemen as had dared to incur professional odium by teaching in it.

In reply to this, Dr. Maybury declared that "he knew some of his nurses who could hardly read the directions accompanying a prescription, who entered the woman's college, and emerged shortly after, fully equipped with their legal diploma."

Dr. Lee observed that the committee report and its concluding resolution might be considered to read about as follows: "Whereas in the opinion of this society, the female mind is capable of reaching every stage of advancement to which the male mind is competent: and whereas all history points out examples in which females have mastered every branch of science, art and literature: *therefore*, be it resolved, that any member of this Society who shall consult with a female physician, shall forfeit his privileges as a member of this society." "The resolution completely stultifies the report."

Nevertheless the resolution was adopted, and the County Medical Society, notwithstanding so many internal protests, reaffirmed its former position. The doughty little society from Montgomery then rushed to the rescue with a counter resolution, flung at its big Philadelphia neighbor like the pebble of David at the face of Goliath:

"Whereas the Woman's Medical College *is* properly organized, with an intelligent and efficient corps of instructors, in posses-

---

* The distinguished ovariotomist, one of the earliest in the country.

sion of good college buildings, and of all the appliances necessary for medical instruction ; that the students and graduates are irreproachable in habits and character, as zealous in the pursuit of knowledge, as intelligent and conscientious, as any of their male compeers ; we hold it to be illiberal and unworthy the high character of our profession to withhold from them the courtesies awarded to male physicians."—E. M. Corson, M.D., Recording Secretary.

In 1870, the Montgomery County Society elected Dr. Anna Lukens to membership.

In these debates the reasoning of the "opponents," was always secretly hampered by the lack of a definite standard with which the curriculum of the condemned female schools could be compared. It was perfectly true that the idea prevailed in them, that the real preparation for medical practice was to be "picked up" by beginning to practice; and that, when a legal diploma had once been obtained, all essential difficulties had been removed, and the graduate could at once enter upon her "life work," with a light heart and assured prospects of success. But then this same idea prevailed also in the men's schools, that were nevertheless recognized as perfectly "regular," and whose graduates were readily admitted to membership. On this account, detailed argument upon a legitimate basis soon broke down, and resolutions were substituted which declared the views of the Supreme Being in regard to female physicians.*

The question was now transferred to the larger area of discussion in the American Medical Association. This is a great national body, composed of delegates from all the State societies, and meeting only once a year in a session of three days, at different portions of the country. In 1871, the annual meeting was held at San Francisco, and the "female physician question" was there subjected to a long and animated debate.†

The preceding year, 1870,‡ Dr. Hartshorne of Philadelphia, a physician of excellent standing, and professor of physiology in the Woman's Medical School, had moved such an amend-

---

* Quite a number of the members of the Society defied the authority of its resolution, and "consulted" with women or even taught them. Among the latter, Dr. Hartshorne, who became an able professor of the Woman's College, was the only one who took the trouble to withdraw from the County Medical Society on account of his relations with the woman's school.

† *Boston Medical and Surgical Journal*, May 25, 1871.

‡ The matter had apparently first been brought forward in 1868, at a meeting held at Washington, D. C., by a resolution offered by Dr. Bowditch of Boston.—*N. Y. Med. Record*, 1868.

ment to the constitution as would permit teachers in such schools (if men) to be received as delegates of the association. In 1871, Dr. Harding of Indiana moved the adoption of the resolution. But Dr. Davis of Illinois asked solemnly whether "the time had come by deliberate action to open the door and welcome the female portion of the community, not only into our profession, but into all professions. Do we desire this time ever to come? Is there any difference in the sexes? Were they designed for any different spheres? Are we to heed the law plainly imprinted on the human race, or are we as a body to yield to the popular breeze of the times and say it must come, and therefore we will yield to it?"

Dr. King of Pittsburgh remarked that this matter had been debated in the society many years, and on one occasion a vote was taken, 47 on one side, 45 on the other, a majority of only two against the women. This war against women was beneath the dignity of a learned society of scientific men. Prof. Gibbons of California said: "If a woman showed herself to be the equal of a man, I cannot for the life of me see what objection there should be to it."

Prof. Johnson of Missouri did not understand that woman has asked admission to this floor. The questions only related to the admission of her teachers as delegates to the association. "I am wholly opposed to the admission of women here. Let women have their own associations. This body will stultify itself by the admission of women."

Dr. Atlee of Philadelphia remarked that the opposition to female colleges generally comes from the professors or controllers of other colleges. These women's colleges stand in many respects better than many of the colleges represented in the association; they give obstetrical and clinical instruction, *as is not given in a majority of the colleges represented here.* . . . By the rules of our medical association, I dare not consult with the most highly educated female physician, and yet I may consult with the most ignorant masculine ass in the medical profession."

Prof. Thomas asked that a committee be appointed to examine the Woman's College, [which, amid all the discussions, had never yet been done, and indeed never was done.] The Pennsylvania State Medical Society had never dared to enforce its resolutions of excommunication. One physician had even challenged it publicly to "dare to enforce this most unjust law."

Dr. Johnson pointed out that the president of the association, Dr. Stillé, was, by its rules, under the ban, because he was in the habit of consulting with women.

Dr. Storer of Boston seized the occasion in the evening session to pronounce a discourse on his favorite subject, the physiological incapacities of women. Dr. Storer had been for two years a visiting surgeon to the New England Hospital; but the boldness and ill success of many of his operations having alarmed the women physicians and the trustees, rules were passed subjecting future operations to the decision not only of the surgical, but of the medical, staff. Such rules were distinctly contrary to medical etiquette, and possibly unnecessary for the purpose in view. Dr. Storer resigned, which was not altogether unreasonable, but the letters in which he proclaimed his annoyance to the world exhibited less of reason than of irrelevant petulance. The main argument of this earlier letter was now reproduced in the memorable San Francisco debate,—although this, on the face of it, was not concerned with the philosophy of the female physician at all.

"There is," declared the Boston orator, "this inherent quality in their sex, that uncertain equilibrium, that varying from month to month in each woman, that unfits her from taking those responsibilities which are to control questions often of life and death."

To this Dr. Gibbons of San Francisco replied: "If we are to judge of this proposition by the arguments of my friend from Boston, I think it would prove conclusively the weakness of his side of the question. . . . It is a fact that a large majority of male practitioners fluctuate in their judgment, not once a month with the moon, but every day with the movement of the sun. I ask whether it be not true that one half of the male practitioners of medicine are not to a greater or less extent under the influence of alcohol at some period of the twenty-four hours? I do not say that they get drunk, but their judgment is certainly more or less affected." A rude rejoinder to a gentleman who had traveled all the way from Boston to San Francisco to make himself heard on the eternal verities of physiology and psychology in regard to "female physicians," which must be rescued from the "popular breeze" of contemporary opinion!

Notwithstanding the warm championship of many of the debaters, including the venerable president, the distinguished Dr. Stillé, Dr. Hartshorne's motion was lost, and the whole subject laid on the table without a vote. This, however, seems to have been the last occasion on which the matter was discussed. For in 1876, when the Association met in Philadelphia, Dr. Marion Sims being president, a woman delegate appeared, sent by the Illinois State Medical Society, Dr. Sarah Hackett Stevenson, of Chicago. Dr. Brodie, of Detroit, moved that hers, "and all such names, be referred to the Judicial Council." A motion that this resolution be laid upon the table was carried by a large vote, amid considerable applause. The president asked if this vote was intended to recognize Dr. Stevenson's right to a seat. Loud cries of yes, and cheers, emphatically answered the question.* Thus this mighty question, which had disturbed the scientific calm of so many medical meetings, was at last settled by acclamation. The following year at Chicago, Dr. Bowditch of Boston, being president, congratulated the Association in his inaugural address that women physicians had been invited to assist at the deliberations.

The State Medical Society of Pennsylvania, where the discussion originated, did not really wait for the action of the National Association to rescind its original resolution of 1860. This did not refer to the admission of women as members, that was not even considered, but forbade "professional intercourse with the professors or graduates of female medical colleges. "In 1871, when the Society met at Williamsport, Dr. Traill Green moved to rescind this resolution, and, " amid intense but quiet excitement," the motion was carried by a vote of 55 yeas to 45 nays.

"Thus," writes the now venerable champion of the women, Dr. Hiram Corson, "ended successfully the movement originated by Montgomery County, to blot from the transactions of the State Society a selfish, odious resolution adopted eleven years before. . . . . This report gives but the faintest idea of the bitterness of the contest, of the scorn with which the proceedings of the Montgomery County were received, and the unkindness manifested against all who from year to year asked for justice to women physicians. . . . . What would now be their status, had not the blunder of the Philadelphia Medical Society been committed?" † In 1881, the first woman delegate was admitted as member of the State Society; and in 1888, the Phila-

* *New York Medical Record,* June 10, 1876.

† "History of Proceedings to procure the Recognition of Women Physicians by the Medical Profession of the State." By Dr. Hiram Corson. Philadelphia, 1888.

delphia County Society also yielded, and admitted its first woman member, Dr. Mary Willets.*

Pennsylvania was not the first State to admit women to medical societies. It has been mentioned that the American Association, at its Centennial year meeting, received Dr. Sarah Stevenson from the Illinois State Medical Society. But, earlier than this, women had been received in New York State and city. The very first occasion was 1869, when the Drs. Blackwell were accepted as members of a voluntary "Medical Library and Journal Association," which held monthly meetings for hearing papers on medical subjects read by its members.† In 1872, a paper was read before this society by a young lady who had just returned from France with a medical diploma, the first ever granted to an American woman from the Paris *École de Médecine*.‡ In 1873, Dr. Putnam was admitted without discussion to the Medical Society of New York county, at the suggestion of Dr. Jacobi the president, whom she married a few months later. In 1874 she was sent as a delegate from the County Society to the State Medical Society, at its annual meeting at Albany. She also became a member of the Pathological, Neurological and Therapeutical societies, but was excluded from the Obstetrical Society by means of blackballs, although her paper as candidate was accepted by the committee on membership, and she received a majority vote. Finally, and a few years later, she was elected, though by the close majority of one, to membership in the New York Academy of Medicine.

The facile admission of Dr. Putnam to these various privileges, in New York, at a time that the propriety of female "recognition" was still being so hotly disputed in other cities, was due partly to the previously acquired honor of the Paris diploma; § partly to the influence of Dr. Jacobi. This phy-

* "It must be acknowledged that the strictly regular instruction imparted in the principal medical schools for women has excited respect, and greatly tended to overcome former prejudices. The admission of women is now a fixed fact."—*Phil. Med. Times*, 1883.

† This society no longer exists; but it can hardly be said to have died from the admission of women, as it never had but three female members.

‡ Mary Putnam, who was in fact the first woman to be admitted to the Paris School, though Miss Garrett of London was the first to graduate from it. The paper read before the New York Society was on Septicæmia, and seems to have been the first read by a woman physician in the United States, before a medical society.

§ Miss Putnam's graduating thesis had moreover secured a bronze medal, the second prize awarded.

sician may be said to have accomplished for women in New York what was done in Philadelphia by Drs. Hartshorne, Atlee, Stillé, and Thomas; in Boston by Drs. Bowditch, Cabot, Putnam, and Chadwick; in Chicago by Dr. Byford. The door was opened, other women entered without difficulty. The County Medical Society was expected to register all regular and reputable practitioners in the city, and at the present date contains the names of 48 regular physicians.

Four other women became members of the Pathological Society,* two of the Neurological Society,† one of the Neurological Association,‡ and two of the Academy of Medicine.§ No new application has been made to the Obstetrical Society, a private club. But the obstetrical section of the Academy contains one female member.‖

In Boston the "admission" of women was debated in three directions: to the Harvard Medical School, to the Massachusetts State Medical Society, and to the Boston City Hospital. The application of Miss Hunt to the Harvard Medical School in 1847 and 1850 have already been described. After the final discomfiture of this first applicant, no other attempt to open the college doors was made until 1879,¶ when a Boston lady, Miss Marian Hovey, offered to give $10,000 toward the new building the college was about to erect on condition that it should receive women among its students. A committee was appointed from among the overseers of the university to consider the proposition;** and after a year's consideration reported, with one dissenting voice, in favor of accepting the conditions. The committee outlined a plan for medical co-education, substantially like that already adopted at the Michi-

---

* Drs. Cushier, McNutt, Withington, Dixon Jones.

† Drs. Peckham, Fiske-Bryson.

‡ Dr. McNutt.

§ Drs. Peckham, Cushier.

‖ Dr. Cushier.

¶ In 1876, the Boylston Prize, conferred every two years by Harvard University for a medical essay, was won by Dr. Mary Putnam Jacobi. The prizes were awarded in ignorance of the names of the writers, and consequently of their sex; but this was the first occasion on which a woman had competed. The subject was, "The Question of Rest for Women during Menstruation."

Dr. Boylston, the founder of the prize, had been the first colonial physician to practice inoculation, after this had been suggested by Cotton Mather.

** The committee consisted of Prof. Alexander Agassiz chairman, Dr. Morrill Wyman, President Eliot, Mr. J. Elliott Cabot, Dr. Le Baron Russell.

gan University, where certain parts of the instruction should be given to both sexes in common; for others, where embarrassment might occur, the instructions should be duplicated. The one dissenting voice, that of Le Baron Russell, disapproved of co-education in any shape, but urged that Harvard University should charge itself with providing a suitable independent school for women.

The majority report expressly advised against the establishment of a separate school for women because "A considerable number of the most highly cultivated women physicians of the country state that the same intellectual standard cannot be maintained in a school devoted to women alone, and that the intellectual stimulus obtained by female students from their association with men is an all-important element of success." *

To guide its deliberations the committee had sent questions to 1300 members of the State Medical Society, to which 712 answers were received; of these 550 were in favor either of admitting women to the school, or of providing in some way for their education and recognition. These answers helped to decide the affirmative character of the majority report. Upon its reception, the Board of Overseers recommended the Medical Faculty to accept Miss Hovey's $10,000 and admit women to the school. But of the 21 members of the Medical Faculty, seven were strongly opposed to the admission of women, six were in favor of admitting them under certain restrictions, eight were more or less opposed but were willing to try the experiment. It was generally considered too rash an experiment to be tried, at the moment that the school was already embarked on certain improvements in its course of education, which threatened to cause a falling off in the number of its students. So the proposition was finally rejected by a vote of 14 to 4. The overseers of the university, having no actual

---

* *Boston Medical and Surgical Journal*, May 22, 1879. The editor expresses surprise at "so frank a confession of inferiority." Although it was only a few years since women physicians were ostracised on the ostensible ground of the necessary inferiority of their means of education, the Boston editor now, in order to confute the claim of necessity for the Harvard education, passes in most flattering review the existing schools for women at New York, Philadelphia, and Chicago, and insists that these offer all the advantages any reasonable woman can want. Thus (this in 1879):

Philadelphia, 29th year, class 90 students.

New York, 10th year, class 47 students.

Chicago, 9th year, class 32 students.

"Answers to letters of inquiry show that these schools for women are looked on with great favor."

control over the decisions of the Medical Faculty, were therefore compelled to decline Miss Hovey's offer. But, in doing so, they strongly recommended as expedient that, "under suitable restrictions, women should be instructed in medicine by Harvard University."

The defeat at Harvard in May was, however, followed by a triumph in another direction in October of the same year. On Oct. 9, 1879, an editorial in the *Boston Medical and Surgical Journal* says: "We regret to be obliged to announce that, at a meeting of the councilors held Oct. 1, it was voted to admit women to the Massachusetts Medical Society."

This society is not, like that of New York and many of the States, composed of delegates from county societies, but it comprises, and indeed consists of, all the legally qualified practitioners of the State. Refusal to enroll women among its members, therefore, meant a refusal to recognize the legality of diplomas that the authority of the State had conferred. The profession, therefore, in this matter deliberately set itself above the law, a most exceptional act in American communities. A precedent for such action had previously been established when the society refused to recognize homœopathic and eclectic physicians, who also held diplomas by legal authority, inasmuch as their schools were chartered by the State. The action of the Medical Society towards women was, in fact, intended as a means of permanently relegating women among classes of practitioners pronounced inferior and unscientific, and whose legal rights merely sufficed to save them from prosecution as quacks, and to recover their fees from such persons as were foolish enough to employ them.

For twenty-five years the battle was waged, and arguments advanced pro and con, of substantially the same nature as those which have already been sufficiently quoted. A circular was sent to the 1343 members of the society, asking the following question: Do you favor the admission of women to the Society on the same terms with men? To this circular, 1132 replies were received, of which 709 were in the affirmative, 400 in the negative, while 23 were indifferent. "It was thus evident that a considerable majority of the Society, seven to four of all who answered the circular, favor the admission of women." *

In June, 1875, a committee of five was chosen from the

---

* Chadwick, "Admission of Women to the Massachusetts Medical Society," *Boston Medical and Surgical Journal*, 1881.

society to report whether duly educated women could not be admitted to membership. In October a majority reported in favor of examining for membership men and women without distinction. But the minority objected so vigorously, that the whole matter was postponed indefinitely. In 1878, another committee was appointed: in June, 1879, the members were found equally divided; the subject was referred back to the committee, who, in October of the same year, advised no action. But this time the minority reported to instruct the censors to admit women for examination. The councilors voted, 48 to 38, to adopt the minority report.*

But the end was not yet, for in February, 1880, the censors of Suffolk County (including the city of Boston), voted that the society be advised to rescind its vote of October. This, however, was never done; but, after some further delay, the first female candidate, Dr. Emma Call, a graduate from Ann Arbor, passed a satisfactory examination and was admitted. The decisive step once taken, other women passed in readily, and 1889, ten years from the date of the conclusion of the famous controversy, a dozen women sat down to the annual banquet of the society, among whom was one invited guest from another State. The "moral tone" did not seem to be "perceptibly lowered," on this occasion.

In 1882, Dr. Chadwick published a tabulated summary of the dates at which various State societies had admitted women to membership.

In 1872, Kansas, Iowa; in 1874, Vermont; in 1875, Maine, New York, Ohio; in 1876, California, Indiana; in 1878, New Hampshire; in 1879, Minnesota, Massachusetts; in 1880, Connecticut; in 1881, Pennsylvania.

Rhode Island, Illinois, and Oregon also had women members, but the date of their first admission was not known. Thus seventeen societies contained, in 1882, 115 female members—that of New York alone having forty-two, much the largest of all.

* The editor of the *Boston Medical and Surgical Journal* announced this decision with great regret. The writer declared it "to be impossible that women can frequent our public meetings or lecture-rooms when certain topics are discussed, without breaking through barriers which decency has built up, and which it is for the interest of every lady and gentleman to preserve. . . . The moral tone of the society will soon be perceptibly lowered." —(*Loc. cit.*, October, 1879.)

The success of the movement was due to the chivalrous energy of a group of younger members, especially Drs. James and Charles Putnam, Dr. Chadwick, Dr. Cabot, and Dr. Derby.

From this time the question of the official "recognition" of women might be regarded as settled. Another question of equal, if not greater importance, now came to the front,—namely, the extension to women of opportunities for study and practice in great hospitals, opportunities absolutely indispensable both to obtaining and maintaining a valid place in medical practice and the medical profession. The discussion of this question belongs to the seventh period of the history.

For this purpose the small hospitals conducted by women were (and are) quite insufficient. There is such a demand upon their slender accommodations and resources for obstetric and gynæcological cases, and the claims of such cases to the special advantages of these hospitals are so paramount, that they have so far tended to a specialism, which, though useful for the patients, is detrimental to the physicians who must find all their training in them. Efforts, therefore, have constantly been made to widen the range for women, by securing their admission as students, internes, or visiting physicians to the great hospitals, which constitute the medical treasure-houses of the country.* In describing the actual condition of the medical schools, mention has been made of the hospital advantages which have been, little by little, secured for their undergraduate students. In Boston, where there is no school for women but the homœopathic school of the Boston University, fewer opportunities exist than anywhere else.

The Massachusetts General Hospital is reserved exclusively for the students of the Harvard Medical School. But the City Hospital remained unappropriated, and in 1886, the President and Trustees of the Boston University petitioned for permission for their female students to visit there, on the same terms as the young men. A committee was appointed to consider the matter, and after an elaborate report on the contemporary usage in ninety-one hospitals throughout the United States, advised that the request be granted. This enabled the female students to attend the public lectures given and the

---

* It will be remembered that it was the experience gained in the rude hospitals of the Revolutionary War, which, by affording American physicians for collective observation of the sick on a large scale, first breathed some scientific spirit into the profession. Similar experience was afterwards gained in the epidemics of yellow fever and of spotted fever, that at different times ravaged the country. An analogous influence was exercised by the Civil War, which influence is becoming most distinct a quarter of a century after its close.

operations performed in the hospital amphitheatre about once a week.*

Similar, though more frequent, opportunities for clinical instruction had been previously secured for women at the city hospitals of New York (Bellevue), Philadelphia (Blockley), and Chicago (Cook County). At the Pennsylvania Hospital in Philadelphia, moreover, the women from the Medical School had been admitted to lectures on special days, when no male students were present. These scanty privileges (for not much can be learned about a patient by spectators seated on the benches of an amphitheatre) were only obtained after a series of collisions with the men students, occasionally rising to the dignity of a row, as upon one memorable occasion at the Pennsylvania Hospital; † more often consisting in petty teasings and annoyances, which bore considerable resemblance to the pranks of schoolboys. To students habituated to the daily visits in the wards of the vast European hospitals, this form of clinical instruction, where the patient studied is seen but once, and then at a distance, must seem ludicrously inadequate.‡ From these defects, however, the male and female students suffer alike. But the former have, until recently, retained the monopoly of the hospital appointments, whereby a certain number of graduates are enabled to acquire real clinical instruction. This monopoly is only just beginning to break down.

Apparently the first general hospital in the country to confer a hospital appointment on a woman, was the Mt. Sinai Hospital of New York. Here, in 1874, Dr. Annie Angell, a graduate of the Infirmary School, was made one of the resident physicians, at the instance of several members of the medical staff.§ She served three years very acceptably.

In 1884 Dr. Josephine Walter, another graduate of the In-

---

* It was also ruled that "any cases deemed improper for a mixed audience should be reserved for the end of the lecture, and that the surgeon before proceeding with them may require the withdrawal of all male or female students as the case may be"; further, "No female patient shall be taken into the amphitheatre without the attendance of a female nurse: and no operation upon a female patient requiring special exposure shall be performed in the presence of male visiting students."

In this simple and even-handed manner were adjudged the vexed questions that had been declared so insoluble.

† *New York Medical Record*, Jan. 1, 1870.

‡ These inadequacies might be rectified, without necessarily introducing into clinical practice the brutalities that so often disfigure the European treatment of hospital patients.

§ Including Dr. Jacobi, Dr. Emil Krackowizer, Dr. Guhleke. The two

firmary School, was admitted as interne after a severe competitive examination, among nineteen candidates, of which only two could be appointed. She also served three years in the hospital, and then spent two years in Europe in medical study.

Since her appointment, none others have been made, or indeed applied for, in this or any other hospital in the city. Even in the Woman's Hospital, with exclusively female patients, and a host of female nurses, the medical staff have repeatedly expressed their formal opposition to the admission of female internes; and the Board of Lady Managers, oblivious of the first resolution of the first founders of the hospital, have so far remained indifferent to the anomalous injustice of the situation.*

Among dispensary services, however, many women have found places. Dr. Angell and Dr. Putnam Jacobi founded a dispensary at the Mt. Sinai Hospital, and for a year conducted it exclusively themselves. It was then systematically organized by the directors of the hospital, and has since always had women on the staff. In 1882, a school was open for post-graduate instruction in New York, and Dr. Putnam Jacobi was invited to a place in its faculty, as the clinical lecturer on children's diseases, the first time a lectureship in a masculine school was ever, in this country, filled by a woman. In the same school, another woman, Dr. Sarah McNutt, was also appointed as lecturer, and founded a children's hospital ward in connection with the school. The positions at present held by women physicians in New York dispensaries may be thus summarized, exclusive of the dispensary of the Infirmary:

Demilt Hospital, 3; Mt. Sinai Hospital, 2; St. Mary's Hospital for Children, 1; Hospital for Ruptured and Crippled, 4; Manhattan Eye and Ear Infirmary, 1; Foundling Hospital, 1 (resident physician); Nursery and Child's Hospital, 1 (resident at country branch); Babies' Hospital, 1.

In Philadelphia, the Blockley Hospital, the first in the United States to allow a woman to visit its wards,† appointed a female interne upon competitive examination, in 1883.‡ Since this date, eleven other women have received such appointments,—

---

former were German radicals of 1848, and in this action remained consistent with philosophic principles of their youth.

* It has been said that if any woman was admitted on the staff of internes, all the patients would demand her for the personal services now rendered by young men, and which are now accepted, though under protest, for the sake of the special skill of the distinguished visiting surgeons of the institution.

† Elizabeth Blackwell in 1848.

‡ Dr. Mary P. Root.

of whom four in 1889. Dr. Clara Marshall and Dr. Hannah Croasdale were put on the visiting staff in 1882. Chicago, however, is the city where the hospital privileges have been most equitably distributed, though the opportunity has been obtained by a struggle rendered severe, not from the opposition of those adverse to women physicians, but from the inadequate instruction given by those who had professed to be their friends.

In 1877, an invitation was sent to the senior class to take part in the examination for internes at the Cook County Hospital. "To go meant to fail. We decided to go, if only to show how little we had been taught in surgery." This was really an heroic determination; and the ordeal was severe. "The students and other spectators received us with deafening shouts and hisses. . . . The gynæcological and obstetrical examiners made vulgar jokes. The surgeon tried to wreck us. We forced things as best we could, but of course no one received an appointment."* As a rather unusual result of this trial, the professor of surgery at the Woman's College was roused to exertion, and for two years taught so well, that on another competitive examination the Woman's College was said to have stood first. However, no woman was appointed, but a relative of the commissioners, without an examination. Still the women's pluck and determination held out; they came up a third time,—and then, in 1881,—the coveted position was gained, and a young woman only twenty-one years of age was nominated as interne. Since then, appointments have multiplied, thus:

Name of Hospital.	Date of Appointment.	No. of Women Physicians.
Cook County Hospital	1881	1
	1888	2
	1889	2
Illinois Woman's Hospital	1882	1
	1887	1
	1888	1
	1889	1
Wesley Hospital	1889	1
State Insane Asylum	Unknown	2

Finally, it is noteworthy that Dr. Sarah Hackett Stevenson holds an appointment to the Cook's County Hospital as visiting physician, and Dr. Marie Mergler a similar appointment to the Woman's Hospital.

* Dr. Marie Mergler, *loc. cit.*

A special and extremely interesting branch of the struggle for hospital positions for women physicians has related to their appointment in the female wards of insane asylums. This movement also originated in Pennsylvania, and in the personal efforts of Dr. Corson, supported, as before, by Dr. Atlee. At the annual meeting of the State Society in 1877, the following preambles and resolution were read :

"*Whereas*, The State Medical Society has taken a deep interest in the welfare of the insane during the last few years; and

"*Whereas*, The inmates of our State hospitals are in nearly equal numbers of the sexes; and

"*Whereas*, We have many female physicians who are eminent practitioners, and one at least * who has had experience in the medical management of the insane : therefore,

"*Resolved*, That a committee of three persons be appointed by the president of this society, to report at its next annual meeting on the propriety of having a female physician for the female department of every hospital for the insane, which is under the control of the State."

A committee was appointed,† and reported at length in favor of the resolution. Just emphasis was laid on the fact that the very first attempts ever made to reclaim the insane asylums of the State from a condition of utter barbarism were due to a woman, Miss Dorothy Dix, whose name has been a household word in America, as that of Elizabeth Fry in England. The fact that at present there were no women who had received the special training requisite for the scientific treatment for the insane was offset by the other facts, that the existing medical superintendents were charged with the business responsibilities of the asylum, and thus had entirely insufficient time to devote to the medical care of the patients ; and that the subordinates, upon whom such care practically devolved, were usually recent graduates, who were entirely destitute of special training, and indeed for whose education in psychiatry no provision anywhere existed.

A bill was drafted, to be presented with a memorial to the Legislature, making the appointment of a female superintendent

---

* Dr. Mary H. Stinson, of Norristown, Pa.

† Dr. Hiram Corson, Dr. A. Nebinger, Dr. R. L. Sibbett.

obligatory in all asylums with female patients. The legislative committee returned the bill to the House with an affirmative recommendation.

A counter memorial was, however, sent to the Senate judiciary committee, protesting against the appointment of a female superintendent as liable to cause clashing in the management of the asylum. The memorial said that assistant female physicians could already be employed wherever deemed expedient. The memorial was so copiously signed as to suggest that much other opposition than that of superintendents, dreading collision, had been marshaled to defeat the proposed law.*

Another counter thrust, however, was given by the trustees of the State Lunatic Hospital at Harrisburg, who warmly supported the bill. Before the adjournment of the Legislature, the bill was in fact enacted, but so altered that the trustees are not obliged to appoint a woman chief physician, but only empowered to do so. At this same time, a new hospital for the insane was opened at Norristown, not far from Philadelphia ; and to this Dr. Alice Bennett, a graduate of the Woman's Medical College of Philadelphia, was elected by the trustees as chief physician of the female department. Dr. Annie Kugler was appointed assistant. Three months later, in September, 1880, the trustees of the asylum at Harrisburg elected Dr. Margaret Cleaves to a position as assistant.† Legislative action analogous to that initiated in Pennsylvania was not long afterward taken in Massachusetts and Ohio, and finally, during the current year, 1890, in the State of New York.‡

In New York, the bill required the employment of a woman physician in every State insane asylum where women are confined. It passed with only two negative votes in the Assembly, and three in the Senate.§

---

* It was signed first by Dr. Kirkbride, superintendent of the Pennsylvania Insane Asylum, and then by the surgeons and physicians, the consultants and the assistants, the in-door and out-door staff of thirteen colleges and hospitals, of which only one received insane patients, the Blockley. In addition were the names of nineteen physicians unconnected with any institution.

† Dr. Bennett's nomination was indorsed by eminent physicians from Philadelphia, Drs. Joseph Leidy, Wm. Pepper, S. Weir Mitchell, H. C. Wood, W. W. Keen, S. D. Gross. The latter venerable surgeon had formerly been bitterly opposed to women physicians.

‡ "The only regret and wonder are that a provision so humane and natural and consoling for these unfortunate wards of the State, has not yet been made law."—*Harper's Weekly*, 1820.

§ *Woman's Journal*, April 26, 1890.

Previous to the enactment of this law, however, women assistants had served for a year at the Willard Asylum for the chronic insane,* and in 1888, two other women, Dr. Steadman and Dr. Wakefield, were appointed in the New York City Asylum on Blackwell's Island. Similar appointments have been voluntarily made in ten other States, and more than twenty women are now serving as physicians in insane asylums.† The latest appointment was the greatest innovation, for it was in a Southern State, Virginia, at Staunton, and a Southern candidate, Miss Dr. Haynes, was appointed.‡ The *Springfield Republican* concludes its notice of this event (see note), with the remark: "This reform is steadily advancing, and it will not be long before the opposition to it will be as obsolete as it is now indecent."§

Thus the last word, (so far) like the first in this long controversy, is indecency. And it is characteristic of the world-old social position of women that it should be so; since women have in the mass, never been publicly and officially regarded as individuals, with individual rights, tastes, liberties, privileges, duties, and capacities, but rather as symbols, with collective class functions, of which not the least was to embody the ideals of decorum of the existing generation, whatever these might happen to be. These ideals once consigned to women, as to crystal vases, it became easier for men to indulge their vagrant liberty, while yet leaving undisturbed the general framework

---

* Rhoda Wilkins, in 1885, a graduate of the New York Infirmary School.

† The following is a partial list of the women now or recently holding such positions, in addition to those already named: Helen Bissell, Kalamazoo, Michigan; Alice M. Farnham, Hart's Island, New York City; Alice Wakeman and Augusta Steadman, Blackwell's Island, New York; Jane Garver, Harrisburg, Pa.; Amelia Gilman, Blockley Insane Hospital, Philadelphia; Laura Hulme, Worcester, Mass.; Martha Morgan, Harrisburg, Pa.; F. McQuaide, Norristown, Pa.; Martha Perry, Taunton, Mass.; Alice Rogers, Taunton, Mass.; Julia K. Cary, Danvers, Mass.; and others in Maine, Minnesota, Indiana, Illinois, Iowa, Nebraska, and California.

‡ "It was a great step for Virginia, thus taken by the trustees, and required considerable effort on the part of some members of the board. . . . Massachusetts is the only State where it is absolutely required by law that every such hospital shall employ one woman assistant physician."—*Springfield Republican.*

§ The Directors of the Woman's Educational and Industrial Union of Buffalo wrote to the superintendents of insane asylums in 38 States, asking their opinion on the law pending in the New York Legislature during its session of 1889–1890. Forty-six answers were received from 32 States, of which 33 favored the law, 5 were opposed, 5 non-committal, and 3 not prejudiced.

of order and society. But all the more imperative was it, that the standard of behavior, thought, and life for women should be maintained fixed and immovable. Any symptom of change in the status of women seems, therefore, always to have excited a certain terror. This is analogous to the fierce conservatism of savage communities, ready to punish by death the slightest deviation from established custom, because, as Mr. Bagehot observes, without such strenuous care their entire social structure is liable to fall to pieces. It is perfectly evident from the records, that the opposition to women physicians has rarely been based upon any sincere conviction that women could not be instructed in medicine, but upon an intense dislike to the idea that they should be so capable. Failure could be pardoned them, but—at least so it was felt in anticipation—success could not. Apart from the absurd fear of pecuniary injury, which was only conceivable so long as women were treated, not as so many more individuals in the community, but as a separate class, and a class alien to men of their own race and blood and even family,—apart from this consideration, the arguments advanced have always been purely sentimental. There has always been a sentimental and powerful opposition to every social change that tended to increase the development and complexity of the social organism, by increasing the capacities and multiplying the relations of its members. The opposition to women physicians is, in its last analysis, only one of the more recent manifestations of this universal social instinct. So true is this, that in the strife physicians have abandoned the sentiments proper to their own profession, and have not hesitated to revile and defame it, in order to prove that it was unfit for the delicacy or virtue of woman. They have forgotten the tone of mind, the special mode of vision that becomes habitual to every one who has really crossed the threshold of the sublime art; they have talked of "revolting details" and "disgusting preliminaries," like the veriest outside Philistine. There are horrors in medicine, because there are horrors in life. But in medicine these are overcome or transformed by the potency of the Ideal; in life they must be borne unrelieved. The women, who, equally with men, are exposed in life to the fearful, the horrible, the disgusting, are equally entitled to access to those regions of knowledge and ideas, where these may be averted, or relieved, or palliated, or transformed.

Again: A mother occupied with her young child offers a spectacle so beautiful and so touching, that it cannot fail to profoundly impress the social imagination. Contemplating this, it is easy to feel that all the poetry and romance, all the worth and significance of women are summed up in the exquisite moments of this occupation ; easy to dread the introduction of other interests lest the women be unduly diverted from this, which is supreme. Yet nothing is more obvious than that diversion comes, a thousand times, from frivolity, but never through work ; and that these moments are preceded by many years, and followed by many years, and for many women, through no fault of their own, never come at all. The seventy years of a lifetime will contain much waste, if adjusted exclusively to the five or six years of even its highest happiness. The toiling millions of women of every age of the world have not been permitted to make such an adjustment, even if they should wish to do so. They have always worked ; but they demand now, and simply, some opportunity for a free choice in the kind of work, which, apart from the care of children, they may perform. The invasion of the medical profession is one of the more articulate forms of this demand.

Although, according to the census of 1880, there were 2432 women registered as physicians throughout the United States, and several hundred must have graduated in the last ten years, it is probable that many of them have received an education too irregular and imperfect to justify their claim to the title in any serious sense. Thus the numbers are still too small, the time too short, to begin to estimate the work of women physicians. A large number of the women recorded in the census tables will not be found among the graduates of any suitable colleges, or on the registered lists of regular physicians, and these cannot be counted in an estimate like the present. Thus the census of 1880 records 133 women physicians in New York, but the medical register of ten years later contains the names of but 48. There seem to be about fifty at present in Philadelphia, twenty or thirty in Boston. Eighteen are said to be practicing in Detroit. The great majority are scattered through the country in small towns or country villages.

It is irrelevant to inquire with Waldeyer, "What women have done?" from the scientific standpoint, because the problem given was to enable them to become observant, faithful, and skillful practitioners of medicine, and this is possible without the performance of any really scientific work.

It is premature to make such inquiries, except for single cases which serve to illustrate the possibility, for it is but little more than a generation that the first school was opened to women ; it is not more than a dozen years since the official education attainable has approached any degree of effectiveness. What women have learned, they have in the main taught themselves. And it is fair to claim, that when they have taught themselves so much, when they have secured the confidence of so many thousand sick persons, in the teeth of such vigorous and insulting opposition, and upon such scanty resources and such inadequate preparation ; when such numbers have been able to establish reputable and even lucrative practice, to care for the health of many families over long terms of years, to sustain medical institutions of their own, almost exclusively dependent upon the good-will of citizens who have closely watched their work,—to serve in public hospitals in competition with men, to care for many thousands of sick poor, to whom abundant other medical aid was accessible, had it been preferred,—to restore to health many thousand women who had become helpless invalids from dread of consulting men physicians, or from delay in doing so,—to hold their own in private practice, in matters of judgment, diagnosis, medical and operative treatment, amidst the incessant and often unfair rivalry of brother competitors,—to do all this, we repeat, itself demonstrates a very considerable, indeed an unexpected amount of native ability and medical fitness on the part of women. With longer time, with more solid and varied opportunities, and with extension to the many of those which have hitherto been shared only by a very few, the amount of work accomplished may certainly be expected to increase, and in geometrical progression.

It could be wished that space remained to bring to light the obscure heroisms of the many nameless lives, which have been expended in this one crusade. It has been fought, and modestly, in the teeth of the most painful invective that can ever be addressed to women,—that of immodesty. Girls have been hissed and stampeded out of hospital wards and amphitheaters where the suffering patient was a woman, and properly claiming the presence of members of her own sex ; or where, still more inconsistently, non-medical female nurses were tolerated and welcomed. Women students have been cheated of their time and money, by those paid to instruct them : they have been led into fields of promise, to find only a vanishing mirage. At what sacrifices have they struggled to obtain the elusive prize ! They have starved on half rations, shivered in cold rooms, or been poisoned in badly ventilated ones ; they have often borne a triple load of ignorance, poverty, and ill health ; when they were not permitted to walk, they have crept,—where they could not take, they have begged; they have gleaned like Ruth among the harvesters for the scantiest crumbs of knowledge, and been thankful. To work their way through the prescribed term of studies, they have resorted to innumerable devices,—taught school, edited newspapers, nursed sick people, given massage, worked till they could scrape a few dollars together, expended that in study,—then stepped aside for a while to earn more. After graduating, the struggle has continued,—but here the resource of taking lodgers has often tided over the difficult time.

These homely struggles,—the necessity in the absence of State aid, of constantly developing popular support and sympathy for the maintenance of the colleges and hospitals, has given a solidity, a vitality to the movement, which has gone far toward compensating its quaint inadequacies and inconsistencies. On the European continent, the admission of women to medical schools has depended on the fiat of government bureaus, prepared in this matter to anticipate a popular demand, and to lead rather than to follow public opinion. In America, as in England, the movement for such extension of privilege has sprung from the people, it has fought its way,—it has been compelled to root itself in popular sympathy and suffrage. Hence a feeling of enthusiasm widely diffused among the women students, the sense of identification with an impersonal cause, whose importance transcended that of their individual personal fortunes, and yet which could only be advanced by the accumulation of their individual successes. The ill-taught girls at Chicago, who, sure in advance of defeat, resolved to face ridicule and contempt at the competitive examinations, in order to make a road for their successors, really exhibited, in a moral sphere, the heroism of Arnold Von Winklereid on the old Swiss battlefield.

The change from the forlorn conditions of the early days has been most rapid, and those who survived the early struggle, and whose energies were not so absorbed by its external difficulties that not enough were left for the intrinsic difficulties of medicine, have been really invigorated by the contest. Indeed one of the ways in which women have secured the infusion of masculine strength essential to their success, has been by successfully resisting masculine opposition to their just claims. It is as in the fable of Antæus,—those knocked down to the earth gained fresh strength as they touched the ground. The character and self-reliance natural to American women have thus been reënforced even by the adverse circumstances of their position. And, conversely, those for whom circumstances of fortune and education have been apparently the most propitious, even those who have received the best theoretical education, have not unfrequently been distanced, or even altogether dropped altogether out of the career, because of an incurable dilettantism, for which the remedy had not been found either in practical hardship or in native intellectual vigor.

Efforts have several times been made to estimate the actual proportion of markedly successful practitioners among the women now engaged in medicine.* The two monographs cited below are both based upon circulars of questions sent out to as many women physicians as possible.† The answers to these inquiries are necessarily very partial, and can be quoted rather as illustrations than as statistics. Among such illustrations, the statements of the pecuniary results of practice are interesting. Dr. Bodley received answer from 76 ladies, and their total annual income, if divided equally among the 76, amounted to about $3000.‡ Among these, however, ten earned between $3000 and $4000 a year, five between $4000 and $5000, three between $5000 and $15,000, and four between $15,000 and $20,000.

In Dr. Pope's paper, 138 women reported on their income, and out of them only eleven had then practiced over two years and failed to become self-supporting. Another item of interest is, that 32 per cent. of these women report that they have one or more persons partially or wholly dependent on them.§

---

* "The Practice of Medicine by Women in the United States." Paper read before Social Science Association, by Emily H. Pope, M.D., Sept. 7, 1881; and "The College Story,"—address at Woman's Medical College of Philadelphia, by Dean Rachel Bodley, March 17, 1881.

† Dr. Bodley sent circulars only to the graduates of the Philadelphia school, of whom, in 1881, there had been 276. Of these, 189 answered the circular. Dr. Pope sent circulars to 470 graduates of all schools, and received 390 answers, many, however, duplicating those of the Philadelphia circular of March.

‡ $2907.30 exactly.

§ The writer knows personally of two women physicians, one in large general practice including much surgery, the other at the head of a Sanitarium, who have each brought up and educated twelve children. One of these ladies was a widow, with one child, when she began to study medicine; the other was never married. A very large number of childless women adopt children, or contribute to the education of the children of brothers or sisters.

So great are the imperfections, even to-day, of the medical art, so numerous all the difficulties of applying even all existing resources, so inevitable are the illusions in regard to the real cause of either success or failure, that it is the most difficult thing in the world to estimate the intrinsic ability of a physician, even by his success in practice. A large practice certainly always testifies to some kind of ability; but this is not always strictly medical. The essential test is that of accuracy in diagnosis, and this test cannot, by means of any public documents accessible, be applied. Its successful application can only be inferred by the gradual development of confidence in women, both among the more intelligent and critical of the laity, and among the more unbiassed of the professional observers, who, in consultations, have had ample opportunity to scrutinize diagnoses.* For a dozen years it has become customary in America for the most distinguished members of the profession, even in large cities, to send patients to women physicians, in any case where the circumstances of the illness lead the patient to prefer a woman.† The same is done when, from personal acquaintance, or on account of public reputation, the patient has confidence in some special woman physician, and desires her counsel therefore, for other reasons than those of delicacy.

The women physicians of America share, while rather intensifying, the main characteristics of their medical countrymen. They have, as a rule, little erudition; but they have great capacity for bringing to bear all available and useful knowledge upon practical issues. They certainly do not read enough; and there is, therefore, a noticeable thinness in their discussions of medical topics when they meet in isolated council. But they have a resolute helpfulness in dealing with the individual cases entrusted to their care, and a passionate loyalty to those who have put their trust in them. They are possessed of abundant motive power for concrete intellectual action, though they might lack this power, if the work depended exclusively on abstract intellectual interest. And, after all, it is this habit of mind which most distinctively marks the modern practicing

---

* A distinguished surgeon recently wrote to a woman physician, when he had confirmed her diagnosis in a serious case, where the family then requested the presence of the consultant at the operation the woman physician was to perform: "I shall be out of town for a week; you had better not wait for me—go ahead and operate yourself." Which she did successfully.

† The above form of consultation has greatly extended the facilities of medical treatment for unmarried women and young girls.

physician, and without it the advances in medical science would be of little profit to the sick; indeed, would often not be made. And, what is often overlooked, it is precisely these mental habits here described which have been usually considered as particularly characteristic of women. Thus the introduction of women into medicine demands no modification of the typical conception traditionally held of women, but only an enlargement of the applications which may be made of this characteristic type.*

In nothing are popular views about women more at variance with fact than in regard to their capacity for operative surgery. The popular conception of surgery is itself entirely false, being inherited from a by-gone period, when hospital operations were conducted in the wards, filled with shuddering patients awaiting their own fate; amid clouds of steam from burning irons, torrents of blood, and the groans and shrieks of the victim.† But to-day, with anæsthetics, hæmostatics, and antiseptics, the surgeon may operate as calmly as on an insensible wax figure; and, moreover, with a reasonably correct technique, be assured of success in a vast majority of cases whose result was formerly, even under the best skill, always doubtful. The very greatness of the achievements of surgical genius have lessened the amount of ability requisite to perform many surgical operations; and especially have the modern conditions of operating removed the perturbating influences which female nerves might be supposed unable to resist. Moreover, the technique has become so precise that it can be taught; and women, even when defective in power of original thought, are extremely susceptible of being trained by exact drill. On this very account the model of a practical medical school should be that of a military academy, where every operation, mental or manual, that the graduate is subsequently expected to perform, will be rehearsed before graduation.

Now the remarkable thing about women surgeons is, not that

---

* "I believe that the department of medicine in which the great and beneficent influence of women may be especially exerted, is that of the family physician. Not as specialists, but as the trusted guides and wise counselors in all that concerns the physical welfare of the family, they will find their most congenial field of labor." Elizabeth Blackwell, "The Influence of Women in the Profession of Medicine." Address before London Medical School for Women, 1889.

† See Tenon's report on the Hôtel Dieu of Paris, made to the National Assembly in 1789. He describes the usage of the time, which eight centuries of hospital existence had not taught how to improve.

they have learned how to operate when they have been taught, but that, with very insufficient teaching for the most part, they have contrived to learn so much, and to operate so successfully. Obstetrics and gynæcology have here again offered peculiar advantages, in presenting a series of cases for operation which vary from the most trifling* to the most serious capital operations in surgery. The latter have only been attempted in the last decade, and it is worth while to quote such statistics as I have been able to obtain, even though they are necessarily incomplete:

New York Infirmary: From 1875 to 1890; 535 operations (29 laparotomies); operators, chiefly Dr. Elizabeth Cushier, but in a smaller number of cases, Drs. Blackwell, Peckham, McNutt, Putnam Jacobi.

New England Hospital: From 1873 to 1890; 829 operations (48 laparotomies); operators, Drs. Dimock, Buckel, Keller, Berlin, Whitney, Smith, Crawford, Bissell, Kellogg, Angell, Pagelson.

Chicago Hospital: From 1884 to 1888; 206 gynæcological, 114 general surgery. Dr. Mary Thompson operated on all the gynæcological cases, except four; the report does not state whether she also operated on the others.

The reports of the Philadelphia Hospital do not give the total number of operations performed in it, but through the kindness of Dr. Fullerton, resident physician, I have received a report of the capital operations, nearly all abdominal:

Women's Hospital, Philadelphia: From 1876 to 1889; 91 operations (all laparotomies, including several Cæsarean sections). Operators, chiefly Dr. Anna Broomall; for a small number of cases, Drs. Croasdale and Fullerton.†

In addition to the above, Dr. Marie Werner of Philadelphia reports 23 laparotomies from private practice.

Other personal statistics I have not been able to obtain. Some are quoted in the list of Literature.‡ These statistics,

---

* Dr. Sims, in his treatise on Uterine Surgery, declared that the local treatment of uterine diseases was, almost always, surgical.

† During this year Dr. Broomall has gone to Asia, to make a tour of the different missionary stations where there are women physicians, and there perform capital operations on the cases which have been accumulating. This is an expedition unique of its kind in history.

‡ At the meeting of the Philadelphia Alumnæ Association, held in March, 1889, six successful cases of capital operations in abdominal surgery were reported by members, including two Cæsarean sections and one hysterectomy. Sixteen laparotomies were further reported from the Woman's Hospital, but these have been included in the statistical table.

though still on a small scale, are, for the time in which they have accumulated, and for the extremely meagre opportunities which have been so far afforded, not at all unsatisfactory.

Written contributions to medical literature are also, though not abundant, at least sufficient to prove that "the thing can be done." The 145 citations made in the list * all belong to the period ranging between 1872 and 1890, a period of eighteen years.

The intellectual fruitfulness of this period is not to be compared with that exhibited by other and contemporary classes of medical workers, but rather with that of the first 150 or 200 years of American medicine. For, until now, it is a mentally isolated, a truly colonial position, which has been occupied by the women physicians of America. When a century shall have elapsed after general intellectual education has become diffused among women; after two or three generations have had increased opportunities for inheritance of trained intellectual aptitudes; after the work of establishing, in the face of resolute opposition, the right to privileged work in addition to the drudgeries imposed by necessity, shall have ceased to preoccupy the energies of women; after selfish monopolies of privilege and advantage shall have broken down; after the rights and capacities of women as individuals shall have received thorough, serious, and practical social recognition; when all these changes shall have been effected for about a hundred years, it will then be possible to perceive results from the admission of women to the profession of medicine, at least as widespread as those now obviously due to their admission to the profession of teaching.

NOTE.—While these pages are passing through the press, the important announcement is made that the trustees of the Johns Hopkins University—in view of a gift of $100,000, presented by women to the endowment fund of the medical department,—have consented to admit women to the medical school of the Johns Hopkins Hospital, so soon as that school shall be opened. This is the first time in America that any provision for the medical education of women has been made at a university of the standing of the Johns Hopkins. It is expected that the medical education of the future school will be especially directed for the benefit of selected and post graduate students, for such as desire to make special researches and to pursue advanced studies in medical science. The admission of women to a share in these higher opportunities is a fact of immense significance, though only a few should profit by the advantage, the standing of all will be benefited by this authoritative recognition of a capacity in women for studies, on this higher plane, on equal terms and in company with men.

---

* See APPENDIX D.

The directors of the Johns Hopkins have in this matter shown the broad and liberal spirit which befits the noble trust they are called upon to administer. It is characteristic of America that the stimulus to the trustees' action came from without the university, from the initiative of women. This time, women have not only asked but they have at the same time given. The $10,000 gift originally offered by Miss Hovey to Harvard on condition of its admitting women, and declined by its medical faculty, has been enrolled in the gift now accepted by the Johns Hopkins. Half of the whole donation is the noble gift of one woman, Mary Garrett,—daughter of one of the original trustees of the Johns Hopkins University. The formation of committees among women in all the principal cities of the United States, for the purpose of raising money for the woman's part of the endowment fund, and even for the remaining amount needed to open the school, is itself a most important fact, for it indicates that interest in the intellectual advancement of women, and especially interest in the success of women in the medical profession, has at last become sincere and widespread in quarters where hitherto it has been entirely and strangely lacking.

Hardly had we pronounced the present position of women in medicine to be "colonial," when, by a sudden shifting of the scene, barriers have been thrown down that seemed destined to last another half century; an entire new horizon has opened before us. *Sic transit stultitia mundi.*

VIII.

WOMAN IN THE MINISTRY.

BY

(REV.) ADA C. BOWLES.

THE entrance of women upon the work of the Christian ministry in America waited for no ordaining council and imposition of hands, but may be said to have begun with the preaching of Anne Hutchinson. Arriving in Boston in 1634, and being admitted to membership in the church, she forthwith began the advocacy of her peculiar doctrines, which carried with them her commission to preach. Believing that "the power of the Holy Spirit dwells in every believer, and that the inward revelations of the spirit, the conscious judgment of the mind, are of paramount authority," what need could she feel of other sanction? Large numbers of women gathered to the meetings in which she boldly discussed the sermons of the preceding Sabbath, as was the custom of the men of the congregation, and set forth her own belief. The dispute among her followers and their opposers, according to Bancroft, "impressed its spirit into everything. It interfered with the levy of troops for the Pequot war; it influenced the respect shown to the magistrates, the distribution of town lots, the assessment rates, and, at last, the continued existence of the two opposing parties was considered inconsistent with the public peace."

In 1637 a synod of the church was called at Newtown and, although Cotton, Vane, and Wheelwright, together with all but five members of the Boston church, had become warm partisans of Mrs. Hutchinson, her tenets were among the eighty-two opinions condemned as erroneous. A few months later, she was summoned before the General Court and, after a trial of two days, sentenced to banishment from the territory of Massachuestts.

That her loss was felt by the church which had excommunicated her may be inferred from the effort made to reclaim her by a deputation sent for that purpose to the Island of

Aquidneck, afterward called Rhode Island, where she had found a refuge. After the death of her husband in 1642, she removed to the Dutch settlement, then at war with the Indians, by whose hand she, with all her family, save one child (carried captive), cruelly perished.

This experience of the church was not calculated to encourage the public preaching of women, nor incline it, a score of years later, to receive with open-armed hospitality the two Quaker women, Mary Fisher and Ann Austin, whose books and trunks were burned on shipboard, and who, upon landing, were haled to prison, in the same spirit of persecution which had driven them from England to the West Indies, and thence to this so-called "land of liberty." Vainly searched for signs of witchcraft, they were then banished for heresy.

Yet the mild doctrines of the Quakers were destined to take root upon American soil, and do their full share in the liberalizing of thought and especially in securing to woman that freedom to preach which has made itself felt in other Christian denominations. The name of no preacher among the Quakers, or "Friends," as they prefer to be called, stands above the name of Lucretia Mott, whose history is too well known to demand more than a word concerning her call to such public service, as given by herself:

"At twenty-five years of age, surrounded by a little family and many cares, I felt called to a more public life and devotion to duty, and engaged in the ministry in our Society, receiving every encouragement from those in authority, until a separation from us, in 1827, when my convictions led me to adhere to the sufficiency of the light within us, resting on truth as authority, rather than taking authority for truth."

This step into the larger freedom of the Hicksites, or Unitarian branch of Quakers, proved no mistake for one whose heart and life could not measure themselves by theological creeds. To use her own words, "I have felt a far greater interest in the moral movements of our age, than in any theological discussion." And her eloquent pleadings and practical charities for three-quarters of a century are ample witness of her sincerity. The domestic life of Mrs. Mott was in itself a noble refutation of the assertion that eminent public service by women is incompatible with home making, since few homes could show such perfect conjugal union and such thrifty household management. There are about three hundred and fifty women preachers in this branch of the Christian church at present.

The sect of Shakers, or "United Society of Believers in Christ's Second Appearing," originating near Manchester, England, about 1770, as an offshoot of the Society of Friends, and following the same spiritual authority, gave to its women an equal share with men in its service and government.

In 1770, Ann Lee, one of the members of this sect, professed to have received a special illumination, in the name of which she was accepted as the "Christ of the female order." Her followers believing that "God was revealed as a dual being, male and female, to the Jews, that Jesus revealed to the world God, as a Father," received "Mother Ann" as "God revealed in the character of Mother, the bearing spirit of all the creation of God." In 1774, obedient to another revelation of the spirit, Mother Ann, with nine of the more prominent members of her society, emigrated to America and began her work in the State of New York, from which center ardent missionaries propagated the new faith.

When we consider the essential doctrines of this sect,—human brotherhood, exemplified in a community of goods, non-resistance, non-participation in government, strict celibacy, and perfect chastity,—we must confess that Ann Lee, possessing not even a rudimentary education, must nevertheless have been gifted with extraordinary powers of persuasion thus to have secured the founding of the various communities of Shakers in the United States, among which her name is still reverenced in its deific relations.

If allowed to follow what might be called natural lines, for the highest ecclesiastical freedom for women, the Roman Catholic Church would seem a proper starting point. Its exaltation of "Mary, Mother of God," the canonization of devout women, its many sisterhoods, its deep indebtness to women in every age and every land, seem a fitting foundation upon which to build an ecclesiasticism which should at least consider woman to be as well endowed by her Creator for a celibate priesthood as the sex ignored in providing the world's Redeemer. Yet no church more rigidly excludes women from the priestly office or gives less indication of change in this regard; nor can it be expected in a non-progressive system, crystallized around the dogma of infallibility.

Nor shall we, though continuing along the lines of natural expectation into the largest Protestant church of America, the Methodist Episcopal Church, find a radical change, although Susanna Wesley was called the "real foundress of Methodism" in England, and Barbara Heck is given equal credit for the first impulse given the church in America. Landing in New York in 1760, in company with the first local preacher and class leader, Philip Embury, Mrs. Heck seems to have "kept the faith" more loyally, in the midst of the distractions and downward tendencies of the new life, than did the preacher. Five years passed and, so far as known, he did nothing to keep together the few Wesleyans, or add to their number. There was much moral degeneration, which no doubt greatly troubled the soul of Mrs. Heck. On a certain occasion, while visiting at a house where were gathered a number of friends and acquaintances, finding them engaged in card playing, "her spirit was roused, and, doubtless emboldened by her long and intimate acquaintance with them in Ireland, she seized the cards, threw them into the fire, and then most solemnly warned them of their danger and duty. Leaving them she went immediately to the dwelling of Embury, who was her cousin. After narrating what she had seen and done, under the influence of the Divine Spirit and with power, she appealed to him to be no longer silent, but to preach the Word forthwith. She parried his excuses and urged him to begin at once in his own house and to his own people. He consented, and she went out and collected four persons who, with herself, constituted his audience. After singing and prayer, he preached to them and enrolled them in a class. He continued thereafter to meet them weekly," * and thus began the work of Methodism in America. When the rigging loft, which had succeeded the house for preaching purposes, had also been outgrown, it was "Barbara Heck, the real founder of American Methodism," who was ready with plans for a chapel, which still stands, a sacred memorial of her zeal and that of the man recalled to his duty by her burning words.

Nor can the work of the Countess of Huntingdon be overlooked in this connection, although the scene of her labors was in another land, since its fruits were here so largely shared through the work of Whitefield. Not merely as the builder of sixty-four chapels, the founder and supporter of a college for the education of ministers, many of whom were maintained by her, is she to be remembered. In the volume just quoted from, we read that, "Under the influence of Whitefield and the Countess of Huntingdon, the Calvinistic non-conformity rose, as from the dead, to new life, which has continued ever since with increasing energy. By the same means, with the co-

---

* Centenary of American Methodism.

operation of Wesley, a powerful evangelical party was raised up in the establishment, and most of the measures of evangelical propagandism which have since kept British Christianity alive with energy, and extended its activity to the foreign world, are distinctly traceable to this great revival. . . . . About the end of its first decade, a scarcely parallel interest had been spread and sustained throughout the United Kingdom and along the Atlantic coast of America. . . . . It had presented before the world the greatest pulpit orator of the age (if not of any age), Whitefield; also one of the greatest religious legislators of history, Wesley, a hymnist, whose supremacy has been but doubtfully disputed by a single rival—Charles Wesley; and the most signal example of female agency in religious affairs which Christian history records, the Countess of Huntingdon."*

Remembering that the churches established by this gifted woman were not known by the names of the men associated with her, but as "Lady Huntingdon's connection," some evidence of the leadership of women will be apparent in the American Methodist Church. Strange to say, this is far from being the case. Although Wesley had encouraged the preaching of women, and although few men could equal the successful labors of many of them, the Methodist Episcopal Church of America is singularly backward in recognition of its women. According to its "Discipline," "the pronouns he, his, and him, when used with reference to stewards, class-leaders, and Sunday-school superintendents, shall not be construed so as to exclude women from these offices." Notwithstanding this, "in many American churches to-day, a woman class-leader would be almost as great a curiosity as John the Baptist, with his raiment of camel's hair, and a leathern girdle around his loins." †

Women of unquestioned ability, liberal education, and purity of character have in vain applied for ordination, though supported by the record of much successful pulpit and pastoral work as licensed lay preachers, and by many influential friends of the laity and clergy. One of these, of national reputation, ‡ to whom this sanction of ordination was refused, has since been ordained by the Protestant Methodist Church, which, having done so, however, steadfastly declines to add to the number, having apparently exhausted its liberality by this extreme application of the spirit of Wesley.

---

* Centenary American Methodism.

† Rev. Annie H. Shaw.

‡ Christian Womanhood, W. C. Black, D.D.

The small sect of primitive Methodists which adheres most strictly to the methods of Wesley have always employed women preachers as a means of reaching the depraved classes; this being one of the points of difference upon which it separated from the main body.

The United Brethren in Christ, or German Methodists, as formerly called, when their membership was more largely of that element, are to be distinguished as appointing the first woman as "circuit rider," which was recently done by Bishop Kephart of the Wabash Annual Conference, held at Clay City, Ind. The appointee is a young woman eminently adapted to the work and is one of several ordained women elders in this church.

So far as known, the Baptist Church has taken no steps leading to the admission of women to its ministry, save in that division known as Free Will Baptists, which has ordained a small number of women in various parts of the country under its democratic system of government. The Free Baptist General Conference of 1886 adopted the following resolution: "That intelligent, godly women who are so situated as to devote their time to the ministry, and desire to be ordained, should receive such indorsement and authority as ordination involves, provided there are no objections to such indorsement other than the matter of sex. Many of the Baptist clergymen, however, as those of all leading denominations, save the Episcopal and Roman Catholic, freely admit women to their pulpits to speak upon great moral questions, and would welcome them to the ranks of the ministry. Women are also prominent in its conference and prayer meetings.

The Presbyterian Church has been a strongly conservative body, slow to sanction radical change in its polity, but if the Pan-Presbyterian Council, held not long since in London, voices the general sentiment of this large and important denomination, women are to enjoy a more equal power in its administration. For a long period they were carefully excluded; but for a number of years past a more liberal policy has welcomed them to a free utterance in the conference and prayer meetings, which they sometimes conduct, and at synods they often speak upon missionary and other topics. At a Synod of the Reformed Presbyterians held in 1889, it was decided by a vote of 93 to 24 that the ordination of a woman as deacon is in harmony with the New Testament and the constitution of the Apostolic Church.

There are also indications that the long-frozen ground of

orthodox Congregationalism is thawing toward a springtime of more generous recognition of its women. The recent opening of the Hartford Theological Seminary, and the almost immediate presentation to it of a prize scholarship to be competed for by women alone, are notable signs. The general recognition of the fitness of women preachers in missionary fields, the significant fact that Oberlin College, which graduated its first woman theological student * nearly forty years ago and has added but one other since, prints this year, for the first time, the names of these two women upon the Triennial Catalogue, are other straws upon the rising tide of favor toward the woman ministry. Under the Congregational system, any individual church may ordain for itself a woman whom it may choose for its pastor, and this has been done in several instances past, either by the deacons of the church or by a council called for the purpose, the present year recording more such ordinations than any preceding year.†

The German Lutheran Church, as represented in a recent session of the Missouri Synod at Baltimore, feeling compelled to recognize the trend of evangelical Christianity toward a woman ministry, presented for discussion the question, "How far and under what conditions do we allow women to teach?" The decision reached was that they must not teach at all in the pulpit nor in the congregation. As there is absolute parity of the clergy of this church, and the congregation is its ultimate of authority, it is by no means certain that this position can be uniformly maintained.

To this church is due the credit of introducing into the country as early as 1849 the order of Deaconesses as maintained in Europe during the last fifty years. By the persistent efforts of Mr. John D. Lankenau of Philadelphia, an enthusiastic supporter of this institution, America is now provided with the finest "Mother-house" in the world, the immediate result of

---

* Rev. Antoinette Brown Blackwell, the first woman ordained in this country.

Mrs. Blackwell writes: "At the time of my ordination I was pastor of the church of 'South Butler and Savannah,' New York State. The church called a council to ordain me and install me as the regular minister. It was an orthodox society in good and regular standing among other Congregational churches, and the ordination was quite according to precedent; though doubtless the Congregational body as a whole never would have ordained a woman either then, thirty-seven years ago, nor yet to-day."—Ed. note.

† Rev. Louise S. Baker, pastor of the Orthodox Congregational Church, in Nantucket, Mass., was ordained by the deacons of that church in 1884, two of the four deacons being women.

which has been a rapid increase of the order in various denominations, in all parts of the country. This magnificent edifice, built by Mr. Lankenau as a memorial of his wife, at a cost of half a million of dollars, has been presented as a free gift to the German Hospital Corporation of Philadelphia. "The western wing of the building is used as a home for aged men and women, the eastern wing as a residence and training school for the deaconesses, the chapel uniting the two, and the whole being known as the Mary J. Drexel Home and Mother-house of Deaconesses." * †

The Protestant Episcopal Church has for many years recognized the value of "sisterhoods" of consecrated women, more or less closely affiliated, for carrying on its various branches of philanthropic service, from which the growth and efficiency of the church has received no small degree of impetus and importance. Among these sisterhoods are numbered two orders of deaconesses, one of which has been changed into the "Sisterhood of St. John the Evangelist"; which, in view of the growing hospitality of thought toward preaching by women, carries in its title a certain suggestiveness. Fourteen sisterhoods, a religious order of widows, and two orders of deaconesses are reported in 1888 for this church.

The church polity of the "Christian Connection," better known as the Christian Church, as its name implies, is placed upon a broad foundation, by which each church is an independent republic, and women are thus eligible to its pulpits; one woman, ordained to its ministry in the State of Illinois, having at the present time charge of three prosperous churches.

---

* Report of the Dedication of the Mary J. Drexel Home and Mother-house of Deaconesses, December 6, 1888. In 1887 Mrs. Lucy Rider Meyer, M.D., connected with the Chicago Training School, with a few women to assist, gave the first impulse to the Deaconess movement in the Methodist Episcopal Church, which has resulted in the establishment of Mother-houses in Chicago, New York, Boston and other large cities. The church, seeing the measureless opportunities offered by such an institution, has wisely been prompt to adopt it, and this will doubtless encourage the adoption of the order by other denominations.

† The Grace House Training School for Deaconesses was opened for the admission of candidates October (1890), in New York, adjoining Grace Church. The General Convention of the Protestant Episcopal Church in October, 1889, provided that every candidate for the office of Deaconess, before she is set apart, shall have had "an adequate preparation for her work, both technical and religious, which preparation shall cover the period of two years." The Grace House Training School is provided to furnish this preparation.—Ed.

The Universalist Church has been the first to open the doors of its theological schools for the training of women for the ministry, and by its established forms ordain them to its full fellowship. This was not, however, considered a part of its ecclesiastical system until made practically such by the admission of the first woman candidate,* who, denied entrance to the Meadville Theological School (Unitarian), applied in 1860 to the President of St. Lawrence University to be admitted to its theological department. In his reply, the fair-minded president candidly wrote: "No woman has ever been admitted to this college, and, personally, I do not think women are called to the ministry, but that I shall leave with the great head of the church. . . . . I shall render you every aid in my power." A graduate of Mt. Holyoke Seminary and of Antioch College, at which she received the degree of A.B., this well-equipped pioneer for a larger place for women in the Christian church soon verified her credentials, and the president, always her steadfast friend, preached her ordination sermon. Since her ordination, she has enjoyed a number of successful pastorates, with the duties of which marriage and motherhood have not proved incompatible.

About fifty women have been ordained in this church, and all its schools and colleges, save one, are now co-educational. There is also, with scarcely an exception, among its clergymen a feeling of cordial fellowship toward women preachers.

Would the limits of this article permit, sketches of the work accomplished by its pioneer women preachers would furnish not uninteresting reading, since their fields of labor have been some of the most difficult in their respective churches. They have been called to the building of new churches in unbroken fields, or to those so dead or dormant as to be apparently beyond the reach of men workers, and yet we hear of no failures among them to raise these churches to new life and prosperity or to organize new material upon strong foundations. In one notable instance, in a suburb of Chicago, a ten years' pastorate has resulted in the building of one church edifice which, speedily outgrown, has made necessary a more spacious and elegant one; and there is no disposition to exchange this successful woman minister for a masculine successor.

The Universalist Register for 1889, contains, in its list of ministers, the names of thirty-five women, being the largest

* Rev. Olympia Brown Willis.

number of ordained women for any year, and the largest number in any denomination.

In just a decade after its refusal to admit a woman, the Meadville Theological School (Unitarian) opened its doors to women students, since which time it has received sixteen. About one third of these have graduated, while others have taken but a partial course, as wives or prospective wives of ministers, in order to be more truly "help-meets" in the pulpit work of their husbands. "Among these graduates," writes a member of the faculty, "every woman has been above the average. Our experience indicates that for success in our ministry, care should be taken to encourage only such women as, together with personal fitness for the work, can easily maintain this high rank."

An amusing incident in the domestic life of one of these women pastors may indicate a possibility of growth in the woman ministry likely to startle conservative minds. A little boy and girl, the children of a mother whose work as a minister evidently contained no surprises for them, were discussing plans for their own future. "I shall help mamma preach," said the little girl. "I shall preach, too," stoutly said the small brother. His sister, looking thoughtfully and doubtfully at him, said slowly, "Yes, mens do preach sometimes."

The woman ministry in America has had no warmer friend than Mrs. Julia Ward Howe, herself a preacher of well-known ability, occasionally preaching in the pulpits of this country, and having preached in Rome, Jerusalem, and Santo Domingo while sojourning in those places. In 1873 Mrs. Howe succeeded in securing a convention of such ministers as were within convenient distance of Boston during Anniversary week, at which addresses were made and the communion observed, Rev. Lorenza Haynes and Rev. Mary H. Graves officiating.

Since that time eight annual conventions have been held in Boston; and in the Hollis Street Church, on June 2, 1882, the "Woman's Ministerial Conference" was formed, Mrs. Julia Ward Howe, president. This is not a working body, but a fellowship of women preachers, whether ordained or not, representing all denominations. Its present officers are: Mrs. Julia Ward Howe, president; Rev. Mary H. Graves, corresponding secretary; Rev. Ada C. Bowles, recording secretary. These, with the additional names of Rev. Louise S. Baker and Rev. Mary T. Whitney, form its executive committee. The title of Rev. is never applied save to those who have been regularly ordained in their respective denominations.

That women bore an important part in the planting and early growth of the Christian church needs no argument. That the plain teaching of Paul should have been so perverted as to mean their exclusion from the office of public teaching is to be explained only by the fact of a departure from the methods of the primitive church, through a purely masculine interpretation and application of regulations which, entirely adapted to the age and country in which uttered, were never intended to be prohibitive of women's preaching in that, or at any later, period.

The establishment of the Diaconate, in which, as an order of the clergy, women administered the sacraments, interpreted and promulgated doctrines, in connection with the practical work of charity and benevolence, are matters of history.

In its periods of persecution, the church received no more devoted service than that given by its consecrated women. For its sake, they cheerfully accepted martyrdom, in its most cruel forms. Princesses of the blood and other women of noble birth left the allurements of courts for the studious seclusion of the cloister, or, seeking out the poor and needy, they divided with them their substance. No conditions of miserable poverty or loathsome disease hindered the most tender devotion. In all ages and in all lands women have given proof of a loyalty to Christianity as sincere as it was serviceable. By their proselyting power in converting royal relatives, they were the means of bringing not only Rome but France, England, Spain, Hungary, Poland, and Russia under Christian rule.*

Is the church to-day less in need of such service than in the past, that it will seek in any way to circumscribe the work of its faithful women by denying to them such sanction, through its prescribed forms, as it bestows freely upon like qualified men, is the question which presses itself persistently forward for settlement.

Certain it is that, as ecclesiastical despotism loses its hold upon the people, they will more readily seek spiritual guidance under a broader law of adaptation and natural fitness, in which women must stand at least an equal chance with men. What the world has already lost by their exclusion from a controlling influence in the church, finds its most painful illustration in the widespread and deep depravity of the masses in our

* "Biography of Distinguished Women," Sarah J. Hale.

great cities, which the church, in none of its branches, has materially lessened. From the efforts now being made in America for the restoration of the Diaconate of woman, it is safe to argue a change for the better in this respect. The new departure in methods has also an important illustration in the city of Chicago, where, under the leadership of D. L. Moody, gifts amounting to $250,000 have been secured for a theological school and home, to be conducted under the auspices of the Chicago Evangelical Society, which is to be open to both sexes upon the same terms. Its object is the evangelization of the unchurched masses of that great city.

The evils which have resulted to society, and which threaten the very life of the nation by the long neglect to establish proper relations between the vast army of ignorant and degraded beings throughout the land with the active life of Christianity, have become too appalling to be contemplated with indifference, even by the most callous and selfish. The call for service of a most heroic kind is urgent and pressing. For this work of redemption, women have an especial fitness. Invested with all the sanction the church can bestow, supplemented by municipal authority where necessary, let the Christian womanhood of America rise to the level of the demand; "In His Name," their motto, In His spirit, their inspiration. No pure-hearted, strong-purposed woman but can find a place here to labor as "a minister of the sanctuary and of the true tabernacle, which the Lord pitched, and not man."

IX.

WOMAN IN LAW.

BY

ADA M. BITTENBENDER.

THE history of various ages and nations, since the days of the prophetess Deborah, who filled the office of judge among the children of Israel (Judges iv. 4), records the names of women distinguished for their legal learning, some of whom were also successful advocates. Among the latter we content ourselves with mentioning Aspasia, who pleaded causes in the Athenian forum, and Amenia Sentia and Hortensia in the Roman forum. But, alas, the right of Roman women to follow the profession of advocate was taken away in consequence of the obnoxious conduct of Calphurnia, who, from "excess of boldness" and "by reason of making the tribunals resound with howlings uncommon in the forum," says Velerius Maximus, was forbidden to plead. (Velerius Maximus, Hist. lib. viii. ch. iii.) The law, made to meet the especial case of Calphurnia, ultimately, "under the influences of the anti-feministic tendencies" of the period, was converted into a general one. In its wording the law sets forth that the original reason of woman's exclusion "rested solely on the doings of Caphrania." (Lex. 1, sec. 5, Dig. iii. i.)

This exclusion furnished a precedent for other nations which, in the course of time, was followed. Dr. Louis Frank, of the Faculty of Law at Bologna, in a pamphlet entitled "La Femme Avocat," translated by Mary A. Greene, LL.B., of Boston, and published in 1889 in serial form in the *Chicago Law Times*, in speaking on this point, says :

"Without taking time to discuss the rudimentary law of the ancient German Colonies, we recall only that institution of Germanic origin, the *vogt* or *advocatus*, whose care it was to represent every woman at the court of the suzerain, in judicial acts and debates. . . . . The ancient precedents were conceived and established in a spirit which was extremely favorable to woman. There is not a trace in them of the privileges of masculinity. They allowed woman to be a witness, a surety, an attorney, a judge, an arbitrator. Later, under the influence of the canon law, and in the early renaissance of juridical study, under the action of the schools of Roman law, a reaction made itself felt against the rights of women, and the old disabilities of Roman legislation reappeared and became a part of the legal institutions."

Further on, Dr. Frank says:

"The forwardness of Calphurnia appeared to all the ancient jurists a peremptory reason for excluding women from the forum."

From among his citations to prove this assertion we extract the following:

"Boutillier tells us that a woman could not hold the office of attorney or of advocate. 'For know, that a woman, in whatever state she may be, married or unmarried, cannot be received as procurator for any person whatever. For she was forbidden (to do) any act of procuration because of Calphurnia, who considered herself wiser than any one else; she could not restrain herself, and was continually running to the Judge without respect for formalities, in order to influence him against his opinion.' (Somme Rural, Edit. Mace, Paris, 1603, L. i. tit. x. p. 45.) Further on, designating those 'who may be advocates in court and who not,' Boutillier cites as incapable minors, the deaf, the blind, clerks, sergeants, and women. 'For women are excluded because of their forwardness, like Calphurnia, who could never endure that her side should be beaten nor that the judge should decide against her, without speaking forwardly to the judge or to the other party.' (*Id.* L. ii. tit. ii. p. 674.) . . . . In Germany as in France, the inferiority of woman was justified upon the same grounds. 'No woman,' says the *Miroir de Souabe*, 'can be guardian of herself nor plead in court, nor do it for another, nor make complaint against another, without an advocate. They lost this through a gentlewoman named Carfurna, who behaved foolishly in Rome before the ruler.'" (*Miroir de Souabe*, T. ii. ch. xxiv., Lassberg, 245.)

The prohibition against women acting as advocates, or barristers, the latter being the term used to designate the office in England, wherever adopted, has continued in force to the present time outside of the United States of America. In England women are permitted to qualify for and practice as attorneys at law and solicitors in chancery, but have not been permitted to become barristers and exercise the rights of that rank in the prosecution of their cases. Were it not for the Calphurnian decree, they still would be ineligible because of being denied admission to the four Inns of Court, where barristers are trained and ranked. These Inns of Court are voluntary societies from whose power to reject applications for membership there is no appeal.

The common law of England becoming the law of this country, its women were thought also ineligible to admission to the bar, and but one woman, so far as we know, attempted to test the matter until within the last quarter of a century. This exception was a very notable one in colonial days. It was the case of Margaret Brent, spinster and gentlewoman. She and her sister Mary, kinswomen of the first Lord Proprietary and Governor of Maryland, came to the Province in 1638, "bringing over nine colonists, five men and four women. They took up manors, imported more settlers, and managed their affairs with masculine ability." So says William Hand Browne in his "History of a Palatinate." The Governor, Leonard Calvert, died the 9th of June, 1647, leaving Mistress Brent his sole executrix. At the time of his death, he was attorney for his brother, Cecilius Calvert, second Lord Baltimore, the Lord Proprietary. Mistress Brent succeeded him as attorney for his lordship. Her right to act in this capacity, which she at first claimed "on the strength of her appointment as executrix," was questioned in the provincial court, where she had occasion frequently to appear in regard to his lordship's "private estate and transactions in the Province." The Court ordered that she "should be received as his lordship's attorney." The question came up in court on the 3d day of January, 1648, of which record was made as follows:

"This day the question was moved in court whether or noe, Mr. Leon. Calvert (remayning his L^p^'s sole attorney within this Province before his death, and then dying) the said Mr. Calvert's administrator was to be received for his L^p^'s Attorney within this Province untill such time as his Lordship had made a new substitution, or that some other remayning uppon the present Commision were arrived into the Province. The Governor demanding Mr. Brent's opinion upon the same Quere. Hee answered that he did conceive that the administrator ought to be looked uppon as attorney both for recovering of rights into the estate and paying of dew debts out of the estate and taking care for the estate's preservation: But not further, untill his Lordship shall substitute some other as aforesaid. And thereuppon the Governor concurred. It was ordered that the administrator of Mr. Leon Calvert aforesaid should be received as his Lp's Attorney to the intents above." (Archives of Maryland, vol. iv. p. 358.)

The provincial court records show that Mistress Brent not only frequently appeared in court as his lordship's attorney, in which capacity she continued to act for some years, but also in prosecuting and defending causes as attorney for her brother, Capt. Giles Brent, and in regard to her personal affairs, and as executrix of Leonard Calvert's estate (the record calls her "administrator"; she was appointed by the testator to execute his will). There is no record of any objection being made to her practicing as attorney on account of her sex. At that time the provincial court at St. Mary's "was the chief judicial body in the Province, being not only a court of first instance for all matters civil, criminal, and testamentary for the city and county of St. Mary's, but having also appellate jurisdiction over the county courts. It was composed of the Governor as presiding judge, and one or more of the members of the council asassociate judges." (Archives of Maryland, vol. iv. preface.)

Unmindful of the words "but not further" in the opinion, Mistress Brent asked for voice and vote in the General Assembly on account of her position as his lordship's attorney. This request was denied. Whether her sex entered into the denial is a question without solution. The Assembly proceedings for January 21, 1648, make mention of the fact in these words:

"Came Mistress Margarett Brent and requested to have vote in the howse for herselfe and voyce allso, for that att the last court, 3d Jan., it was ordered that the said Mistress Brent was to be looked uppon and received as his Lps Attorney. The Govr denyed that the said Mistress Brent should have any vote in the howse. And the said Mistress Brent protested against all proceedings in this present Assembly, unlesse shee may be present and have vote as aforesaid." (Archives of Maryland, vol. i. p. 215).

The first woman since the days of Mistress Brent to ask for and obtain admission to the bar of this country was Arabella A. Mansfield of Mt. Pleasant, Iowa. She studied in a law office and was admitted to the Iowa bar in June, 1869, under a statute providing only for admission of "white male citizens." The examining committee in its report, which is of record, said:

"Your committee have examined the provisions of section 2700 of chapter 114, of the Revision of 1860, concerning the qualifications of attorneys and counselors in this State [section 2700 provided for the admission of "white male persons." ED.], but in considering the section in connection with division 3 of section 29, chapter 3 of the Revision, on construction of statutes [section 29 provided that "words importing the masculine gender only may be extended to females." ED.], we feel justified in recommending to the court that construction which we deem authorized, not only by the language of the law itself, but by the demands and necessities of the present time and occasion. Your committee take unusual pleasure in recommending the admission of Mrs. Mansfield, not only because she is the first lady who has applied for this authority in this State, but because in her examination she has given the very best rebuke possible to the imputation that ladies cannot qualify for the practice of law."

At the time of Mrs. Mansfield's debut into the profession without opposition, Myra Bradwell, of Chicago, having studied law under the instruction of her husband, ex-Judge James B. Bradwell, was unsuccessfully knocking at the door of the Supreme Court of Illinois for admission. To give an understanding of the case, and line of argument used in denying her application, we extract from the opinion of the Court, delivered by Mr. Justice Lawrence, the following:

"Mrs. Myra Bradwell applied for a license as an attorney at law, presenting the ordinary certificates of character and qualifications. The license was refused, and it was stated, as a sufficient reason, that under the decisions of this court, the applicant, as a married woman, would be bound neither by her express contracts, nor by those implied contracts, which it is the policy of the law to create between attorney and client.

"Since the announcement of our decision, the applicant has filed a printed argument, in which her right to a license is earnestly and ably maintained. Of the qualifications of the applicant we have no doubt, and we put our decision in writing in order that she, or other persons interested, may bring the question before the next Legislature. . . . . It is to be remembered that at the time the statute was enacted [the statute under which admission was sought, which provided that "no person shall be permitted to practice as an attorney or counsellor at law," etc. ED.] we had, by express provision, adopted the common law of England, and, with three exceptions, the statutes of that country passed prior to the fourth year of James the First, so far as they were applicable to our condition. It is also to be remembered that female attorneys at law were unknown in England, and a proposition that a woman should enter the courts of Westminster Hall in that capacity, or as a barrister, would have created hardly less astonishment than one that she should ascend the bench of bishops, or be elected to a seat in the House of Commons. It is to be further remembered that when our act was passed, that school of reform which claims for women participation in the making and administering of the laws, had not then arisen, or, if here and there a writer had advanced such theories, they were regarded rather as abstract speculations than as an actual basis for action. That God designed the sexes to occupy different spheres of action, and that it belonged to men to make, apply, and execute the laws, was regarded as an almost axiomatic truth. It may have been a radical error, but that this was the universal belief certainly admits of no denial. A direct participation in the affairs of government, in even the most elementary form, namely, the right of suffrage, was not then claimed, and has not yet been conceded, unless recently, in one of the newly settled territories of the West. . . . . But it is not merely an immense innovation in our own usages, as a court, that we are asked to make. This step, if taken by us, would mean that, in the opinion of this tribunal, every civil office in this State may be filled by women ; that it is in harmony with the spirit of our constitution and laws that women should be made governors, judges, and sheriffs. This we are not prepared to hold. . . . . There are some departments of the legal profession in which woman can appropriately labor. Whether, on the other hand, to engage in the hot strifes of the bar, in the presence of the public, and with momentous verdicts the prizes of the struggle, would not tend to destroy the deference and delicacy with which it is the pride of our ruder sex to treat her, is a matter certainly worthy of her consideration. But the important question is, what effect the presence of women as barristers in our courts would have upon the administration of justice, and the question can be satisfactorily answered only in the light of experience." (Supreme Court Reports of Illinois, vol. lv. p. 535.)

The Supreme Court of Illinois having refused to grant to Mrs. Bradwell a license to practice law in the courts of that State, she appealed the case to the Supreme Court of the United States, where the judgment of the State court was affirmed. She was there ably represented by Mr. Matthew

Hale Carpenter. Mr. Justice Miller delivered the opinion of the court. In affirming the judgment, the refusal being made on the ground that women are not eligible under the laws of Illinois, the court held that "such a decision violates no provision of the Federal Constitution"; that the right to practice law in the State courts is not "a privilege or immunity of a citizen of the United States, within the meaning of the first section of the fourteenth article of amendment of the Constitution of the United States"; and that "the power of a State to prescribe the qualifications for admission to the bar of its own courts is unaffected by the fourteenth amendment, and this court cannot inquire into the reasonableness or propriety of the rules it may prescribe." (16 Wallace's Reports, Supreme Court U. S., p. 130). Mr. Justice Bradley, while concurring in the judgment, gave expression to his views in a separate opinion in which he took occasion to say that, "The constitution of the family organization, which is founded in the divine ordinance as well as in the nature of things, indicates the domestic sphere as that which properly belongs to the domain and functions of womankind." The Chief Justice, Salmon P. Chase, "dissented from the judgment of the court, and from all of the opinions."

The Legislature of Illinois, in 1872, enacted that "No person shall be precluded or debarred from any occupation, profession, or employment (except military) on account of sex." But Mrs. Bradwell, ever since being occupied with editorial work on the *Chicago Legal News*, which she founded in 1868, and with the publication of Bradwell's Appellate Court Reports and other legal works, did not renew her application for a license to practice law. The sequel is this, copied from the *Chicago Legal News* of April 5, 1890: "We are pleased to say that last week, upon the original record, every member of the Supreme Court of Illinois cordially acquiesced in granting, on the Court's own motion, a license as an attorney and counselor at law to Mrs. Bradwell."

The next court case was that of Mrs. Belva Ann Lockwood, of Washington, D. C., who graduated from the Law School of the National University, and was admitted to practice before the Supreme Court of the District, in 1873. The same year a motion was made for her admission to the bar of the U. S. Court of Claims. This Court refused to act upon the motion, "for want of jurisdiction." The opinion concludes in these words: "The position which this Court assumes is that under the Constitution and Laws of the United States a court is without power to grant such an application, and that a woman is without legal capacity to take the office of attorney." (Court of Claims Reports, vol. ix p. 346.)

At the October term, 1876, of the Supreme Court of the United States, Mrs. Lockwood applied for admission as practitioner of that court. Her application was denied. The decision has not been officially reported, but, upon the record of the Court, it is thus stated: "Upon the presentation of this application the Chief Justice said that, notice of this application having been previously brought to his attention, he had been instructed by the Court to announce the following decision upon it: By the uniform practice of the Court from its organization to the present time, and by the fair construction of its rules, none but men are admitted to practice before it as attorneys and counselors. This is in accordance with immemorial usage in England, and the law and practice in all the States, until within a recent period; and the Court does not feel called upon to make a change until such a change is required by statute or a more extended practice in the highest courts of the States."

Mrs. Lockwood continued practicing before the courts of the District and elsewhere, outside of United States courts, until Congress passed a bill providing, "That any woman who shall have been a member of the bar of the highest court of any State or Territory, or of the Supreme Court of the District of Columbia, for the space of three years, and shall have maintained a good standing before such court, and who shall be a person of good moral character, shall, on motion, and the production of such record, be admitted to practice before the Supreme Court of the United States" (Approved, Feb. 15, 1879). Mrs. Lockwood drafted the bill and secured its passage. She was the first woman to be admitted under the law and to practice before this Supreme Court. (Since then, six others have been admitted, viz.: Laura De Force Gordon of Stockton, California; Ada M. Bittenbender of Lincoln, Nebraska; Carrie Burnham Kilgore of Philadelphia; Clara M. Foltz of San Diego, California; Lelia Robinson-Sawtelle of Boston, and Emma M. Gillet of Washington, D. C. Mrs. Bittenbender moved the admission of Miss Gillet, the first instance of one woman moving the admission of another to the highest court in the country.) A few days after Mrs. Lockwood's admission, she received word from the Court of Claims that she could now plead before it.

The next State court to be heard from on the subject was

the Supreme Court of Wisconsin, in 1875. The matter was the motion to admit Miss R. Lavinia Goodell to the bar of that court. Miss Goodell, the year before, had been admitted to the bar of the circuit court of Rock county in that State. The argument, read on the hearing of the motion by I. C. Sloan, Esq., was prepared by her. The motion was denied, it being held that "To entitle any person to practice in this court, the statute requires that he shall be licensed by its order, and no right to such an order can be founded on admission to the bar of a circuit court. The language of the statute relating to the admission of attorneys (which declares that '*he* shall first be licensed,' etc.) applies to males only; and the statutory rule of construction that 'words of the masculine gender *may* be applied to females,' 'unless such construction would be inconsistent with the manifest intention of the Legislature,' cannot be held to extend the meaning of this statute, in view of the uniform exclusion of females from the bar by the common law, and in the absence of any other evidence of a legislative intent to require their admission." Chief Justice Ryan delivered the opinion of the Court. The following extract from that opinion we believe will be read with interest, and remain of historic value as showing the fossilized misconceptions woman combated with in attaining the generally acceptable position in the legal profession in this country which she now holds :

"We cannot but think the common law wise in excluding women from the profession of the law. The profession enters largely into the well-being of society ; and, to be honorably filled and safely to society, exacts the devotion of life. The law of nature destines and qualifies the female sex for the bearing and nurture of the children of our race and for the custody of the homes of the world and their maintenance in love and honor. And all life-long callings of women, inconsistent with these radical and sacred duties of their sex, as in the profession of the law, are departures from the order of nature ; and when voluntary, treason against it. The cruel chances of life sometimes baffle both sexes, and may leave women free from the peculiar duties of their sex. These may need employment, and should be welcome to any not derogatory to their sex and its proprieties, or inconsistent with the good order of society. But it is public policy to provide for the sex, not for its superfluous members ; and not to tempt women from the proper duties of their sex by opening to them duties peculiar to ours. There are many employments in life not unfit for female character. The profession of the law is surely not one of these. The peculiar qualities of womanhood, its gentle graces, its quick sensibility, its tender susceptibility, its purity, its delicacy, its emotional impulses, its subordination of hard reason to sympathetic feeling, are surely not qualifications for forensic strife. Nature has tempered woman as little for the juridical conflicts of the court room, as for the physical conflicts of the battle-field. Womanhood is molded for gentler and better things. And it is not the saints of the world who chiefly give employment to our profession. It has essentially and habitually to do with all that is selfish and malicious, knavish and criminal, coarse and brutal, repulsive and obscene, in human life. It would be revolting to all female sense of the innocence and sanctity of their sex, shocking to man's reverence for womanhood and faith in woman, on which hinge all the better affections and humanities of life, that woman should be permitted to mix professionally in all the nastiness of the world which finds its way into courts of justice ; all the unclean issues, all the collateral questions of incest, rape, seduction, fornication, adultery, pregnancy, bastardy, legitimacy, prostitution, lascivious cohabitation, abortion, infanticide, divorce."

Ah, dear sir, it is largely to "mix professionally in all the nastiness of the world which finds its way into courts of justice," that many, very many women seek admission to the bar. In every case involving any one of the "unclean issues" or "collateral questions" you have named, some woman must appear as complainant or defendant, or be in some way associated. What more proper, then, than that some other woman should be in court, clothed with legal power, to extend aid and protection to her sister in trouble, that justice may be done her, and the coarse jest and cruel laugh, so proverbial in social impurity cases before woman's advent as pleader, prevented! And we respectfully call upon the mothers of every land to see to it that in no instance in the future of the world shall a woman be summoned to the bar of justice as a party or witness in any case involving one of these "unclean issues" or "collateral questions" without being accompanied by one or more of her own sex of irreproachable character. When such emergencies are otherwise unprovided for, let the "good mothers of Israel" in the place convene and depute one or more of their number to perform this duty. It is a duty, unquestionably, to be performed in the interest not only of one sex, but of mankind generally ; for what affects one sex for good or evil, affects both.

Aye, Mr. Chief Justice, "the profession enters largely into the well-being of society"; and it is because of this fact woman desires and ought to enter it. This is the best of reasons. As to her motherhood prerogatives, experience has shown her able to perform these as the Father of the Universe and Mother Nature would have her, and still not to be precluded from giving the profession the necessary "devotion" to the end that it shall be "honorably filled and safely to society." If "the law of nature destines and qualifies the female sex . . . . for the custody of the homes of the world and their maintenance in love and honor," as you say, Mr. Chief Justice,—we say "if" because we believe the male sex to be joint-heir,—that does not mean that all women, or any woman, should stay inside of four walls continually to cook, wash dishes, sweep, dust, make beds, wash, iron, sew, etc. Oh, no! A woman may properly act as the custodian of a home and maintain it in love and honor, and do none of these things. Instead of such "lifelong callings of women" being "departures from the order of nature, and, when voluntary, treason against it," as you think, Mr. Chief Justice, we hold that to stifle the longings of an immortal soul to follow any useful calling in this life, to be a "departure from the order of nature, and, when voluntary, treason against it."

A law was promptly enacted enabling women to practice law in Wisconsin, under which Miss Goodell was admitted to the Supreme Court of the State.

Next following Miss Goodell's case, came that of Lelia J. Robinson of Boston, in 1881, the Supreme Judicial Court holding that under the laws of Massachusetts "an unmarried woman is not entitled to be examined for admission as an attorney and counselor of this court." In the opinion of the Court it is stated that "this being the first application of the kind in Massachusetts, the Court, desirous that it should be fully argued, informed the executive committee of the Bar Association of the city of Boston of the application, and has received elaborate briefs from the petitioner in support of her petition, and from two gentlemen of the bar as *amici curiæ* in opposition thereto." The statute under which the application was made provided that, "A citizen of this State . . . . may, on the recommendation of an attorney, petition the Supreme Judicial or Superior Court to be examined for admission as an attorney, whereupon the Court shall assign a time and place for the examination, and if satisfied with his acquirements and qualifications he shall be admitted." The Court said that "the word 'citizen,' when used in its most common and most comprehensive sense, doubtless includes women ; but a woman is not, by virtue of her citizenship, vested by the Constitution of the United States, or by the Constitution of the Commonwealth, with any absolute right, independent of legislation, to take part in the government, either as a voter or as an officer, or to be admitted to practice as an attorney." (Mass. Supreme Court Rep., vol. cxxxi. p. 376.) The opinion was delivered by Chief Justice Gray. The Legislature, in 1882, passed a statute providing for the admission of women upon the same terms as men. Miss Robinson, now Mrs. Sawtelle, immediately took the examination and was admitted to the Suffolk County Bar. The next year the Legislature extended the powers of women attorneys in an act "to authorize the Governor to appoint women who are attorneys-at-law special commissioners to administer oaths and to take depositions and the acknowledgment of deeds." This legislation became necessary on account of a decision of the Supreme Court of the State in which it was held that "a woman cannot lawfully be appointed a justice of the peace, or, if formally appointed and commissioned, lawfully exercise any of the functions of the office." (Mass. Supreme Ct. Rep., vol. cvii. p. 604.) The power "to issue summonses for witnesses" was added in an act of 1889.

Mary Hall of Hartford, Connecticut, in 1882, after having completed the prescribed term of study and passed the required examination, applied to the Superior Court in Hartford county for a license to practice law. The statute under which her application was made provided that the Superior Court "may admit as attorneys such persons as are qualified therefor agreeably to the rules established by the judges of said court." This statute had "come down, with some changes, from the year 1750, and in essentially its present form from the year 1821." The bar of Hartford county "voted to recommend the admission of the applicant subject to the opinion of the Court whether, as a woman, she could be legally admitted, and appointed Messrs. McManus and Collier to argue the case before the Court." The Court reserved the application for the advice of the Supreme Court. The latter Court "held, that under the statute a woman could be admitted as an attorney." This being contra to the holdings of the United States and State courts in similar cases, which we have cited, was refreshing indeed. The opinion merits quotation quite at length. It was delivered by Chief Justice Park. The part selected reads :

"No one would doubt that a statute passed, at this time, in the same words would be sufficient to authorize the admission of women to the bar, because it is now a common fact and presumably in the minds of legislators, that women in different parts of the country are and for some time have been following the profession of law. But if we hold that the construction of the statute is to be determined by the admitted fact that its application to women was not in the minds of the legislators when it was passed, where shall we draw the line? All progress in social matters is gradual. We pass almost imperceptibly from a state of public opinion that utterly condemns some course of action to one that strongly approves it. At what point in the history of this change shall we regard a statute, the construction of which is to be affected by it, as passed in contemplation of it? When the statute we are now considering was passed it probably never entered the mind of a single member of the Legislature that black men would ever be seeking for admission under it. Shall we now hold that it cannot apply to black men? We know of no distinction in respect to this rule between the case of a statute and that of a constitutional provision. . . . . Events that gave rise to enactments may always be considered in construing them. This is little more than the familiar rule that in construing a statute we always inquire what particular mischief it was designed to remedy. Thus the Supreme Court of the United States has held that in construing the recent amendments of the Federal Constitution, although they are general in their terms, it is to be considered that they were passed with reference to the exigencies growing out of the emancipation of the slaves, and for the purpose of benefiting the blacks. But this statute was not passed for the purpose of benefiting men as distinguished from women. It grew out of no exigency caused by the relation of the sexes. Its object was wholly to secure the orderly trial of causes and the better administration of justice. . . . . We are not to forget that all statutes are to be construed, as far as possible, in favor of equality of rights. All restrictions upon human liberty, all claims for special privileges, are to be regarded as having the presumption of law against them, and as standing upon their defense, and can be sustained, if at all by valid legislation, only by the clear expression or clear implication of the law.

"We have some noteworthy illustrations of the recognition of women as eligible, or appointable to office under statutes of which the language is merely general. Thus, women are appointed in all parts of the country as postmasters. The act of

Congress of 1825 was the first one conferring upon the Postmaster-General the power of appointing postmasters, and it has remained essentially unchanged to the present time. The language of the act is, that "the Postmaster-General shall establish post-offices and appoint postmasters." Women are not included except in the general term "postmasters," a term which seems to imply male persons. . . . . The same may be said of pension agents. The acts of Congress on the subject have simply authorized "the President, by and with the advice and consent of the Senate, to appoint all pension agents, who shall hold their offices for the term of four years, and shall give bond," etc. At the last session of Congress a married woman in Chicago was appointed for a third term pension agent for the State of Illinois, and the public papers stated that there was not a single vote against her confirmation in the Senate. Public opinion is everywhere approving of such appointments. They promote the public interest, which is benefited by every legitimate use of individual ability, while mere justice, which is of interest to all, requires that all have the fullest opportunity for the exercise of their abilities. . . . . We have had pressed upon us by the counsel opposed to the applicant, the decisions of the courts of Massachusetts, Wisconsin, and Illinois, and of the United States Court of Claims, adverse to such an application. While not prepared to accede to all the general views expressed in those decisions, we do not think it necessary to go into a discussion of them, as we regard our statute, in view of all the considerations affecting its construction, as too clear to admit of any reasonable question as to the interpretation and effect which we ought to give it." (Conn. Supreme Ct. Rep., vol. l. p. 131).

We have a record showing that there were fifty-six women attorneys in the country at the time this last decision was rendered, in July, 1882, of whom thirty-one had graduated from law schools. Five of the fifty-six have gone to the spirit land. The first to go was Lemma Barkaloo, of Brooklyn, N. Y., the second to be enrolled as an attorney, and the first to try a case since the days of Mistress Brent. She was refused admission to the Law Department of Columbia College, and entered that of Washington University at St. Louis, in 1869. Without completing the course, she was admitted to the Circuit Court of St. Louis, and to the Supreme Court of the State in 1870. She died the same year of typhoid fever. The St. Louis Bar resolved "that in her erudition, industry, and enterprise, we have to regret the loss of one who, in the morning of her career, bade fair to reflect credit upon our profession and a new honor upon her sex." Alta M. Hulett, of Chicago, died in 1877. She prepared the bill to secure admission of women in Illinois and lectured in its interest during its pendency. She was admitted on her nineteenth birthday. Ellen A. Martin, in speaking of her in an article on "Admission of Women to the Bar," published in the initial number of the *Chicago Law Times*, says: "Miss Hulett was a young woman of remarkable energy and push, and of excellent ability and business judgment. She had tact and skill in the acquisition and management of business, and was a capable and efficient lawyer. She had a wonderful faculty for making friends who interested themselves in her success, and in the three years of her practice acquired an amount of profitable business that is not generally expected in law practice until after a much longer period. Her successful, and it may fairly be termed brilliant, career had a marked influence in producing a favorable attitude of the public toward woman practitioners." Lavinia Goodell, daughter of the well-known Abolitionist, Rev. Wm. Goodell, was the pioneer lawyer of Wisconsin. She was admitted to the bar, after passing a brilliant examination, in 1873. The case which greatly extended her reputation throughout the State and country was one involving twelve hundred dollars, in which her client was a woman. The case was carried from the county court to the circuit court, and appealed from that to the supreme court, where she won. According to the law of Wisconsin, Miss Goodell's admission to the circuit court admitted her to all courts in the State except the supreme court. Upon carrying up her case, and applying for admission to this, the chief justice (Ryan), refused her on the ground of sex. The arguments appear in substance in vol. xxxix. of Wisconsin reports.

She afterward reviewed the chief justice's decision in the *Chicago Legal News* and unquestionably had the better of him in argument. She also prepared a bill and sent it to the State Legislature, providing that no person should be refused admission to the bar on account of sex. A petition asking for its passage was signed by the circuit judge and every member of the bar in the county. In such high esteem was Miss Goodell's practice held, that her best paying clients were women. She was admitted to the supreme court in 1875.

She did much work for temperance and woman suffrage, two subjects which were very near her heart. Her life was devoted to good deeds, which only ended here when she was called up higher. She died in 1880, in Milwaukee, where she had gone for medical treatment.

M. Fredrika Perry, of Chicago, died in 1883. She graduated from the Law School of Michigan University in March, 1875, was immediately admitted to the Michigan bar, and in the fall to the Illinois bar. Soon afterward, on motion of Miss Hulett, she was admitted to the United States circuit and district courts for the Northern District of Illinois, Miss Hulett being the first woman admitted to these courts and to any United States court. She continued in practice in partnership with Miss Martin, under the name of Perry & Martin, until her death (the result of pneumonia). Speaking of her, Miss Martin says: "Miss Perry was a successful lawyer and her success was substantial. She combined in an eminent degree the qualities which distinguish able barristers and jurists; her mind was broad and catholic, clear, quick, logical, and profound; her information both on legal and general matters was extensive. She had a clear, strong, and pleasant voice, and was an excellent advocate, both in presenting the law to the court and the merits of a case to the jury. She was a skillful examiner of witnesses, and understood as few attorneys do, save practitioners who have grown old in experience, the nice discriminations of Common Law Pleadings and the Rules of Evidence, the practical methods by which rights are secured in courts. All her work was done with the greatest care. She was engrossed in the study and practice of law, appreciating its spirit and intent, and gained steadily in efficiency and practical power, year by year. She had the genius and ability for the highest attainment in all departments of civil practice, and joined with these the power of close application and hard work. She belonged to the Strong family, which has furnished a great deal of the legal talent of the United States. Judge Tuley, before whom she often appeared, said of her at the bar meeting called to take action upon her death, "I was surprised at the extent of her legal knowledge and the great legal acumen she displayed." Tabitha A. Holton, of Dobson, North Carolina, died in 1886. She was admitted to the Supreme Court of the State in January, 1878, having passed a highly creditable examination. She practiced in Dobson, in partnership with her brother, Samuel L. Holton, devoting herself chiefly to office work and the preparation of civil cases, until a short time before her death.

Ada H. Kepley, of Effingham, Illinois, was the first woman to graduate from a law school in this or any other country.

She took her degree in June, 1870, from the Union College of Law, Chicago.

The major part of law schools of the United States now freely admit women when applied to for that purpose. Among those still refusing are the law departments of Yale, Harvard, and Georgetown universities, and Columbia College; the Cumberland University Law School of Lebanon, Tennessee, the Law Department of the Washington and Lee University in Lexington, Virginia, and the Law Department of the University of Virginia. "One woman, however, does wear the honors of the degree of Bachelor of Laws as conferred by Yale. This is Alice R. Jordan, now Mrs. Blake, who, after a year of study in the Law School of Michigan University and admission to the bar of Michigan in June, 1885, entered the Law School at Yale in the fall of the same year, and graduated at the close of the course with the degree as already stated. Dean Wayland, of Yale Law School, sends me a catalogue of the University, and writes that the marked paragraph on page 25 is intended to prevent a repetition of the Jordan incident. The paragraph referred to appears on the page devoted to departments of instruction, and reads: 'It is to be understood that the courses of instruction above described are open to persons of the male sex only, except where both sexes are specifically included.'"—(Lelia J. Robinson, LL.B., in an article on "Women Lawyers in the United States," in *The Green Bag*, January, 1890.) As to the relative standing of the sexes as students in law schools, Hon. Henry Wade Rogers, dean of the department of law of Michigan University, says: "The women who have attended the Law School have compared favorably in the matter of scholarship with the men. They are just as capable of acquiring legal knowledge as men are." This law school has graduated more women than any other in the country. Hon. Henry Booth, dean of Union College of Law, gives the standing of women in scholarship as that of a fair average, and says: "We discover no difference in the capacity of the sexes to apprehend and apply legal principles. We welcome ladies to the school and regard their presence an advantage in promoting decorum and good order."

A law school for women has recently been opened in New York City. Its founder is Madame Emile Kempin-Spyri, a graduate of the School of Jurisprudence, of the University of Zurich, in 1887. Her application for admission to the order of advocates of her native country, Switzerland, being denied, she emigrated to the United States. She is the counsel of the Swiss Legation in Washington.*

Women lawyers of this country are entitled to practice before all courts, State and national, the same as male lawyers. When not admitted under existing statutes, the respective legislatures, so far, with two exceptions, have promptly passed enabling acts. Women anxious for admission were the first to advocate these. One exception to the usual legislative promptness is found in the case of Annie Smith, of Danville, Virginia. The Judge of the Corporation Court, to whom she applied in 1889 for a certificate to enable her to be examined, refused it on the ground that for a woman to obtain license the present statute would have to be amended. Mrs. Smith, aided by her husband, an attorney, vainly endeavored to secure the necessary enactment during the last session of the State Legislature. The bill, a general one, was voted down ; but a private bill, to enable Mrs. Smith only to obtain license, was favorably reported. The Legislature, however, adjourned before final action on it. Mr. and Mrs. Smith will continue their efforts until successful.

The other exception was a prior one, but admission came without legislation. This is found in the case of Carrie Burnham Kilgore, of Philadelphia. Speaking of her twelve years' struggle for admission, Miss Martin, in her article on "Admission of Women to the Bar," already cited, says : "In December, 1874, Carrie Burnham (now Kilgore), of Philadelphia, began the long and tedious warfare that she has been obliged to wage for admission in Pennsylvania. The Board of Examiners refused to examine her, because there was 'no precedent for the admission of a woman to the bar of this county,' and the Court refused to grant a rule on the board requiring them to examine her. Mrs. Kilgore then tried to have a law passed forbidding exclusion on account of sex, but the Judiciary

---

* Dr. Kempin writes : The Law School for women was a private undertaking, but founded with the aim to connect it with an already existing institution after having proven its vitality. With the help of the Women's Legal Education Society, an incorporated body of women interested in the higher education of their sex, the Law School succeeded in connecting itself with the University of the City of New York. In response to a request of the Women's Legal Education Society the doors of the Law Department of the University were thrown open to women on the same terms as to men, and a lectureship created to which I was selected as a lecturer on the same footing as other lecturers in the Law Department and especially to instruct classes of non-matriculating students who desire a knowledge of law for practical guidance and general culture.—ED.

Committee of the Senate took the position that the law as it stood was broad enough, and so it would seem to be. The Act of 1834 declares, 'The Judges of the several Courts of Record in the Commonwealth shall respectively have power to admit a competent number of persons of an honest disposition, and learned in the law, to practice as attorneys in their respective courts.' The Senate finally passed the clause desired, at two or three sessions, but it was never reached in the House. Finally Mrs. Kilgore gained admission to the Law School of the University of Pennsylvania in 1881, where she had previously been denied, and by virtue of her diploma from there, in 1883, was admitted to the Orphans' Court of Philadelphia. She was then admitted to one of the Common Pleas Courts, but denied admission to the other three, though it is the custom when a person has been admitted to one, to admit to the rest as a matter of course. As soon after admission to the Common Pleas Court as the law allows, two years, and in May of this year, 1886, Mrs. Kilgore applied and was admitted to the Supreme Court of the State, and by virtue of this admission, all the lower Courts are now compelled to admit her. Thus, Pennsylvania has accomplished after twelve years, what Iowa did seventeen years ago without any ado, and with a statute that might have afforded a reasonable ground for refusal, which the Pennsylvania statute did not." Since her admission, Mrs. Kilgore has been in active general practice. Her husband, an able lawyer, in whose office she studied and worked, died two years ago, in 1888. He had a large clientage. After his death, Mrs. Kilgore was requested to take charge of his cases in all but one instance. She is the attorney for Harmon Lodge, I.O.O.F., and the Relief Mining and Milling Company. Several times she has been appointed master and examiner by the courts. A special correspondent of the *Chicago Daily Tribune*, in its issue of April 5, 1890, speaking of Mrs. Kilgore's efforts and successes concludes with: "She has several interesting children and a delightful home, neither her struggle for woman's rights nor her devotion to her professional concerns having interferred with her domestic duties nor estranged her from the hearth."

This reminds us of many interesting cases of motherly care and devotion on the part of women practitioners, two of which we cannot refrain from mentioning. One is in regard to Ohio's first woman lawyer, Annie Cronise Lutes, of Tiffin, who was admitted to practice before the courts of that State in April, 1873. Her sister, Florence Cronise, was admitted in

September of the same year. These two sisters, since their admission, have pursued the steady, straight practice of law without deviation. For several years they were law partners. In 1880, Mrs. Lutes and her husband, who had been fellow students in the same office, and were admitted to the bar at the same time, formed a partnership. (This left Miss Florence to practice alone, which she has since done with signal success.) Mr. and Mrs. Lutes were married in 1874. They have three daughters. The two eldest (aged fourteen and twelve respectively) are attending the Heidelberg University, at Tiffin, taking the full classical course, *for which they were prepared under the instruction of their mother*, never having attended public school. The full force of this fact will become apparent further on. In 1881 Mr. Lutes became *totally deaf*. In a letter showing the extent of their law practice, which was published in the article on "Women Lawyers in the United States," already cited, Mr. Lutes says:

"Our practice is general in character, and extends to the courts of this State and the United States courts for the Northern District of Ohio. The following facts will enable you to form an estimate as to the nature and extent of Mrs. Lutes's pratice and experience at the bar. The bar of this county has forty-five members. The total number of civil cases on the trial docket of the term just closed was 226; of that number, our firm was retained in fifty cases, which is probably a fair average of our share of the business for this county, and our practice also extends to a considerable extent to the adjoining counties of this district."

Mr. Lutes's infirmity necessarily imposes extra duties on his faithful partner, which the following extract from the *Chicago Daily Tribune*, of April 5, 1890, graphically pictures: "Mr. Lutes is totally deaf, but his wife sits by him in court and repeats word for word what is said, and although her lips make no audible sound, every word said by judge, jury, or opposing counsel is understood. Without her assistance he would be perfectly helpless, so far as his law practice is concerned. The two work together on every case that is brought to them, and it is seldom a person sees one without the other. Their practice is lucrative and extensive."

The other case is that of Clara S. Foltz. Her married life was unfortunate. She had the family to support. This she did by undertaking dressmaking and millinery, and then conducting classes in voice culture and keeping boarders. An attorney who "admired her keen reasoning powers and her incisive logic," one day said: "Mrs. Foltz, you are such a good mother that I believe you would make an able lawyer. Here is a copy of Kent's Commentaries. I wish you would take it home and read it." She did so as she nursed her babies—five of them now. Shortly afterward she began the study of law in an office. Subsequently she secured a divorce and the custody of her children. In September, 1878, she was admitted to practice and removed to San Francisco for a course in the Hastings Law College. She made application for admission as a student in the college and the dean permitted her to attend the lecture for three days, while the directors were deciding what to do about it. They refused her application on the ground that it was "not wise or expedient, or for the best interest of the college, to admit any female as a student therein." Mrs. Foltz informed the dean that she meant to attend the lectures—peaceably if she could, but forcibly if she must. She promptly commenced action for a mandate to compel the directors to admit her. She won. The directors appealed the case to the State Supreme Court. Mrs. Foltz appeared and argued her side of the case, making the point that the Law College was a branch of the University, and that woman's right to enter the latter was unquestioned. The Court agreed with her, and held that "An applicant for admission as a student to the Hastings Law College cannot lawfully be rejected on the sole ground that she is a female." (Foltz *v.* Hoge, *et al.*, Cal. Supreme Court Rep., vol. liv. p. 28.) She entered the college and remained there eighteen months, attending three classes daily to overtake her class. Finally overstudy, lack of means, and the care of her children, prostrated her. It was a severe disappointment not to be able to complete the prescribed three years' course and win her degree. She will yet gain it. Mrs. Foltz thus tells the story of her first case:

"I firmly believe in the Infinite. The day the Supreme Court admitted me—it was on Thursday—I traveled from San Jose to San Francisco. An old gentleman who knew of my struggles and ambitions was on the train. He explained in an apologetic way that he thought perhaps I would be willing to assist him in finding a land claim that he had pre-empted, and which another settler contested. My would-be client had all the necessary proofs and witnesses ready, and the case was to come up at ten o'clock the following day. I had never been in a land office. I was ignorant of the methods of procedure, but I could soon learn. I accepted the case.

"That day was a crisis in my life. To pay the ten dollar

fee of the Supreme Court I pawned this breastpin—dear old pin! Next morning, before I was up, a knock came to my door as the clock struck seven. My client was there. I dressed myself and carried on a conversation through the door. What would I charge for my services, he asked. I did not know, but ventured a guess at the correct figure. I would undertake the case for $25. He hesitated a little, and said that after witnesses fees and other expenses were paid he would have but $15 left, and that if I had a mind to take that sum it would be all right. I accepted eagerly, for I needed the money. Next I invited the witnesses in and questioned them. We parted to meet at the land office, but I went down in advance to see the Surveyor-General. I hold that the truth is always the best, so I told him that I had a case at ten o'clock, but knew nothing about land-office matters, and that I wanted to learn the law. He was very kind and furnished me with a pamphlet of instructions. Then I ventured to request that the case might go over to 1 P.M. He found that it could. I was immensely relieved and hastened off with my precious pamphlet. Client and witnesses were on the stairs. I informed them of the change in time and turned back. Didn't I get that pamphlet by heart though! And I won my first case, redeemed my cherished pin, and paid my board bill."

Laura De Force Gordon, who was also denied admission to the Hastings Law College, and aided Mrs. Foltz in her mandamus case, successfully defended a Spaniard charged with murder, within two months after her admission to the bar in 1879. "Among her most noted criminal cases was that of The People *v.* Sproule, which was indeed in some respects the most remarkable trial in the whole range of criminal jurisprudence in California. The defendant had shot and killed a young man named Andrews, by mistake for one Espey, the seducer of Sproule's wife. It was a fearful tragedy, and the excitement was so great that the jail had to be guarded for a week to prevent the lynching of the prisoner. Mrs. Gordon undertook his defense, against the advice of the most distinguished lawyers in the State, and obtained a verdict of "Not guilty" amid the most deafening cheers of men and hysterical cries of women, half-weeping jurymen joining in the general clamor of rejoicing." ("Women Lawyers in the United States," in *The Green Bag*, January, 1890.)

In speaking of her practice, Mrs. Lockwood says: "My first was a divorce case and I won it, but the man refused to pay the alimony. The judge told me there was no law to make him pay it. I told him there was, and I showed him I could issue a *ne exeat.* I issued the writ, and the man was clapped into prison until he agreed to pay the alimony. Years afterward a similar case came up and the men who were the lawyers asked if there was no way to compel a man to stay in the District until he paid the alimony. The clerk said: 'Belva Lockwood is the only one who has ever issued a *ne exeat* in the District; you had better consult her.' Many a time I have been saved by a little wit. Once my client, a woman, got upon the witness stand, in spite of all I could do, and acknowledged she had committed the crime of which she was accused. It was for shooting a constable, and that woman described the whole thing, talking until I was glued to my seat with fright. When she stopped and I had to get up I didn't know what I was going to say, but I began, Gentlemen of the jury, the laws must be enforced. My client has committed the double offense of resisting an officer of the law and shooting a man. The District is under the common law. That law says a woman must obey her husband. Her husband told her to load a gun and shoot the first officer that tried to force his way into the house. She obeyed him. Gentlemen, I claim that that husband loaded the gun and shot the officer, and as the judge will not postpone this case until I can have the husband brought from the West, where he is, I claim you are not trying the right prisoner. You would not have a woman resist her husband?' The jury brought in the verdict of 'Not guilty,' and the judge, a crusty gentleman, said, when the next case was brought up: 'I will call a new jury for this case, as the old one has just done a hard day's work.'"

Col. C. K. Pier, his wife, and three daughters, of Madison, Wisconsin, are widely known as "the Pier family of lawyers." The Colonel is a lawyer of long standing. Mrs. Pier and their eldest daughter graduated from the Law Department of the University of Wisconsin in 1887. All three practice together. The two younger sisters, Carrie and Harriet, have nearly finished the course in the law school from which their mother and sister graduated. Miss Kate, in her twenty-first year, appeared before the Supreme Court and won her case, the first to be argued by a woman in the supreme tribunal of the State. A newspaper, commenting on the fact, says: "Her opponent was J. J. Sutton, a veteran practitioner. The gray-haired patriarchs of the profession smoothed the wrinkles out of their waistcoats and straightened their neckties, and then wiped the specks off their spectacles. The audience was one before which any young man might readily have been excused for getting rattled. There were present Gen. E. E. Bryant, dean of the law faculty, ex-Secretary of the Interior William F. Vilas, and a host of visiting legal lights. Even the dignified judges were compelled to affect an extra degree of austerity to conceal their interest in the young attorney. But Miss Pier showed no sign of embarrassment. Her argument was direct and to the point, and, moreover, relieved of the superfluities that frequently characterize the verbose utterances of more experienced attorneys of the male sex. She stated her case unhesitatingly, and frequently turned to and cited authorities, showing an acquaintance with the law and a degree of self-possession which indicated that she was truly in love with her profession. She showed she possessed the true mettle for success, and two weeks later, when the judges rendered their decision, she had the pleasure of winning her first case. Since then both she and her mother have frequently argued cases before the Court."

Almeda E. Hitchcock, of Hilo, Hawaii Islands, graduated from the Law Department of the Michigan University in 1888, and was admitted to the Michigan bar. Her father is one of the circuit judges of that far away island. On her return home she was admitted to the Hawaiian bar on presentation of her license from the Michigan Court, the first instance of a woman's receiving license to practice law in that kingdom. The same day she was appointed notary public and became her father's law partner.

Marilla M. Ricker, while a resident of the District of Columbia, was appointed Commissioner and Examiner in Chancery by the Supreme Court of the District, and several cases were heard before her. Other women lawyers, in various parts of the country, have been appointed examiners in chancery and examiners of applicants for admission to the bar. Mary E. Haddock, LL.B., in June, 1878, was appointed by the Supreme Court of Iowa to examine students of the State University for graduation and admission to the bar. She was reappointed for two successive years. Ada Lee, of Port Huron, Michigan, the year following her admission in 1883, was elected to the office of Circuit Court Commissioner, having been nominated, without solicitation on her part, by the Republican, Democratic, and Greenback parties of St. Clair county. "She performed the duties of this office, and held it until the expiration of her term, despite the fact that thirteen suits were begun to oust her, during which time two hundred and seventeen cases were tried before her." Mrs. J. M. Kellogg acted as Assistant

Attorney-General during the time her husband was Attorney-General of Kansas. They are law partners.

Phoebe W. Couzins, LL.B., was chief deputy United States Marshal for the Eastern District of Missouri during the time her father was the Marshal. At the death of her father she was named his successor, which position she held until removed by the in-coming Democratic administration. Catherine G. Waugh, A.M., LL.B., was for a year or two Professor of Commercial Law in the Rockford (Ill.) Commercial College. Mrs. Foltz delivered a legal address before the students of Union College of Law in 1886. Mary A. Greene, LL.B. recently delivered a course of lectures before the students of Lasell Seminary on "Business Law for Women."

Several able articles have been written for law journals by women lawyers of this country. Of books, M. B. R. Shay, is author of "Students' Guide to Common Law Pleading" (published in 1881.) Of this work, Hon. R. M. Benjamin, dean of Law Faculty, and Hon. A. G. Kerr, professor of Pleading of Law Department of the Illinois Wesleyan University, say, as published in Callaghan & Company's annual catalogue of law books:

"We have examined with considerable care Shay's Questions on Common Law Pleading, and can cheerfully recommend them to students as admirably adapted to guide them to a thorough knowledge of the principles of pleading as laid down by those masters of the system, Stephen, Gould, and Chitty."

Lelia Robinson Sawtelle is author of "Law Made Easy" (published in 1886). Of this work, Hon. Charles T. Russell, professor in Boston University Law School, says: "For the end proposed, the information and instruction of the popular mind in the elements of law, civil and criminal, I know of no work which surpasses it. It is comprehensive and judicious in scope, accurate in statement, terse, vigorous, simple, and clear in style. My gratification in this work is none the less that its author is the first lady Bachelor of Laws graduated from our Boston University Law School, and that she has thus early and fully vindicated her right to the highest honors of the school accorded her at her graduation." Mrs. Sawtelle has since written a manual entitled "The Law of Husband and Wife," which likewise has been well received. She is now at work upon another to be called "Wills and Inheritances."

We have already spoken of Myra Bradwell as the editor of the *Chicago Legal News*. Catharine V. Waite, LL.B., edits the *Chicago Law Times*, which she founded in 1886. Bessie Bradwell Helmer, LL.B., compiled, unassisted, ten volumes of

Bradwell's Appelate Court Reports. Cora A. Benneson, LL.B., was law editor for the West Publishing Company of St. Paul, Minnesota, in 1886.

The first association of women lawyers is called "The Equity Club." This was organized in October, 1886, by women students and graduates of the Law Department of Michigan University, having for its object "the interchange of encouragement and friendly counsel between women law students and practitioners." It is international in scope. Each member is required to contribute a yearly letter, "giving an account of individual experiences, thoughts on topics of general interest, and helpful suggestions," for publication and distribution among members of the association.

Another association of women lawyers, organized in 1888, is the "Woman's International Bar Association," having for its object:

1. To open law schools to women.
2. To remove all disabilities to admission of women to the bar, and to secure their eligibility to the bench.
3. To disseminate knowledge concerning women's legal status.
4. To secure better legal conditions for women.

Women lawyers are welcomed as members of bar associations established by their brothers in the profession. Many have availed themselves of this privilege.

For various reasons quite a number of women admitted have not, so far, identified themselves with law practice. Others have allowed themselves to be drawn into temperance and other reform movements; but the greater portion at once settled down to follow their chosen pursuit with no deviation, and are ripening into able, experienced lawyers, and winning their fair share of clientage. Some confine themselves mainly to an office practice, seldom or never appearing in public; others prefer court practice. Those who enter the forum are cordially countenanced by brother lawyers and acceptably received before court and jury. As a rule they are treated with the utmost courtesy by the bench, the bar, and other court officers.

Woman's influence in the court room as counsel is promotive of good in more than one respect. Invectives against opposing counsel, so freely made use of in some courts, are seldom indulged in when woman stands as the opponent. And in social impurity cases, language, in her presence, becomes more chaste, and the moral tone thereby elevated perceptibly. But there should be one more innovation brought into general vogue, that of the mixed jury system. When we shall have women both as lawyers and jurors to assist in the trial of cases, then, and not until then, will woman's influence for good in the administration of justice be fully felt. In Wyoming and Washington the mixed jury system has been tried and found perfectly practicable.

There has not been time enough yet for a woman to develop into an Erskine or Burke, an O'Connor or Curran, a Webster or Choate. But few men have done so, if history correctly records. Woman has made a fair beginning, and is determined to push on and upward, keeping pace with her brother along the way until, with him, she shall have finally reached the highest pinnacle of legal fame.

X.

WOMAN IN THE STATE.

BY

MARY A. LIVERMORE.

No one who has studied the history of the world, even superficially, will dispute the statement that over the female half of the human family there has steadily brooded a cloud of hindrance and repression, of disability and servitude. The long past has denied to women the possession of souls, and they have been relegated to the ignorance and injustice to which men have always doomed those regarded as their inferiors. Until within a few years, comparatively speaking, the world has been under the dominion of brute force, and might has made right. Every one has been welcome to whatever he has had the brawn and muscle to win and to hold, and all have yielded to the rule of physical force, as to-day we respect the decisions of the courts. All through these ages the history of woman has been disastrous. Her physical weakness, and not alone her mental inferiority, has made her the subject of man. Toiling patiently for him, asking little for herself and every thing for him, cheerfully sharing with him all perils and hardships, the unappreciated mother of his children, she has been bought and sold, petted or tortured, according to the whim of her brutal owner, the victim everywhere of pillage, lust, and war. And this statement includes all races and peoples of the earth from the date of their historic existence.

Among the Hindoos, woman was the slave of man; bought, sold, lent, gambled away, and taken for debt, with the very power of life or death held over her by some irresponsible husband, father, or other man. She was forbidden to speak the language of man, and was condemned to use the patois of slaves. Under the old Roman law, the husband was the sole tribunal of the wife. He controlled her property, earnings, and religion: she was allowed no rights in her own children; and she could invoke no law against him. The Greek law regarded woman as a child, and held her in everlasting tutelage from the cradle to her gray-haired old age. Aristotle, and they of his school, called her a "monster," an "accidental production." The Hebrews pronounced her an afterthought of the Deity, and the mother of all evil. Throughout the entire Orient, her condition has been one of such compulsory servitude, that the phrase "Oriental degradation of woman," remains to-day the synonym of the deepest debasement woman has ever known.

When the councils of the medieval church came together to decide on the instruction needful to the young, they hastened to count women out, and to declare them "unfit for instruction." And they, who in defiance of this decision—kind-hearted nuns of the Catholic Church—established schools for girls, were publcily stoned when they were met on the streets. The early Christian fathers denounced women as "noxious animals," "painted temptresses," "necessary evils," "desirable calamities," and "domestic perils." From the English Heptarchy to the Reformation, the law proclaimed the wife to be "in all cases, and under all circumstances, her husband's creature, servant, and slave." Herbert Spencer, writing of English laws, in his "Descriptive Sociology of England," says: "Our laws are based on the all-sufficiency of man's rights, so that society exists to-day for woman only as she is in the keeping of some man." To Diderot, the French philosopher, even in the eighteenth century, so persistently do the traditions of the past make themselves felt, woman was only a "courtesan." To Montesquieu, she was "an attractive child,"—to Rousseau "an object of pleasure to man." To Michelet, nearly a century later, she was "a natural invalid."

This subjection of woman to man, which has hindered her development in normal ways, has created a contemptuous opinion of her, which runs through the literature and legislation of all nations. It is apparent to-day in unjust laws and customs, which disgrace the statute books, and cause society to progress with halting step. There still exist different codes of morals for men and women, different penalties for crime, and the relations of the sexes to the government are dissimilar. In marriage, the husband has control of the wife's person, and, in most instances, ownership of her earnings, and of her minor children. She is rarely paid the same wages as man, even when she does the same work, and is his equal only when punishment and the payment of taxes are in question. All these unjust inequalities are survivals of the long ages of servitude through which woman has passed, and which have not yet ceased to exist. During their existence, says Mme. de Staël, "woman was able to exercise fully but one of the faculties with which nature has gifted her—the faculty of suffering."

Born and bred under such conditions of injustice, and with arbitrary standards of womanly inferiority persistently set before them, it has not been possible for women to rise much above them. Here and there through the centuries, exceptional women, endowed with phenomenal force of character, have towered above the mediocrity of their sex, hinting at the qualities imprisoned in the feminine nature. It is not strange that these instances have been rare. It is strange, indeed, that women have held their own during these ages of degradation. And as by a general law of heredity "the inheritance of traits of character is persistent in proportion to the length of time they have been inherited," it is easy to account for the conservatism of women to-day, and for the indifference and hostility with which many regard the movements for their advancement.

For a new day has dawned, and humanity is moving forward to an era when oppression and slavery are to be entirely displaced, and reason and justice recognized as the rule of life. Science is extending immeasurably the bounds of knowledge and power. Art is refining life, and giving to it beauty and grace. Literature bears in her hands whole ages of comfort and sympathy. Industry, aided by the hundred-handed elements of nature, is increasing the world's wealth, and invention is economizing its labor. The age looks steadily to the redressing of wrong, to the righting of every form of error and oppression, and demands that law and justice be made interchangeable terms. So humane a spirit dominates the age in which we live, that even the brute creation share in it, and we have hundreds of societies organized to prevent cruelty to animals. It could not be possible but that women should share in the justice and kindliness with which the times are fraught, and the last quarter of a century has lifted them to higher levels. How has this been accomplished?

While progress is the method of man, his early progress was inconceivably slow. He had lived on the earth long ages before he knew enough, or cared enough, to make a record of what he did, thought, felt, hoped, or suffered for the benefit of posterity. The moment he began to make a record of his daily life, history began. And history takes us back, according to the popular conception, only five or six thousand years—authentic history to a period much less remote. From the early civilizations that flourished in the valleys of the Nile and Euphrates, this age has inherited very little. What we possess that may seem a transmission from that earlier time has been for the most part rediscovered, or reinvented by the civilizations of the present.

To the Greek civilization we are indebted for a marvelous development of the beautiful in art. And when our art students have exhausted all modern instruction, they are compelled to go back thousands of years, and sit down at the feet of the dead Greeks, and learn of them, through the mutilated remains of their masterpieces. To the Roman civilization we owe a wonderful development of law. The Roman code of laws is to-day the basis of the jurisprudence of the civilized world. Very little more than these survivals of the Greek and Roman civilizations have come down to us. For the barbarian hordes of the North and the East crushed out the life of the "Eternal City," pillaged what they did not destroy of its treasures, despoiled the cities in its vicinage, and ground to powder its boasted greatness and its strong arm of power. The phenomenal dark ages set in, and for a thousand years the world groped in ignorance and darkness, and very little progress was made in any direction.

But civilization is not artificial, but real and natural. It is to the race what the flower is to the bud, and the oak tree to the acorn,—growth, development. Again the divine in man asserted itself, and again there came into the world a quickening spirit. Four great events occurred, of world-wide importance, each following quickly its predecessor, and an impetus was given to humanity which has never spent itself, but has steadily gained in power and momentum. The revival of classical learning had a powerful influence upon woman as well as man. The invention of the art of printing enabled the race to retain whatever knowledge it acquired, whereas, before, it lost as fast as it gained. The discovery of this continent opened a new world and limitless possibilities to the pent-up, struggling spirits of the East, longing for a larger and better life than was possible under the depressing conditions of that day. While the great Reformation, begun by Luther, released both men and women from the almost omnipotent control of the Church. Demanding the right of private judgment in matters of religion, it wrought out a great development of religious liberty, which has been succeeded by a greater outcome of civil freedom.

These four events, occurring almost simultaneously, were the precursors of our present civilization. They kindled the souls of men into a flame which has burned steadily to this hour. The development of the present day dates from them, and the civilization begotten by them is endowed with earthly immortality. It abounds in the elements of perpetuity, which the earlier human growths by the Nile and Euphrates never possessed. Slavery has almost entirely disappeared from the world under its influence. Liberty has infected all races with its divine contagion, and has driven from the western hemisphere every crowned head. Laws and law-makers, trade and commerce, public and private life, church and state are examined by the highest ethical standards. And through the last three centuries, there has rung out a growing demand for human rights, and human opportunity, which has now culminated into a mighty and imperious demand that cannot be much longer denied. It is the people's hour. In this trumpet call for right and justice are heard the multitudinous voices of women, who have caught the ear of the world, and to whose banner are daily flocking new recruits, and at last the woman's hour has also come.

During the centuries that preceded the Christian era, and for centuries after, there were, here and there, in many countries, eminent women who came into possession of power and privilege; sometimes they were used wisely, and sometimes wickedly. But there were others, on whose histories women will always dwell with fresh delight, and refuse to believe the inuendoes of contemporary writers concerning them. We read of Aspasia, the preceptress of Socrates, the wife of the great Pericles of Athens, and the friend of the Greek philosophers. Summoned for trial before the Greek Areopagus, she was charged with "walking the streets unveiled, sitting at table with men, disbelieving in the Greek gods, believing only in one sole Creator, and with entertaining original ideas concerning the motions of the sun and moon." She was in advance of her time, and the age could not understand her.

We linger over the sad story of Hypatia, whose father, Theon the younger, was at the head of the Platonic school at Alexandria at the close of the fourth century. He was also the commentator on Ptolemy, and the editor of "Euclid," adding here and there a demonstration of his own. All that he knew he imparted to his daughter, and Hypatia occupied a position unparalleled in ancient or modern times. Before she had reached her twenty-seventh year she had written a book on

"The Astronomical Canon of Diophantes," and another on "The Conics of Apollonius." One of her enemies, the historian Socrates, tells us that when she succeeded her father in the Platonic school derived from Plotinus, and "expounded the precepts of philosophy," studious persons from all parts of the country flocked to hear her, and that "she addressed both them and the magistrates with singular modesty." But alas! she paid the penalty of her great superiority. And because she was suspected of having "an influence in public affairs," and was deemed "worthy to sit in the councils of church and state," she was brutally murdered by a savage mob, that regarded superiority in a woman as an arraignment of inferiority in men.

We are familiar with the story of Zenobia, Queen of Palmyra, who reigned A.D. 267, of whom reluctant history tells us that she was a woman of great courage, high spirit, remarkable beauty, and purity of moral character. Her literary acquirements were unusual, and she spoke Latin, Greek, and the Oriental languages with fluency; while in the admistration of her government she combined prudence, justice, and liberality, so that nearly the whole of the eastern provinces submitted to her sway.

It is a matter of history that 320 B.C., Martia, Queen of London, first formulated the principles of the English common law in her judgments and enactments. Her "Martian Statutes" outlived the Roman, Anglo-Saxon, and Norse invasions. Holinshed, who is regarded as good authority, says that Alfred the Great, after twelve hundred years, revived her Briton laws, and enforced them among Anglo-Saxons and Danes. Two centuries later, they were again re-enacted under Edward the Confessor, and a century after they were again re-enacted by Stephen. The earliest laws of Great Britain, therefore, the substance of which has been in force twenty-two hundred years, were made by a woman.

Tacitus says of the Britons that sex was ignored in their government. Cæsar says that women had voice in their councils, and power in their courts, and often commanded in war. Plutarch says that women, among the Britons, took part in deciding on war and peace, as members of the councils, and that differences with their allies were decided by the women.

Until the time of the Reformation, Catholicism was the state religion of Britain, and nunneries were established and regulated by law. The Superiors were elected by the nuns and represented their constituents in the Wita, or legislative council; and in this way the right of women to representation in governments was recognized. The Domesday Book, compiled under William the Conqueror, in 1070, enumerated the inhabitants of each village who were entitled by existing Saxon law to vote for local officers, and included many women. Women were chosen members of many Saxon local assemblies by their own sex, and shared authority as members.

It has never been questioned that women have the right to vote in secular corporations where they are stockholders. It has been taken as settled that women have a right to vote in the enactment of corporation statutes, in deciding who shall be intrusted with the powers conferred on the corporation by law, and in electing persons to administer those powers. Women have always shared control of the immense Bank of England, with its enormous power over the currency and fortunes of the world. In still more important corporations this has been the case. "Women were at liberty to take part as stockholders with full powers to vote on all questions in the 'Virginia Company,' which peopled Virginia, and in the company which populated part of New England, and for a time governed it. The same was true of the Hudson's Bay Company, which for centuries ruled half North America. It was also true of the East India Company, which for about the same time ruled absolutely one of the greatest empires of earth."

When the barons wrested Magna Charta from King John, one of the rights for which they contended, and forced him to grant, was the right of women to a vote in the House of Lords. He was compelled to summon to that House all earls, barons, and others who held lands directly from the king, and he summoned to the very first Parliament the countesses of Pembroke and Essex. In the reign of Edward I. ten ladies were summoned as entitled to seats There is conclusive evidence that during the first three reigns of the existence of Magna Charta, women had a right to a voice in the English government, and exercised it.

John Stuart Mill declares that "the list of women who have been eminent rulers of mankind swells to a great length, when to queens and empresses there are added women regents, and women viceroys of provinces." "It is a curious consideration," he continues, "that the only things which the existing laws exclude women from doing, are the things which they have proved they are able to do. There is no law to prevent a woman from having written all the plays of Shakspere, or composed all the operas of Mozart." But it is almost everywhere declared that women are not fit for power and cannot be made so, and that they cannot take any part in civil government. The laws have been cunningly framed to prevent their taking the first step in this direction, and a public sentiment has been created as the bulwark of the law. "And yet," says Mill, "it is not inference, but fact, that a woman can be a Queen Elizabeth, a Deborah, a Joan of Arc,"—an Isabella, a Maria Theresa, a Catherine of Russia, a Margaret of Austria.

"If a Hindoo principality is strongly, vigilantly, and economically governed," continues this earnest friend and student of woman, "if order is preserved without oppression; if cultivation is extending, and the people prosperous, in three cases out of four that principality is under a woman's government." And he tells us "he has collected this fact from a long official knowledge of Hindoo governments." "There are many such instances," he continues. "For though, by Hindoo institutions, a woman cannot reign, she is the legal regent of a kingdom during the minority of the heir. And minorities are frequent, the lives of the male rulers being so often prematurely terminated through the effect of inactivity and sensual excesses. When we consider that these princesses have never been seen in public, have never conversed with any man not of their own family except from behind a curtain, that they do not read, and if they did there is no book in their language which can give them the smallest instruction in political affairs, the example they afford of the natural capacity of women for government is very striking."

It was not, however, until the fifteenth century that there was a marked tendency to recognize the general equality of women with men. During the days of feudalism, it was debated, very earnestly, whether women should be educated or not, and it was generally believed that a knowledge of letters would put into their hands an additional power to work evil. Nevertheless, at all periods, whenever and wherever we can trace a literature, we find women shining in it. Feudalism may be considered to have perished at the beginning of the fifteenth century, and a new period of transition had arrived, to which historical writers have given the name of "The Renaissance."

In 1506, Cornelius Agrippa, eminent in the literary society of his time, wrote a book not only to prove that men and women are equals intellectually, but that woman is superior to man. In 1552, another work of similar scope appeared, based on the Platonic philosophy, the purpose of which was a defense of woman's superiority. In 1599, Anthony Gibson sent into the world a third volume, again reiterating "the superiority of women to men, in all virtuous actions, no matter how fine the quality of men may be proved to be." At the same time books were also being published by other vigorous writers of the day, who stoutly denied to women the possession of reason, and maintained their eminence in iniquity only.

In 1696, Daniel Defoe contended for the better education of women, declaring his belief that if men were trained in the same deplorable ignorance as women, they would be vastly more incompetent and degraded. In 1697, Mary Astell "distinguished for literary and theological labors," wrote a letter in "Defense of the Female Sex," which passed through three editions. An appeal to women written by the same author, entitled, "A Proposal to Ladies for the Advancement of their True Interests," advocated their general education, and besought their co-operation in some worthy educational scheme. It so wrought on Lady Elizabeth Hastings, a wealthy noble lady, that she immediately offered ten thousand pounds for the establishment of a college for women. It was a grand proposition, and would have been carried out but for the opposition of the bigoted Bishop Burnet.

At that time Italy led all other nations in literary activity, and then, as now, was remarkable for her pride in her learned women. Lucrezia Marinella of Venice wrote a work entitled, "The Nobleness and Excellence of Women, together with the Faults and Imperfections of Men." The University of Bologna, which admitted women as students, and conferred degrees upon them as early as the middle of the thirteenth century, at last elevated them to professorships, where they taught law and philosophy, physiology and anatomy, Latin and Greek. The annals of Italian literature, scholarship, and art, are radiant with the names of women who distinguished themselves in various departments, and were honored by the men of that day, who proudly testified to their abilities and achievements. Women of France and Italy interested themselves in medical science, and we read of a woman who lectured in the sixteenth century on obstetrics "to large classes of both sexes."

In England, there was the same mental quickening among women, as on the continent. Queen Elizabeth ascended the throne, and found herself immediately confronted with perplexities, embarrassments, and anxieties. She was obliged to face religious bigots at home, and unscrupulous kings abroad; her people were rent with differences of religious belief, were rude, ignorant, and inert; her noblemen were factious, her exchequer empty, her parliaments jealous of her; there was neither army nor navy, and the nation was poor and embarrassed with debt. But her stout heart, strong will, and wise head were soon felt in every part of her kingdom. The Reformation begun by Luther had stimulated England to great activity, had loosened the hold of the church upon both men and women, and the way was being prepared for that grand development of religious and civil liberty which has since followed.

During the Elizabethan era, the great ideas were born which immediately underlie our present civilization. Government, religion, literature, and social life were then discussed as never before, earnestly, and by great thinkers, and reforms were inaugurated that lifted the world to a higher level. Not only was the age enriched by great men of marvelous political wisdom, financial skill, comprehensive intellect, and original genius, but there were noble women in England, who, holding high social position, devoted their leisure and their wealth to studious pursuits, and emulated the superior men of the day. How grandly they illuminated the circles that gathered about them, while the majority of their sex wasted their time in frivolous pursuits!

It was in the midst of this intense intellectual ferment, and as the result of it, that the settlement of our country began. While the Church of England had emancipated itself from the Papal power at immense cost of life and treasure, and after generations of conflict, it had not learned the great law of religious freedom. Our forefathers made war on the divine right of bishops, and the authority of the church to control their consciences, and were driven by persecution to America. Here they prospered, were subject to Great Britain, and for a time were contented. But when in America they were denied the rights granted to Englishmen living in England, their discontent became general, and the Declaration of Independence and the War of the Revolution followed. They were not hot-headed philosophers, crazed by the theories of the French revolution, as many to-day would have us believe. The "glittering generalities" of the Declaration of Independence, as Rufus Choate sneeringly called the immortal principles of our great charter of liberty, were not deductions from Rousseau, Voltaire, or any other French philosopher. They were simply the reiteration of the rights of English citizenship, expanded and adapted to the exigencies of the new world in which the colonists had planted themselves. For the American civilization is only a continuation of the English civilization, under new conditions—some of them more favorable, and others less so. Before there was a revolution in France, or a democracy in France, Jefferson's most democratic words had been spoken in America. And all the facts go to show that if there was any learning from each other in political science, between him and the French philosophers, they were the pupils, and not Jefferson. They were men of untarnished moral character; religion and patriotism were to them synonymous terms, and their love of liberty developed into a passion. The world has never seen grander, more versatile, nor more self-poised men, than the founders of our nation.

What of the women associated with these heroes? "The ammunition of the Continental soldiery in the war for freedom came from the pulpit, and the farmer's fireside," said one of the orators on a recent centennial occasion. The men of the Revolution had no cowardly, faint-hearted mothers and wives to hang about their neck like millstones. Their women were as heroic in fiber as themselves. Patriotic mothers nursed the infancy of freedom. They talked with their children of the wrongs of the people, and of their invaded rights, and uttered their aspirations for a better state of things in language of intensest force. Sons and daughters grew sensitive to the tyranny that oppressed their parents, and as they came to maturity burned with a desire to defend their rights to the utmost.

During the French and Indian wars of the country that preceded the war of the Revolution, women learned to rely on themselves, became experts in the use of fire-arms, and in many instances defended themselves and their children. They were fired with the same love of liberty as the men—they were equally stung with the aggressions of the British government, and as resolute in their determination to resist them. They encouraged them to enter the army, cheered them when despondent, toned them to heroic firmness when wavering, and cheerfully assumed every burden which the men dropped to repel the invaders of their country and their homes.

Not only did women mingle their prayers with those of men at the family altar, beseeching Divine guidance, but their own counsel was sought by men, and given, in the deliberations which resulted in the nation's independence. Less than half a century ago, Mrs. E. F. Ellett took on herself the task of collecting the facts, and sketching the biographies, of the women who were known to have contributed to the success of the country in its struggle for independence. She was successful beyond her expectations, and published three volumes of about three hundred pages each, containing biographical sketches of nearly one hundred and seventy women. Despite the light esteem in which the service of women has been held, and the ease with which it has been forgotten, their record had been preserved, and their memories tenderly perpetuated for three-quarters of a century.

Foremost among them stands Mrs. Mercy Warren, wife of Joseph Warren, and sister of James Otis, author of the never-to-be-forgotten axiom, that "Taxation without representation is tyranny!" She possessed the fiery ardor and patriotic zeal of her distinguished brother, with more political wisdom and sagacity. She was the first one to suggest the doctrine of the "right to life, liberty, and the pursuit of happiness as inherent, and belonging equally to all mankind"; and the patriots of that day accepted her teaching. She first of all counseled separation from the mother country as the only solution of the political problem. She so impressed her convictions upon Samuel and John Adams that they were foremost in their advocacy of "independence," and received, at first, marked discourtesy from their contemporaries for their imprudence.

She corresponded with the Adamses, Jefferson, Generals Gerry and Knox, Lee and Gates, and others who sought her advice. She entertained General and Mrs. Washington, supplied political parties with their arguments, and was the first woman to teach political leaders their duties in matters of state. She kept a faithful record of events during the Revolutionary War, drew her own conclusions as a philosopher and politician, and at the close of the struggle published a history of the war, which can be found in some of the New England libraries, and which contains faithful portraits of the most eminent men of the day. Rochefoucauld, in his "Tour of the United States," says of her, "Seldom has a woman in any age acquired such ascendancy by the mere force of a powerful intellect, and her influence continued through life."

So grand a leader had plenty of followers, and while there appears to have been no other woman of the time whose influence was as powerful, there were not a few who almost reached the altitude of her rare development. The *morale* of these women penetrated the men of the time with a sinewy courage that neither weakened nor flagged. They enforced their words of cheer by relinquishing prospects of advantage for themselves, renouncing tea and all other imported luxuries, and pledged themselves to card, spin, and weave the clothing of their households, and as far as possible of the army. They gave their own property for the purchase of arms and ammunition for the soldiers, and melted their wealth of pewter ware, in which many of the colonial households were rich, and ran it into bullets for the army. They raised grain, gathered it, and caused it to be ground for bread, that the poor and feeble might be fed.

They visited the hospitals with proper diet for the sick and wounded, sought out the dungeons of the provost and the crowded holds of the prison-ships, with food and medicine in their hands and heroic words on their lips. They unsparingly condemned coldness or backwardness in the nation's cause, and young girls refused the suits of lovers till they had obeyed the call of their country for military service. They received their beloved dead, slain in battle, and forbore to weep, although their hearts were breaking. They even hushed the bitter resentment of their souls, which had been aroused by British invasion, and gave Christian burial to their enemies, who, but for them, at times would not have received it. They trained their little children to the same uncomplaining patience, the same steely endurance, and the same heroic love of liberty which fired their own hearts, until boys and girls gloried in danger and privation. What wonder that the heroes of the Revolutionary War proved invincible!

John Adams, the second President of the Republic, knew the women of the Revolution well, and was able to measure a superior woman wherever he found her, and to estimate her influence. His own wife, Mrs. Abigail Adams, was the personal friend of Mrs. Mercy Warren, and every whit her peer. Her husband was proud to acknowledge her as his equal in all save early education, which was accorded him in large measure and wholly denied her, as she never attended school a day in her life. In one of his letters to his wife Mr. Adams comments on the futile efforts of the British General Howe to obtain possession of Philadelphia, which the colonists foiled for a long time. He writes her, "I do not believe General Howe has a very great woman for a wife. A smart wife would have put Howe in possession of Philadelphia a long time ago."

In the winter of 1780, the resources of the country touched their lowest point, and allowed but the scantiest supply of food and clothing for any one. British cruisers on the coast destroyed every hope of aid from the merchant vessels, and the cup of misfortune pressed to the lips of the struggling colonists overflowed with bitterness. Even the ability of the wealthiest and most generous was exhausted by the repeated drafts made on them. So great was the need of the army, that General Steuben, who had been aid-de-camp to the king of Prussia, and had learned the art of war from the renowned Frederic the Great, declared that "there was not a commander in all Europe who could keep his troops together a week in such suffering and destitution."

But when all despaired the women rallied. All else was temporarily forgotten. The women of Philadelphia went forth from house to house, soliciting money, or whatever could be converted into money. They asked for cloth, garments, and food. Rich women stripped themselves of jewels that were heirlooms in their families, pillaged their parlors of antique bric-a-brac, with the hope that it might find purchasers, and emptied their purses of the last penny they possessed. More than seventy-five hundred dollars in specie were collected, when hard money was at its highest value. One woman cut five hundred pairs of pantaloons with her own hand, and superintended their manufacture. Mrs. Bache, a daughter of Dr. Franklin, was a leading spirit in these patriotic efforts. When a company of French noblemen called on her, she conducted them to her parlor, and showed them a pile of twenty-two hundred shirts for the army, collected by herself, each one marked with the name of the woman who had cut and made it.

Nor was this a mere spasm of helpfulness, that soon died out in forgetfulness and inaction. All through that dreary winter women continued their visits to Washington's camp, fortifying the men with their own inflexible spirit, and tiding them over this darkest passage in their experience, with steady streams of beneficence. They always went laden with comforts for the needy and the sick, and were prepared to serve as cook or seamstress, amanuensis or nurse, equally prompt with hymn or story, Bible-reading or prayer, as occasion demanded.

While the colonial women were a mighty bulwark of strength to the struggling men of the embryo nation, some of them were unforgetful of their own rights, and in advance of the formation of the new government asked for recognition. Abigail Smith Adams, the wife of John Adams of Massachusetts, was a woman of strong convictions, and of large intellectual abilities. She wrote her husband, in March, 1776, then at the Colonial Congress in Philadelphia, and urged the claims of her sex upon his attention, demanding for them representation when the government was organized. She wrote as follows:

"I long to hear that you have declared an independency; and in the new code of laws, which I suppose it will be necessary for you to make, *I desire that you will remember the women, and be more generous and honorable to them than your ancestors.* Do not put such unlimited power in the hands of husbands. Remember all men would be tyrants if they could.

"If particular care and attention are not paid to the ladies, we are determined to foment a rebellion, and *will not hold ourselves bound by any laws in which we have no voice nor representation.* That your sex is tyrannical is a truth so thoroughly established as to admit of no dispute; but such of you as wish to be happy, willingly give up the harsh title of master for the more tender and endearing one of friend. Why then not put it out of the power of the vicious and lawless to use us with cruelty and indignity? Superior men of all ages abhor those customs which treat us as the vassals of your sex."

When the Constitution of the United States was framed without any recognition of the rights of women, the disappointment of Mrs. Adams almost culminated in indignation. She felt most keenly the discrimination of the law against her sex, and wrote her husband again, as follows:

"I cannot say that I think you are very generous to the ladies, for while you are proclaiming peace and good-will to all men, emancipating all nations, you insist on retaining absolute power over wives. But you must remember that absolute power, like most other things which are very bad, is most likely to be broken."

She was especially solicitous that there should be equal advantages of education for boys and girls. "If we mean to have heroes," she writes, "statesmen, and philosophers, we should have learned women." And again, "If you complain of lack of education for sons, what shall I say in regard to daughters who every day experience the want of it!"

Nor were the women of the South forgetful of their rights, and at an early day they also put in a demand for political equality. The counties of Mecklenburg and Rowan in North Carolina blazed with the fiery patriotism of their women. And in their defiant conversations with British officers, who were quartered in the houses of the wealthiest and most intelligent of these Southern matrons, as also in their debates with the men of their own community, officers, judges, and clergymen, they unhesitatingly declared their right to legal equality with men, in the new government, whenever laws should be formulated for the infant republic.

Two years after the Declaration of Independence was adopted, the sister of General Richard Henry Lee, Mrs. Hannah Lee Corbin of Virginia, wrote to her brother, declaring that women should be allowed the franchise, if they paid taxes. He replied that in Virginia women already had the right to vote, and "it is on record that women in Virginia did exercise the right of voting at an early day." On the second day of July, 1776, the right to vote was secured to the women of New Jersey, and they exercised it for over thirty years. Our country began its very existence burdened with the protests of our great fore-mothers against violation of the immortal principles which were its corner-stone. "All just governments derive their powers from the consent of the governed," was the startling announcement the Fathers thundered into the ears of the monarchs of the old world. And many of their wives and daughters contended, with invincible logic, that this axiom included women as well as men.

The long struggle of American women for education, opportunity, and political equality which has since followed, dates, therefore, from the hour of the nation's birth. It is the legitimate outcome of American ideas, for which the nation contended for nearly a century. Absorbed in severe pioneer work, inevitable to life in the wilderness, and denied education themselves, the first care of our revolutionary mothers was for the literary and religious instruction of their children. As far back as the year 1700, a woman, one Bridget Graffort, had given the first lot of ground for a public school-house, although at that time, and for long years after, no provision whatever was made for the education of girls. There was a bitter prejudice against educated and literary women in the early days of our history. And even after five colleges had been founded for young men,—Harvard, Yale, Princeton, Columbia, and William and Mary, Virginia,*—a young woman was regarded as well educated who could "read, write, and cipher."

If, however, school privileges were denied them, the education of the early American women proceeded, through the very logic of events. In laying the foundations of the new government all questions were discussed that touched human interests, not only publicly but privately—from the pulpit, and around the fireside. Women listened to them, and took part in them. The famous book of Mary Wollstonecraft, "A Vindication of the Rights of Woman," was published in Lon-

* Harvard chartered 1650; Yale, 1701; Columbia, 1754; William and Mary, 1693.—Ed.

don in 1790, and found its way into American circles. It received the unsparing condemnation meted out to all efforts put forth in advance of the age, for the world has always stoned its prophets. It demanded for women every opportunity accorded to man, and the same rights in representation, before the law, in the courts, and in the world of work. Torrents of the vilest abuse were heaped on the author, and formed the answer vouchsafed by the public. It educated not a few women, however, who in turn preached the same gospel, and made for women the same demands.

In 1831 the first real grapple began with American slavery, through the establishment of the *Liberator* by William Lloyd Garrison. He flung out his banner, which he never lowered, demanding immediate and unconditional emancipation of the slaves of the South, and after a struggle of forty years, his demand was granted. Slavery was fastened on our coast long before the birth of the republic. In the century before 1776, three and a quarter millions of negroes had been taken by Great Britain from African shores for her various colonies in the new world. And at the close of the Revolutionary War, when the population was but three millions, six hundred thousand of these were black slaves, even then a menace to the peace of the nation. Against the protests of some of the noblest and wisest of the revolutionary patriots slavery, was introduced into the National Constitution in 1787, and was fastened on the national life.

The aggressions of the slaveocracy during the first half century of our national existence alarmed the non-slaveholding portion of the country. And almost at the same time, in the progress of civilization, the era was reached when the enlightened conscience of the civilized world demanded the abolition of slavery. Slowly routed from the dominions of other nations by the manumission of the bondmen, or the purchase of their freedom, slavery seemed at last to have intrenched itself on American soil, and to dominate American civilization. A struggle with it was inevitable. Some of the grandest men and women of the nation entered the lists against it, for the early Abolitionists were remarkable people. It is only necessary to mention the names of some of the leaders in that holy war, to summon up visions of manly beauty and womanly grace, men and women endowed with ability, culture, character, refinement, courage, and social charm. Their public speech blazed with remorseless moral logic, and thrilled with matchless eloquence, so that crowds flocked to hear them, wherever they spoke. Garrison and Phillips, Sumner and Parker, Birney and Pierpont, Gerrit Smith and Theodore Weld—what men of their day surpassed them in manliness, moral force, and persuasive and convincing speech? They were supplemented and complemented by noble women, unlike them, and yet every whit their peers—Maria Weston Chapman and Lydia Maria Child, Sarah and Angelina Grimke, Lucretia Mott and Abby Kelly, Helen Garrison and Ann Greene Phillips. *

Mrs. Chapman and Mrs. Child put to the service of the great reform pens tipped with flame, and wielded with consummate energy and skill. And the Grimke sisters, who had manumitted their slaves in Charleston, S. C., and come North to advocate Antislavery doctrines, with Lucretia Mott and Abby Kelly, entranced large audiences with their eloquent discourse, and roused the dormant moral sense of their hearers into protest against the colossal sin of the nation. Conservatives in church and state were alarmed. War was declared against the eloquent women, and it was decided that they should be silenced, and not allowed to act or vote in the business meetings of the Antislavery Society. This brought about a division in the organization before it had reached its first decade.

A double battle was now forced on the Garrisonian Abolitionists—a battle for the rights of woman as well as for the freedom of the slave. The doctrine of human rights was discussed anew, broadly and exhaustively, and it was demonstrated that the rights of man and woman were identical. Antislavery platforms resounded with the demand that liberty, justice, and equality be accorded to women, and the antislavery press teemed with arguments for women's rights, which are repeated in the woman suffrage meetings of the present time.

In 1840 a "World's Antislavery Convention" was held in London, and all Antislavery organizations throughout the world were invited to join in it, through their delegates. Several American societies accepted the invitation, and elected delegates, six or eight of whom were women, Lucretia Mott and Mrs. Wendell Phillips among them. The excitement caused by their presence in London was intense, for the English Abolitionists were very conservative, and never dreamed of inviting women to sit in their Convention. And these women who had come among them had rent the American Antislavery Societies in twain, had been denounced from the pul-

* See chapter on The Work of Antislavery Women —Ed.

pit, anathematized by the press, and mobbed by the riffraff of the streets. "They who have turned the world upside down have come hither also," was the affrighted cry, nor was the alarm of the English Abolitionists lessened when they saw that those of the women delegates who were not Quakers, clad in the traditional garb of that sect, were young, cultivated, and refined.

A long and acrimonious debate followed on the admission of the women, during which many of the men delegates from America showed the white feather and sided with the English opposition. Again the tyranny of sex was combated, and the doctrine of woman's equality with man enunciated, and again the battle for woman's rights was fought with moral force and logical correctness, as it had been in America the year before. Some of the noblest women of England were in attendance as listeners and spectators,—Elizabeth Fry and Lady Byron, Mrs. Anna Jameson and Mary Howitt,—and, judging by later events, the lesson was not lost upon them. When the vote was taken, the women delegates were excluded by a large majority. William Lloyd Garrison did not arrive in London until after the rejection of the women. When he was informed of the decision of the Convention he refused to take his seat with the delegates. And throughout the ten days' sessions he maintained absolute silence, remaining in the gallery as a spectator. Only one other of the delegates joined him, Nathaniel P. Rogers of Concord, New Hampshire, an editor of an Antislavery paper.

The London Convention marked the beginning of a new era in the woman's cause. Hitherto, the agitation of the question of woman's equal rights had been incidental to the prosecution of other work. Now the time had come when a movement was needed to present the claims of woman in a direct and forcible manner, and to take issue with the legal and social order which denied her the rights of human beings, and held her in everlasting subjection. At the close of the exasperating and insulting debates of the "World's Antislavery Convention," Lucretia Mott and Mrs. Elizabeth Cady Stanton agreed to hold a Woman's Rights Convention on their return to America, and to begin in earnest the education of the people on the question of woman's enfranchisement. Mrs. Stanton had attended the Convention as a bride, her husband having been chosen a delegate.

Accordingly the first Woman's Rights Convention of the world was called at Seneca Falls, New York, on the 19th and

20th of July, 1848. It was attended by crowds of men and women, and the deepest interest was manifested in the proceedings. "Demand the uttermost," said Daniel O'Connell, "and you will get something." The leaders in the new movement, Lucretia Mott and Mrs. Stanton, with their husbands, and Frederick Douglass, acted on this advice. They demanded in unambiguous terms all that the most radical friends of woman have ever claimed: "equal rights in colleges and universities, trades and professions; the right to vote; to share in all political offices, honors, and emoluments; to complete equality in marriage; equal rights in property, in wages for equal work, and in minor children; to make contracts; to sue and be sued; to personal freedom; and to serve on juries, especially when women were tried."

The Convention adjourned to meet in Rochester, New York, August 2, 1848. There were the same crowds in attendance, the same deep interest, and the same earnest debates and discussions as had characterized the meeting at Seneca Falls. Women soon adapted themselves to the situation, increased in efficiency and courage, participated in the debates, and elected a woman president, in spite of the ridicule occasioned by the suggestion. She discharged the duties of the office admirably, and the ridicule was soon merged in applause. A third Convention was held at Salem, Ohio, in 1850; a fourth in Akron, Ohio, in 1851; a fifth in Massillon, Ohio, in 1852; another at Ravenna, Ohio, in 1853, and others rapidly followed. The advocates of woman suffrage increased in number and ability. Superior women, whose names have become historic, espoused the cause—Frances D. Gage, Hannah Tracy Cutler, Jane G. Swisshelm, Caroline M. Severance, Celia C. Burr, who later became Mrs. C. C. Burleigh, Josephine S. Griffing, Antoinette L. Brown, Lucy Stone, Susan B. Anthony, Paulina W. Davis, Caroline H. Dall, Elizabeth Oakes Smith, Ernestine L. Rose, Mrs. C. H. Nichols, Dr. Harriot K. Hunt; the roll-call was a brilliant one, representing an unusual versatility of culture and ability.

The First National Woman Suffrage Convention was held in Worcester, Massachusetts, October 23 and 24, 1850. It was more carefully planned than any that had yet been held. Nine States were represented. The arrangements were perfect—the addresses and papers were of the highest character—the audiences were at a white heat of enthusiasm. The number of cultivated people who espoused the new gospel for women was increased by the names of Ralph Waldo Emerson, Theodore Parker,

Bronson and Abby May Alcott, Thomas W. Higginson, William I. Bowditch, Samuel E. and Harriet W. Sewall, Henry Ward Beecher, Henry B. Blackwell, Ednah D. Cheney, Hon. John Neal, Rev. William H. Channing, and Wendell Phillips. Space fails for a detailed statement of the grand personages who gave of their talents, their wealth, and themselves, that the cause of woman's elevation might be advanced.

Meetings were now of frequent occurrence in various parts of the country. The ridicule of the press, the horror of conservatives, the anathemas of the pulpit, and the ostracism of society began to abate. Petitions to legislatures, that were at first received with derisive laughter, and then laid on the table, now received attention. Unjust laws, that bore down upon women with cruel severity, were modified. And papers established in the interest of women found their way to the people, increased in circulation, and their influence was felt for good. A dozen years were spent in severe pioneer work and then came the four years Civil War. All reformatory work was temporarily suspended, for the nation then passed through a crucial experience, and the issue of the fratricidal conflict was national life or national death.

The transition of the country from peace to the tumult and waste of war was appalling and swift, but the regeneration of its women kept pace with it. They lopped off superfluities, retrenched in expenditures, became deaf to the calls of pleasure, and heeded not the mandates of fashion. Their work was that of relief and philanthropy, and, for the first time in the history of the world, the women of America developed a heavenly side to war. They cared for the needy families of soldiers, nursed the sick in camp and the wounded in hospitals, ministered to the dying in the rear of battle-fields, and kept the channels of beneficence full to overflowing, which extended from Northern homes to the army at the front. For their multiform work they needed immense sums of money, and now the latent business abilities of women began to show themselves.

They went to Washington, and competed with men for government contracts for the manufacture of army clothing, and obtained them. When their accounts and their work were rigorously inspected by the War Department they received commendation, and were awarded larger contracts. They planned great money-making enterprises, whose largeness of conception and good business management yielded millions of dollars, to be expended in the interest of sick and wounded soldiers. The last two of the colossal Sanitary Fairs, held in

New York and Philadelphia, yielded respectively $1,000,000 and $1,200,000. Women were the creators, the inspiration, and the great energizing force of these immense fairs, and also, from first to last, of the Sanitary Commission. Said Dr. Bellows, "There was nothing wanting in the plans of the women of the Commission, that business men commonly think peculiar to their own methods." Men awoke to the consciousness that there were in women possibilities and potencies of which they had never dreamed.

Clara Barton, doing clerical work in a department of the government, and declining to receive compensation therefor, attracted no attention. But Clara Barton in hospitals, and on hospital transports, bringing order out of chaos, hope out of despair, and holding death in abeyance—Clara Barton at Andersonville, where twelve thousand soldiers had succumbed to the horrors of life in the military prison of the enemy and had been ignominiously buried in long trenches, unpitied and unknown, aroused the attention and awakened the gratitude of the nation. For she ordered the trenches opened, the unknown dead exhumed and decently buried, each man in a separate grave, with a headstone recording his rank, his name, and the date of his death, when it could be ascertained.*

Anna Dickinson, working for a pittance in the Philadelphia mint, and making speeches, on occasion, in behalf of the enslaved black man, was regarded as a nuisance. But Anna Dickinson on the platform, with impassioned speech and fervid moral earnestness pleading the cause of the slave before large audiences, and receiving one and two hundred dollars a night for the service—Anna Dickinson in the Connecticut and New Hampshire Republican campaigns, thrilling both States with her eloquence, and capturing both for Abraham Lincoln and Republicanism, became the heroine of the hour, and was hailed as the Joan of Arc of the century.

The development of those years, and the impetus they gave to women, which has not yet spent itself, has been wonderfully manifested since that time. At the close of the war there was but one college open to women, and that was grand old Oberlin in Ohio. Vassar received its first class of students in September, 1865, and now the colleges and universities which admit women are more in number than those which reject them. Dr. Elizabeth Blackwell graduated from a medical college in Geneva, N. Y., in 1849, and afterward had access to the highest instruction and the best *cliniques* in Paris. She

---

* See chapter on Red Cross.

became the pioneer of the great host of women physicians and surgeons, who, since the war, have entered the ranks as medical practitioners, and have been thoroughly trained and duly qualified for their profession. Reverend Antoinette L. Brown was graduated from the theological school at Oberlin, Ohio, in 1850, and ordained in 1853. But not until after the war were theological schools opened to women in the Methodist, Unitarian, Universalist, Christian, and Free Baptist denominations. The United States Census of 1880 gave the number of women ministers as one hundred and sixty-five, resident in thirty-four States. During the last twenty-five years law schools have admitted women, and the National Census of 1880 states the number of women lawyers as seventy-five. The next Census will reveal a great increase in the numbers of women physicians, lawyers, and ministers.*

It has been since the war, and as the result of the great quickening of women which it occasioned, that women have organized missionary, philanthropic, temperance, educational, and political organizations, on a scale of great magnitude. Without much blowing of trumpets, or unseemly boasting, they have overcome almost insuperable obstacles, have brought business abilities to their management of affairs, and have achieved phenomenal success. Their capacity for public affairs receives large recognition at the present time. They are elected, or appointed to such offices as those of county clerk, register of deeds, pension agent, prison commissioner, state librarian, overseer of the poor, school superintendent, and school supervisor. They serve as executors and administrators of estates, trustees and guardians of property, trusts, and children, engrossing clerks of State legislatures, superintendents of women's State prisons, college presidents and professors, members of boards of State charities, lunacy and correction, police matrons, and postmistresses.

They are accountants, pharmacists, cashiers, telegraphers, stenographers, type-writers, dentists, bookkeepers, authors, lecturers, journalists, painters, architects, and sculptors. In many of these positions women serve with men, who graciously acknowledge the practical wisdom and virtue that they bring to their duties. "And although many women have been appointed to positions in departments of government, and to important employments and trusts," said Senator Blair of New Hamp-

---

* See chapters on Woman in the Ministry, Woman in Law, Woman in Medicine.—ED.

shire, from his seat in Congress, "as far as your committee are aware no charge of incompetence or malfeasance in office has ever been sustained against a woman."

Only a little more than a quarter of a century ago women were allowed to enter very few remunerative occupations. In 1836, when Harriet Martineau visited this country, to study its new institutions, that she might be able to forecast the type of civilization to be evolved from them, she especially investigated the position of women in the young republic. She was surprised to find them occupying a very subordinate position in a country calling itself free, and to find that they had entered only seven paying occupations. They were allowed to teach, to be seamstresses, tailoresses, milliners, dressmakers, household servants, and factory operatives. Hon. Carroll D. Wright, Chief of the National Bureau of the Statistics of Labor, in a recent report, has announced the number of remunerative professions and occupations in which women are working as three hundred and forty-two. In the cities of Boston, New York, Philadelphia, Chicago, Minneapolis, and San Francisco, women have established hospitals, and have managed them with admirable wisdom.* Two of the ablest legal journals of the West have been established by women, who are their editors and proprietors.

Side by side with this phenomenal development of women, and always subsidiary to it, when not its direct cause, the movement for woman's enfranchisement has proceeded with deepening earnestness, urged onward by the spur of continual victories. A great host of women have come to regard this as the largest question before the world to-day, and as underlying and involving the just settlement of the great social and moral problems of the time. It is not possible for one sex to settle aright the matters that equally concern both sexes, like questions of marriage and divorce laws, the regulation of the liquor traffic, the management of public schools, the care and cure of insane and criminal people, and many others that may be mentioned. There is not a question casting its shadow athwart the political horizon that is not underlaid by a moral basis, and women have a vital interest in all moral matters. This has greatly extended the area of the woman suffrage debate, and added to its ranks large numbers of able workers, who stood aloof while the reform was treated as an abstraction.

---

* See chapter Hospitals and Training Schools managed by Women.—ED.

It is not possible to rehearse, in detail, the progress of the movement since the close of the war. The brief space allotted in these pages is insufficient for its complete history—volumes would be necessary. There can be recorded here only the briefest mention of its unflagging struggle, and its steady gains, year by year. In 1869, two great National organizations were formed. One styled itself "The National Woman Suffrage Association," and the other was christened "The American Woman Suffrage Association." The first established its headquarters in New York, and published a weekly paper, *The Revolution*, which was ably edited by Mrs. Stanton and Miss Anthony. *The American* made its home in Boston, and founded *The Woman's Journal*, which was edited by Mrs. Mary A. Livermore, Mrs. Julia Ward Howe, Mrs. Lucy Stone, William Lloyd Garrison and Thomas W. Higginson.* The State Woman Suffrage Associations became auxiliary to one or the other of these parent societies, and very frequently to both. "The National" invariably held its annual meetings at Washington, while Congress was in session. "The American" itinerated from State to State, and held its annual meetings where it was thought they would do the greatest amount of missionary work.

After twenty years of separate activities, a union of the two national organizations was effected in 1890, under the composite title of "The National-American Woman Suffrage Association."

These bare statements of fact do not give a hint of the vast labor, sacrifice, and expenditure of time, brain, and money which have been put into the woman's cause during the last quarter of a century. Hundreds of noble men and thousands of earnest women have toiled, unsparing of themselves and their substance, to bring in the day when, for women, law and justice shall be interchangeable terms. Many have died in the harness, reconciled to their discharge from the battle, because they saw from afar the victory which is to infold unborn millions in its benefactions. Others have dropped away from the work from failing health, the pressure of other duties, and some from cessation of interest. But the vacant places have been filled by new recruits, unweary and zealous, who have brought versatile abilities to the service, and have kept the ranks more than full. Other organizations, formed for various purposes, have adopted our cause as their own, and have again

---

* See chapter Woman in Journalism.—Ed.

and again rendered all women their debtors by their generous aid.

Chief among these is the Woman's Christian Temperance Union, with a membership of nearly two hundred thousand, whose greatly beloved president, Frances E. Willard, is as earnest an advocate of the ballot for woman as a temperance measure, as she is for prohibition.* Before she was elected the president of the National Woman's Temperance Union, she had presented a petition with one hundred and eighty thousand signatures to the Legislature of Illinois, asking for the women of the State the right to vote on the question of license or no license in their respective districts. Under her grand leadership that great organization has become a mighty factor in the work for women's enfranchisement. Its large membership, its perfect organization, its loyalty to its president, its relations to the church, its successful publishing house, its ably conducted official paper, *The Union Signal*, with a subscription list of eighty thousand,—all these combined advantages enable it to wield an influence in woman's behalf more effective than all other agencies united.

It has pushed through the legislatures of thirty-seven States and Territories the laws that now compel, in all public schools, instruction in the nature and effect of alcoholic drinks and narcotics on the human system. It has successfully engineered other legislation in many States, concerning other matters in which it is interested—notably the passage of laws forbidding the sale of tobacco to minors under sixteen years of age. It lent a hand toward the enactment of the petition-vote in Texas, for school officers, and in Arkansas and Mississippi, for and against liquor license. What may not be expected of this grand body of women, when it becomes more firmly welded, has grown even more skilled in its work, and more fully conscious of its great power!

The Woman's Journal has recently employed an efficient woman in Washington to make a complete summary of the laws of every State and Territory in the Union, as they affect women's right to vote, or take part in the management of the public schools, either as State or county superintendents, or as members of school boards. She was detailed to this work, and furnished with the sources of information, by Hon. William T. Harris, National Superintendent of Education. Her statements may be relied on, therefore, as accurate, and complete to

---

* See chapter on Woman's Work in the W. C. T. U.—Ed

date. We append this valuable summary, which shows rapid gains in a very short time, and demonstrates an evolution in self-government that cannot stop at any half measure, but must go on yet farther.*

The States and Territories which confer certain rights and privileges upon women are twenty-eight, as follows:

CALIFORNIA—No person shall on account of sex be disqualified from entering or pursuing any lawful business, vocation, or profession. Women over the age of twenty-one years, who are citizens of the United States and of this State, shall be eligible to all educational offices in the State, except those from which they are excluded by the constitution. And more than this, no person shall be debarred admission to any of the collegiate departments of the university on account of sex. [Sch. Law, 1888.]

COLORADO—No person shall be denied the right to vote at any school district election, or to hold any school district office on account of sex. [Sch. Law, 1887.]

CONNECTICUT—No person shall be deemed ineligible to serve as a member of any board of education, board of school visitors, school committee, or district committee, or disqualified from holding such office by reason of sex. [Sch. Law, 1888.]

ILLINOIS—Women are eligible to any office under the general or special school laws. [Sch. Law, 1887.]

INDIANA—Women not married nor minors, who pay taxes, and are listed as parents, guardians, or heads of families, may vote at school meetings. [Decision of attorney-general.] The attorney-general questions the constitutionality of an act to authorize the election of women to school offices, approved April 14, 1881. The State constitution reads, "No person shall be elected or appointed as a county officer who shall not be an elector of the county."

IOWA—No person shall be deemed ineligible, by reason of sex, to any school office in the state. No person who may have been or shall be elected or appointed to the office of county superintendent of common schools, or school director, shall be deprived of office by reason of sex. [Sch. Law, 1888.]

KANSAS—Women over twenty-one years of age, residents of the district, are allowed to vote at district meetings. [Sch. Law, 1885.]

KENTUCKY—Widows qualified to pay taxes, and having

* See APPENDIX E, for Civil Rights of Women.--ED.

children of school age, may vote at elections for district school trustees. [Sch. Law, 1886.]

LOUISIANA—Women over twenty-one are eligible to any office of control or management under school laws of the State. [Constitution, Art. 232.]

MAINE—Women are eligible to the office of supervisor of schools and superintending school committee. [Sch. Law, 1889.]

MASSACHUSETTS—Women are eligible to serve on school committees, and to vote at school meetings for members of school committees. [Sch. Law, 1883.]

MICHIGAN—Women are eligible to election to district offices, to the office of school inspector, and are qualified to vote at district meetings. [Sch. Law, 1885.]

MINNESOTA—Women of twenty-one and over who have resided in the United States one year, and in this State for four months preceding the election, may vote for school officers, or for any measure relating to schools which may come up in school district meetings. Any woman so entitled to vote may hold any office pertaining to the management of schools. [Sch. Law, 1887.]

NEBRASKA—Women twenty-one years of age, resident of the district and owners of property, or having children to educate, may vote in district meetings. [Sch. Law, 1885.]

NEW HAMPSHIRE—Women may vote at school district meetings if they have resided and had a home in the district for three months next preceding such meeting. They may hold town and district school offices. [Sch. Law, 1886.]

NEW JERSEY—Women over twenty-one years of age, resident of the State for one year, and of the county for five months preceding such meeting, may vote at school meetings. They are eligible to the office of school trustee. [Sch. Law, 1887.]

NEW YORK—No person shall be deemed to be ineligible to serve as any school officer, or to vote at any school meeting, by reason of sex, who has the other qualifications now required by law. This permits women to act as school trustees, and to vote at district meetings, if residents of the district, holding taxable property, and over twenty-one years of age. [Sch. Law, 1887.]

OREGON—Women who are widows and have children to educate, and taxable property in the district, shall be entitled to vote at district meetings. [Sch. Law, 1887.]

PENNSYLVANIA—Women twenty-one years of age and upwards

are eligible not only to the office of county superintendent, but to any office of control or management under the school laws of the State. [Sch. Law, 1888.]

RHODE ISLAND—Women can be elected to the office of school committee, and a woman is as eligible as a man for school superintendent. [Sch. Law, 1882.]

VERMONT—Women have the same right to vote as men have in all school district meetings, and in the election of school commissioners in towns and cities, and the same right to hold offices relating to school affairs. [Sch. Law, 1881.]

WISCONSIN—Every woman who is a citizen of this State of the age of twenty-one years or upward (except those excluded by Sec. 2, Art. 3, of the Wisconsin constitution) who has resided within the State one year, and in the election district where she offers to vote, ten days next preceding any election pertaining to school matters, shall have a right to vote at such elections. Every woman of twenty-one years of age and upwards may be elected or appointed as director, treasurer, or clerk of a school district, director or secretary of a town board, under the township system, member of a board of education in cities, or county superintendent. [Sch. Law, 1885.]

ARIZONA TY.—The territorial law provides that no person shall be denied the right to vote at any school district election or to hold any school district office on account of sex. [Biennial Report, 1883–84.]

* DAKOTA TY.—In all elections held under the provisions of this act, all persons who are qualified electors under the general laws of the Territory, and all women of twenty-one years and over, having the necessary qualifications as to citizenship and residence required by the general laws, and who have children of school age under their care or control, are qualified voters. Women having the requisite qualifications are eligible to the office of school director, judge or clerk of election, township clerk, or county superintendent of public schools. [Sch. Law, 1887.]

IDAHO—The right of citizens of any school district to vote at any school election, or upon any school matter, or for county superintendent, or to hold office as school trustee or county superintendent, shall not be denied or abridged on account of sex. [Sch. Law, 1885.]

* MONTANA—Every person, without regard to sex, over twenty-one years of age, resident of a school district, and a taxable inhabitant, is entitled to vote at the annual school meeting for the election of trustees. All persons otherwise quali-

fied are eligible to the office of county superintendent of common schools without regard to sex. [Sch. Law, 1887.]

WASHINGTON—Women over the age of twenty-one years, resident of the school district for three months immediately preceding any district meeting, and liable to taxation, are legal voters at any school meeting. They are also eligible to hold or be elected to any school office. [Sch. Laws, 1885–86.]

WYOMING—Every woman of the age of twenty-one years, residing in the Territory, may, at every election to be holden under the laws thereof, cast her vote, and her rights to the elective franchise and to hold office shall be the same under the election laws of the Territory as those of electors. [Revised Statutes, 1887.]

All States marked with a star, thus (*), were Territories at date of laws. In Montana, those women who pay taxes will vote on all questions submitted to the vote of tax-payers. In Washington and South Dakota, the question of giving women full suffrage is hereafter to be put to vote, and on this question women already qualified as voters for any purpose can also vote. In Kansas, women have now the right to vote at municipal elections, and in Wyoming women have had full suffrage on the same terms as men for twenty years. The constitution of Wyoming, besides the equal suffrage provision, establishes the reading test, as in Massachusetts, and the Australian ballot for voters. At this present time of writing, Wyoming's admission to the Union as a State is pending in Congress. The House of Representatives has voted the Territory qualified for statehood, and to give her admission. It is believed the Senate will confirm this action and that the bill will be signed by the President, when Wyoming will enter the sisterhood of States with equal suffrage for men and women incorporated in her constitution.*

The States and Territories which, according to the latest issue of their school laws, do not give women any voice in school affairs are nineteen, viz.: Alabama, Arkansas, Delaware, Florida, Georgia, Maryland, Mississippi, Missouri, Nevada, North Carolina, South Carolina, Ohio,† Tennessee, Texas, Virginia, West Virginia, Alaska, Indian Territory, and New Mexico.

In Texas, the school officers are chosen by petitions to the

* Wyoming was admitted to statehood, with equal suffrage for men and women incorporated in her constitution, by an Act of Congress, July, 1890.

† And yet coeducation had its birth in Ohio (Oberlin, 1833).—ED.

county judge for their appointment, and he appoints those whose petitions are most largely signed. These petitions women can sign on the same terms as men, and thus practically vote without leaving home. The question of liquor license is decided in Arkansas and Mississippi in the same manner. In the territory of Utah women had full right to the elective franchise, and to hold office for many years. But in the winter of 1886–87, women suffrage was abolished, and the Territory redistricted for voting purposes. This was done by the Edmunds bill as a means to destroy polygamy. In Washington, women had exercised the right of suffrage conferred on them by the territorial legislature for two or three years. They were deprived of it by the decision of a territorial judge, some two years since, who gave an adverse decision on the question, when it came before him. His unjust act was performed in the interest of the liquor saloons, whose hostility to woman suffrage is immitigable everywhere.

It will be seen, therefore, that there are thirty-one States and Territories which have conferred the franchise on women in some form, from the petition-vote of Texas, Mississippi, and Arkansas, to the full suffrage exercised by the women of Wyoming for twenty years. This has been accomplished not by the fanaticism of a few abnormal and unbalanced women, as many superficial objectors declare. It is the legitimate outgrowth of the principles of Republican government, and has come naturally from the evolution of woman as a human being, which has proceeded through the ages. No one who has studied the question can lack faith in its ultimate success, and the beneficent results it is sure to accomplish. For the ballot in the hands of woman is the synonym of her legal equality with man, and legal justice has always preceded social equity. Woman has wrought more of good than evil in the world during her ages of ignorance, bondage, and degradation. What then may not be expected from her in righteousness and helpfulness, when she is accorded freedom, equity, and opportunity!

XI.

WOMAN IN INDUSTRY.

BY

ALICE HYNEMAN RHINE.

IN treating of woman's industrial career in America the subject falls naturally into periods, each one of which seems to possess some distinct characteristic. These periods can in no sense be considered arbitrary divisions, for the changes in woman's industrial position in America have been the result of slow transitions from one state to another. The fact that is emphasized is, that certain causes can be observed which had the effect at stated times of forcing old conditions to give way to new. By taking up in their order each of these epoch-shaping factors, we can discern most easily the part women have played in the progress of American industries.

The first of these periods embraces those years of primitive social conditions when people labored to supply the simplest needs of life; when men were engaged principally in agriculture and commerce, and women carried on the work of manufacturing clothing, and attending to the wants of the household. In those days, almost every family owned a loom, spinning-wheel, reel and knitting-needles, and the family comfort depended largely on the degree of skill and industry with which these manufacturing implements were handled. In some homes, hundreds of yards of "homespun" were made yearly. The New York *Mercury* for 1768 credits one family, living in Newport, Rhode Island, with having within four years "manufactured nine hundred and eighty yards of woolen cloth, besides two coverlids (coverlets), and two bed-ticks, and all the stocking yarn of the family."

In those days neither wealth nor position afforded women an excuse for idleness. Nor did their labors cease with the home. It was considered so unbecoming to be unemployed that even hours of social enjoyment were devoted to useful occupations. During the enforcement of the non-importation acts, when, among other things, cloth and stockings were prevented from coming into this country from England, a letter written from Newport tells of a social gathering where "it was resolved that those who could spin ought to be employed in that way, and those who could not, should reel." At a similar meeting in Boston, "a party of forty or fifty young women, calling themselves 'Daughters of Liberty,'" amused themselves at the house of their pastor with spinning, during one day, "two hundred and thirty-two skeins of yarn, some very fine." No woman considered herself too elegant

To guide the spindle and direct the loom,

or knit the stockings which, since stocking-frames were interdicted as articles of import, had to be made for the whole people by slow process of hand. As indicative of the simple and industrial habits of Mrs. Washington, it is related that when, in 1780, a party of the leading ladies of Morristown called upon her by appointment at her husband's headquarters, Mrs. Washington appeared before them in a plain gown of "linsey woolsey," and, while she entertained them with pleasant conversation, her busy fingers never ceased plying the knitting-needles.

Prior to and long after the Revolution, stocking knitting was an industry large enough to claim most of what were termed woman's "spare moments." With the assistance of child and slave labor, large quantities were made for sale or exchange. Legislators, to stimulate busy fingers to fresh exertions, offered bounties for their increased production. In Virginia, prizes of fifty pounds of tobacco (the currency then) were given "for every five hundred pairs of men's and women's stockings produced, worth from three to five shillings the pair, with the privilege of buying them at an advance of seventy-five per cent. on those prices."

Except among a few German settlers in Pennsylvania, no attempt was made for many years to change stocking-making from a domestic into a factory industry. Until 1826 the manufacture of stockings remained woman's almost exclusive province. Then knitting-machines were set up in several of the States, but, as if there was some peculiar fitness in this remaining woman's department, the employees in knitting-works have always been, even down to 1889, "nearly all women and children."

Never did women work harder than during this domestic

period of labor. The slave women of the South, in addition to going through all the processes of manufacturing woolen and cotton cloth, which they afterward cut and made into garments, attended to both in and out-of-door labor. They tilled the rice fields, planted tobacco, sowed the cotton seed, and helped with the harvesting. The women in the North, though not "put into the ground," as the early adventurers termed field-work, engaged energetically in other industries. History tells of women who helped build their own homes, wielding the ax and carrying the water to mix mortar with which to build chimneys. On the farms, it was women who raised the garden truck of vegetables and herbs, attended to poultry breeding, milked the cows, made butter and cheese, did the sewing, and performed all the household chores now classed in industrial statistics as "domestic service."

Outside the strictly necessary occupations of manufacture, household service, clothing, and garden-work, from quite early times women in America turned their attention to speculative labor and to trade. When James the First, thinking to utilize mulberry trees that were indigenous to our soil, forwarded silk-worm cocoons to America, when dazzling dreams of wealth to come from the successful culture of the silkworm were indulged in by people on both sides of the Atlantic, and when bounties of money and tobacco were offered for spun and woven silk, according to its weight and width, most of these prizes were obtained by women. The success obtained by women in feeding the worms, and reeling, spinning, and weaving the silk, caused this industry, during the varying fortunes that preceded the establishment of silk-weaving as a factory industry, to be carried on mainly by them. History has preserved the names of three women famous before the Revolution as silk-growers and weavers: Mrs. Pinckney, Grace Fisher, and Susanna Wright. While silkworm culture was a failure in spite of all the fostering care bestowed upon it, and none of the pioneers realized any of the golden visions of rivaling the productions of Spain and the Indies, the efforts made by them paved the way for future cultivation.

Along with the silk industry, another of scarcely less importance was growing up quietly in New England. This was the manufacture of straw goods, the products of which now amount to many millions annually. Straw, applied to so many purposes to-day, owes its origin as an article of manufacture to a young Massachusetts girl. In 1789 Miss Betsy Metcalf discovered the secret of bleaching and braiding the meadow-grass of her native town of Dedham, and of ingeniously making this braid into a bonnet. Although scarcely more than a child, the chronicles tell that she taught others to do what she had done, and started a business by which the want of bonnets and hats for summer-wear was supplied. From using straw for head-gear, its manufacture spread to other things, and developed an industry that, in 1880, employed nearly eleven thousand operatives. Of these over seven thousand were women.

Whether it was the active out-door life led by the American women of the eighteenth century, or the wide-awake interest circumstances obliged them to take in the concerns of the family and of men; whether the stirring times in which they moved, or the deferential attitude of men stimulated them to do things that the women of other nations were not doing, it is certain that the American women of a century ago were far in advance of their times in all things except a knowledge of light literature, which the circulating libraries of Europe placed within the reach of women there, and a scarcity of books denied them here. That this was more of a gain than loss, by giving women time to think, is shown in the energy with which they went to work in helping to build up the nation. They engaged in mercantile affairs with such success that, it is said, "many Boston fortunes owed their rise to women." The active interest taken by them in politics gave, even before the Revolution, some representative women to journalism." Out of the seventy-eight newspapers published in the colonies, sixteen were edited by women, and all but two of them championed the cause of liberty and justice. The first paper to publish the Declaration of Independence was edited and printed by a Mrs. Reid. In medicine, women confined themselves into distilling herbs into remedies which it was said "could kill or cure with any of the faculty." In the practice of midwifery, history has preserved the name of a Mrs. Robinson, of New London, who continued to practice to an advanced age, and who "delivered twelve hundred mothers without losing a patient."

The inventive faculty, so distinctive a trait in the character of the American man, was also a gift of the American woman. How many women were inventors will never be known, as they timidly shielded their identity behind men. This is said to have been the case with the cotton-gin. Credited through all the years to Eli Whitney, modern writers claim that it was the fruit of the inventive powers of Mrs.

Nathaniel Green,* widow of Gen. Green of revolutionary fame. The story runs that Mrs. Green, a native of Rhode Island and familiar with the working of the anchor forge belonging to her husband's father, set her wits to work while visiting her Georgia plantations, to lessen the labor of cleansing the cotton. When this difficulty was solved, she permitted Mr. Whitney to claim the patent, through fear of the ridicule of her friends and loss of social position recognition of her work might have entailed.

By whomever invented, no other instrument has been so fruitful of consequences. In 1793, when the cotton-gin was made, cotton, instead of being King, was a humble garden plant, grown for home consumption in the regions from Georgia to New Jersey. When its snowy blossoms ripened, women gathered them, plucked the seeds from the fiber, and got it ready for spinning. So difficult was this process, that to remove the seed from one pound was considered a good day's work. By the operation of the cotton-gin, in the time it had taken to cleanse one pound, three hundred-weight could be got ready for market. By this, cotton was transformed at once into a valuable commercial product that required for its successful cultivation an enormous increase of land and labor. It instilled such new life into the almost dying institution of slavery that the cotton-gin may well be said to have been the foster-mother of slavery in America.

As the immediate effect of the cotton-gin in the South was to give an enormous value to the slave, its invention was followed in the North by the cotton factory. The cotton factory was the northern complement of the cotton-gin. To women it had the momentous results of transferring them from the home to the factory; of taking them out of the family farm-house to the manufacturing towns and villages, and, by making them for the first time the wage-earning competitors of men, altering their whole status in the labor market of America.

With the factory came a new epoch for women in America. The War of the Revolution and the War of 1812 had been ended long enough to induce a general feeling of security concerning the future of the republic. For a large number of people, the hard work and deprivations of the past were as a dream; peace and plenty promised to abound. Wealth came

---

* "Women as Inventors." Mrs. Gage, *North American Review*, 1883, p. 478.

flowing from all directions in a steady stream into the country through the various channels of commerce and agriculture. Numerous business enterprises were undertaken, principal among which were the factories for weaving cotton and wool into cloth. The earliest of these was built in Massachusetts, where numerous swift-flowing rivers abound, capable of being utilized for moving machinery. Through the energetic, progressive spirit of the descendants of the Puritans, it was not long before New England began to rival Old England in manufacturing the increased production of cotton grown in the United States. The first cotton mill erected in Lowell, Massachusetts, in 1822, was followed so quickly by others, that by 1839 there were in Lowell ten companies incorporated with a capital of $13,000,000. These produced 2,463,000 yards of cloth per week, of which all but 91,000 were cotton. The number of operatives employed were 12,507, and in the cotton mills the majority of these were women. From the amount of capital invested and the number of operatives employed, Lowell was termed, in the period between 1840 and 1850, "the Manchester of America."

But in nothing—except that Lowell and Manchester were places filled with the hum of machinery tended by human workers for their own livelihood and the profits of others—was there any resemblance between Manchester and Lowell. The recorded condition of the English operatives, especially women, at that time reads like a page torn from some canto of Dante's "Inferno;" while that of Lowell, pictured by women who worked as ordinary mill-hands in the Lowell factories, seems in comparison like a Utopian idyl evolved from the brain of dreamers.

According to writers, the women operatives who entered the Lowell mills came from the New England farms, not from stress of circumstances, but to get wage-money to help lift a mortgage from the family farm, or to assist some son or brother in obtaining an otherwise impossible university education. A large majority entered the mills to secure independence, or household and dress adornments. Not a few entered so as to be near circulating libraries and schools, with the opportunities for self-culture which these afforded. Coming from the agricultural class, which considered itself among the aristocracy of America,* no class distinctions were made, and the factory

* "For generations," writes Johnstone, in his 'History of Connecticut,' "merchants and mechanics had been outranked by farmers."

young women were welcomed into the best social circles of Lowell. Well but simply dressed, as was the fashion of the times, they were to be seen at church, Sunday-schools, and social gatherings at the parsonages and elsewhere, receiving the same consideration as those whom circumstances had placed above the need of work. The girls themselves felt no loss of caste or diminution of self-respect. Most of them expected to marry—many did—and withdraw from the factory, and failing this, when factory work became disagreeable, to retire to the family home. The factory was an episode, not, as it later became too frequently elsewhere, the burden of this chapter in woman's life.

The factories *per se* were as remarkable as the women who operated them. Kept as clean as the nature of the work would admit, with plants growing in the windows trained to shade the glass, the rooms seemed redolent of the country. Fronting one side of the building were the banks and waters of the swift-flowing Merrimac, which, as it hastened on to meet the sea, turned the wheels of the machinery, ignorant as yet of steam. On the other was the bright, new village, looking, as Dickens said in 1843, "as if every kind of store had taken down its shutters for the first time and started in business yesterday." Standing on the hill was the prettiest building in the place, which was the hospital where girls when sick were tenderly cared for. Those unable to pay the weekly charge of three dollars, had it provided for them by the corporations. Seldom were the latter put to this expense, for Yankee girls had a horror of being placed under money obligations. Boarding-houses, erected by the mill-owners, were given in charge of reputable women. The charge for board in them, including the mid-day meal,—which was taken in civilized fashion at the boarding-house tables,—and washing to a certain extent, was fixed at the small sum of $1.50. Wages, counting in those of the little doffers, averaged $3.75 per week. Weavers, drawing-in girls, warpers, and spinners, who tended extra work, could earn from six to eight dollars per week. These wages, with the low price of board and the economical style of dress common in those days, enabled the mill operatives to place a large part of their earnings in the savings bank established for their use by the corporations. In 1841, one hundred thousand dollars, a sum which was a source of pride to all concerned, was deposited to the credit of the girls of Lowell.

Happy in their social position, and in the good feeling existing between employers and employed, free from pecuniary care for the necessities of life and in command of some of the best luxuries, the Lowell girls reached an intellectual height unique in the history of industrial workers. When the twelve or fourteen hours that then constituted a day's work were ended, buoyant with the health of generations of out-door workers, the Lowell women were fresh enough to enjoy in various ways what was left of their evenings. In most of the boarding-houses there were pianos, the joint property of the girls. Some played, others sang. Books were read, topics discussed, and poems, stories, and essays written. These formed the pages of the "Lowell Offering," a monthly magazine composed entirely of articles by the girls. The literary merit of these articles astonished people from abroad. Harriet Martineau republished some of them in England under the title of "Mind among the Spindles," while Dickens claimed that, independent of the fact that the articles were written by girls after a long, hard day's work in factories, they "compared favorably with those of many English periodicals." In character, the stories differed from the sentimental love-tales common to women's writings of that period. Simple in style, they were mostly descriptive of human life and the beauties of nature that the girls had left behind them, and what was best in their Lowell environments. Among the contributors, who attained national reputation, were Lucy Larcom, the poet; Margaret Foley, the sculptor, and Mrs. H. H. Robinson, the author.* These women always spoke with affectionate respect of their factory experiences. Mrs. Robinson, at the International Council of Women, held at Washington in 1888, after telling how she had entered the Lowell mills as a "doffer" when a child, and remained there until she married in 1848, said: "I consider the Lowell mills my *alma mater*, and am as proud of them as most girls of the colleges in which they have been educated."

When factory towns sprang up in the suburbs of the large cities of New York, Pennsylvania, New Jersey, etc., they did so under conditions different from those of Lowell, and, of course, had other results. There was no need in these places for corporations to offer exceptional wages and treatment to women to induce them to enter the mills. Already at hand, and eager to accept any conditions, were the thousands of

* Material for the account of Lowell has been taken from Mrs. H. H. Robinson's interesting paper on Early Factory Life in New England, Dickens's American Notes, Lowell Offering, and Appleton's American Cyclopædia.

women who had been deposited on the shores of America by the tidal wave of immigration, which set in from Europe during the decade of 1845–55. For these women, who labored for bread and butter and not for knick-knacks, no effort was made, as in Lowell, to surround them with a favorable social atmosphere. How women spent their evenings, what were their pleasures or sorrows and how they lived, in a country where the necessities of life were dear, on their weekly wages of $2.63 to $4.99 per week (the average wages of factory women from 1850 to 1860), was inquired into by none. Employers and employed both felt that all responsibilities began and ended with the money given and received on pay-days.

This indifference concerning working-women was not confined to the factory, but was so general that even the National Census Report did not take the trouble to classify woman's work separately from man's, until it was found that in some departments of industry women exceeded men in point of numbers almost in the ratio of two to one. In the cotton factories of twenty-five States, in 1850, the number of women employed was 62,661, against 32,295 men. In 1860, the average number employed in the cotton factories was, according to official returns, 75,169 women against 46,859 men. It was computed that in the woolen goods manufactories of the six New England States, there were 29,886 men and 51,517 women employed. Hosiery, an industry belonging to women since days when Shakespeare wrote of

> The knitters in the sun,
> And the free maids who weave their thread with bones,

employed in 1860 almost three times as many women as men. Large numbers of women made rubber clothing. Half as many women as men were engaged in the manufacture of paper. Women filled places in bookbinderies, printing offices, and newspaper establishments. The number of women engaged in domestic service (never an exactly ascertainable quantity) formed a bulk equal to the factory population; while the ranks of needle-women were, as usual, larger than all of those industries combined, excepting domestic service. In 1850, the number of women engaged in the making of men's and boys' clothing alone numbered 61,500; the number of men being 35,061. In 1860, owing to the invention of the sewing-machine, these figures were partially reversed; the number of women employed was diminished and that of men increased.

The sewing-machine was one of several factors that about 1860 inaugurated for women another industrial period. From its invention by Elias Howe the sewing-machine properly belonged to 1846, but the business of making and selling them was not fairly started before 1853. Then the sales of all the manufacturers amounted to only 2529. In 1860 they had reached to about 50,000. This increase showed that the sewing-machine results must be dated from the year of its acceptance into popular favor. Mr. Howe's invention, like all other labor-saving machines, intended to be a blessing by lightening the burdens of workers, proved a curse by taking away their accustomed pursuit from those who depended on the skill by which they drove

The patient needle through the woven threads.

Brought into competition with machines that could do more and better work in one day than was possible for six women, working twenty hours apiece, to accomplish, these had either to starve, or force their way into some other wage-earning industry. An example of how this displacement affected needle-women can be gleaned from Appleton's Cyclopædia for 1862, which cites a single establishment in New York, employing four hundred machines and producing about ten thousand shirts a week, whose estimated savings (in wages) were about $240,000 per annum. In the same year, the following sums were saved in wage-time by the sewing-machines in the manufacturing industries :

Men's and boys' clothing in New York City	$7,500,000
Hats and caps	462,500
Shirt bosoms	832,750

Calculating that each machine did the work of six girls, and estimating that one girl operated each machine, there were 73,290 women displaced by the machines on which these savings were made.

Contemporary with the general acceptance of the sewing-machine, and intensifying the distress of the wage-worker, was the Civil War, which, in 1860, began to decimate the ranks of men and to convert into wage-earners large numbers of women who had been wage-expenders. Delicate women in the South, reared in affluence, waited upon by slaves, were thrown, by losses of male relatives and property, among the bread-winners. Numbers of these journeyed to Northern cities to hide their poverty as well as to gain entrance into the larger field of industries the North was supposed to offer. But here they were met by thousands of other women, native to the North, who, like their sisters of the South, through the death of those who had hitherto fought the battle of life for them, were obliged to become producers in the place of being consumers.

The distress experienced by workers of this class wrought that great revolution in thought which involved the education of women. This is one of the accepted factors of the present period. At that time agitation was rife as to what should be done for the advancement of women as workers. Miss Virginia Penny, in a book called "Think and Act,"* advocated the entrance of women into the trades and professions that were monopolized by men. "Apprentice," she says, "ten thousand women to watchmakers; train ten thousand for teachers to the young; make ten thousand good accountants; put ten thousand more to be deaconesses trained by Florence Nightingale; put some thousands in the electric telegraph offices all over the country; educate one thousand lecturers for mechanics' institutes; one thousand to read the best books to the working-people; train up ten thousand to manage washing-machines, sewing-machines, etc. Then the distressed needle-woman will vanish, the decayed gentlewoman and broken-down governess cease to exist."

Writers like Gail Hamilton in the North and Catherine Cole in the South urged the higher education of women; their right to be educated the same as man; "to enter the same pursuits, receive the same wages, occupy the same posts and professions, wield the same influence, and, in a word, be independent of man as a means of support."

These strangely reasonable, though novel propositions, met with as much public condemnation at the time as though, in place of being suggestions for elevating women into skillful, rational workers, they had advocated turning them into gamblers and drunkards. The fact was ignored that the majority of women had always been engaged in carrying on some kind of necessary industry, if only in untaught, helpless ways. Hence it became fashionable to say that "woman as a worker was a product of modern times." Her entrance into the ranks of wealth-producers and wage-earners was called the "New Departure," and was deplored by writers as calculated, by thwarting nature's evident design in making her child-bearer, child-trainer, and house-mother, to rob her of special gifts of

* "Think and Act," "Men and Women," "Work and Wages." Virginia Penny, 1869.

grace, beauty, and tenderness. The error of the day, it was argued, lay in the thought that woman should be self-supporting, and she was implored to stop and consider what homes would become,

> Where woman reigns, the mother, daughter, wife,
> Strews with fresh flowers the narrow way of life,

if "woman was to take her place beside man in every field of coarse, rough toil."

The peculiarity of these arguments, intended to dissuade women from being workers, was, that while poets, philosophers, and essayists were picturing women as weak, tender creatures, clinging for protection to man as the vine to the oak, the lovely presiding geniuses of homes, the expenders of wealth produced by man, there were, according to the census of 1860, one million women working by the side of men in various domains of "coarse, rough toil." These writers, clergymen for the most part, made the mistake, common to people in comfortable circumstances, of looking on the small, glittering world of dazzling drawing-rooms and boudoirs, where an elegant, dainty womanhood presides, as "woman's world." Living in this, they became blinded to that other, larger world of women without homes, with no time for the cultivation of the graces or personal adornment, who were obliged to work if they would live.

According to the newspapers of 1867 and of 1870, out of seventy thousand women (wage-earners) in the city of New York, not including domestics, twenty thousand were in a constant fight with starvation and pauperism. Seven thousand lived in cellars. Those who got sewing to do worked from seven in the morning until midnight making shirts at six cents apiece. The most rapid workers could scarcely, even with those long hours, make one dozen shirts and thus earn their seventy-two cents per day. The pay for drawers, undershirts, and blouses was in proportion. We read that in Boston there were, in 1868, "twenty thousand women working at starvation rates; eight thousand workers at twenty to twenty-five cents per day, twelve thousand workers for less than fifty cents, and even at these rates there was little work." These women lived at times, it is said, "on one cracker a day for breakfast, dinner, and supper," working from "dawn to dawn" to "get one mouthful of food." In this same year, the New York journals reported thirty thousand girls struggling in that city with starvation and cold, making shirts and furnishing the thread at sixpence each. The condition of seventy-five thousand working women in the city beggared description. The New York *Herald* described them as living in "nasty tenement houses, in cellars unfit for human habitation, in pools of foulness, where every impurity is matured and every vice flourishes." Women who could get sewing-machines worked at them for $2.50 per week, and the forty-one cents per day that they earned represented the work, if not the wages, of six other women.

The helplessness, the misery, the degradation of womanhood, laboring and starving on beggarly wages in rich and prosperous cities, arrested the attention of the thinking class to woman's needs as it has never been arrested before. How to help woman to better her condition became, in 1868, one of the burning questions of the day. Gail Hamilton, Mrs. Stephens, Miss Penny, and others, attributed the distress of the factory and needle-women to the lack of educational training which obliged women to crowd into occupations requiring little, if any, skill. To remedy this, the establishment of industrial schools was advocated. Men, it was reasoned, had their trades' apprenticeship system, schools, and universities, by which they were educated into a knowledge of many things; and by applying the same method to women, giving some thousands of them a professional training in each of the various trades, arts, and sciences useful to mankind, the ranks of the factory-seekers and needle-women in search of employment would be thinned sufficiently to cause the anomaly to vanish of millions of adult human beings laboring as men for the pay of children, and yet paying as men for whatever they got. Other remedies agitated were those of woman suffrage and the organization of women into societies for mutual protection and benefit.

Small private attempts at industrial schools for the advancement of women, such as the "Wilson Industrial School" in New York, had been started by the benevolence of individuals as early as 1856; but the first serious attempt to give practical shape to the question of higher education for women was undertaken when Peter Cooper made the advantages of the institute founded by him and bearing his name, free in all its departments, to women as to men. The Cooper Institute, opened to the public in 1859, had its free art classes for women, where art was taught in its application to the industries. The Cooper Art School is said to be, even now, "the largest in the world for women." From its inception a few women were found ready to avail themselves of the opportunity given them to study art in its various income-producing forms. But not until after the close of the war, when conditions made it urgent upon women to work on new lines, did the classes increase to any extent. (Then hundreds more than could be accommodated applied for admission.) Names were placed in the roll-book a year ahead, and the classes, through their increased size, overflowed into rooms not intended for their use. The number of students in the free art classes, for the season of 1889–90, was 310. For this season there were 693 applicants for admission to the free art classes. The accommodations do not admit of but few over 300.

In this one phase of work accomplished for women in the United States, there was much that was attractive to the class drawn into the Cooper Institute, a class that belonged neither to the rich nor to the extremely poor. The large, light, airy rooms were formed, many of them, into charming studios, filled with tasteful studies, articles of bric-a-brac, stuffs, and, occasionally, growing plants. Books, pictures, and engravings on art were supplied them in the art rooms. Descending three flights of broad stone steps, lined on each side with studies in plaster and on paper, there was the free library, a room of magnificent proportions, 125 x 30 feet, glass-domed, and containing 21,276 bound volumes, nearly 5000 unbound, and having always on file 189 magazines and 393 of the best newspapers, American and foreign. It can be imagined what godsends these treasures of art and literature were to women of talent, whose work had hitherto been conducted without any, or the most meager, advantages. To add to their value, the work of training pupils was intrusted to teachers capable of drawing out latent possibilities. The line of industrial work done in the Cooper Institute consisted of the arts of design as applied to making patterns for stained glass, wall-papers, oil-cloths, textile fabrics, carpets, and adapting the patterns of Oriental rugs for the American market. Other forms of art consisted in coloring photographs, portrait crayon drawing, and in late years wood-engraving, for which women developed an unusual aptitude. When pupils attained sufficient proficiency in any of these branches, they were permitted to add to their incomes by executing orders from business firms for pay. Profits from this source almost maintained some of the most expert during their last school years. The students in 1889, and the graduates of May, 1888, earned in this way, during the year, $17,805.

A wise discretionary power given the trustees of the Cooper Institute, "to add such other art or trade to the curriculum as would tend to furnish women with suitable employment," led to the establishment, in 1869, of a class in telegraphy and in 1884, of a stenographic and type-writing class. Both of these combined, educated about one hundred women yearly in those professions. The expense of carrying on all the departments of woman's work was, in 1889, one-fifth of the whole expenses of the building, and barely reached $10,000—an outlay surprisingly small for the equipment of about four hundred women, educated to maintain themselves, and influence, by teaching and example, the minds of the many with whom they come into contact.

Significant as was the work performed by this institution, devoted to art and science, it was, nevertheless, felt by charitable individuals that something more was needed in the way of instruction for the mass of women who toiled without chance of coming within the sphere of its beautiful influence. Wealthy philanthropists, whose sympathies were touched by the lives of the workers, sought to help women in many other ways. The Young Women's Christian Association of New York recognized early the necessity of educating self-supporting women in many of the skilled industries. This association, which, of late years, has become a power for good in almost all the large cities of the United States, instituted in New York, as part of its plan of work, free classes for training women in commercial arithmetic, penmanship, book-keeping, and type-writing. An industrial department was created for teaching dressmaking in all its branches of cutting, fitting, hand and machine sewing. In imitation of the Cooper, art classes were formed for teaching the retouching of photo-negatives, photo-coloring, mechanical and free-hand drawing, modeling, and design. To still further carry out its program "to care for the temporal, mental, and moral welfare of the self-supporting women of New York City," a free library was attached to the building and a series of free concerts, readings, and lectures provided for. Through these and other means of physical culture, Bible and choir classes, employment bureaus, board directories, and a department for the sale of goods made in sewing-classes, about five thousand persons were reached during the year of 1887. The number of pupils in all classes was reported as 965. But with the best intentions, this organization, like the Cooper, failed to reach the women who live and work in the city's slums. Its applicants were those who had first graduated from the public schools and then, helpless as babes, had availed themselves of the splendid opportunity it offered for gratuitous instruction in some wage-earning industry. When Miss Graffenried, of the United States Labor Bureau for 1889, went among the women in tenements, factories, and shops, out of three thousand interviewed, she said, "Not one was known to have come under the influence of this noble organization."

Besides schools such as the Cooper and the Woman's Christian Union, that were specially designed for educating women in industrial trades, so many other ways were thought out for bettering their condition, that one might well call the years from 1868 on, the philanthropic era for women. So numerous were the societies started for their relief that scarcely a need existed that an organization of some kind did not attempt to fill, and each in its particular way emphasized Emerson's truth, "there is more kindness in the world than ever was spoken." Through the efforts of a few liberal-minded, energetic men and women, there was established in New York, in 1868, a society called the "Working Woman's Protective Union," that purposed to provide "women with legal protection against the frauds and impositions of unscrupulous employers, to assist them in procuring employment, and to secure them such suitable departments of labor as are not occupied by them." From the start, the novel work done by this society was appreciated by the class it was intended to help. Perfectly unsectarian, with all its services *gratis*, the rooms, first on Bleecker Street, and for the past twenty years on Clinton Place, were thronged by women in distress desirous of legal counsel, matronly advice, or help to better work. At all times chance visitors could see women waiting in the front room, while the superintendent gave sympathetic ear in the rear apartment to some earlier comer. One day in each week was known as "complaint day." On that day the legal representative of the Union received and examined the complaints that the superintendent deemed worthy of prosecution. What the society has done in the twenty-five years of its existence is summed up in the statement that on an annual outlay of $5000 it has fought and won the legal battles of 12,000 women, who would otherwise have been defrauded of their hard-earned wages by unscrupulous employers. It has collected by legal processes $41,000, in sums averaging $4 each, and supplied in twenty-five years more than 300,000 applicants with employment, advice, or relief. As many of these applications were made by the same person three or four different times, there were represented, perhaps, 10,000 applicants annually. It was of this society that Henry Ward Beecher said the Union's greatest and best work was "the mere fact of its existence," as this fact made employers more careful in withholding from the working-woman her just dues.

When a plan to redress a wrong succeeds, it is sure to have imitators. Societies in other cities followed the example of the Woman's Protective Union, and some of these branched out in directions unthought of by the founders of the parent institution. The Woman's Educational and Industrial Union, in Boston, besides securing wages unjustly withheld from working-women, added the task of investigating advertisements for work to be done at home, and, if found fraudulent, warning women against them. It procured situations for the unemployed ; sold on commission the fruits of woman's work ; opened a lunch-room where women could have varied bills of fare at moderate prices, or where they could sit and eat the luncheons brought from home. It included in its scope the instruction of women in various points of law, such as those regarding the relations between employer and employed, the hiring of rooms, and the detention of property. It detailed agents to look up titles to furniture that, by means of mortgage or insufficient payment of the installments, might not belong to the seller. A feature was made of holding lectures and mothers' meetings, the purpose of the talks being to lead women into higher planes of thought and action. One of the most active endeavors was made in the line of securing the appointment of police matrons in large cities.*

The honor of originating the parent Woman's Protective Union in New York belongs to men ; but the establishment of both similar and widely different societies in the United States is due to the zealous energy of women themselves. The Woman's Club in Chicago instituted, in 1866, a Protective Agency that had for its objects the protection of woman's purity and honor, and her deliverance from swindlers and extortionists. In the first year of its existence, it examined 156 complaints, fifty-one of which were claims for money,—chiefly wages. These aggregated $992.89. It is said to be the design of this agency "to establish in the near future a loan fund for the benefit of those in need of temporary assistance, and who, under existing conditions, are obliged to pay usurious interest for money."

Better than anything else, philanthropic work undertaken by

---

* See chapter, Aid for the Criminal Classes.—Ed.

women in America shows the difference between past and present generations. A few decades ago, woman's attention was absorbed in organizing small, local, sectarian sewing societies, Sunday-school classes, and church fairs. After the Civil War these few circumscribed channels no longer sufficed for woman's activity, and an expansion took place that made itself felt in the organization of societies for working-women. These took no heed of sects, restricted in no way the compass of the schools designed for them, and worked for humanity as a whole. In their management of these institutions, women displayed an amount of executive ability and enlightened interest in public need that surprised men. Because they had never attempted organization on a large scale, they were supposed to lack constructive talent. Some, with true conceptions of what society should be as a whole, endeavored here and there to take away from the institutions they founded, and over which they presided, the semblance of that offensive charity which plumed itself formerly in making petticoats for the poor,—

> Because we are of one flesh after all.
> And need one flannel (with a proper sense
> Of difference in the quality),

or distributing stale bread and thin soup, together with homilies on the virtues of contentment and the blessing of poverty and work. Along with men, they fell into the swim of modern thought which attempted to render institutions self-supporting through the co-operative efforts of those availing themselves of their privileges. It was on these broad lines of non-sectarianism, diversity of teaching for a sisterhood of women, and the co-operative society in which there is strength, that there was built up for the use of the working-women the various boarding-homes, industrial schools, and stores for the disposal of woman's handiwork. To soften the harshest experiences of women thrown upon their own resources for necessities of food and shelter, philanthropic women, and men, too, made it their business to establish "boarding-homes," where the price of entrance was fixed at sums low enough to come within the reach of the average wage-earning woman. The clean, quiet streets usually chosen for these homes, contrasted with the filthy, crowded thoroughfares where the cheap lodging-houses—the only resorts the average friendless working-woman could afford—were most apt to be situated. The difference within was as great as without. In place of the cold, comfortless rooms which, as a rule, were destitute of fire or carpet, and where there was neither reception-room for visitors, nor bath nor laundry for inmates; the model boarding-houses had spacious, well-ventilated bedrooms attractively adorned, with a neat parlor, usually a library or reading-room, well warmed, brightly lighted, and inviting. Privileges of bath-rooms and laundries were added to increase the comforts of the boarders. Two of the best of these homes are to be found in Boston, one on Warrenton, the other on Berkeley Street. These structures, built under the auspices of the Woman's Christian Association, are provided with electric bells, ventilating appliances, and safeguards against fire. Both houses have, besides offices and attendants, handsome parlors, well-stocked reading-rooms, libraries, and lecture halls. One of them possesses a fine gymnasium. The price for board and lodging varies from $3 to $5.50 per week, but more than one-half of the guests pay from $3 to $4 per week. In the two homes there exist accommodations for about three hundred women. The sums named secure pleasant rooms, well-prepared and neatly served meals, and include, besides washing and ironing, heating and lighting of rooms, the use of reading-rooms, library, parlor, and admission to all entertainments of the association.

In thirteen other cities in the United States there have been established, by the same energetic society, one "home," smaller, but similar in character to the Boston homes. Connected with all of these, and adding greatly to their usefulness, are departments for giving instruction in sewing, teaching the art of dressmaking, and training woman in housework. Chautauqua circles were organized among the residents, and classes gotten up in which, for nominal sums, girls could be taught the languages, book-keeping, type-writing, stenography, painting, drawing, calisthenics, etc. Employment bureaus were attached, which, by personal application or through correspondence, obtained situations for those who were on its registers for services to be given, or received. To still further extend their helpfulness, another department, called the "Travelers' Aid," employed agents to meet incoming steamers and direct unprotected girls to the Association Homes, advise them as to the best and most economical means of transportation, and the best way to secure employment. Several smaller organizations, such as the "Helping Hand," "Girls' Friendly Society," etc., instituted homes that were carried on in much the same way. The benefits of ventilation, cleanliness, and decent behavior were rigidly enforced, while in general the most strenuous efforts were put forth to make the homes so far self-supporting that their residents could look on them as co-operative enterprises, in which, by combination and judicious management, the funds each expended singly, brought them all unitedly, comforts which would have been impossible without such action.

To propagate the idea of the value of co-operation among women, whether workers or not, was perhaps the most useful thing accomplished by the boarding-home societies. So far the number of these institutions has been limited, so that they suggest what could be done rather than indicate what has been accomplished in brightening the lives of the great mass of homeless working-women. In Boston, where these "homes" are most numerous, there are, for a population of eighty thousand wage-earning women, but six of these dwellings. Altogether, the limit of their accommodations is about 387 boarders. In these meager results, for so much energetic, philanthropic work, the abortiveness is shown of private individualistic attempts to supplant by means of model co-operative boarding-homes, the cheap and nasty tenement lodging-houses, situated too often in close proximity to gin-shops, gambling dens and brothels. By the numbers who vainly seek admission into the few boarding-homes that have been established in various large cities, the fact is proved that were the idea of co-operative homes carried out to largest national issues and placed everywhere within reach of wage-earning women, all but the most debased would avail themselves of their privileges, and thus secure the comforts and good living enjoyed so rarely by women whom circumstances compel to labor.

Another phase of work initiated by women, and which, like the boarding-homes, needs only to be carried out on the broad and liberal lines of a national co-operation to become a power for universal good, were the exchanges, or stores, instituted for the purpose of selling hand or machine-made articles of woman's manufacture, and which gave the maker the full price they brought, less a ten per cent. commission and a membership fee of $5 for maintaining the establishment. In this way, the founder of the Woman's Exchange hoped to solve the ever-perplexing problem of finding a remunerative market for the work that women had been taught to do in the various art and industrial schools. At the time the first exchange was planned in New York, some ten years ago, thousands of women, graduates from the various art schools, were at work in stores and factories decorating china, painting household adornments such as portières, screens, wall-hangings, and doing all kinds of fancy work at prices but little, if any, beyond the wages of the average worker on men's and women's clothing. To direct this work into a channel, where the maker and not the employer would receive the profit, was what the originator of the exchange proposed to do for women pressed by poverty into the ranks of the bread-winners.

From the first, the exchange became popular with a certain class, and had a most phenomenal growth, forty having come into existence during the last decade, all of which are working successfully on the same general plan. A walk through the rooms of the parent institution, now established in a handsome building at 329 Fifth Avenue, shows the number and variety of workers who availed themselves of its privileges. In the salesrooms, hand-painted and embroidered tapestries hang on the walls; artistic screens, painted or embroidered on all conceivable materials, stand in every nook and corner; elaborately decorated china for ornament or table use lies piled on shelves; while textile fabrics of all kinds, made up into articles for wall decorations, bed and table use, or personal wear, are tastefully arranged on counters or within glass cases. On the upper floors in the building, women are kept constantly at work inspecting, marking, and ticketing goods sent in by consignees. In the basement are the storehouse and restaurant for receiving and selling cakes, pickles, preserves, and other edibles, sent to be disposed of for the benefit of the makers.

In this one establishment the sales for the year 1888 amounted to $51,180.26. The aggregate sold in the cake and preserve department amounted to $13,256.89. One consignee of chicken jelly, etc., got during the year $1,256.89. Of two consignees in the cake and preserve department one received $1,019.73, the other $772.42. Things sent to the lunch-room for Sunday night teas brought one consignee the comfortable little income of $965.78. From the sale of children's wrappers alone, one consignee received $548.66, and one woman for screens, decorated frames, etc., $1105.71. One consignee received during the spring and fall months $217.35 for articles which she had previously made for manufacturers at $2.50 apiece, and which were sold for $35 each. In the order department connected with the exchange, the work done consisted of 1263 pieces of plain sewing, 1784 pieces of English embroidery, 1100 painted articles, and 2033 fancy articles. From the forty other societies then in existence the reports showed a grand aggregate of over one million dollars from sales during the year.

These figures demonstrate how thoroughly practical the scheme is of sending hand-made articles to special magazines to be disposed of for the makers' benefit. The woman who, by sending her work to the exchange, got $35 for what she, as a wage-earner, had received $2.50 from the manufacturer, got the profit that had previously gone to swell the bank-account of the manufacturer, middle men, and retail dealers. This was the same with all contributors to the exchanges ; by employing their own labor they accumulated the premiums which, under the old factory and store system, inured to the benefit of their employers. In establishing the woman's exchanges, the difficulty was to secure enough women of intelligence to be their own employers and to interest enough women in woman's work to become patrons of the exchanges instead of the stores. For instance, to meet the expenses of the Fifth Avenue establishment in 1888, the income from all sources was $13,589.56, while the expenses of carrying on the business amounted to $16,318.48. This left a deficit of $2723.92 that had to be met by donations, and which kept the institution on a partly charitable instead of wholly self-supporting basis. As this deficit had lessened with each year, some optimistic thinkers began to hope that the time was coming when it would disappear altogether, and thus allow them to become strictly co-operative instead of philanthropic concerns. A conclusion reached was, that were they once to become independent of charitable donations, they would branch out largely enough in most of the worst paid departments of woman's work so as to force out those employed on such labor for the vast retail stores. But it was found that an insuperable obstacle to the extension of the exchanges lay in the utter lack of system with which contributors worked. In the matter of production, the regular stores had but little system; still some attempt was made in them to regulate the supply of manufactured goods to meet a possible or expected demand. Contributors to the exchanges had no such guide. Those who made and sent articles for sale could have no opportunity for knowing what others were making and sending. The result was that women living near or afar off in town and country worked completely in the dark. With no finger on the public pulse in the matter of supply and demand for goods, they were obliged for this haphazard work to purchase their own material in small quantities in the retail markets, while the merchant-manufacturers bought theirs in bulk in the cheapest. This could only mean more failures than successes in the disposal of goods made under such conditions. Again, only women possessed of some means could afford to lay out money for materials and wait the uncertain chances of its returning to them with a profit. In consequence, most of those contributing articles to the exchanges for sale were "reduced gentlewomen," who made use of this means of becoming their own employers, not so much for support, as to better their conditions of living, without the publicity consequent upon working for manufacturers. This in itself made it impossible for the exchanges (as was claimed by their supporters) to have "*helped women in general to have hushed the 'Song of the Shirt.'*" * To the women of the proletariat, the exchanges were not only unknown mediums by reason of their situation in fashionable thoroughfares, but forbidden factors because of their attendant risks and expenses. The number of sewing women helped in them to increased earnings was too insignificant to warrant any hope that the co-operative principles underlying their business methods would ever spread far enough to leave any impress upon prevailing modes of work in the business world. Like all other remedies, instituted by wealthy philanthropists to assist the working-women, they were palliatives for the ills of a few, not curatives for the sufferings of the many.

Much more satisfactory than anything which had been accomplished in the name of philanthropy or charity for working-women were the labor organizations founded by the proletariat and sustained by their own energy and contributions. About 1870, associations of working-people (including women) were inaugurated for the purpose of gaining better social conditions. These were more attractive and beneficial to the laboring class because they lacked that element of restitution of a modicum of withheld wages which tainted all that wealth did for the alleviation of the condition of wage-earning women,† and, moreover, was built upon the sounder philosophy

---

* Speech of Mr. Frederic Coudert at the Lenox Lyceum, April 7, 1890.

† This thought of the greater benefit to be derived from the organizations of labor as opposed to the philanthropic work done by the employing classes for the people who work, has been ably carried out in a paper read by Mrs. Florence Kelley Wischnewtzky before the New York Association of Collegiate Alumni, May 14, 1887, entitled "The Need of Theoretical Preparations for Philanthropic Work." This essay will appear in an early number of the Boston "Nationalist."

of an endeavor to organize into bodies capable of striving collectively for their own deliverance, that class of women whom the industrial schools, women's exchanges, etc., could not reach. The most important of these bodies was the Knights of Labor. Organized openly in 1881 at the Detroit Convention, but more secretly some years before, this body welcomed women into its ranks on the ground of seeking "to gather into one fold all branches of honorable toil, without regard to nationality, sex, creed, or color." Trade assemblies, composed entirely of working-women, were formed, and the members were taught the beautiful principles on which the order was founded. In amalgamating with knights, women assumed the duties of the new chivalry. Engaging as equals in the undertaking, helping with time and money to carry out the new mission, they sought by Agitation, Education, and Organization to lighten the burden of toil, and to elevate the moral and social condition of mankind. In 1883, one local assembly, composed entirely of women, counted fifteen hundred members. These must all have given adherence to that order's doctrine of "Equal pay for equal work," and "woman's equitable consideration with man in the Nation's government." Mrs. Leonora Barry, who had been a factory worker for some years in Central New York, became the chief officer of a trade assembly of nine hundred and twenty-seven women. Later, in 1886, she was elected a delegate to the general assembly, by which she was commissioned "to go forth and educate her sister working-women and the public generally as to their needs and necessities."

The open declaration of this powerful organization,—that women possessed equal rights with men,—showed, as much as anything else, the advance of public sentiment in regard to women. Its educational influence extended outside the ranks of the order. Most of the women members were drawn from the employees in factories producing clothing, textile fabrics, food, tobacco, etc., and from the trades of typography, telegraphy, and stenography. In the mixed local assemblies women have an equal chance with men to express their views upon subjects bearing on the labor question. And even where women sat quiet, as most frequently happened, without taking share in the debates, one of the valuable purposes of the order was said to be served by the information and larger views which came to them through these discussions. In assemblies composed entirely of women, of whom not one, perhaps, could boast of more than a minor part of a common school education, ideas were advanced for their financial as well as educational benefit. Factory operatives, coming under their influence, became shareholders in co-operative concerns. Co-operative shirt factories, conducted solely by women, were established in Baltimore and New York. A co-operative knitting mill was set up at Little Falls, N. Y., while other co-operative industries throughout the land came, through co-operative principles, into the possession of the workers. A co-operative tailoring establishment in Chicago had its rise in the lock-out of a few factory girls who attended a labor parade without permission. With the luck that comes with pluck, they became possessed of $400, through soliciting subscriptions. With this they went into business and succeeded. It is claimed, that inside of nine months they had done $36,000 worth of business, besides having the gratification of being their own employers.

This departure from the custom prevailing among the proletariat to sell their services for wage-hire, was due largely to the demand made in the nineteenth plank of the platform of the Knights of Labor for the abolition of the wage system and a national system of co-operation in lieu thereof. The insertion of such a demand proved the founders of the order to have been thinkers radical enough to go a step beyond the old idea of trades organizations with their petty notions of each trade working solely in its own interests. In comparison with the broad and lofty conception of the Knights of Labor, which sought to include in its benefits all women and men engaged in every department of industrial work, other organizations, such as the American Federation of Labor, which is a mere rope of sand, showed themselves away in the rear-guard of progressive civilization by placing themselves solely on the old competitive and selfish trades union basis.

The next largest organization that took women into its body on terms of equality was "The Granger Association of Western Farmers." * Founded in 1870, this association of the agriculturists of the country proposed to do for women on the farms what the societies had done for them in the other industries. They formulated as a principle "that no Grange should

* Since the Grangers were first organized, that body has amalgamated its efforts with those of the Farmers Alliances and these again with the Knights of Labor. The Alliances are in many respects more socialistic than the Socialists, inasmuch as the last-named have only proposed, by a transitional and constitutional method, to arrive at the demands now made by the Alliances, and these only after the altruistic and industrial planks in their platform have been gradually conceded by National and State Legislatures. The

be organized, or exist, without women." This act was held to be the emancipation of women on the farms, as that of the Knight of Labor had been in the trades. In their public meetings, women were invited to take part in the discussions of plans for mutual benefit, for usefulness and culture. The principles of co-operation, which brought them together, extended to the buying of all descriptions of goods in bulk. This, by increasing the purchasing power of limited incomes, increased the comforts and attractions of homes that would otherwise have been deprived of them. The women who entered the Granges held a conspicuous place in the national census of agricultural operators and producers of national wealth. They were engaged in the farm labors of milking, making butter and cheese, raising poultry, preserving eggs, and gathering honey for market and home consumption. Vegetable gardens, fruit orchards, viticulture, berry plants, and shrubs of many millions' value were largely attended to by them ; while planting, weeding, haying, harvesting, tilling the soil, and caring for live-stock were rapidly added to the list of women's occupations on the farm. To bring a new brightness into the lives of these toilers was an avowed object of the Grange. It proposed, by bringing men and women together with communities of interests, to effect a great moral and social good, and thus elevate them from slaves and drudges into a "better and higher manhood and womanhood."

As "the thoughts of men were widened by the processes of the suns," the idea gained ground that if organization was good for women in one direction, it might be good in all. Men began, about 1884, to receive women into their trades' unions, and a few energetic women in various States started working-women's unions that comprised the members of different trades. The Cigar and Typographical Unions were among the first to admit women into their bodies. The Cigar-Makers' Union of Denver, a branch of the International Cigar-Makers' Union, admitted women to membership and made no distinction on account of color. Through the efforts of the union, the hours of labor were reduced from ten to eight, and the

---

Farmers Alliances, which number possibly 5,000,000 members, demand the immediate ownership by the people of all the means of transportation and communication, railways, canals, telegraphs, telephones, etc. But more than this, their platform calls upon the nation through Congress and the Treasury department for a system of sub-treasuries, which have to aid directly in the purchase, storage, and distribution of the products of farms and plantations—that is of all grain, tobacco, and cotton.

rate of wages, as they expressed it, "raised from a mere pittance to respectable living wages." Typographical unions were much praised for their gallantry in forcing employers to agree to their terms of "Equal work, equal pay, equal terms of apprenticeship for both sexes." This chivalric aspect was somewhat dimmed by the refusal afterward of some union men to work in the same offices with women. Employers were frequently given the option of choosing between having all men or all women at the cases, and the struggle usually ended in favor of the men. How this worked to the disadvantage of women can be seen by referring to the California Bureau of Labor Statistics for 1889, where the statement is that the book and job printing houses in San Francisco employing union help had only three women in three separate printing establishments as against one hundred and nineteen men; while in the non-union, the proportion was forty-eight women against eighty-five men. Since the investigations of the Bureau, the number of union women employed is said to be "much increased." This in regard to wages means a great deal to women, as the unions have a fixed scale which ranges from eighteen to thirty dollars for week or time work. In one of the largest printing establishments in San Francisco, women compositors not in the unions received as wages nine dollars per week as against fifteen dollars for men; proof-readers, nine dollars against eighteen dollars for men. Forewomen and foremen were paid in the same ratio. Discrepancies like these, of fifty per cent. difference in the wages of women, because they were women, proved the value of an association that insisted upon the justice of "equal pay for equal work."

Trade organizations composed exclusively of women were instituted timidly and tentatively in the large cities.* Though protective rather than educational, the instruction given in the few trades unions established by and for women possessed a very broadening character. Able speakers, frequenting the meetings, familiarized the members with the economic theories advanced as to the value of the co-operative principle, the duties owed by the strong to the weak, and the correlation between woman's best interests and the interests of the State. The experience of the trades unions proved the absurd fallacy of the time-worn objection against women's guilds, "that it would unsex them," for the effect of their organizations was to make their

* The first one established of any note was that of the Daughters of Crispin, in Massachusetts, an organization of shoemakers, incorporated in 1872.

members more unselfish and more womanly, more apt to think of the good of all than of a part, and, through the importance of being one of a large body working for some common weal, less inclined to frivolous ends.

To wage-working women, one important practical result of labor combinations was the concession made by legislators, through fear of losing the labor vote, to the demand for Bureaus of Labor Statistics, which should show the actual condition of men and women engaged in any and every department of labor. Massachusetts, always first in the field of reform, established such a bureau of labor statistics in 1869. Other States followed slowly in her wake. By 1887 twenty-two States had recognized the importance of having similar bureaus. Among them was "the Department of Labor," instituted in Washington in 1885, for the purpose of doing collectively for the whole people what the individual States were to accomplish separately. When the Massachusetts Labor Bureau went into operation, its chief, General Henry K. Oliver, a man of liberal views, endeavored to ascertain the conditions under which industrial women worked. The means employed were :

I. Personal investigation.

II. Distribution of printed forms with blanks for employed and employers to fill.

III. Summons to witnesses from the employed and employing classes to testify.

IV. Soliciting information through correspondence.

Through the recommendation of ladies interested in the question of ascertaining the conditions of working-women, General Oliver associated one of their own sex, Miss Adeline Bryant, with the work of the bureau. In the third year of the bureau's existence five women were placed on the staff of helpers. The precedent set by Massachusetts of employing women as investigators was followed in turn by the other State bureaus and by the "Department of Labor" at Washington.

The investigations of the bureau of 1869 covered the thirty-five industries in which the working-women of Massachusetts were then engaged. Published in 1870, the report of the bureau corroborated the accounts given by the press of that year concerning the low wages, long hours of work, and miserable state of living that was the lot of the wage-earning women in the manufacturing towns of Massachusetts. General Oliver himself assisted in the personal investigation carried on in Boston. Accompanied by the Chief of Police, he visited the homes of "poor-paid laborers,"—women and men,—and found that the homes of the laborers are a pretty accurate index of the social, industrial, sanitary, educational, and moral standard of the laborers themselves. The result of his work was a recommendation for further and more thorough research. "Such investigations," he said, "will reveal a state of things at which the people of Massachusests will gaze with amazement, disgust, and anger, and demand a bettering of the wrong."

Investigations by blanks and by summons to witnesses was less successful than the personal interview. The mass of the people were ignorant of what the bureau sought to accomplish by their questions; hence not more than twenty per cent. of the employers and thirty-three per cent. of the employed addressed returned replies. A dread on the part of manufacturers and shopkeepers, lest "out of their own mouths they should be condemned," prevented them from answering, and those under them were restrained to silence through fear of losing employment. In spite of the risk, courageous women replied to the blanks and gave personal testimony sufficient to enable the commission to form a partial estimate of the social and economic conditions of the whole. The statistics presented by the bureau were said to have reached "the very verge of human society." Said Mrs. Atkinson, speaking of the reports on the working-women, "The stern fact, the thrilling incident, the woeful spectacle, the harrowing sight of squalor and wretchedness are marshaled before our eyes in a great and terrible array." The subjects investigated were: Housework, Hotel and Saloon work, Home work, Store work. Under the Home work was classified sale work; under Store work, clerks, accountants, saleswomen, and cash girls. All that could be found out concerning women in these employments was printed and presented by General Oliver to the Legislature and to the public, without any of the softening touches common to later reports.

The next extended investigation into the occupations and history of wage-earning women was made in 1884, at the instigation of Mr. Carroll D. Wright, who, in 1874, had superseded General Oliver as chief of the Massachusetts Bureau. The research undertaken by Mr. Wright had for its object the ascertainment of the "moral, sanitary, physical, and economical" condition of all wage-earning women in Boston, except those employed in domestic service. This was a larger field than that covered in 1869. Woman's occupations had multiplied in the earlier year five-fold over what they were in 1840, when, to Harriet Martineau's surprise, seven vocations, outside of housework, were all into which the women of the United States had entered. In 1884 they were more than ten times seven. Methods of working had also become more difficult to classify. One by one domestic industries were relegated from the home to the factory. And in most of these, what had been done by one person had become differentiated into numerous parts, requiring the co-operation of many workers. Thus, in the occupation of making men's and women's clothing, there were classified in 1884 as many as 103 subdivisions. Altogether, in the seventy distinct industries catalogued, there were 354 subdivisions of industries, and each one of these parts employed a different set of workers. It was important that a number of representative women should be interviewed in each of these departments; for, even where each branch formed part of a distinct whole, each worker in those branches had interests at variance with the others.

The force of women engaged in the industries of Boston had also seemingly almost doubled in the five years from 1880 to 1885. Exclusive of domestic service, the number of women in all other industries was estimated in the United States census of 1880 at 20,000; in the Massachusetts Census Report for 1885 at 39,647. With this apparent doubling of the population, the amount distributed in wages had not doubled, and so all that had been bad in the conditions of wage-earning women in previous years was heightened because there was nothing to relieve it. On account of all this, the appearance of the report of 1884 was anxiously looked for by large numbers of persons who had become familiar with the line of work of the bureaus. Great, therefore, was the public surprise at finding the whole report so biased in favor of the law-making, shop-keeping, manufacturing class as to prove valueless as an investigation into the condition of women dependent on wages for their living. The statistical information it contained, although arranged in the formidable manner common to the expert statistician, needed no careful scrutiny of its figures to establish the truth of Disraeli's proposition that "nothing is so unreliable as facts, unless it is figures."

However, the work done by the Boston Bureau, although misleading in itself, had the good effect of stimulating similar research in other places. In the following year, 1885, the first part of the Third New York Report was devoted to an investigation of the condition of the working-women of New York City. It was estimated that in that year over two hundred thousand women were employed in the various trades of that city, exclusive of those in Brooklyn. The number of industries, exclusive of domestic service, and without counting subdivisions, was ninety. Scarcely any European city offered so wide and diversified a field for inquiry as this; and yet the commissioner, Mr. Charles F. Peck, claimed that, through lack of time, in place of any close and searching inquiry "into special conditions of the effects of these employments on the physical development of women and its relation to the social, commercial, and industrial prosperity of the State," he was obliged to content himself "with a general survey, instead of that minute and detailed examination which the subject would justify."

Mr. Peck discovered, as his predecessors in Massachusetts had done, that at all times the questions involved in the conditions of working-women resolved themselves into those of "wages, hours, health, and morals." With regard to the first, he found that the wages of women, as a rule, were, in 1885 as in 1869, less than one-half that obtained by men,—the remuneration being widely different even where the work performed was the same. In those professions or trades in which women were organized, and for equal work received equal pay with men,—as printers, cigar-makers, and hatters,—the men themselves received very low pay. In the tenement-house factories, the women engaged in cigar-making numbered four thousand. These were employed in the branches paying the lowest wages, as stripping and binding. For these, the pay seldom averaged $5 per week, and then was not steady the year round. The manufacturers gave as reason for hiring so many women, "That they could get them for fifty per cent. less than men." Capmakers earned from $3 to 4.50 per week; compositors all the way from $8 to $16 per week. One of the new branches of work into which women had entered was that of polishing marble. The manager of the Niagara Marble Works testified that they employed from twenty-five to thirty women, whose wages averaged from $4.50 to $8 per week, men getting for the same kind of work from $1.50 to $3 per day. When asked if "they could get men to work for the same wages as women?" the reply was, "Hardly, unless they were boys, and then they would not be so skillful."

But it was in the class of work that has always been called "woman's work" that the bureaus found the most beggarly wages paid. A manufacturer of pants, vests, shirts, and overalls testified that he gave from fifteen to thirty-five cents apiece for making vests; seventy-five cents to $1.50 per dozen for shirts, and from twelve and a half cents to twenty-five cents a pair for pants. Boy's gingham waists, with trimming on neck and sleeves, were paid for at the rate of two and a half cents each. By working steadily at the machine from six o'clock in the morning until one at night, the seamstress could make twenty-five cents a day at this "shop work." The inmates of several charitable institutions in the city were found by the commissioner crocheting ladies' shawls for twenty-five cents apiece. An expert, he was told, could finish one in two days. This was all that the several Blanks & Co. would pay, because competition for this kind of work was so great they were able to get the work done for almost any price.* On woman's wear, the wages had been so reduced that it was alleged that a full day's work on a cloak brought from fifty to sixty cents. The visits of the commissioner to some of the attic tenement-house rookeries, where this work was carried on under the direction of "sweaters," disclosed numbers of cloak-makers working sixteen hours a day for fifty cents. In those dens he saw stacks of cloaks piled on the floors ready to be sewn together by women scantily clad, with hair unkempt, and whose pale, abject countenances formed such pictures of physical suffering and want as he trusted "he might never again be compelled to look upon." The style and quality of the cloaks upon which these women toiled were of the latest and best. They were lined with quilted silk or satin and trimmed with sealskin or other expensive material, and found ready sale in the largest retail stores in the city at from thirty-five to seventy-five dollars each.

To give some idea of how the cloak-makers lived on this pittance the bureau gave a realistic engraving, done from a drawing taken on the spot, in which it was endeavored to reproduce the outlines of one room (as a sample exhibit of the rest) where six women sat at work under the directions of sweaters. In size the room might possibly have measured twelve by fourteen feet, and perhaps nine feet high. The atmosphere was next to suffocating and dense with impurities. On one end of a

* One evil that shirt-makers and seamstresses of all kinds had to contend with was that the work was given out to contractors, families, and institutions, principally to the Roman Catholic Protectory and the House of the Good Shepherd.

table, at which four of the women sat, was a dinner-pail partially filled with soup (that is what they called it) and a loaf of well-seasoned bread. These two courses, served with one spoon and one knife, satiated the thirst and hunger of four working-women. In an adjoining side room, without means for ventilation or light, the deadly sewer gas rose in clouds from a sink. On the floor lay a mattress which partook in appearance of the general filth found throughout the building. On this mattress the cloak-makers, tired out by the long day's work and faint for want of food, threw themselves down and awaited the coming day's awful toil for bread. This, it was claimed, was neither a fanciful nor exceptional picture; that a degree of want, misery, and degradation existed among the working-women living in tenement houses next to impossible to describe. "Certainly," said the commissioner, "no words of mine can convey to the public any adequate conception of the truly awful condition of thousands of these suffering people. Formerly," he wrote, "Hood's 'Song of the Shirt' gave sentimental celebrity to the wrongs of the sewing-women, but it is not the shirt (alone) now, but the woman's cloak and the man's coat or pants that draw tears and groans from the overdone sewing-woman."

Testimony elicited as to the workers in some of the trades, particularly tobacco, was even more revolting than that concerning the sewing-woman. In the report, wood-cuts were given of rooms such as a large proportion of cigar-makers worked, lived, ate, and slept in. "These people," it was said, "worked till twelve P. M. or one o'clock A. M., then slept by the machine a few hours, and commenced work again." The description of women sitting "surrounded by filth, with children waddling in it, whose hands, faces, and bodies were covered with sores," were sickening. Cankerous sores were "even on the lips of the workers, they all the time handling the tobacco that was made into cigars." In the scale of sanitary conditions of homes and workrooms, the cigar-makers were among the lowest. Of bunch-makers and rollers, who replied to the questions of the sanitary condition of their homes, but two out of 118 answered, "good." All of the rest wrote, "bad," "very bad," the "worst you ever saw," "miserable," and "poor." As to their workrooms, out of one hundred and thirty, one hundred and three were without means for free circulation of air. *One* only possessed no offensive odors. The unhealthfulness of the workrooms of the cigar-makers, the coat-makers, the tailoresses, and the cloak-makers was about the same.

Among this latter class of seamstresses 38 out of 41 answered that their surroundings were very offensive through being "near offensive stables." The order of the day was, "general filth, water-closets, bad sewerage, dirty neighborhoods, overcrowding, and poor ventilation." Similar complaints came from compositors in printing-offices, women in type-foundries, kid-glove sewers, carpet-factory operators, and silk weavers.

While in many of the large factories the sanitary conditions were good and proper, ventilation being secured,—when it did not interfere with the work carried on,—there were other features that if less injurious to health were quite as objectionable to the wage-worker. In the carpet and silk factories, women were obliged to stand all day, as, though seats were provided in many instances, fines were exacted from those using them. It was the same with washing facilities; women employed in silk establishments in weaving light-colored or white silks were fined as high as fifty cents for washing their hands, and fines were also imposed if spots got on the goods. Women testified that they were fined "if discovered reading a letter, or a paper, or spoke to one another." The proprietor of one of these factories stated that the fines he collected in this way he gave away in "charity," and, "That five dollars a week was enough for a girl to live on." In some carpet factories the system of fines was even more excessive. Women were docked as much as five dollars if any accident happened to the machinery, which they were compelled to clean while it was in motion. In one mill, they were "not allowed to talk to one another during working hours or at noon, under penalty of being docked or discharged." The fine in some places for being five minutes late was twenty-five cents, while a half-hour over-time was exacted. How disproportionate this punishment was is evident; those women who were fined at the rate of thirty dollars per day, were being paid at the rate of eight cents an hour. When women were not fined for being five minutes behind time, they were "locked out" for two hours. These were the hands employed on piece work, and the loss of two hours made, as it was intended, a large hole in the day's earnings. In most cases it was claimed that the amount of fines exacted was optional with the foreman or superintendent, and that frequently they were so excessive as to affect the whole pay of employees for weeks ahead.

The tyranny of the strong and powerful over the weak and helpless,—which found expression in the exaction of fines from those who were termed variously "white slaves," "slave girls," "prisoners of poverty," etc.,—existed in another form in the long hours of labor demanded by the Legrees of the industrial world from the wage-working women. While in many factories the legal limit of sixty hours per week for minors, and women under twenty-one, was observed, there were grave and numerous exceptions to this rule among tobacco-workers, seamstresses, bakery employees, etc., etc. In the cigar factories, the great majority of bunch-makers and rollers, whether employed at home or in the factory proper, were worked fifteen, sixteen, seventeen, and even eighteen hours a day. Operatives on clothing worked from nine to sixteen hours per day. In the collar, cuff, and shirt-making factories in Troy, as well as the laundries in that place, the hours were uniformly ten, and in New York from eight to twelve. Milliners worked nine hours in factories and from fourteen to sixteen at home. Feather-workers in factories nine to ten. Operatives on ladies' underwear eight to ten in factories; twelve to fourteen hours at home. While this made a good showing for the factories engaged in these industries, it must be remembered that much of the work quoted as done "*at home*" was only a continuation of factory labor, as work was in many cases taken home from these, either to supplement the day's earnings, or to oblige (?) employers, who withheld extra compensation for the extra work exacted. In occupations requiring a different kind of skill, or impossible at home, the hours were found to be sometimes less than the legal limit. Those for compositors were from eight to ten. Type-foundry operatives, seven and a half to nine. Stenographers, telegraphers, and typewriters, from five and a half to six, seven, and eight. Saleswomen, again, worked many hours over-time in all except the largest houses, and during the holiday season these largest stores were no longer exceptions. In fancy-goods stores, millinery shops, bakeries, candy stores, etc., etc., no limit was placed through the holidays,—that were in no sense holidays to employees,—except the limit of physical endurance. In return no portion of the extra profit this extra work brought was shared by proprietors with their overtaxed employees.

Economically speaking, the worst of all the evils society perpetrated against the working-women was that of forcing her into long hours of continuous labor; for, whether standing at the looms and in the stores, or sitting at the sewing-machine, specific diseases of the sexual organs were induced, causing marriage to be followed by miscarriage or sickly children. No original statistics were collected by the bureau to show how far the health and morals of women engaged in industries were affected by their employments, and what relation this influence exerted in reference to woman's position in the State. While this prevented the report from being of full service to the political economist, to the historian its pages were valuable as forming a succession of *genre* pictures, otherwise unattainable, of the proletarian women, as they lived, labored, and suffered in New York City in 1885.

An epidemic of investigation into women's condition as wage-workers followed the New York report. Five States—Maine, California, Colorado, Iowa, and Minnesota—prepared separate chapters on the subject of the working-women for their Bureaus of Labor Statistics for 1887–1888. In New Jersey, although no original investigation was made by the State, the bureau reprinted in 1887 a large portion of an excellent report on "Woman's Work and Wages," gathered by Mrs. Barry in 1886 by order of the Knights of Labor. The latest, and what should have been the best report, was a national research into the social and economic environments of wage-earning women in twenty-two of the largest and most representative cities in the United States. This investigation, conducted under the auspices of the Central Bureau at Washington, comprehended statistics gained through interviewing and questioning personally 17,427 women engaged in industrial pursuits. Undertaken in 1888, this national report was printed in 1889, under the title of "Working-women in Large Cities." It formed a volume of 631 pages, mostly statistical tables, framed so as to seem to cover the most important points concerning women as industrial workers.

To two grades of readers these bureau publications were most welcome. First, to the more intelligent among the working-class, "in whose humble cabins," it was said,* "complete sets of Bureau Reports could be found preserved in calico covers having as many colors as 'Joseph's coat,' and presenting as much evidence of constant use as the old-time spelling-book in a country school-house that was passed from scholar to scholar until it has made the round of the school." Second, to the students of sociology, who pored over their pages, hoping to gain clear ideas of what was going on in the working world of men and women. Excellent though they were, these reports were nevertheless disappointing, at least as far as they related to facts concerning woman's industrial position.

* Ohio Report for 1887. L. McHugh, commissioner.

The first and greatest disappointment for readers was the fact that the number of wage-earning women interviewed in any one place by the bureau agents was too small to give even an approximate idea of the whole ; e. g. the statistical tables of all industries for New York City were founded on the testimony alone of 2984 women, while at that period (1889) the number of wage-earning women in that city and Brooklyn was estimated at 300,000.(?) As this method of taking one per cent. of the population of women as a guide by which to estimate the conditions of all the others prevailed everywhere, conclusions drawn from the presented statistics were, of necessity, vitiated. To a certain extent they had to be accepted with allowance.

With all that this limitation implies, the bureau statistics are, nevertheless, interesting as comprising the best data we have on which to base assumptions of the industrial status of wage-earning women. In regard to wages, the conclusions, though obviously inexact, still show plainly enough that wages were regulated everywhere by the prices of rent and food, and that only so much was paid as would keep life in the worker. In the appended table, taken from the National Report for 1889, it will be seen that in the South, where living is comparatively cheap, wages are lower than in the West, where life's necessaries come higher. In the East they are a mean between the two.

AVERAGE WEEKLY EARNINGS, BY CITIES.

Cities.	Average Weekly Earnings.	Cities.	Average Weekly Earnings.
Atlanta	$4.05	New Orleans	$4.31
Baltimore	4.18	New York	5.85
Boston	5.64	Philadelphia	5.34
Brooklyn	5.76	Providence	5.51
Buffalo	4.27	Richmond	3.93
Charleston	4.22	St. Louis	5.19
Chicago	5.74	St. Paul	6.02
Cincinnati	4.59	San Francisco	6.91
Cleveland	4.63	San Jose	6.11
Indianapolis	4.67	Savannah	4.99
Louisville	4.51		
Newark	5.10	All Cities	$5.24

In the 343 industries named in this report, for 1889, it will be seen that the conditions under which women gained their livelihood had not been bettered, and that, on the contrary, the testimony as published in the other State reports disclosed a state of affairs similar to that which Engels* described as existing among the same class of laboring women in England in 1844. Nothing worse can be found in any of Engels' descriptions than the following account (given in the New Jersey Report for 1887–1888) of the tyranny practiced upon the linen thread spinners of Paterson: "In one branch of this industry," it is said, "women are compelled to stand on a stone floor in water the year round, most of the time barefoot, with a spray of water from a revolving cylinder flying constantly against the breast; and the coldest night in winter, as well as the warmest in summer, these poor creatures must go to their homes with water dripping from their underclothing along their path, because there could not be space or a few moments allowed them wherein to change their clothing."† Another account, which calls up the experiences at Leeds and Lancaster in 1844, is taken from the Wisconsin Report for 1888. In the prosperous city of Janesville, in that highly favored State described as a paradise for workers, the report tells of a factory "in which some three hundred women and children are employed, who work eleven and a half to twelve hours per day and night, the night being the time most of the children are employed." Although eight hours is the legal working day in Wisconsin, and fourteen years the age limit at which children may be employed, "many of the children are under fourteen years of age, and all have to work eleven and a half hours. The thermometer averages, in the heated season, about 108 degrees . . . . and loss of health follows women by reason "of the intense heat at night and insufficient sleep in the day-time."

These by no means exceptional cases show how conditions of work for laboring women were increasing in intensity in the United States. That they were becoming worse in other ways was evidenced in New England manufacturing towns, where employment of women and children as the cheaper wage-taking

---

* Condition of the Working Classes in England in 1844, Frederick Engels. Translated by Florence Kelley Wischnewetzky.

† In England this outrage on humanity was forbidden, in 1878, by Clause No. 35 of the Factory Bill, which provided that "no young person, or woman, shall be employed in any part of a factory in which the wet spinning of flax, hemp, jute, or tow is carried on, unless sufficient means be employed and continued for protecting the workers from being wetted, and, where hot water is used, for preventing the escape of steam into the room occupied by the workers."

element was gradually extinguishing the male operative.* In the manufacturing towns of Fall River, Lawrence, Lowell, etc., the family life was so demoralized that men were obliged to be supported in idleness by mothers, wives, or sisters or children, because no work was to be had for them in the mills. It was said that some of these men, displaced by the light-running machinery that a child's hand might guide, remained at home and did the housework and minded the children, while the women went forth as the breadwinners ; others, less patient, took to loafing, and ended generally in prisons. "This," as Engels termed it, "insane state of things" affected all unfavorably. Women learned to care so little for themselves that it was said "a girl in Fall River comes out of the mill with bare feet and a shawl thrown over her head, and all she cares for is a loaf of bread and a mug of beer." Children, going too early into the mills, were corrupted, morally and physically; yet mothers, unable from their own slender wages to support the family, were tempted to swear "false oaths in regard to their children's ages, so as to get them into the mills and thus make more money."

This Moloch of cheap labor, which demanded both women and children, did not stop at making mothers commit perjury for the sake of bread ; it rifled the eleemosynary institutions of little ones left there for safe keeping, and sent them in ship or car loads to the West.† The claim was made in New York in 1888 that ‡ "during the last forty years not less than two hundred thousand children had been sent into the Western States, many of whom had been sold outright," by managers of asylums, who refused to allow the names of these little ones to be known, for fear that parents or relatives, who had surrendered them in seasons of distress, might wish to reclaim them when

* Fall River, Lowell, and Lawrence. Thirteenth Annual Report, Massachusetts Bureau Statistics of Labor.

† Public attention was first directed to this hideous phase of the child labor question through the discovery of the fact that large numbers of orphan children, varying from eleven to fourteen years of age, were being exported from St. John's Asylum, Brooklyn, N. Y., to the glass factories of Fostoria and Findlay, O. Other asylums, including the organization known as the Children's Aid Society, were said to be equally guilty with St. John's Home in carrying on the business of child trading for a money consideration.

‡ New York newspapers November 23-26, 1888 ; *Brooklyn Citizen*, November 23, 1888 ; Correspondence of Factory Inspectors, Harry Dorn, Ohio, November 1888 ; Correspondence of Factory Inspectors, John Franey, Albany, N. Y., November, 1888.

fortunate enough to procure work. These children, not sold in the open market as their black brothers and sisters had been, but disposed of in the name of *Charity*, had their identity concealed by change of name ; cases are on record where brothers and sisters have grown up, met, and married, and "after marriage learned to their horror that they were children of the same parents."

Thus factory and farm-house had begun to stand in the United States as they had in England from Queen Elizabeth's days—as the fabled ogre's castles of ancient legend, which drew women and children into them to serve and suffer hopelessly, unless relieved from captivity and death by a stronger power. History repeated itself in this exploitation of women and children and in the plans made for their relief. The broad system of factory legislation, inspired in England by the revelations of the cruelty practiced upon the most hapless portions of its population, began to be imitated in the United States. Massachusetts, the pioneer State in introducing salutary reforms, took the initiative, and in 1874 forced its Legislature to recognize that it was the duty of the State to regulate the hours of labor of women and children engaged in the manufactures. In that year, after a long series of discussions between radicals and conservatives, the Ten-hour Factory Bill was passed. It is doubtful if the radicals would have triumphed even then, had they not been able to demonstrate that there was "a limit to human endurance, which, once transgressed, was not only disastrous to the operative but unprofitable to the mill-owners."

Having once committed itself to the precedent of interfering to protect the weak against the strong, Massachusetts had no alternative but to advance in the same direction. By degrees, twenty-four distinct points were covered by factory legislation.* Nine other States followed Massachusetts in the enaction of factory laws, and all made provision for bureaus of factory inspection to see that the laws were obeyed. These factory laws, as far as they concerned women, besides limiting the hours of labor, obliged "employers to provide seats for women and grant them permission to use them when not actively engaged in the duties for which they were employed." Fire-escapes were to be provided, and proper safeguards thrown

---

* New Jersey, 1883 ; Ohio, 1884 ; New York, 1886 ; Wisconsin, Rhode Island, 1887 ; Connecticut, 1888 ; Maine, 1888 ; State factory inspection in Pennsylvania in 1889 ; municipal factory ordinance in Chicago, 1889.

around machinery. Women under twenty-one years were not to be allowed to clean machinery while in motion. Suitable wash-rooms and other conveniences were to be furnished them. Forty-five minutes were to be given for the noon-day meal at a uniform and proper time. Locking of doors—that travesty upon free labor—was prohibited during working-hours. Sanitary regulations of work-rooms and weekly payments were to be enforced. The trusteeing of wages was abolished. Cellars were forbidden to be used as work-rooms. "No plea," it was said, "and no subterfuge should be permitted to justify the use of any underground apartment for purposes of human habitation."

Delegating to States the privileges of exercising supervision over manufactories, etc., for the benefit of labor, was a long step forward in the path of progress; a signal triumph of radicalism over conservative obstructionists denying the right of the State to protect its citizens. But if the reformer gained his points, the manufacturer contrived, as far as possible, to make the victory an empty one. Only so far as employers could not prevent was labor legislation effective. With the ten-hour working day, while employers complied with the letter of the law, a large majority defied the spirit. No fact was better known than that the ten-hour law for women and children was disregarded whenever possible. In factories where notice was given that ten hours would constitute a day's work, the clause "unless otherwise ordered," usually accompanied it; and the "otherwise ordered" came whenever the manufacturer's convenience demanded it. Other factory legislation fared little better. When, according to law, seats were placed in mills, factories, shops, and stores, women were, in general, forbidden to use them, under penalty of discharge. Locking of doors, when employees were at work, although less common, was still continued. Labor commissioners, wishing to enter factories employing many women, "had much difficulty in getting inside, so securely was every gate and door locked and barred." Sanitary work-rooms remained the exceptions; underground places continued to be used for human habitations, workshops, and salesrooms. Cellars were converted into bazaars in which hundreds of women and children were employed, and where they lived the year round in the glare of electric lights, never seeing daylight except in the morning hours, on Saturday half-holidays, and Sundays. One obvious reason why factory laws were disregarded so flagrantly was that the working force of factory inspectors in every State but Massachusetts was so limited as to make it impossible for them to visit even once during the year half the factories under their supervision. In many cases their powers were so restricted that when they caught an offender against the laws, they had to act on Dogberry's advice "to take no note of him, but let him go."

Despite the fact that laws, made for the protection of women in the industries, were not always enforced,—enough good resulted from them to increase the tendency everywhere of looking to the State for further legislation. In the pages of the labor reports containing the replies made by working-women to the question of what, in their opinion, would remedy the wrongs of industrial workers, one response was, "The power to vote, as the right of suffrage, will place the services of women on an economic basis with those of men." Women working in factories asked to have inspectors appointed of their own sex, on the ground that women could understand and protect the interests of women better than men. In States where the statutory age for protection under the eight or ten hour factory law was below twenty-one, women over twenty-one desired the law extended so as to embrace those of all ages. Employees in mercantile houses doing duty as clerks, cashiers, saleswomen, etc., desired "that the same protection given to women in factories be extended to them, as their duties are fully as onerous as those of the average female in the mill or factory."

As almost all reforms have originated with the educated, and have gathered strength for fruition by rolling onward among the people, the value of these suggestions was enhanced by reason of being the expression of the most intelligent of the working-women interviewed by the Labor Bureau agents. Private philanthropic efforts of all kinds had yielded no effectual help to women, and it was small wonder if the more thoughtful among them turned to the power of the State as the only adequate means for relief from conditions which new inventions of machinery—dispensing with men and employing women and children as guides—and a mania for money-getting at the expense of the proletariat, had rendered intolerable. Though a few stenographers, telegraphers, type-writers, teachers, with some workers in the industrial arts, had gained better breathing-places upon the middle rungs of what was called the "social ladder," the struggle for life had been constantly growing fiercer among those crowded *en masse* at the bottom. Everywhere production was carried on with less regard for the life, health, and comfort of the working-women. Women were employed in even greater numbers in the poisonous, dusty, dangerous, and laborious industries, all of which were much more injurious to them, as child-bearers, than to men. The long hours of exhaustive work, destructive of family ties ; the starvation wages obtained during seasons of work ; the misery of seasons of lock-outs from work, led too frequently to the chaffering of their bodies on the street corners for bread, or the finding of a refuge from starvation in a leap from some house-top or a plunge into the river. The stories of the suffering endured by women engaged in the industrial occupations of the country, as told by capable investigators like Helen Campbell, proved that everything made by women, not excepting the whitest, daintiest robes, had crimson spots on them,—the blood-splashes of the toilers,—that, although unseen, no cleansing could wash away. Not a shop-made garment, a web of silk, cotton, or flax, or wool, a pair of gloves, shoes or stockings, any knitted thing,—machine or hand-made,—a woven carpet or piece of furniture, an artificial flower, feather, or piece of lace, a hat for a man or bonnet for a woman, a piece of table-glass, pottery, or cutlery, a lucifer match, an article of jewelry, or even a printed book, but over them all flitted the ghosts of women twice murdered in their making : once by their own pangs, and again by the sufferings of the little children, flesh of their own flesh, who toiled beside them wearily—

> Weeping (working) in the play-time of the others,
> In the country of the free.

The publication of Helen Campbell's "Prisoners of Poverty," with frequent repetitions, from other sources, of the wrongs endured by industrial women, caused a great wave of indignation to sweep over society. Many good men and women carried on crusades against the purchase of ready-made garments—sad misnomer for things so hardly made. One of their war-cries was, "An honest woman's back is not the place for a dishonestly manufactured article," and another that, "It is better for a woman to wear a coat with a hole in it than one with the stain on it of blood-guiltiness." Economically unwise and impossible of success as this crusade was, it was important as showing that a higher ideal of Justice had begun to enter into woman's mind. Hitherto people had partaken of the fruits of labor unthinkingly. Now the time was seen to have come when an awakened public began to question the propriety of purchasing and using things made through the abuse of their fellow-beings. As Emerson said of his charity-given dollar that "it was a wicked dollar he would yet learn to withhold," so women were teaching themselves to withstand desires for articles which helped to perpetuate wicked systems of work.

To the political economist, the part that woman was taking in the country's industries became a subject of national importance. After frequent investigations into the nature of their occupations, the question was propounded, "Whether it would not be expedient, for the good of the State, to altogether forbid the employment of women in factories?" The position taken by Mr. Wright, the leading authority in American labor statistics,—not prominent, however, as an advanced reformer,—was "that married women ought not to be tolerated in the mills at all," as "the employment of mothers is the most harmful wrong done to the race." "Vital science," he observes, "will one day demand their exclusion, as the effect of such employment is an evil that is sapping the life of our operative population andm ust, sooner or later, be regulated, or more probably, stopped." *

It will be seen at once that this suggestion of Mr. Wright lies directly on the plane of modern socialism or nationalism. To advocate taking two million women forcibly from certain harmful occupations is a tacit admission that the individual has no right to dispose of herself to the disadvantage of the State. Physicians had long sounded notes of warning of a race deterioration that was going on in consequence of the employment of women under bad conditions of labor, and the claim was made that "at all hazards the State must protect itself." To do this, however, involved consequences that the advisers, perhaps, foresaw. As legislation excluding women and children from factories would interfere directly with their support, the logical conclusion would be that the State, to keep them from actual starvation, would be bound to interfere again to the extent of furnishing them with such means of living as would make them—what the State wanted—happy, healthy, capable mothers of the race. And, as it would be obviously impossible to discriminate between those engaged in one pursuit at the expense of those employed in others, it would follow that the State, by supporting the factory work-

* Massachusetts Bureau of Labor Statistics, 1875, pp. 183–84.

ers, would place itself under obligations to clothe, feed, shelter, and educate all women.

This second proposition is so necessary a corollary of the first as to make Mr. Wright's suggestion almost conclusive evidence that his investigations had led him to accept the nationalistic theory of State interference with the liberty of labor, as the sole remedy for the evils sapping the life of our female operative population. And as no student of practical economics would consent to the entire withdrawal from the productive industries of so large and capable a body of workers as the three millions women now engaged in them, Mr. Wright must have also given acceptance to that other part of the nationalistic creed—growing so fast into popular favor—of its being the duty of the State to regulate the hours of labor so that work may be the promoter of health in women in place of being its destroyer.

Even if the results of Mr. Wright's investigations into the hard facts of woman's industrial condition in America had been to throw him into accord with what is termed "scientific socialism," * his experience would have been simply that of most honest investigators. Helen Campbell, converted to socialism while gathering material for her books illustrative of women as workers, claimed in her latest volume that "In socialism . . . . in its highest interpretation, lies the only solution for every problem on either side the great sea, between the eastern and western worker." Instances of similar experience might be multiplied, but are rendered unnecessary by the

* Whenever "socialism" is referred to in this essay, by the term should be simply understood the meaning given to the word in recent editions of Webster's "Unabridged Dictionary of the English Language," viz.: "A theory of society which advocates a more precise, orderly, and harmonious arrangement of the social relations of mankind than that which has hitherto prevailed." This necessarily is the very opposite of anarchy, described, in the same authority, as "The state of society where there is no law or supreme power, or where the laws are not efficient and individuals do what they please with impunity." Socialism is therefore the antithesis of anarchism. The former is constructive and altruistic, the latter destructive, and the absolute sovereignty of the individual, consequently, disregard of others. Nor is by socialism meant communism. Socialism recognizes the right of the individual to the product of his own labor and certainly not the division thereof; whereas communism means that common ownership of property which has only been successfully carried out in the conventual orders of the Roman Catholic Church and in the Buddhistic Lamaseries. This is the position taken in a recently published article from the pen of the well-known social-economist Charles Sotheran, formerly literary editor of the New York *Star*, but better known under his *noms-de-plume* of "Colmolyn" and "Southernwood."

rapidity with which the doctrine has spread in the past ten years throughout Europe and America, and the honored names which have become identified with its support. According to its adherents, one phase of applied socialism will consist in a consolidation of the splendid processes of organization and co-operation inaugurated by the various labor societies and speculative enterprises of to-day. In its results, it aims to benefit woman: (1) by recognizing woman as the perfect equal of man, politically and socially; (2) by fixing woman's means of support by the State so as to render her independent of man, and thus insure her that freedom and dignity which is hers of right as the mothers of the race; (3) by permitting them to withdraw from maleficent industries; (4) by shortening the legal working day so as to afford her leisure for the higher things of life. As women are also in greatest measure the teachers of the race, socialism victorious would secure for them a complete system of technical, art, and professional schools, so as to make the education of women universal and rounded in place of partial and incomplete. To-day, scarcely one-third of the population has been taught so much as to read and write understandingly.

The students of woman's present position in and outside the named industries make the claim that nothing less radical than such reforms as are contemplated by the socialists will avail to better their condition. A charge made and sustained by them is that existing labor legislation, as well as charitable donations of schools, libraries, etc., built by bourgeois manufacturers out of the "skimped" wages of employees, have all been futile. Whatever has been done, the fact remains, as Victor Hugo tersely put it, "The paradise of the rich is made out of the hell of the poor." Dives grows richer with the years, the purple and linen of his wives and daughters more costly, their fare more sumptuous. While Lazarus, with his women, whose toil supplies the fine raiment and choice delicacies, crouches outside the gates in rags, grown more beggarly, and whose food becomes daily more loathsome and scant.

Nationalism proposes to call this injustice to a halt. With Herbert Spencer it says, that "One [woman] will not be suffered to enjoy without working that which another produces without enjoying." It preaches the brotherhood of man, the sisterhood of women; the creed heroic in its grandeur of the abolition of alms-giving Charity, and the substitution for this outgrown goddess of past ages a divine spirit of Justice, whose fiat is to be obeyed though the heavens fall. "The growth within the mass of the population of these principles is," says a recent writer in the *Forum*, "one of the most formidable symptoms of the 'times.'" In this remark there lies all the pungency of truth. Earnest men and women are preaching the doctrines of Nationalism with all that intensity of faith which characterized the disciples of the anti-chattel slavery movement. To most, its tenets have become a religious as well as a political belief. To hasten the time of its adoption, women's voices are being heard in lecture halls and wayside inns, in meeting-houses, in the school-room, at the hearth-stone, and through the medium of the printing-press—speaking with the same enthusiasm for the redemption of the white slave as the Lucy Stones and Harriet Beecher Stowes did before 1866 for the enfranchisement of the black slave. That woman's duty to woman is taking this noble shape of pleading the cause of humanity, as though every industrial worker in factory, field, mill, and shop were her own mother, children, sisters, brothers, is the light in the heavens showing that the darkest hour before dawn has been reached, and is passing away from the horizon of the industrial population.

XII.

CHARITY.

BY

JOSEPHINE SHAW LOWELL.

To make even a superficial study of the work done and being done by American women to help their suffering fellow-beings must fill the heart with gratitude for the wisdom and devotion displayed, and with a rejoicing hope for the future. To know that all over this vast continent, intelligent and unwearying women are thinking and working and praying for the needy, the wicked, the ignorant, the weak, and the down-trodden, is a joy and an inspiration.

Necessarily, everything that is attempted is not accomplished, nor are all the attempts wise, but, nevertheless, it is encouraging to find, in looking over the whole field, that it has been very uncommon for any women, in this country, to rest content to feed the body of their suffering fellow-creatures, ignoring the wants of the brain, the heart, and the soul. However imperfectly accomplished, there always seems at least an attempt to reach beyond the material need and minister to some higher want ; to add at least a little to the character of those they have sought to help, and where the ministering to the higher wants has been made the real aim of the work, where the command, "Seek ye first the Kingdom of God and His Righteousness," has been followed, the results are, as I have said, full of encouragement.

It would be impossible in this article to give a detailed history of the charitable work of American women, nor would it be especially useful, because in each community very much the same course is followed, and nothing would be gained by describing what is so well known. I shall, therefore, attempt nothing beyond a general sketch of the usual fields of women's work, pausing to give a more careful description only of such enterprises as seem to me to contain something original, and which may serve as an inspiration and example. Nor can I dwell at length even upon these.

Apart from those who compose our own circle of family and friends, there are four classes of our fellow-men upon whom we may exercise our "Charity,"—that is, whom we may serve.

I. Those who have already reached the lowest depths, who have given up even the pretense of independence, who are housed in "public institutions," in poorhouses, prisons, insane asylums. Much may be done for these to render their lives more bearable, to help them to accept the hard lessons of their purgatory, and to learn, before they die, that one lesson which no other experience of life has succeeded in teaching them, the lesson of self-control. This has been recognized by women for years, and they have carried comfort and help, both physical and spiritual, to these unhappy beings. It has not been common, however, for women, until within a few years, to concern themselves with the management of the public institutions themselves, and although Miss Dorothea Dix began very early to devote herself to this work and spent her life in bringing about reforms in the insane asylums of many different States, still it is scarcely twenty years since such work has been generally considered to be within the sphere of women. There are now four States, Massachusetts, Connecticut, New York, and Wisconsin, in which women have accepted positions on the State Boards of Charity, and they have in these positions been very useful in bringing their critical and criticising powers and their knowledge of detail to bear upon the management of State and County institutions, besides forcing into prominence the moral aspects of the questions dealt with by the official Boards of which they are members.

The first volunteer association established to visit and improve the public institutions (as distinguished from the individual inmates), and the agency which first turned the attention of women generally to their duty in this direction, and convinced men that it was one which women were competent to perform, was the State Charities Aid Association of New York, founded in 1872 by a woman, who, during the war, had discovered and proved the working powers of women in the societies auxiliary to the Sanitary Commission. The Association consists of a central body of men and women, giving much time and thought to the study of the theory and history of all questions relating to the public care of the suffering and dependent, and of an associated committee in each county of the State, engaged in active inspection of the local method of caring for these unfortunates. These County Committees appeal to the central body for advice and instruction as to the best means to overcome the evils they discover, and furnish it with facts and figures to aid its study of general principles.

An immense good has been accomplished all through the State of New York by the Association by means of the public opinion aroused in relation to matters concerning which, before its formation, the public conscience seemed to be dead. All matters relating to the causes and prevention of pauperism are dealt with by it; it deserves the thanks of the whole country for having been the means of establishing the first training-school for nurses ever opened here, and it was very active in securing the passage of the New York law forbidding the detention of children between the ages of two and sixteen years in poorhouses.

In New Jersey there is a similar association, working upon very much the same plan, and modeled upon that of New York.

In Pennsylvania the saving of children from the contamination of the vile associations of the poorhouse was also due to women, and they have founded a society to take charge of those children who would, but for their labors, be public dependents.

The following extracts from the reports for 1885 and 1886 of the Pennsylvania Children's Aid Society will suffice to show its objects and methods, and also, let us hope, to incite other women in other States, where it is still neglected, to take up the work of gathering together and turning into the noble river of working humanity the little rills, which, if left to trickle into the great slough of pauperism and vice, only serve to increase its slimy foulness, and require deep and expensive channels to carry them off after they have become corrupt and poisonous in its depths.

The *object* of the Children's Aid Society is to provide for the welfare of destitute and neglected children by such means as shall be best for them and for the community. Our *method* of accomplishing this object is:

1. By placing such children in carefully selected private families, mostly in the country, paying a moderate rate of board where necessary, and following up each case with such inquiry and supervision as may secure to the child the conditions of physical and moral well-being.

2. By utilizing existing institutions for children as temporary homes, while permanent family places are being sought.

3. By putting, so far as possible, the support of a child upon its relatives or parents, legitimate or otherwise, and by preventing the needless separation of mothers and children.

4. By keeping an open office (39 South Seventeenth Street, Philadelphia),

where any citizen can receive free information about public provision and private opportunities for homeless children.

5. By organizing, in the cities and counties of Pennsylvania, auxiliary societies under the direction of capable and willing women, who will not only help find good country homes for the poor children of Philadelphia, but will also care for the destitute and pauper children of their own localities.

Our experience and observation abundantly confirm the following conclusions:

1. That there is no need of any more public institutions for the care of destitute children, and that much of the money now devoted to orphanages, etc., might be more usefully spent in securing homes for such children in private families and paying their board.

2. That there is no serious difficulty in finding suitable private homes, on the boarding-out plan, for all homeless children, excepting such as require treatment in hospitals or training in idiot asylums.

3. That children brought up in institutions are not so well fitted for their later life outside such institutions as those reared in families. Congregated in large numbers, they run greater risks of contagious disease; they lead an unnatural life of monotony or stimulation; they must all be treated alike, with a minimum of personal regard; they are often at the mercy of hired care-takers with little parental feeling.

4. Child-caring institutions are nevertheless important as temporary homes, or as receiving and forwarding houses for the children, while permanent places are being found.

5. The law forbidding the detention of children in almshouses can best be carried out by the co-operation of the Directors of the Poor, with voluntary associations of discreet and benevolent women, who are willing to find places for the children, look after their welfare, and report to the Directors. It is for the interest of the tax-payers that these children be taken out of the pauper class as soon as possible and absorbed in the community.

6. In a county where such an association exists, and where the Directors make fair allowance for the support of the children, there is no excuse for detaining any child in the headquarters for paupers and no need for creating an institution for pauper children. . . . . A very important and constantly increasing feature of our work seeks the welfare of the child by promoting that of the mother. Almost every day women bring their babies to the office with a pitiful tale of poverty, misfortune, and alas! often of crime, asking sometimes to have their little ones taken and provided for either to save themselves the burden, or to conceal their own disgrace.

The Society has always felt and endeavored to perform its solemn duty in such cases, which consists in keeping the child and mother together, making each the guardian of the other, and preserving the tie as the strongest incentive to a better life on the part of the mother. The interests of the child demand this, unless its natural protector should prove herself totally unfit for the simplest duties of motherhood.

Many respectable families in the country are glad to receive the services of an able-bodied, though inefficient woman, in return for low wages, and the privilege of allowing a small child to run about the house. In this way, these poor creatures are encouraged to regain the path of honesty and virtue, and, as the child grows older, its love and helpless demands form the strongest barrier which can surround the mother's life.

The work of placing these women at service has increased to such an extent that the entire attention of one person might be given to this department.

Besides the mother and her child the Society deals with a third member of this caricature of family life, namely, the father. Here the strong arm of the law is required to fix the responsibility, secure support for the child, and, if possible, to punish the wrong-doer. The services of our Solicitor are in constant requisition for this retributive task. . . . .

The Children's Aid Society of Pennsylvania has forty-four County Committees, besides its Central Board in Philadelphia.

In Connecticut, County Homes have been opened (under Laws of 1883–4–5) to receive temporarily children dependent upon the public, and committees, composed almost exclusively of women, appointed to supervise these Homes and find permanent homes in families for the children.

In Massachusetts, women are appointed as members of the Board of Managers of the State schools for delinquent and dependent children, and a very important work for women has been developed in caring for such children outside the schools. In order not to injure the boy or girl by longer retention in the school than is absolutely required for training, each one is, at the earliest moment when his progress warrants the trial, placed in a family to work ; but that the trial may be as favorable as possible, for each child so placed, a volunteer friend is found by the Board in the neighborhood, who is to watch over and give advice and assistance both to the child and its guardian. There are at present (October, 1889) eighty-four of these women visitors, officially appointed and recognized by the State as part of its system of caring for dependent and delinquent children. Of these children, thus freed from the weakening influence of a too long extended institution life, there are now in Massachusetts 1063 boys and girls under this State care.

This special work (of taking dependent children from poorhouses and other public institutions and placing them in private families, thus returning to a natural and happy life those who, but for such transplanting, would have been doomed to grow up tainted with pauperism and vice) owes its inception to the personal devotion and the labor of years of individual women in certain counties of Massachusetts, Connecticut, and New York. But for the proof of its wisdom and practicability which they gave by their successful work, it would never have assumed the position it now holds. These women have not only saved the individual children whom they took from vile surroundings, amid the contaminating companionship of the lowest of men and women, but they have set an example which is spreading over the country and which will change for the better the future of whole States.

The Women's Prison Association of New York visits the prisons of New York and Brooklyn, and within a few years the Women's Christian Temperance Union has organized a department of prison work, which will be spoken of elsewhere in this book,* but until their attention was thus called to the horrible evils of the county jails of this country, its women, with the rarest exceptions, seemed absolutely ignorant of this great national wickedness. In Massachusetts women are, and have been for a few years, members of the Prison Board, and in Massachusetts, Indiana, and New York, there are State prisons and reformatories for women under the charge of women officers.

Women are peculiarly fitted for the work of inspecting public institutions, and it would be much better if, in every community, instead of starting so many private institutions of charity, they would give their attention to the oversight of the public institutions, already necessarily existing, and which, too often, by their mismanagement, very much increase, not only the sufferings of the miserable people already in them, but also the number of those who will hereafter have to be supported as inmates.

II. Another class of sufferers needing tender care are the inmates of private Homes for old people, convalescents, and incurables; and of hospitals, reformatories, and asylums for children. Such institutions as these are usually established and managed by women, excepting the hospitals, which, though under the care of men, often have an associate board of women to take the oversight of the daily comfort of the patients.

The Homes for the aged in our cities are many of them established by churches for their dependent members, and in almost all an entrance fee is required. There are Homes for aged married couples in some of our cities, and in many, also, a free Home for old men and women, maintained by the Roman Catholic Little Sisters of the Poor, who receive inmates, however, of every faith.

Of Homes for convalescents and incurables there are very few, comparatively, though it would seem as if the hard lot of these two classes of sufferers would appeal most strongly to tender-hearted women. In no one community, however, have we adequate provision for them, and they languish, unwelcome inmates of hospitals and poorhouses. There is a small Home for Incurables in Boston, founded by a young Roman Catholic Irishwoman, who earned her daily bread by hair-dressing, and

---

* See chapter, Work for the Criminal Classes.—Ed.

who for four years had given all her spare time and money to the care of one dying girl after another, until she was enabled, by the help of friends for whom she worked, to open the Channing Home, which from that time to this (now long after her death) has been a refuge for poor consumptive girls and crippled women.

Reformatories for women are, strangely enough, often established by men. It would seem as if no work could be more appropriate to women, and as if there were no field which they should more quickly have occupied entirely to the exclusion of men; but although there are a number of such institutions for both girls and women in different parts of the country, to whose management good women have devoted themselves, there is still room for many more, in which women (especially young women) who are a danger to themselves and others, ought to be shut away from temptation and the opportunity to tempt.

Women's work in hospitals and in care for the sick is to be treated elsewhere in this book.

The Homes for children, which abound in almost every part of the country, have all had their growth in less than ninety years, the very first one established being the Boston Female Asylum, opened in 1800, and incorporated in 1803, established by women whose granddaughters and great-granddaughters are now numbered among the managers.

There is a great deal of devoted, earnest work given both by the outside Boards who control these Homes and by the officers who take the daily care of the thousands of children in them; there is the wish to do real good, and, especially among the Sisterhoods, whose whole lives are given up to the work of ministering to these children, there is often absolute self-sacrifice; but it is too frequently open to question whether the real benefit done is equal to the benevolence which prompts the doing. In these institutions the children are generally treated kindly, but the managers, unfortunately, too often fail to see the bad effects of the institution life both upon the child and upon society as a whole; and, though they may suspect their existence, they usually feel helpless to remedy these evils, scarcely having courage to enter on new ways of caring for their charges.

One institution, which for thirty-one years had continued in the old way, was closed under circumstances most creditable to the managers, and the history of the Union Temporary Home of Philadelphia deserves a place in this article as an example to the management of other similar institutions.

At the thirty-first annual meeting in January, 1887, the following resolution was adopted:

Resolved, That in the judgment of this meeting it is advisable that our building be closed at an early day; that all our property be converted into an income-bearing fund; that under the direction of a special executive committee chosen from the Council, or the Board of Managers, or both, said income shall be applied, according to the declared object of our constitution, in paying for the temporary board and care of "children of the poor;" that the term "Home" be construed to include any house or household in which such children are placed; and that the machinery of the Children's Aid Society be used for obtaining, investigating, and supervising such boarding-homes; that all the rights of parents be duly respected, and they still be held to pay a share, wherever practicable; and that our Board of Managers, or such committees as they may appoint, represent this corporation in carrying out these arrangements, and in the performances of whatever duties may be required to secure the execution of our trust and the welfare of the children.

Some of the reasons for this action are given in the following extracts from a paper submitted by the managers to the meeting:

In taking action which looks toward co-operation with another body, we have been moved by considerations which affect profoundly three interests: (1) Those of the parents and guardians of the children admitted to the Home; (2) those of the public which is asked to give it support; (3) most of all, those of the children.

I. Since the Home was started, thirty years ago, the population of Philadelphia has increased from about 500,000 to nearly 1,000,000. In such a vast and dense mass of human beings, personal relations between giver and receiver have become more difficult, and the indiscriminate charity which encourages pauperism has been a cause of growing concern. A habit of dependence, which takes advantage of every opportunity to live by public or private charity, is widespread; and the growth of false, communistic views makes necessary more guarded methods than those which may serve in smaller communities, with simpler social conditions.

The history of our own institution, as the managers well know, shows a constant pressure for the admission of children whose parents are able to support them, but are naturally disposed to do this at the lowest possible cost, and that we have also been furnishing easy facilities for those who desire, for selfish reasons, to rid themselves of the presence and care of their little ones. The charitable feature of the institution, or the fact that a part of the expense is borne by our contributors, is disguised by the fact that we are accustomed to charge $1.25 to $1.50 a week for each child, so that the institution is regarded by such parents simply *as a cheap boarding-house for children.* We believe that many, who could themselves bear the entire cost with no serious hardship, are tempted to magnify their own disability by the fatal facilities afforded by a well-meant charity. Some of this class are doubtless in need of help, but it should not come in this delusive form. They may want friendly counsel and wise direction in finding suitable homes; and they may sometimes be assisted by kindly oversight of these homes and of their children. It is in our power to secure for them these advantages, with added pecuniary assistance where needed, by utilizing the methods of the Children's Aid Society, which is also a Bureau of Information.

* * * * *

III. The most important consideration relates to the children. No mere saving of money would justify a change which threatened injury to the least of these little ones. But a majority of the managers are convinced, by observation and experience, that life in the average institution is not so good for children as life in the average household. None can realize that so fully as those who are best acquainted with the inner workings and vicissitudes of child-caring institutions. We have sought to guard our children from the worst effects by providing a kindergarten for the younger ones, and by sending the elder to the public schools; and they have enjoyed the care and kindness of an exceptionally competent and faithful matron; but the total result has compelled us to the same conclusion with many tried workers in charity,—viz.: that the children can best be fitted for the life they must live in the world by being placed in good families.

The testimony of two gentlemen on our Board of Council, both experienced as heads of great industrial enterprises, is that institution boys are generally the least desirable apprentices. They have been dulled in faculty by not having been daily exercised in the use of themselves in small ways. . . . have had all particulars of life arranged for them, and, as a consequence, they wait for some one else to arrange every piece of work, and are never ready for emergencies or able to "take hold."

One great evil of institutions for children is quite overlooked—the effect on the parents of relieving them of the care of their children,—because the attention of the managers is almost exclusively devoted to the care of the children while in the institution; they do not think it part of their duty to study the family from which the child was taken, or the influences which surrounded it before it came under their charge; nor do they, with rare exceptions, follow the children's lives with any systematic care after they leave them. They thus know nothing of the results of their own work, and may be doing great evil, where they wish only to do good.

In Dorchester, Mass., there is a small "Industrial School for Girls," which seems to be especially distinguished from most other Homes of the kind, by the thorough and systematic manner in which the children who have left the school are watched over. Besides the standing committee on "placing out," which is required to report to the managers once in three months concerning the girls under its charge (those who, having been fitted in the school for household work, have been put into places to earn their living), a "Committee on Friendly Guardianship" has been created, whose duties are thus described in the report of the school for the year 1887: "To keep a list of all girls leaving the school, who, through the expiration of the papers placing them under our care, are no longer formally wards of the school; to keep up a knowledge of these girls and to report concerning their welfare twice a year, such report to be added to the secretary's records. The term Friendly Guardianship is used to distinguish this oversight, which does not carry with it any formal authority, from the usual school guardianship of girls who are placed under our care for a period beyond that passed at school, and which is recognized as authoritative by the girls themselves and by their relatives, if they have any."

In the report for 1888, it is stated that there are thirty-four girls under direct school guardianship, thirty-five under the charge of the Friendly Guardianship Committee, and an account is given of the present condition of fifty-eight earlier school graduates. The following reflection, found in the report, applies equally to other institutions of the same character:

"The expense of caring for a child at the Industrial School is large as compared with the cost of boarding in a private family, and this expense can only be justified by keeping up a high standard in the school, and by adding a large amount of personal work outside and beyond the school for the girls who have gone out from it."

Another Boston society (in whose establishment and management women have always had a large part) is also distinguished for the continued oversight of its charges after they have quitted the institutions it has established. The Boston Children's Aid Society maintains three distinct farm schools for boys, in each of which a small number of boys (it is the intention never to have more than thirty in any one school) are under the care of a farmer and his wife, who teach them to work, while they receive a common school education from a teacher in the house. The majority of the boys, when received, are either under arrest, or are threatened with arrest, and they are committed to the care of the society for reformation. After such a term of training, as seems needed in each case, the boys are generally sent to work in the country, and a paid agent (a lady) has the oversight of them, writing to them and visiting them. For the boys who have returned to Boston, a club has been formed "to afford opportunities for studying the careers of the boys, noting their progress, learning the plans of such as had plans, and stimulating those who had none to form them, and in general arousing the boys to a livelier sense of their duties and opportunities."

The Boston Children's Aid Society has also a certain number

of girls under its care, either at work or boarded in private families. The aim of the society is to put the children in its charge into private families as soon as they are fitted for such a life, and it had in 1888 more children outside its farm schools than in them to take care of.

We have so far been speaking of people living in institutions, living, that is, under unnatural conditions, uprooted, as it were, from their own place in life, and set in artificial surroundings. There are a third and fourth class still to consider.

III. The third class are those who neither support themselves entirely in self-respecting independence, nor are subject to the discipline of an institution, those who are constantly being tempted to depend upon others, to think their circumstances too hard for them, to regard as unattainable the heights of self-support which the mass of mankind reach,—the weak, the inefficient, the unwise, the self-indulgent,—in a word, those who are unequal to the demands of life. They need all the "help" they can get, but not of the kind which is usually given to them, not that which enervates them, which encourages all their weaknesses, which makes the dependent more dependent, the inefficient more inefficient, the self-indulgent more self-indulgent. They need *real help*, help to stand upon their own feet, help to respect themselves, help to play their part in life with energy and intelligence, help to be men and women, strong, self-dependent, ready to help others.

The "relief" which is poured out indiscriminately simply serves to check their efforts at self-support, and to turn all their energies to the pursuit of more "relief." It is not that they are different from other people ; no human being will put forth greater exertion to sustain himself in the way he likes than is required for that purpose. No man will devote more time or more labor than is necessary to maintain himself and his family at his own standard. If his standard is so low that what comes to him in "relief" is enough for him, why should he spend time and strength in getting more ? But if his standard is so low, then the help he needs is that which will raise his standard, but not his standard of physical life only ; far more important is it to raise his moral standard,—to raise his character, so that degrading surroundings cannot be endured, so that they cannot exist.

By the different kinds of "help" offered to those in want, they may be trampled down into the mire and left, body and soul degraded, a curse to themselves and others, or they may be lifted into the healthy, self-respecting life of the men and women who do the work of the world, of the mass of the people, who lead hard lives of struggle and self-sacrifice, but whose intellects are strengthened, whose characters are strengthened, whose souls are strengthened, by the daily and hourly trials they meet and overcome.

The account of the way in which American women have dealt with these suffering people, those upon whom most of the experiments of the benevolent are tried, is not, as I have already said, entirely discouraging. In all their dealings with them, they always seem to have had a latent consciousness at least that they had minds and souls, and not bodies only. I think women have seldom been responsible for the "charities" which were satisfied to give one meal to a hungry fellow-being and then turn from him with no further sense of responsibility for any subsequent meal. They have usually sought to enter into some sort of human relation with those they tried to help, to make material relief the vehicle for moral and spiritual relief, and even when the material relief was actually doing far more harm in undermining character and self-dependence than could be counteracted by all the teaching given, still this sad fact was not recognized, or at least not realized, and the intention was far better than the performance.

Within the past ten or fifteen years, all over the country, an awakening of conscience in regard to these subjects has been taking place, and in almost all the larger cities and in many of the towns of our country there are already formed associations whose object it is to cure and prevent pauperism. This movement is in this country due in a great degree to women, and in all the sixty or seventy societies which now exist men and women work together, and in many of them women take the lead. The "old charity" sought mainly to relieve physical suffering by physical relief; the "new charity" seeks to relieve physical suffering by raising the character of the sufferer and by discovering the underlying causes of the suffering both in himself and in his surroundings.

IV. The fourth class whom we can serve are the people who are generally thought to need no "charity" at all, and who indeed get but little of it, either by word or deed—the wage-earners of the world—those who dig and hammer, who sew and scrub, who toil and sweat, to feed and clothe themselves and all the world besides.

Fortunately, there has, within the past few years, grown up a strong conviction among those who seek to serve their kind, that to help these men and women, to strengthen them, to teach them, is the real means of lifting the race, and hence have been developed (especially by women, and for women and children) many plans for making their lives not only easier, but richer and nobler, and more what a human life should be.

In all such plans education is involved, and there are many inspiring instances of really great changes wrought by women in the system of education in our large cities, whose influence for good will never cease. The introduction of kindergarten teaching for little children, which many of those who study the dark problems of pauperism and crime believe will do more to destroy the misery of mankind than any other one educational agency, was due to Miss Elizabeth Peabody, herself a teacher in her youth, who in her middle age was filled with enthusiasm by the beautiful new teaching, and has lived to see it, in her old age, incorporated, mainly by the exertions of women, into the public school system of many of our large cities, where the need of the reform was greatest.

In St. Louis, the first city to adopt the kindergarten, it was a woman who proposed it. In Boston, one woman herself established and maintained for nearly ten years thirty-one kindergartens, and finally, having by this long experience proved their value, persuaded the Board of Education to accept them as part of the public school system.

In Philadelphia, another woman, inspired by the good she saw accomplished in Boston by the kindergartens established by her friend, in 1879 opened one in that city, and gradually, following her example and under her leadership, others were opened; and in 1881 the Sub Primary School Society was incorporated for the purpose of establishing and maintaining kindergartens in Philadelphia, and continued its work until in December, 1886, this was consummated, when it presented to the Board of Education thirty-two kindergartens, to be in future carried on as part of the school system.

In California, the Golden Gate Association has founded, by the help of a few rich people who have given money, and of many devoted women who have watched over the enterprise and given time and thought to its success, a large number of free kindergartens, and the same is true of many other cities in the country.

In other ways, also, the public schools have been benefited by the volunteer work of women, not only as members of School Boards, which position they have accepted in Boston, New York, and Philadelphia, but especially in leading the way in demonstrating the possibilities and value of industrial education.

In New York, the Industrial Education Association was founded by men and women for the purpose of bringing this most important subject before the public, and of training teachers for all branches of manual education.

Industrial schools have been established and carried on by women in many different localities,* and all over the country church societies conduct sewing classes, and classes in domestic training for girls. In many of our cities, women have established vacation schools to save the children from the demoralization of the long summer idleness, and have, in some places, obtained the use of the public school buildings for this purpose. In Boston "The Emergency and Hygiene Association" (composed of men and women) has a "Committee on Playgrounds," which, in the summer vacation of 1888, opened seven of the public school yards as play grounds for children, and three more as "sand-gardens." In each a matron was present to oversee the games of the children, and in the playgrounds they were supplied with "sand-heaps and shovels, balls, tops, skipping ropes, sand bags, building blocks, flags to march under, and transparent slates to draw on," while in the "sand-gardens" there was only the pleasure of digging in sand heaps. Thus for three hours a day on four fair days of each week during the vacation, hundreds of children spent happy and healthful hours.

The "fresh air work," the "country week," the excursions of every kind, are chiefly carried on by the devotion of women, and all will undoubtedly accomplish a greater good than the temporary benefit to the health and spirits of city children, by implanting a love for country life in many of the little visitors, which may prove in the future an influence to counteract the strange taste which now leads so many people to prefer a crowded tenement to a farm-house and makes them "feel lonesome" within a stone's throw of a dozen neighbors.

Nor have women, although devoting so much of their time to the training of children, neglected those past the age of schooling, those who have grown up without privilege or advantage, especially the young girls who have to work for their living and struggle with untrained hands and brains to support themselves and perhaps many others dependent on them. In almost all our cities women have formed associations especially to help self-supporting young women and girls, and the aim of all is to give happiness and added pleasure, besides the oppor-

---

* See chapter on Woman in Industry.—Ed.

tunity of development in every direction. The Women's Christian Associations,* of which there are more than fifty in the country, open rooms for evening entertainment and study, give instruction in intellectual and manual branches, find situations for those who need them, help working girls in every way, and many are the women who have leisure and education who devote both to efforts to help and succor women who have neither. Most of these associations have Homes for working women, where the inmates are guarded and watched over with kindly care. In other cities the Young Women's Christian Association have no Homes of their own, but select safe boarding places for young women, and direct them to them, and keep boarding registers.

One of the women who knows most of the condition of working women in our cities, says of the "Homes:" "The few hundreds sheltered are in most cases really friendless and deserving women to whom the chief boon is not the cheap board, but the respectable surroundings, which could not be had at all in ordinary lodgings. . . . . The safe-guards thrown about women in these Homes are most desirable. . . . . My objections to them are that they are not radical enough in their reforms, and really bar the truly needy factory girl of the slums; and that by furnishing so many comforts and privileges at low rates they create false expectations and standards. Were the advantages made dependent on co-operative management, were the inmates themselves responsible for the adornment and conduct of the Homes, suffering for extravagance and bad judgment, profiting by foresight and experience, valuable educational training would be secured, and a far more home-like interest."

The Boston Young Women's Christian Association (founded in 1866) in its twenty-third annual report, after describing the employment department, gymnasium, library, entertainments, the travelers' aid, the industrial training department, the evening classes for intellectual work, says:

"Another important work, which has been carried on for some years, is the training of girls for domestic service. . . . They remain three months. . . . . They are instructed in the best possible way, practically, by doing all varieties of domestic work. As this educational work progressed, there opened out another need, and this was an opportunity for preparation on the part of women of intelligence and education, by which

---

* See chapter, Woman in Industry.—Ed.

they could fit themselves for positions as matrons, housekeepers, teachers of domestic economy, etc. For this end a normal class has been organized, and they are now pursuing a course of instruction."

The New York Young Women's Christian Association, founded in 1872, offers to self-supporting women the following privileges:

I. The Bible class.
II. Free concerts, lectures, readings, etc.
III. Free classes for instruction in writing, commercial arithmetic, book-keeping, business training, phonography, type-writing, retouching photo-negatives, photo-color, mechanical and free-hand drawing, clay modeling, applied design, choir music, and physical culture.
IV. Free circulating library, reference library, and reading-rooms.
V. Employment bureau.
VI. Needlework department, salesroom, order department, free classes in machine and hand-sewing, classes in cutting and fitting.
VII. Free board directory.

In the year 1883 was incorporated the Baltimore Young Women's Christian Association, "having in view the improvement of the condition of the working women of Baltimore by providing for them a reading-room, and such other departments as may be found necessary."

I quote from a description, lately written, some account of the work of this association:

"The educating influences of the Young Women's Christian Association has been chiefly social and practical. . . . Classes in reading, writing, book-keeping, and singing were early instituted. . . . . English literature has been taught in simple and effective ways by reading aloud from good authors to appreciative groups of young women, and also by introducing the co-operative method of reading, one girl taking one book by a given author, another girl another, and all reporting on their individual readings to the assembled class. . . . .

"Another excellent branch of committee work is to see that girls who come to the lunch-rooms have proper boarding places. Ladies visit girls in their lodgings. A female physician has lent her services in caring for the sick, and has made herself very useful by keeping a careful watch upon the sanitary condition of shops where girls are employed. . . . ."

Several of the Women's Christian Associations have under their care other branches of charitable work than those above enumerated, and as a rule their benefits seem to be confined more or less strictly to Protestants. There are other organizations for the befriending of young women and girls (helping hands, girls' friendly societies, church societies in great numbers, etc., etc.) which have the same limitation, but there are still others intended to receive all who will join them.

The "Women's Educational and Industrial Unions," existing in thirteen cities of the United States, have for their objects "increasing fellowship among women, in order to promote the best practical methods for securing their educational, industrial, and social advancement." *

The following are extracts from a circular issued by the original Union, founded in Boston, in 1877:

> This institution may be regarded as a social centre, a place of welcome. Any woman, resident or stranger, by coming to the Union will find herself among friends. Its placards in railway stations often bring to us strangers from various parts of the country and from abroad. It invites all women to its reading-room and parlors. It provides lectures, classes, and entertainments. Some of the classes are industrial. It has "Mother's Meetings" and "Talks with Young Girls" from women with high reputation. It affords opportunities for interchange of thought upon the vital questions of the day. It receives and preserves reports of women's associations both near and distant. It is a centre of local information. It gathers in the best ideas and suggestions, and weaves them into plans for the benefit of humanity. It befriends the friendless. It is a tower of strength for the helpless. It secures dues unjustly withheld from working women. It investigates fraudulent advertisements, and publicly warns women against them. So far as practicable, it secures situations for the unemployed. In its salesrooms are found the products of women's industries. . . . . Wise thinkers have the opinion that for removing the ills of humanity primary work is better than after work. The methods of the latter are charities, reformatory crusades, and penal enactments. The evils contended with,—pauperism, drunkenness, vice, crime,—are simply inward conditions becoming apparent in conduct. These conditions are ignorance, selfishness, undeveloped faculties, false rating of values, lack of self-respect and of self-restraint. The effective work is to change such conditions by a kind of education that shall develop the highest and best, thus enabling the individual to stand upright of himself, instead of being held in position by charities, reforms, or penalties.

In New York, in 1879, was founded a Girls' Club, which consisted of the founder, a woman of education and wealth, and ten or twelve factory and shop girls, who met in an upper room in a Tenth Avenue tenement house. During the past ten years, that club has increased to a membership of several hundred, and twenty-two kindred clubs have been formed in New York, eleven in Brooklyn, and eight in Boston and in other cities. These clubs are mainly self-supporting, and their work is the education and elevation of the members in every pos-

---

* See chapter, Woman in Industry.—ED.

sible direction—physical, industrial, mental, and moral. They supply a common ground of meeting for young women who have had the privileges of education, money and leisure, with those who have had the privileges of self-denying, hard-working lives, and the benefits are mutual.*

Women have, in various cities, opened restaurants where good food is provided at moderate prices, for the purpose not only of saving money to those who patronize them, but to give decent and attractive surroundings and a freedom from temptation to drink. In some of these restaurants are rooms where working-girls may eat lunch which they bring from their own homes, and in some the decent toilet provision is spoken of as a great boon to these girls, who work in shops and factories where every requirement of decency is neglected or violated in that particular.

In New York City a small band of educated women have jointly hired a tenement house in the very worst district of the city, politically and morally, and there they intend to live, for the purpose of doing what they can to elevate the tone of the neighborhood. Most of them have their daily avocations, but in the evenings they will give their time to such efforts as they find best suited to attain their end.† Some of them have already taken part in the work of the "Neighborhood Guild,"

---

* The Association of Working Girls' Societies was formed February, 1884, with the following objects:

1. To strengthen, to knit together, and to protect the interests of the several societies.
2. To hold meetings, when reports of the societies shall be presented, and to make more generally known their aims and advantages.
3. To promote the general adoption of the principles upon which the societies have been formed.
4. To secure the services, by co-operation, of good teachers, lady physicians, and lecturers.
5. To keep the several societies informed of such classes and schemes as are proved valuable.
6. To encourage and assist in the establishment of new societies.

In April, 1890, a convention was held under the auspices of the New York, Boston, and Brooklyn Associations of Working Girls' Societies, and the Philadelphia New Century Working Women's Guild. Two hundred and twenty-five delegates, representing ninety-six clubs, and from thirty-eight different cities and towns, were present.—Ed.

† The effort above referred to has during the year taken shape as the "College Settlement," and on September 1, 1890, its first annual report closes with the following words:

"What are the 'results?' Certainly the residents are recognized as the friends of those about them. The children turn to them with the joy of every acquisition and the grief of every loss. The club boys of sixteen

the spirit of which is thus described in its last published circular :

We do not look upon our work as done by one class of society for another class of society ; not as up-town residents, nor from the height of proud superiority to our fellow-men in any regard do we go down to labor in the tenement-house district. All sorts and conditions of men are brought into contact in the Neighborhood Guild. All both give and receive ; all are both teachers and taught ; and the lesson for all is the brotherhood of man. The Guild is not connected with any church or society, whatsoever. But persons of various beliefs are connected with the Guild, and the sense of the brotherhood of all men is their bond of union. The work of the Guild, except in the kindergarten, is done by faithful volunteers, several of whom have resided for many months in the tenement-house district. The spirit of the Guild is against unnecessary absenteeism in good works. It would bring all sorts of men together close enough to feel one another's heart-throbs. It believes in a communism of mental and spiritual possessions.

A somewhat similar society, established both by men and women, in Philadelphia, gives the following account of itself :

The object of this unsectarian association is to establish, in localities most needing them, and chiefly for the benefit of workingmen and their families, convenient centers for social intercourse, amusement, reading, study, restaurant accommodation, etc., without the accompaniment of any demoralizing features.

Our first experiment was to open, on Saturday evenings, the hall on the corner of Twenty-third and Hamilton streets, which seats nearly three hundred people. This was furnished with tables for refreshments, and here we gave a series of light entertainments, sometimes for five cents, sometimes ten cents admission. The next step was to open the house at 2134 Vine street, and start a neighborhood society under the title of Family Guild, No. 1. In order to secure to the house at the start the character desired, we admitted to its privileges, under proper conditions, men, women, and children, and in-

---

and seventeen years are proud of their connection with the house and eager rivals in its good opinion. Even some of the older women turn to the residents as friends upon whom they can rely. Those who know the work best do not look for results other than this friendly relation in any near future. The work, if it is anything, is a process of education. Character is not formed in a year. In all the club work the object constantly sought is helpful, personal contact. All methods are simply a means to this end. For this reason the number of members in each club is limited. If the higher is ever to give an uplift to the lower, must it not be through this method of friendship ? Such a relation implies giving and taking on both sides, and the workers at the Settlement find one of the strongest points gained by residence to be, that their neighbors have a chance to do something for them, a chance which is often improved. The Settlement is one of the influences which go to form the lives of the people in Rivington Street. If it shall create any higher ideals or quicken any aspirations, if it shall awaken one soul to any sense of its own nature, the object of the College Settlement will surely be attained."

stead of separating families, offered special inducements to father, mother, and children to come together.

The advantages of membership are a library, reading-room (with magazines, weekly and daily papers), rooms for games, music classes, accommodations for business and social meetings, etc. The price is one dollar a year for adults, fifty cents for those under seventeen, while a family ticket including father, mother, and all children under seventeen, is one dollar and fifty cents. Class instruction is extra, five and ten cents a lesson, except the manual training, which is free, and the dancing, which is fifteen cents.

The most popular classes last year were cooking, singing, and dressmaking. The cooking class numbered sixteen, dressmaking ten, singing thirty. The number of members enrolled last winter was one hundred and fifty. This does not include all attending classes, some of whom were not members of the Guild.

The experiment of associating the sexes both in study and recreation has proved a success. The class in manual training, which now numbers forty, is composed about equally of young men and women, and the teachers say it is much easier with such a class to keep order and to secure attention to work.

Besides the regular social evenings devoted to plays, singing, dancing, etc., it is not unusual for the members of the evening classes which close at nine to adjourn to the play-room and take a little time for amusement. The managers have naturally kept an anxious watch over these occasions and have found nothing to complain of in the conduct of the young people. . . . .

There will be certain hours of each afternoon devoted to the children of the neighborhood, with the object of teaching them quieter and less brutal ways of playing than they learn on the streets. We also hope to establish a day nursery, which shall obviate the dreadful necessity among working women of locking their children alone in a room for the day. . . . .

In Illinois, women have organized associations for the protection of women and children which seem to be more far-reaching than any such in other States.

The second article of "The Protective Agency for Women and Children of Chicago" reads as follows:

Its objects are to secure protection from all offenses and crimes against the purity and virtue of women and children; protection against any injustice to women or children of a financial character, such as withholding of wages, exacting of exorbitant interest, violation of contract, or fraudulent advertisements of any kind; enforcement of existing laws, and efforts toward the enactment of better ones, for the protection of women and children against wrongs and abuses, of whatever nature; the extension of a wholesome moral support to women and children who have been wronged, discriminating wisely between misfortune and guilt.

For three years the agency has fulfilled its objects and has carried out the wish expressed in its first annual report in the following words: "Justice is better than charity, and we wish to be a terror to evil-doers as well as a good Samaritan to the unfortunate."

The Agency is carried on by a governing board consisting of delegates from sixteen different associations of women in Chicago, and it has taken its stand by the side of the poor and oppressed and demanded and obtained justice for them in the courts. In its third annual report it publishes the following extracts from a letter of John P. Altgelt, Judge of Superior Court of Cook County: ". . . . I wish to express my high appreciation of the work the Agency is doing. . . . . You have rendered a double service to the courts and have materially aided in the administration of justice." In Peoria, Ill., there is also such an Agency, and a National Association has been formed "for the purpose of establishing, or helping to establish, similar societies in different parts of the country."

Another important woman's society is the "Illinois Woman's Alliance," which declares its objects to be: "1. To agitate for the enforcement of all existing laws and ordinances that have been enacted for the protection of women and children, as the factory ordinances and the compulsory education law. 2. To secure the enactment of such laws as shall be found necessary. 3. To investigate all business establishments and factories where women and children are employed, and public institutions where women and children are maintained. 4. To procure the appointment of women as inspectors and as members of boards of education and to serve on boards of management of public institutions."

The Woman's Alliance has already been "largely instrumental in procuring the passage of a compulsory education law, and has secured the appointment of women factory inspectors."

Another branch of work taken up by women in some of our cities is the owning and hiring of tenement houses, for the purpose of improving the houses and thereby serving the tenants and the public. This is done both by individuals, who undertake the oversight of the houses and the collecting of rents themselves (following the example of Miss Octavia Hill in London), and by associations such as the Co-operative Building Association of Boston, which is a joint stock company of men and women, who buy and build houses and oversee their property by means of committees of their own number. The object is to raise the standard of the houses for working people in any given locality, and also to show that such houses, when managed for the benefit of the tenants, may be made to pay a fair return to the owners. This work seems peculiarly fitting for women, who carry sympathy and conscience into their business relations.

Indeed, the work of women seems to be unending, and it is impossible to compute its value. The only feeling evoked by the study of the reports of what is going on all over the country is that of deep gratitude, and of regret that the whole cannot be spread out for the encouragement and inspiration of others, and that so meager an account as this must suffice.

It is strange to remember that all this activity has had its rise in less than a hundred years. The simple story of the first organized charitable work ever done, so far as we know, by women in this country is thus told in an account of the "Female Society of Philadelphia for the Relief and Employment of the Poor:"

"It will be remembered that in the year 1793, the yellow fever made an awful and depopulating visitation to our city, and those who were spared its ravages were left in much distress. Anne Parish, and some other young women, having devoted considerable time and strength in relieving the sufferers, felt called upon to continue their labors when the deadly scourge had passed, as the following minutes, the first on the books, will show:

"'A number of young women, having been induced to believe from observations they have made that they could afford some assistance to their suffering fellow-creatures, particularly *widows* and *orphans*, by entering into a subscription for their relief, visiting them in their solitary dwellings without distinction of nation or color, sympathizing in their afflictions, and, as far as their ability extends, alleviating them, have for this purpose associated together. Their views being humble and funds inconsiderable, yet seeking neither honor nor applause, they only ask a blessing on their feeble efforts, sensible of the obligations they are under to an Almighty Giver for the comforts they enjoy, are desirous of making a grateful acknowledgment by endeavoring to adopt the precept He taught, to visit the sick, feed the hungry, and clothe the naked. They propose to nominate a treasurer, to appoint a committee to visit the poor, and discover their necessities either for immediate relief, or to give them employment.'"

This was in 1795, and it was this same young Quaker woman, Anne Parish, who, in that, or the following year, believing that "ignorance was one great cause of vice and the calamities attendant thereon, and that a guarded education would tend greatly to the future usefulness and respectability of the rising youth," with two friends, opened the first charity school for girls in the United States, teaching them "some of the most useful branches of learning, viz.: spelling, reading, writing, arithmetic, and sewing."

These two little societies, both founded by one young woman, were the pioneers in the work for the desolate and oppressed now being carried on by hundreds of associations and by thousands of women all over our country, and we can only thank God that so many are seeking "to comfort and help the weak-hearted, to raise up those who fall, and to strengthen such as do stand."

XIII.

CARE OF THE SICK.

HOSPITALS AND TRAINING SCHOOLS FOR NURSES MANAGED WHOLLY OR IN PART BY WOMEN.

BY

EDNAH DOW CHENEY.

So soon as the human being emerged from barbarism, and life became precious, the restoration of the sick to health must have engaged attention. The original idea of the hospital was wholly charitable, as it was an obvious duty to take care of the sick, who were unable to help themselves, and under many circumstances this work could be better done in an establishment for that special purpose than in a private home.

Such establishments have existed in very early times and in various countries, and women have always borne their part in the work as nurses, if not as physicians or managers.

Although the hospital, in some form, was not unknown before the establishment of the Christian church, yet that church certainly took the care of the sick as a special province, and found in its orders of monks and nuns very convenient instruments for carrying it on. It was an important adjunct of religion, for the mind and heart, during sickness and convalescence, are open to religious and moral influences, and the grateful patient often became a zealous convert to the church which had given him help in the hour of suffering. The old proverb recognized this :

When the Devil was sick, the Devil a monk would be ;
When the Devil was well, the devil a monk was he.

The earliest known hospital for the sick was founded in the latter part of the fourth century at Cæsarea ; St. Chrysostom built one at his own expense at Constantinople, and Fabiola, the friend of St. Jerome, founded one at Rome.

Many of the present great European hospitals, as the "Hotel Dieu" of Paris, "St. Bartholomew" of London, etc., owe their existence to religious foundations, and the sisters of various orders made it their especial work to labor in them.

Women assisted in these good works. In the old hospital of the Savoy in London, thirteen sisters are on the pay roll. "Queen Mary tried to restore this hospital, and the ladies of the court and maidens of honor stored the same with two beds, bedding, and furniture in very ample manner." The work of the sisters of charity is familiar to all, and Protestants have imitated it by establishing orders of women who devote themselves to the care of the sick.

In addition to the ordinary needs of human life, war brought its large increase of wounds and sickness, which made military hospitals a necessity, and women did not hesitate to follow men to the camp and field to minister to their fellow-beings in distress. In these scenes of war Florence Nightingale began her great work, which has raised nursing to the rank of a skillful profession. Private charity also extended help to the sick, and King James's favorite goldsmith, George Heriot, secured an honorable remembrance in Edinburgh by founding the large hospital which bears his name. Neither has the State forgotten its duty to the sick, not only in providing infirmaries, almshouses, and other institutions, but certainly, in later times, in furnishing hospitals for the poor at the public expense.

In time of war, or when great epidemics devastated cities, the hospitals often became excessively crowded, and offered scenes of misery and horror which justified the dread and disgust felt for them in the popular mind, so that to "die in a hospital" was an expression for the extreme of human misery.

Through all these years women took an active part in hospital work as nurses, and, in the case of infirmaries connected with female convents, must have had charge of the administration; but it is not until our own day that hospitals have been established especially for the benefit of women, and mainly under their own control. As the science of medicine advanced, and physicians were not solitary students but became a body of educated men united in their work and deeply interested in the advancement of their science, the hospital came to be regarded not exclusively as a charity, but also as a school in which the student of medicine could gain experience and knowledge by intimate acquaintance with various forms of disease and the means employed to remove it. This created a vulgar prejudice that the sick were considered only subjects of experiment, without regard to their own good. But, in fact, the constant presence of bodies of intelligent students in hospitals has done much to raise their character and to reform abuses. As Dr. Finlay says, "Clinical teaching benefits the patient, secures careful investigation of his case, and has a bracing effect on the work done in the hospital."

It is in this relation that hospitals have become especially important to women during the last thirty years.

The woman physician was not wholly unknown in America before this time. Anne Hutchinson, of Boston, was doctor as well as preacher. Ruth Barnaby practiced the profession of midwifery forty years, and this branch of practice was fully recognized as belonging to women.* But while the standard of education for women was very low, these were only individuals carrying out the impulses of their genius or their hearts, having no relation to each other and no thorough systematic education.

When Elizabeth Blackwell took her stand for thorough medical education for women, she felt the imperative need of clinical instruction for them. No hospital in America would give to women students of medicine any opportunity to see the work done in it.

The other hospitals, which have been established since these pioneers, have followed their plans so nearly that but few exceptions need be made to the general account. While I cannot be sure that my list is complete, I give the following names of hospitals known to me, similar in character and methods:

New York Infirmary, 1857.†
Women's Hospital of Philadelphia, 1860.
New England Hospital for Women and Children, 1862.†
Chicago Hospital for Women and Children, 1865.
Pacific Dispensary and Hospital for Women and Children.
Ohio Hospital.
Northwestern Hospital, Minneapolis.

The hospital in Chicago, like other promising children of the East transplanted to the West, has outgrown its parents, and is now the largest institution of its kind in this country, and probably in the world. It has eighty beds.

---

* See chapter, Woman in Medicine.—Ed.

† The story of the founding of the New York Infirmary, and the New England Hospital for Women and Children, is told in the chapter on Woman in Medicine.—Ed.

The Massachusetts Homœopathic Hospital was not established for the special benefit of women, but in connection with the medical school of Boston University, but it received the funds of the old Female Medical School, and it has women professors and students, and admits women to the hospital as *internes*.

The hospitals have dispensaries connected with them which are very important aids to the work, both of charity and education. These dispensaries afford the students a wider range of observation and experience than they could gain in the hospitals, since the patients are numbered by thousands, and they bring the poor sick women to the acquaintance of women physicians, to whom they can often confide their troubles more freely than to men. Cases which need the treatment of the hospital are secured admittance to it. In all this hospital work, and especially in that of the dispensary, as indeed in all charitable work, it has been found necessary to guard against the danger of pauperizing those who should be helped. For this reason a small charge is made to dispensary patients, except in cases of known destitution. The patients willingly pay it, feeling their own self-respect increased thereby, and the dispensary may be thus made nearly or quite self-supporting.

The surgical department of hospitals is of special importance to the poor, as it is almost impossible for them to have the conditions in their homes necessary to insure a fair chance of success and recovery in cases of operations. Remarkable success has been attained in this department in some of the hospitals I have named, where the greatest of abdominal operations are performed by surgeons connected with the hospital, with a percentage of recovery equal to that of other good hospitals here or in Europe. This branch of work is of absolute importance to the *internes*, and of the greatest value to the nurses.

Not less interesting or successful is the maternity work of these hospitals. A great deal of the chronic trouble from which working women suffer so severely comes from want of proper care while they are exercising the functions of child-bearing. The poor applicant to the maternity department is seen by the woman physician, who gives her advice as to previous care of herself, and she has in the hospital that thorough rest and care which are indispensable to full restoration to health.

A great moral question forces itself on the consideration of the managers of these hospitals. The applicants to the maternity are very often unmarried girls. Does true humanity require us to refuse help to such women? It is evident that care must be exercised to give no encouragement to immorality, while we must not refuse the aid which is so often absolutely necessary to save life. The problem is a difficult one, but the managers have tried to meet it. They usually make a distinction between the first offense—which is often rather due to weakness and folly than to depravity—and confirmed habits of immorality, and do not receive unmarried women a second time. In one hospital, at least, the directors find the greatest assistance from a committee of ladies who look after the maternity patients, both before they enter and after they leave the hospital. They endeavor to procure work for the mother, and watch over her welfare and that of the child. But they make it their invariable rule to give aid only on condition that the mother makes every effort to fulfill her maternal duties; for they believe there is a regenerating power in motherhood, and that care for her child is the surest safeguard against a mother's committing a second fault.

To many women of good position the maternity is a great blessing, if they have not comfortable homes and friends to care for them. The expense in the hospital is much less than the price for which good medical attendance and nursing can be secured at home.

I need only say of the medical care of women by their own sex in hospitals that its value has been fully proved. Women of all classes seek this aid eagerly, and show full confidence in their physicians and obey them quite as implicitly as they do those of the other sex. Women often say that they have suffered for years without medical or surgical assistance, that might have relieved them, from unwillingness to reveal their troubles to men. The greater freedom of the relation between patients and physicians of the same sex, enables the doctors to exercise much influence over their patients, who learn many good sanitary lessons in housekeeping. A physician was surprised to find the sick room of a poor patient carefully aired: "Why, you know they always do so at the hospital," was the explanation given.

These hospitals have also done much to dispel among the poor the fear of going to hospitals.* Finding their friends

NOTE.—I do not mean to claim that this result, which is very evident in the community, is entirely due to the establishment of women's hospitals, for it is the consequence of a broader feeling for humanity in all institutions; but it is certainly a marked feature of women's hospitals. This note will apply

kindly ministered to by their own sex, they come to regard the hospital as a kindly refuge in sickness, not as the last resort of a homeless and deserted sufferer who will die unfriended and alone.

Besides these hospitals, especially adapted to assist in the medical education of women, are others established by women mainly in the interests of charity. I have, for instance, the twelfth annual report of "The Home of Mercy," in Pittsfield, Mass. It contains about thirteen beds, and the number of patients in a year was one hundred. It was established by a small body of women who felt the need of a place for the victims of accident or disease. Sixty-eight per cent. of the patients are women, and all the officers but the physicians. This institution seems to present a good model for smaller cities and towns where, especially among a manufacturing population, hospital accommodations are often much needed. A training school for nurses is added to its work.

Another step has been taken in the medical education of women in the employment of women physicians, (made obligatory by the Legislature in some States) in State institutions, thus giving them management of the women's infirmary. At the Reformatory prison at Sherburne, Mass., the resident physician has charge of the health of two hundred prisoners. The good care and treatment given them is apparent in the improvement of the health of prisoners during their stay, and in the small number of deaths.

The employment of women physicians in insane asylums is a very valuable measure from which we may hope great good in the future. At present, the most interesting instance of such work that has come to my notice is in the State Hospital for the Insane at Norristown, Pa., where Dr. Alice Bennett, with two women assistants, has charge of over eight hundred patients. Her carefully tabulated statistics throw much light on important questions regarding the causes of insanity and the probability of restoration. Dr. Bennett has introduced beneficial improvements in the treatment of patients in the direction of more freedom and more social life and opportunity of employment. She says in her last report, "No mechanical restraint (by which is meant enforced limitation of free movements of the body by means of jackets, muffs, straps, etc.) is at any time made use of in this department. . . . . There are

to all that I have said of hospitals. My subject is women's hospitals, but I would gladly do justice to the good work done in all hospitals, if it were not too broad a field.

times in the history of many cases, when temporary separation from external cause of irritation is beneficial and necessary . . . . Brush making, basket making, sewing and mending, kindergarten occupations for the feebler-minded and melancholy, and the ever-present "house-work," in all its forms, engage about half the whole number of patients at one time or another. The officers and patients have also organized a 'Lènd a Hand Club.' Dr. Bennett has arranged for a large number of patients to take their meals together, and finds the arrangement very beneficial."

Some of those who are working for the sick have preferred the name of "Hospital Association." Such is the St. Luke's hospital in Jacksonville, Fla., said to be the first one in the State. The officers are women, but the physicians and a board of trustees are men. The main purpose of this association seems to be to relieve the wants of strangers, who so often go to Florida seeking health, but sometimes in vain.

The Women's Homœopathic Association of Pennsylvania was formed for a distinctively reformatory purpose. Its government is composed of women, with the exception of an advisory board of men. The medical faculty is composed of both men and women. This account is given of its origin :

"The motive of starting a women's association was, largely, to correct the abuses that grow out of institutions managed by men. It is here now and has been for many years the custom for hospital or other charitable institutions to have an auxiliary board of women managers, whose duties are to look after the house-keeping department and raise money either by giving entertainments or begging—the expenditure of the money so raised, and general management of hospital work, is considered beyond a woman's ability. This prevents a voice in the higher administration. Some of the women, whose names appear as incorporators of the hospital of this association, desired to open an institution where women could, when in sickness and sorrow, be in the care of women. Out of 213 patients cared for during 1888, 153 were charity cases, 45 partial pay, and 15 cases full pay."

The "Philadelphia Home for Incurables" was established by women, but its bounty is not confined to them ; it admits men as patients. With the exception of a superintendent of the men's department, the management is entirely in the hands of women. This is an effort to meet the crying need of a home for chronic sufferers. Each patient pays one hundred dollars and is kept during her life.

Much other work of the same nature as that I have described is, doubtless, doing in our vast country, of which no account has reached us. One of the many "Women's Clubs" has taken the subject of hospitals into serious consideration. While rejoicing in every such effort, I would like to add a word of caution that every enterprise should be most carefully considered, and the work never allowed to fall below the recognized standard of merit.

When the pioneer hospitals were opened, no other clinical advantages were free to women; now the hospitals are beginning to open their doors to them. The report of the city hospital of Boston says, "The propriety of women practicing as physicians or surgeons, and their comparative ability and fitness to pursue this profession, are not questions for the trustees to consider in the official management of the hospital; they must recognize the fact that women are becoming practitioners in all the schools of medicine; that they are admitted to the Massachusetts Medical and other State societies, and are recognized as practitioners by the community at large; and that they are admitted in common with male students to other leading hospitals of the country. The trustees therefore feel that there is no sufficient reason why women should not be admitted to the public instruction in the amphitheater on the same terms as men, except as to certain operations from which a reasonable sense or regard for propriety may exclude them." This advance in public opinion is most gratifying; but, even when all hospitals are open to women students, the value of those of which I have spoken will not be lost; they will still have special work to do, both in education and charity.

This movement for the clinical education of women in hospitals begun in America, has extended to Great Britain, Switzerland, and Germany, and is now being rapidly introduced into India, where the Women's Hospital is found to be a most important agent in educating and elevating the women of India.

The lamented Dr. Amandibai Joshee, who was the pioneer of medical education for Hindoo women, was a student at the Philadelphia college and an *interne* at the New England Hospital.

An excellent hospital in Burlington, Vt., was planned and endowed by a woman (Miss Mary Fletcher), who gave it her personal supervision. It had no direct bearing on women's education, but was open to all classes of patients. Since Miss Fletcher's death it is called by her name. It is mainly intended for residents of the State, although other patients are received if it is not full. It has no women physicians, but a board of women visitors. It has an amphitheater for clinical instruction, and its buildings are large and convenient.

All these hospitals maintain the principle that those who are treated in them should pay for the care they receive according to their ability. The price of board and treatment varies from five to forty dollars per week, according to the service required and other circumstances; but in all the institutions are free beds, endowed or supported by charity.

Out of this hospital work has grown another very important branch of service in the training schools for nurses. While estimating this new departure at its full value, I wish to pause a moment to pay a deserved tribute to the "old-fashioned nurse." In New England, especially in our country towns, and I presume no less in other parts of the country, the nurse was an important and honored member of society. Although not regularly trained according to the modern demands, she was generally a woman deeply read in the great school of life; often a widowed mother, who earned her bread by giving to others the fruits of her own blighted family life; sometimes a maiden, who, losing the hope of a home of her own, found a wide and useful sphere for her energies and affections in care of the sick; sometimes the girl who had wrecked her life by youthful indiscretion (like Mrs. Gaskell's "Ruth"), in the ministry of help to others found a life which soothed her own sorrows and restored her to the respect of society. The nurse then gathered her knowledge as she could, watching through long winter nights with sick friends, and visiting among the poor when disease came upon them. Dickens has drawn cruel portraits of the nurse of olden time, true, perhaps, to flagrant instances, but forming a pitiful caricature of the whole class. The old nurse was more often the true friend of the family, summoned in every time of trouble, and loving the children whose birth she had watched, almost as if they were her own.

But with the advance of scientific medical practice it became necessary that the physician should have an assistant fitted to carry out his views skillfully as well as faithfully; and the trained nurse was called into being. She, as well as the physician, must have clinical education. How strongly this need was felt is shown by the almost simultaneous establishment of training schools in various countries. To Miss Nightingale is due the impulse which started the general movement.

The New England Hospital claims priority in this country, in announcing the training of nurses as an important part of its work in 1863; but its school was not fully established until the return of Dr. Dimock from Europe in 1869, who placed it on its present foundation. The methods pursued in the various training schools now in operation are very similar, showing that the work has been carefully considered and is being satisfactorily done. Similar difficulties presented themselves to those found in all industrial education, of which one of the greatest was the impossibility of finding teachers trained for the work. Such women as I have described might be very valuable nurses, but they had not acquired their knowledge systematically, and were not skilled in the art of teaching. The doctor knows what qualities are wanted in a nurse, but cannot always give the instruction and discipline which will secure their development. The women physicians had some advantage in this respect. The very general employment of women as teachers has helped to supply this need. A young woman who had a natural aptitude for nursing, and the high moral qualities necessary for a superintendent of nurses, and who also had the experience of a few years of teaching, became well adapted to the new profession, and after a few years the training schools began to furnish graduates who could carry on the work as teachers.

Another difficulty was in the amount of time required for thorough training. The pupils seldom had resources to support them during one or two years of training. It is quite necessary, therefore, to pay the pupils a small salary, after their first month of probation, in addition to their board and lodging. This is sufficient to provide for their inexpensive clothing and all other necessary expenses, so that the graduate leaves the school without arrears of debt and able to look cheerfully forward to the exercise of her profession. A great step has been gained for women in thus raising this humble labor to the dignity of a profession. The woman who has given one or two years to preparation for her life-work, looks upon it very differently from one who has taken it up only on the pressure of necessity and has to learn her business in the doing of it. She feels a conscious strength in her position, which ought to stimulate her intellectual powers and elevate her moral character. It is true that the school gives her only the preparation for her work, and she must get the best part of her education from life, but she goes to her task with tools well sharpened for use, and a trained power of observation which should make every experience doubly valuable. Let her not lose in the pride of her acquisition the lovelier spirit and conscientious fidelity which made the old nurse the useful and trusted friend of the family.

The well-trained nurse is like another eye and hand to the

physician. She notes with reliable accuracy the changes of pulse and temperature, keeps the record of nourishment and sleep, watches every vital function with a practiced eye, and thus can give to the medical attendant a photographic picture of all that has occurred since his last visit. She carries out his directions intelligently, and thus enables him to calculate on strict application of the means he wishes to use.

In 1886, by the report of the Bureau of Education, there were 29 training schools for nurses, 139 instructors, 837 pupils, 349 graduates, in twelve different States and the District of Columbia. Some of these schools are connected with public hospitals, others with private charities. In a few cases the schools are independent of any institution, but the pupils are employed both in hospitals and private families.

The rules of admission are very similar in all schools. The minimum age ranges from twenty to twenty-five, the maximum from thirty-five to forty. As a general rule, twenty-five is a good age at which to enter a training school; the constitution should be well established, the character formed, and some experience of life gained before entering upon this difficult work. Good education and character are required, and in most cases certificates of good health and ability for the work.

The wages paid to pupils vary from seven dollars per month the first year, and twelve dollars the second year, to sixteen dollars per month for the highest grade of nurse, in a New York hospital. The time required for study ranges from one to two years, the last being the rule in a majority of cases. The Philadelphia school, which demands only one year, has an additional course of one year to train superintendents.

The expense of supplying the nursing of the hospital by a training school, in the only case known to me, is found to be about the same as by the old method of hired nurses. Trained nurses receive good pay in comparison with that of the ordinary employments of women, ranging from ten dollars per week upward to twenty, thirty, or even forty dollars, according to the difficulty of the case. While these prices are by no means higher than should reward a nurse who has given years to preparation for her profession and who works faithfully in it, they are yet burdensome to many families. A surgeon will sometimes refuse to take a case unless he can have the skilled nursing that he believes essential to success, and yet the pay of the nurse will take all the earnings of the father, on which the family rely for support.

But, on the other hand, the saving of expense in the number

of physician's visits is to be considered, since he can trust the report of the nurse, and so the patient is better cared for, without additional expense. During the last months of study, the nurse's work is among the poor, under the direction of the dispensary physicians. Not only are the patients much helped by this arrangement, but the experience is of great value to the nurses, as they see a greater variety of work than they can in a hospital and under differing conditions of life, and are thus fitted to meet what comes to them in their future practice.

Societies are also formed by women for supplying nurses to the sick poor. Such associations employ a number of trained nurses in attendance on patients who are unable to pay full price. They work both in connection with dispensaries and independently of them. Usually a nurse makes two visits a day to her patient, doing for her whatever members of the household cannot do, but she is always required to instruct some of the family, if possible, in the simple methods of care of the sick. She also uses her opportunity to enforce common rules of hygiene and sanitary care on all the household. In this way it is hoped that much may be done for the prevention of disease as well at its cure.

The "Visiting Nurse Society, of Philadelphia," may serve for a good model of such associations.*

While it has been impossible in limited space to do full justice to all the good work now doing in the training of nurses, there are yet two directions, of which I wish to speak, in which

---

* In New York city the Woman's Branch of the New York City Mission sends out five nurses among the poor. These nurses have all had a full course of training at some hospital. This mission claims to be the first society in America to have introduced trained nurses in its work.

The Department of United Relief Works of the Society of Ethical Culture, organized in 1879, furnishes nurses to Demilt and New York Dispensaries. During the year 1888–1889 these nurses paid on an average 2800 visits to about 700 patients, including all diseases, even of the most infectious nature, and quite irrespective of creed and nationality.

The Mt. Sinai Training School supplies, at its own expense (being at present a separate organization from the hospital) from among its nurses not yet graduated, but experienced in hospital training, a nurse who administers to the sick irrespective of creed, nationality, or disease, under the direction of physicians attached to what is called "District Poor Service" of Mt. Sinai Hospital. Among the corps of physicians, all of whom give their services free, is one woman, Dr. Josephine Walter, who devotes on an average four mornings a week to this work in some of the poorest and most miserable districts of the city.

The order of Deaconesses, referred to in the chapter on Woman in Ministry, also act in the capacity of nurse. Among them are many regularly trained nurses who serve in the hospitals closely connected with the church.—Ed. note.

it should be extended. It is desirable that women should be especially trained for the care of insane patients, who need peculiar care both in institutions and in private life. The extreme watchfulness and the power of control required for this service seem to demand a special training, which would be unnecessary or even prejudicial in ordinary nursing. This subject is already engaging the attention of those having the care of the insane, and I doubt not they will find means to carry out their ideas.

Again, I believe that nursing would afford a wide field of usefulness for the colored women of our Southern States. Their qualities of patience, sweetness, and affection are well adapted to this profession, and when to these is added the intellectual education which is now within the reach of many of them, there is no reason why, with good training, they should not do excellent service. Many of the best nurses in our Southern cities are of this class. The University of Atlanta, Ga., has made some attempt to introduce nursing into its practical education, and I hope other experiments will soon be made. So far as I know the New England Hospital is the only one that admits colored pupils to its training school. Here this measure has been entirely successful, and no disagreeable feeling has arisen on the part of patients or any one else. The colored students have maintained a fair average in their standing, and some have been superior. A good education is the most important prerequisite to the entrance of colored women into this field.

While my fruitful theme is by no means exhausted, I wish in conclusion to add one thought, viz., that however decidedly these hospitals of which I have spoken owe their existence to women, either as originating or endowing them, in every case within my knowledge there is a union of both sexes in the management of the institution. The arrangements are very various ; in some cases the managers are all women and the physicians are men ; in others all the physicians but the consulting staff are women, while the board of management is divided between the sexes ; in others we find the women have full charge, with an advisory board of men. This proves that women have been more anxious to secure good management than to establish their own claims. It is an earnest of future improvement when both sexes shall work together in all departments of life, each bringing her or his peculiar talents to the work, either as individuals or as representing a part of the community.

XIV.

CARE OF THE CRIMINAL.

BY

SUSAN HAMMOND BARNEY.

WHEN Elizabeth Fry, in 1815, rapped at the prison doors in England, she not only summoned the turnkey, but sounded a call to women in other lands to enter upon a most Christ-like mission. The reports of her work in Great Britain and on the Continent, published at intervals during several succeeding years, extracts of which found their way into American papers, not only awakened admiration for the fearless courage manifested in the self-denying efforts, but marvel at what she was able to accomplish, and, from the reading, a few women in our land arose to ask the question, "Lord, what will *Thou* have me to do?" and in the answer found new light upon the words, "I was in prison and ye visited me."

There was no talk about "going to work," but, from their knees, two or three women in New York, as early as 1830, began in the quietest manner possible to visit the district lock-ups and prisons, making careful inquiries concerning these places and their inmates, thus gathering up food for thought, which sent them back to their prayers with something definite to ask for.

In 1834 these women, with a few others, organized "The New York Moral Reform Society," with Margaret Prior for their first missionary, and they made systematic prison visitation a part of their regular work. From their own records, "Our Golden Jubilee, 1834—1884," we quote: "Our prisons were at that time in a sadly demoralized condition,—as our missionaries went through these public institutions, gathering facts relative to the spiritual condition of the inmates, they saw an urgent necessity of reform and gave themselves no rest till it was accomplished." To their memorials, petitions, and personal appeals, the State Legislature at length responded, and several reforms were inaugurated, among them better arrangements for separation of the sexes and the placing of matrons over the female departments. At this time Mrs. Dora Foster was given charge of women at the Tombs, then used as a police district lock-up, and she proved of such exceptionable character and qualifications as to continue in favor and in office more than forty years. A great change in the moral atmosphere of the place was effected by her discreet management, and many and sore evils were prevented.

SPREAD OF WORK.

Reports of the work were taken to other cities, and in 1839 the society became national in name, with vice-presidents in seventeen different States, and in the next few years, particularly in New York, Pennsylvania, Massachusetts, Rhode Island, and Connecticut, we find the women prominent in anti-slavery and other reforms, giving special thought and personal efforts, toward the amelioration of the condition of persons confined in our various institutions. Thus quietly was the leaven working in many places, hindered, hampered, and limited by prejudice against woman's work, and the fear of their seeing too much, if once admitted and allowed the privilege of inspection.

It is recorded, that on one of the ladies being denied the opportunity which she sought of seeing and ministering to a sick *female* prisoner, while a minister was allowed to go in and on his asking the reason of it, "Why," said the official, "it wouldn't have done, she's too sharp; *she* wouldn't have come in here and just prayed and gone away about her business as you have; *she'd wanted to know the cause*"; and another time when those in authority had been solicited by a public-spirited gentleman to grant permission for women to go in and out these places on their errands of mercy, they explained their refusal by saying, "That until the State was ready to expend money enough for several changes, it would only be inviting trouble to have such women spying round and seeing everything, as they were sure to do."

NEW YORK PRISON ASSOCIATION.

On November 23, 1844, a company of gentlemen gathered in a private parlor in New York City "to take into consideration the destitute condition of discharged convicts"; then a circular was issued, calling for a public meeting on December 6, at which time the following resolution, among others, was offered by Isaac T. Hopper: "*Resolved*, That in the foundation of such a society (the New York Prison Association), it would be proper to have a female department to be especially regardful of the interests and welfare of prisoners of that sex."

Public meetings were held, and in June, 1845, a house was taken, two matrons placed in charge, and a committee of ladies organized to superintend and control its operations. A sewing department and school were established, and at a later day a laundry.

In 1854 the women dissolved all connection with the New York Prison Association, and were incorporated as "The Women's Prison Association and Home." Up to this time the Home had averaged about 150 inmates per year. We quote from one of their reports: "We will not dwell upon the many years of up-hill work through every possible discouragement, but proceed at once to the results of a pre-determined endeavor to take by the hand the unfortunate of our sex and lead them to a better life, where by patient industry they might earn an honest livelihood."

In 1859 the association adopted as a distinctive name for its house department that of "The Isaac T. Hopper Home." The work has gone steadily on, the women of the association having been to the front in every effort for prevention of crime, and reform of the criminal girls and women, and in their forty-fourth annual report, we find, "During the year 119 women have been sent to service in families in the State, and 31 out of the State; 4 were returned to friends." Only those who can read between the lines can understand all that these items mean. To those who talk glibly about "abandoned women" and the "utter hopelessness of trying to save them," the subjoined lines from the same report might seem "mere sentiment," but to those with clearer vision it is the secret of their success. "We believe that woman, in her deepest degradation, holds something sacred, something undefiled; and, like the diamond in the dark, retains some quenchless gleams of the celestial light."

The prison committee, through its chairman, gave in 1887 an exhaustive report upon the condition of prisons and station houses, and in 1888, through their prison visitor, a female M.D., a careful report, both of which contain items which are strange reading for nineteenth century civilization and progress.

PERSONAL WORK.

In the autumn of 1844, Margaret Fuller Ossoli accepted a position on the New York *Tribune*, and became an inmate of the Greeley mansion. The prison on Blackwell's Island was on the opposite side of the river, at a distance easily reached by boat, and Sing Sing was not far off. Margaret was to "write up" these places, and gladly took the first opportunity to visit them. Her biographer says: "She had consorted hitherto with the *élite* of her sex, she now made acquaintance with the outcasts to whom the elements of womanhood are scarcely recognizable. For both she had one gospel, that of high hope and divine love. She seemed to have found herself as much at home in the office of encouraging the fallen as she had been, when it was her duty to arouse the best spirit in women sheltered from the knowledge and experience of evil by every favoring circumstance." She herself said of a meeting where she addressed the female prisoners, "All passed, indeed, as in one of my Boston classes." This was after Mrs. Farnum had been appointed matron, a woman of uncommon character and ability, and the women already showed the results of her intelligent and kindly treatment. Through the letters published in the *Tribune*, on "Prison Discipline," "Appeal for an Asylum for Discharged Female Prisoners," "Capital Punishment," and others, public attention and interest were awakened, and Mr. Greeley says, "I doubt that our various reformatory institutions had ever before received such wise and discriminating commendation to the favor of the rich as they did from Margaret's pen during her connection with us."

Dorothea Dix, of blessed memory, whose specialty seemed the caring for the insane, gave much thought and gracious ministry to those in bonds; and many were indebted to her personal efforts in their behalf, both while in prison and in the trying time of their release. She was also fearless in lifting up her voice against abuses, and in favor of needed reforms. She was so persistent in reiterating her protests, that attention had to be given, and her demands secured changes which are thankfully remembered.

In Rhode Island, as early as 1830, a young and gifted woman, whose heart had been stirred by accounts given by her father, a prominent lawyer, began to visit the institutions of the State; and through a long and eventful life has continued her ministrations. Even now, in her ninety-first year, she has not entirely laid down her work. By voice and pen she has appealed stoutly against wrongs and abuses, and while she has been the spiritual mother of numberless men and women, she has not neglected the financial aid so important to those who emerge from prison life. She was the originator of the "Rhode Island

Prisoners' Aid Association," and the founder of the "Temporary Industrial Home" for released female prisoners, which was opened in 1880, and bears her name, "The Sophia Little Home."

Among the special workers should be named Miss Linda Gilbert of New York, who has devoted much time to prison work, and in fifteen years has procured employment for over six thousand ex-convicts; six hundred of the better class of these she has by her own individual aid established in business in a small way, and in speaking of the results of her ventures in thus assisting them, she says, "I am happy to state that not ten per cent. of the number thus aided have turned out unsatisfactorily." She has also presented twenty-two libraries to prisons in six different States, and among other projects which she hopes to accomplish is the establishing of a national industrial home for ex-convicts, where various branches of labor can be taught and the inmates put in the way of becoming self-supporting. When a little girl of only eight or nine years, she used to visit the prison nearest her home and take some little gift, if only a few flowers, to cheer the prisoners, who learned to look upon her visits to their dark abode as they would a stray sunbeam from heaven.

Elizabeth Comstock, of Michigan, upon whose head in childhood Elizabeth Fry placed her hand as she said the kindly words, "Remember what I tell thee, dear Elizabeth; to be Christ's messenger to those who know him not, that is the happiest life," has so well carried out her avowed purpose, "To bear our Father's message of love and mercy to the largest household on earth, the household of affliction," that in thirty years, mid duties urgent and varied, she has visited over 120,000 prisoners, awakening hope and giving direction to many lives.

A long list of other names might be added, but our space is otherwise needed.

REFORMATORY PRISONS FOR WOMEN.

In the year of 1873 startling revelations concerning immoralities connected with the Indiana Southern Prison led to the immediate occupancy of the buildings in Indianapolis, which had been under way for two years and which were to be known as "The Reformatory Prison for Women and Girls." The institution was officered entirely by women, with Mrs. Sarah J. Smith, one of its chief founders, for Superintendent. The project was looked upon as a doubtful experiment, and the speedy relinquishment of the idea prophesied. The board of managers consisted at first of three gentlemen and two lady visitors. In 1887 Governor Williams approved an act of the Legislature by which the general supervision and government were vested in a board of women managers. This was, at that time, and we believe still is, the only governmental prison known, either in the United States or in Europe, under the entire management of women.

The safe transfer of the women prisoners, seventeen in number, under the charge of warden, chaplain, and matron of the Jeffersonville prison, was considered a great event, "as two were dangerous and others below hope." The present Superintendent says: "We have no weapons of defense, not a gun or pistol about the premises. Kind words and gentleness of manner are almost sure to win. We have eleven lady officers, women of refinement and Christian character, lending every thought to the uplifting of their sex. The financial showing in the seventeenth annual report reflects great credit upon the management, while the large percentage claimed as "permanently reformed," attests to the thoroughness of work and wisdom of methods.

In 1870 a number of influential ladies of Eastern Massachusetts—among whom was Mrs. E. C. Johnson, the present Superintendent of the reformatory—petitioned the Legislature for a separate institution for the reformation of female prisoners, but it was not until the fall of 1874 that ground was broken at Sherborn for the erection of the buildings. In September, 1877, these were occupied, and the work has been eminently successful from the start. The system of grading adopted in 1881 has proved very satisfactory, and over two hundred and thirty inmates, ranging from fifteen to seventy-five years of age, find in it an incentive to order and decorum. The aim is to prepare them, if found trustworthy, to do good work as servants, and this is so far a success that the demand is greater than the supply.

No one familiar with the old régime in connection with women prisoners but would hail with thankfulness the improvements shown under the present administration. Said an English critic after a visit: "I remarked, 'These people are almost of a hopeless type'; the reply came quickly, '*Hopeless* is not a permitted word here, we hope for all.' I came away glad to have seen such an experiment, hopeful for its success, and confident that women had undertaken for women a beneficent work."

Women in other States are agitating the question of separate prisons for women, and in several feel assured of success in the near future.

In 1887 at Hudson, N. Y., The House of Refuge for Women was opened, and an efficient lady superintendent placed in charge. The results reached, even at this short period, have been encouraging in the highest degree, and emphasize the wisdom of the arrangements, which are largely due to the persistent efforts of women in philanthropic circles. We quote from report of "Standing Committee on Reformatories," of which Josephine Shaw Lowell is a member: "To any who have visited even once one of the county jails in this State, and know the condition of young women in them, kept in idleness, in the midst of degraded companions, under the charge of male keepers, frequently not out of sound, sometimes not out of sight of the male prisoners, nothing can be more affecting than to see the young women in the House of Refuge, neatly dressed, always occupied, and constantly under the care of refined and conscientious women."

WOMEN ON STATE BOARDS.

In New York, Massachusetts, Connecticut, and Wisconsin there are women on the State Board of Charities.* In Pennsylvania, the board appoints women visitors to public institutions, and in Rhode Island the Governor appoints a board of women visitors to all institutions caring for women and girls. Massachusetts stands alone in the honor of having women on "Boards of Commissioners of Prisons." This was inaugurated in 1880, and their gracious womanly influence is felt in all the institutions of the State.

In some other States women are coming to be recognized factors in these lines of work, and are cordially invited to fill places of trust. The *Journal of Prison Discipline and Philanthropy*, published by the Pennsylvania Prison Association, in its issue of 1886 says: "This society has profited largely by the recent admission of competent women into the acting committee. Their suggestions have proved of marked advantage, and with the time, intelligence, and high moral force they have given to the work, both in and out of the prison, there has been a gain which promises incalculable good."

DEPARTMENT OF PRISON, JAIL, AND POLICE WORK OF THE NATIONAL WOMAN'S CHRISTIAN TEMPERANCE UNION.

This department is in the eleventh year of organized work, which, under the same Superintendent, Mrs. S. H. Barney, of

* See chapter on Charity.—ED.

Providence, has steadily increased until now her parish is the entire country. The plan of national, State, and local superintendents insures system and supervision all along the lines, and brings out annually the general summary of work attempted and work accomplished.

In the spirit of the department's motto, "*Not willing that any should perish*," the investigations have extended to State prisons, penitentiaries, convict camps, city prisons and jails, houses of correction or refuge, police stations and lock-ups, and reformatories for adults and juveniles.

In many of these places were found a brutality and neglect of the common decencies of life which were disgraceful beyond description. Criminals of all grades herded together irrespective of age, sex, or degrees in vice. Youths of both sexes confined with those hardened in crime, while awaiting trial, became schooled in vice. Thousands, who for some first and trivial offense were lodged in the calaboose or the county jail, exposed to the contaminating influences of indiscriminate companionship, became hardened, and lost all self-respect as they yielded, day by day, to this mind-poisoning, moral miasma.

The first visits of the women to many of these places, where they went unheralded, were unwelcome, and they were sometimes repulsed by officials with, "We don't 'low any women round here ; leastwise, only them that's sentenced." Entrance at last secured, it would have been a picture worthy of some master hand when these women stepped, pale-faced but brave-hearted, into those miserable, crowded corridors. The lewd and profane conversation was hushed, but it could *be felt*, as plainly as could be seen the vilest of obscene prints and the most dangerous kinds of literature.

Nothing was more disheartening than the condition of *women* in these places. Having become criminals, they were generally deemed hopeless, and, on being released, it was expected they would drift back again after a longer or shorter period.

The *call* to the work gained emphasis as it was realized how little this age of boasted civilization and philanthropy had done for unfortunate and degraded women. Arrested by men, given into the hands of men to be searched and cared for, tried by men, sentenced by men, and committed to our various institutions for months and even years, where only men officials had access to them, and where, in sickness or direst need, no womanly help or visitation was expected or allowed.

In one of the New York cities, in a jail, eleven women were found to be in the care of men, and the keys of "the women's quarters" in the hands of one of the *male convicts.* The women, with the intent of being ready for their release, which was near, had removed most of their clothing "for the wash," and were in a semi-nude condition.

A visitor to a county jail in Pennsylvania, writes: "The scene that met our gaze when we entered the jail was indescribable. The prisoners—twenty-six men and two women—were allowed to associate in the open space between the vestibule and the cells. In appearance, they might have been a gang of bandits in a cave. The men were in groups, playing cards on low boxes on the floor. The jail was deficient in ventilation, also in light and cleanliness."

In a New England jail two boys were found under fourteen years of age. The months which would elapse before their trial would be ample time to complete their crime education under the tutelage thus provided for them. Similar sights may be seen in many of the prisons and jails of our land, proving conclusively the need of womanly forethought in these matters, which from a merely economical standpoint need prompt attention. The better care of our juvenile offenders cannot be deferred without irreparable loss, for in a few years we shall have missed our chance to save them, so they will then be found in the ranks of confirmed criminals. Perhaps no work of the department will prove more fruitful in results than the effort to secure *Matrons for the Police Stations.* The movement began in 1877 and has been adopted in one or more cities in twenty States, while in Massachusetts, New York, and Pennsylvania all cities over a given number of inhabitants are required by law to provide matrons to care for arrested women. We quote from an article furnished the *International Review* in 1888 by the present writer:

POLICE MATRONS.

Shall we have police matrons? seems no longer an open question. With the reform inaugurated in twenty cities, and under advisement in as many more, the *idea* may be said to be established. How wide is to be the influence of such an officer, and how effective her work, depend upon the place and the woman. "The place" should be central, with requisite accommodations for the comfort and convenience of the matron, in order that she may economize her time and strength. Official recognition of her work and its importance, with ready co-operation in various ways, will necessarily have much to do with its success; and these have sometimes been won under very trying circumstances. Other points, more or less essential, will occur to those interested, for every conceivable objection and obstacle will be presented, emphasized, and duly magnified while the effort is being made to secure a place.

That secured, then comes the question, "Where is the woman to fill it?" There will be applicants enough, and for them "friends at court" to push their claims, but "the right woman" will have to be sought; and it is better to wait for her, than to inaugurate the movement under too great disadvantages. A middle-aged woman, scrupulously clean in person and dress, with a face to commend her and manner to compel respect; quiet, calm, observant, with faith in God, and hope for humanity; a woman fertile in resources, patient and sympathetic. She could hardly be all this without possessing a generous endowment of "good common sense," and she cannot possibly do the work required unless that is sanctified. It will be seen at once that "the place" is indeed, in a very real sense, "missionary ground," and that "the woman" must necessarily have these qualifications and spirit in order to fill it and meet the demands of the time. Competent and conscientious, the influence of such a woman, in such a position, can hardly be overestimated. Her duties, serious and responsible, but legitimate to the office, will naturally develop as she is given opportunity to work out the problem, "What can be done for women in police stations?" under methods demanded by Christian civilization.

Of course, she will be "on call," and every woman brought to the station will be committed at once into her care, and every duty connected with search, locking-up, and necessary attendance, will be performed by her. The cells for women (entirely separate from the men) will be in her charge, and she will be accountable for them and their occupants. Just what she will need to do in every case, no one could possibly outline. Said the chief of police in ——: "I wish you to state definitely all the duties of a police woman." For answer, I said: "Will you first describe to me the duties of a policeman?" "Impossible," was the reply; "he must be ready for everything." Just so, within the limitations of her office, must the matron be ready for everything.

Women brought to stations are not all drunk, or even bad. Girls or women suddenly set adrift; one who has lost her train and is penniless; or who finds herself deserted; or who, by reason of sudden illness, fainting, or temporary aberration, cannot give her name and residence; the partially insane;

attempted suicides; persons arrested on suspicion (and frequently found innocent); young girls taken up for disorderly conduct or because found in questionable company,—all these are liable to be brought to the station-house, a place which officials represent as "wholly unfit for a decent woman." These arrested women are often irresponsible for the time being, careless of their person, and regardless of the commonest laws of decency. Their clothing is often disarranged and unfastened, and they are liable to be in a condition totally unfit for appearance in court. The matron should be provided with such articles as womanly thought will suggest, and she should accompany her charge to the court room and remain by her until release or sentence removes her from her care. Among these will be found some for whom the matron may intercede, and who, upon her representation, may be taken to some "home," and life for them thus receive an upward lift, instead of the almost fatal plunge downward of the police court. There will be children of varying ages, from the babe born in the station-house to the poor child in short dresses, the victim of home neglect or of some one's vile lust; and drunken women with infants in their arms, who need some woman to rescue them, for the time being, from their own unmotherly grasp, and to prevent them from nursing the alcoholized milk which would be offered them. Night will sometimes be made hideous by women raving with drunken delirium, or maddened by the fiery draught to foulest deeds of rage and shame; but "the right woman" will not fail in such emergencies or be dismayed by such depths of degradation, but rather see in it the *why of her calling*. Any one of the classes named will be better off for the matron's presence, and the worst will be found more amenable to her touch and voice than to the average policeman, be he ever so well disposed. How far police duty and supervision may be combined with the missionary work needed, both in the station and in following up special cases, will depend, of course, largely upon the locality, the number of arrests, and the general demands of the service.

Whatever else may seem uncertain at the beginning of the work, there is one thing sure—"the right woman" will find her time occupied, and exercise for all her tact, patience, and consecration; and any one who takes the position merely for the salary or from sentimental notions, will pretty surely resign at the end of the first quarter, or those interested in the success of the movement will seek for some one else to fill the place. Difficult as it may seem to secure one who combines these qualifications, yet it will doubtless prove, as in many another important position where much is demanded, that the best available person is selected who, under the emergency, develops unexpected fitness, and who in time comes to compel approval and indorsement even from those who hesitated in committing to her this trust.

In every city where the appointment of a police matron is secured, there should be a committee from the Woman's Christian Temperance Union, upon whom the matron can rely for such help as she will assuredly need, and an "Open Door" or "Temporary Refuge" will prove an absolute necessity if much rescue work, which was the primary thought in the reform, is to be undertaken.

In time, there will be womanly supervision in the transportation of women to the various institutions to which they are consigned ; and the police matron will hasten the day, by her womanly forethought, for the women passing from her care, besides strengthening her influence over them. Indeed, *the presence* of the police matron will often prevent carelessness on many points, and deliberate wrong in others. Ten years ago the movement was sneered at ; ten years hence no city will be without one or more such officers.

All along the lines of the National Department advanced plans are yearly sent forth, and every State and Territory made some attempt to carry them out. During the last year hundreds of services have been held in hitherto neglected places. These were of a varied nature, preaching, prayer and conference meetings, Bible classes, Sunday schools, literary and musical entertainments ; in some of which young people and children assisted. Said the keeper of one of the most desolate places : "It's funny to see how the men try to clean up for the women's meetings."

One of the convicts told an officer, "I can stand the chaplains preaching, but those women, with their tearful pleading, break me all up ; home and mother seem realities again."

The Prison Flower Mission, cared for and directed by Jennie Carsuday, from her sick room in Louisville, Ky., has proved a blessed ministry to hundreds, and an opening wedge for the gospel message of hope and help.

Great numbers of bibles, testaments, helps for bible study, prayer, hymn, school, and library books have been supplied, and millions of pages of gospel and temperance leaflets and papers distributed, thus displacing dime novels and cards.

Book-cases, wall-rolls, illuminated mottoes, and pledge cards have been furnished, with Christmas boxes and Easter offerings by the thousands. Organs have been given, and others loaned for chapel services.

Petitions for needed reforms have been widely circulated, co-operation with other organizations gladly given, and scores of articles furnished the press, all of which have helped to arouse to action those not identified with the W. C. T. Union, and who perhaps had larger influence in certain directions.

Letter writing, to and for the inmates, has proved helpful. Visiting the friends of prisoners, giving sympathy, advice, and aid, have proved a practical illustration of the words, "Bear ye one another's burdens, and *so* fulfill the law of Christ."

Several States have inaugurated the "Prison Gate Mission," which is an important branch, and aims to have its missionaries meet the prisoners on their release, with *help* and *hope*, in the most practical ways. "Temporary Homes" and "Open-Doors" are offering shelter and work, and thousands of lives redeemed attest the genuineness of these varied efforts put forth in quietness but with great faith.

Many of the State superintendents of this department have given years of untiring labor, often furnishing their own supplies at great personal sacrifice. Brave, true-hearted, and practical, they have disarmed criticism, walked unharmed in dangerous places; never dropping into sentiment or refusing attention to established rules, they have won recognition from all right-minded officials and citizens.

PAST, PRESENT, AND FUTURE.

Thus, glancing backward, and passing in hasty review what has been attempted and accomplished since 1830, we catch a glimpse of what is now waiting to be done, and the call is so imperative, that we must express our thanksgiving for the past by bringing all the force of combined action to bear upon needed reforms in the present. We believe that woman has special endowments for these lines of work, and that her absence from them has been a source of weakness and failure.

We must familiarize ourselves with the questions of penalogy, the relation of the State to its vicious and dependent classes; contract labor and the lessee system with their attendant evils; congregate and separate imprisonment; prison discipline, with reformatory measures and institutions.

We should demand the absolute separation of the sexes, and

juvenile from older offenders; also *matrons* to care for women arrested or committed.

Visit unannounced police stations and courts, with county jails, where women are under care of men, or "left to themselves," and compare their looks and manners with those in similar places where the right kind of matron bears sway with a firm hand and dignified presence. Women should be associated with men as prison inspectors, and women physicians on boards to care for women and children. Greater efforts should be put forth in the lines of *reclamation*, opening the way to a return to honesty and self-support; but double diligence should be given to *removing the varied causes* of *crime*, thus proving ourselves wise citizens in the truest sense of the word.

XV.

CARE OF THE INDIAN.

BY

AMELIA STONE QUINTON.

THE work of women for the Indians within our national limits has been important and of many kinds. It would require much more than the space of a single volume at all fitly to describe the labor, self-sacrifice, and heroism of women in connection with the various missionary organizations in behalf of the red man. Some of the stories of such work read like heroic romance, are worthy to be recorded in an epic, and glow with delineations that reveal exalted unselfishness,* divine self-devotement, and sometimes a success that seems a fitting crown for such labor, albeit the crown, as so often to high souls in any vocation, comes after the martyrdom.† In the East, in the Southwest, and in the Northwest thrilling annals might be gathered from two centuries, oftenest of those unknown to fame and without even public recognition, who have laid down life in work for the Christianization of Indians, and of some women who as overworked secretaries or other officials have no less laid down life in labor to sustain such missionaries. But this is a realm for the biographer and for the historian of Christian missions, and must not be entered upon or even gleaned from in a sketch so limited as the present one must be.

In the educational work of various types done for the native Indians, noble women have been engaged, and this is notably true of the Hampton, Virginia, and Carlisle, Pennsylvania, Indian schools, where gifted women of high culture have devoted some of their best years to the elevation of the red race. It would seem invidious to name a few where many

---

* See the story of Mrs. McFarland's work, in "Alaska," by Rev. Sheldon Jackson, D.D.

† See "Mary and I," by Rev. Dr. Stephen R. Riggs.

have wrought so well, and this department of labor, like that of missionary effort, should be chronicled elsewhere.

A few women have made philological, ethnographic, and archæological studies among North American Indians and have added the results to the aggregate of scientific knowledge, doing also more or less to preserve Indian records and material objects of value connected therewith, thus increasing the sum of human interest in the red man, and, by the same, his self-respect and therefore his elevation and progress. But the request for this paper was for one regarding the late and general philanthropic work of women in behalf of Indians rather than for one giving the data referred to above, and which are less familiar to the writer.

The name of Helen Hunt Jackson deservedly stands first in the literary world as connected with modern effort by women for the deliverance of our native American Indians from oppression and injustice, as shameful as have been endured in any civilized land or by any race under the guardianship or power of any civilized government. The first letters and articles on this subject from her fascinating and popular pen were in the New York *Tribune*, the *Christian Union*, and other religious and secular newspapers and magazines, and were the outcry of a just and humane soul quivering with a poet's intense feeling and outraged sensibility at the discovery and realization of the unspeakable suffering of a capable and naturally brave race in a position where, to put the case comprehensively, no human right is treated as sacred, and where greed and passion alternately rob and destroy among their victims. Her quotations, from government documents and of proved facts, startled thoughtful readers, and her appeals rang like clarions through the souls of those who really heard them, and with peals whose vibrations have not yet ceased. Soon after she seriously took up the subject she visited, in Philadelphia, the officers of the Women's Indian Association, and expressed herself as delighted and still further inspired to find a group of earnest women already at work to make the facts of the Indian situation known, with the object of moving the people to demand of the government enacted justice for the wronged race. She wrote "A Century of Dishonor,"* a book which every patriotic and intelligent American should read, a condensed library on the Indian question and largely made up of quotations from public and official records, and introduced the book to the press and

* The latest and best edition is by Roberts Brothers, Boston, Mass.

pulpit of the country. She had a copy of it placed on the desk of every member of Congress the day but one before the second annual petition of the Women's Indian Association, of which she became a member, was presented to that body, January 27, 1881, and the writer, at the time also a guest of Miss Seward, vividly remembers with what anxious interest she noted quotations made from her book in the Senate Speeches to which both listened during the four or five days which followed. But the reception of this book was a disappointment to its author, and she said, later, in letters to and in conversation with the writer: "It is not read as I hoped it would be; I can count upon certain thousands who will read what I write because it is mine; but not even all of these will read this book, and they *must* read something on the Indian question. I will write an Indian story." To this resolve her facile pen, her poetic fire, and her genius for graphic delineation and clear, strong statement were given, and the story of "Ramona," the data of which were procured among the Indians of California while she was a government inspector among them, was given to idyllic, classic romance, to the American conscience, and to the humane of all civilized society. She poured her heart into the story and her heart's blood out through its pages. She put the labor of the working years of an average life-time into that half-decade of toil for a hunted race, and so it was again, as not infrequently in this world's story, that the righteous zeal and the intense compassion of a quick spirit "ate up" the life, and another consecrated genius fell, another great heart broke. The massive cone of rocks, cast by loving hands from every State in our Union upon the lonely mountain grave which she asked for among the Indian haunts of Colorado, fitly marks the resting place of her dust, but her "soul is marching on," still rallying, still inspiring unselfish souls to the cause she died for. The life given for others is a sacred life.

Another woman worker who has wrought with entire devotion and with the ability of genius for the Indian race, who began that work a year or two after "H. H." felt her first inspiration, is Miss Alice C. Fletcher. Already a student accustomed to research she first went among Indians, in the summer of 1882, in the interests of scientific observation. Perceiving at once the wrongs and needs of the race, she became their enthusiastic friend, laid aside her scientific pen and pencil, and made a serious study of the situation of the people among whom her labors began, the Omahas of Nebraska. Representing their case to governmental authorities in Washington, and successfully awakening interest in their behalf among legislators, she drafted a bill and had the satisfaction of seeing its passage, and then of allotting their lands under it to these Indians in 1883–84. Nor was this all or even the chief part of her work. Her scientific researches since then, treating in monographs of Indian traditions, customs, ceremonies, music, and other subjects ethnographic, biological, or archæological, have been original and valuable. It was during the period covered by this work that she brought a party of thirty-six young Indians to the Carlisle and Hampton Indian schools, herself raising $1800 with which to meet the expenses of other Indians who begged to join the party and seek an education. She persuaded General Armstrong to undertake at the Hampton school, the training of young Indian married couples, in cottages built by funds she raised for their training, and by the success of this experiment introduced the department of Indian Home Building into the Women's National Indian Association, of which she is an earnest member, and for which department she has raised in all more than two thousand dollars, since expended in building Indian homes, such loan-funds being in various instances returned to the association and reloaned to other Indian beneficiaries. An exhibit of civilized Indian industries for the Exhibition of 1884–85, at New Orleans, was also prepared by Miss Fletcher, and a diploma of honor was awarded her for this labor and for the lectures she gave upon the exhibit during the exposition. Her book, entitled "Indian Civilization and Education," prepared in answer to a Senate resolution of February 23, 1885, under the direction of the Commissioner of Education, is an extended and valuable work, and was supplemented by her late journey to Alaska in behalf of Indian education there. Since that time she has, as a special agent of government, allotted lands in severalty to the Winnebagoes of Nebraska, and is at this date (January 1891) engaged among the Nez Percés of Idaho, having been first for such work an appointee of President Cleveland, July, 1887, and the only woman till recently so commissoned. In addition to these greater services she has rendered many others, such as starting the education of the first Indian woman physician,* and of several Indian students at law or in some course of special training; inciting others to build here a chapel and there a school; doing with unstinted energy and enthusiasm the great service which lay before her, and let-

* This was Susan La Flesche, a sister of "Bright Eyes."

ting no chance slip to render the smaller aid. Possessed of a quick scientific perception, keen sagacity, great executive ability, of undaunted and tenacious purpose, of clear judgment and strong mental grasp, her heroic labors have accomplished important and lasting results for the benefit of the Indian race.

But another chapter of Indian work began six months before "H. H." commenced earnestly to think or write on the Indian question, as she herself told the writer, when a noble woman in Philadelphia, whose attention was just then specially called to the wrongs of the red race by items in the daily press, brought these facts to the notice of a small group of Christian workers. This was Mary L. Bonney,—later the wife of Rev. Thomas Rambaut, D.D., LL.D.,—whose life had been given to educational work, who had liberally aided many Christian and philanthropic enterprises, who had an important share in inaugurating the Women's Union Missionary Society, and who had given largely for the training of young men, both white and colored, for the Christian ministry. President of a missionary circle,* she brought to its monthly meeting, April, 1879, facts regarding the efforts of railroad companies having roads through the Indian Territory, and of western senators and others, to press Congress to open that Territory to white settlement, and to set up there a United States territorial government, though solemn treaties with the civilized tribes bound the nation never to do this without their consent. Her sense of justice was shocked, and she felt that so gross dishonesty must be a vast hindrance to Indian missions, as well as a great injury to the moral sense of our nation. The story of what followed is an interesting one as furnishing another marked illustration of the fact that the human family is but one, and that when any branch of it suffers, the others, upon knowledge of the fact, will rise to the rescue ; and that leaders and groups of workers are separately and individually moved upon in accordance with one great over-plan and its clearly apparent, all-including, redemptive design. Miss Bonney printed a petition to the government, and copies were distributed in an anniversary meeting, but from pressure of business these were left unnoticed in the pews ; the missionary circle adjourned for the summer, and there the matter seemed to end. But, as Miss Bonney states in a sketch of the beginnings

* This was The Women's Home Mission Society of the First Baptist Church of Philadelphia, that of the Rev. George Dana Boardman, D.D., a society organized by the éfforts of Mrs. Boardman, the gifted wife of that distinguished preacher and author, and largely in the interests of Indians.

of the movement, "she presented," a month later, "the facts she had gathered to her friend," and "the two entered into covenant" and "formed their plan of action." * Miss Bonney as the senior principal of the Chestnut Street Female Seminary of Philadelphia, one of the most excellent and widely-known educational institutions for young ladies in the country, originated by herself twenty-nine years before, and which became, in 1883, the Ogontz School, had little time for detailed investigation of wrongs to Indians or to use the avails of such study for arousing the public to their redress; but she had the means required and the heart generously to use these, while her friend the writer, deeply moved on behalf of Indians by the facts of their great wrongs, investigated the subject and gave herself to the work. Seven thousand copies of an enlarged petition,† with a leaflet appeal to accompany it, were circulated during the summer in fifteen States by this volunteer committee of two, and those whom they interested, and the result in the autumn was a petition roll, three hundred feet long, containing the signatures of thousands of citizens. This memorial was carried to the White House, February 14, 1880, by Miss Bonney and two ladies, whom she invited to accompany her; Mrs. George Dana Boardman, who presented the petition to President Hayes, and Mrs. Mariné J. Chase, who arranged the interview, and it was presented by Judge Kelly in the House of Representatives the 20th of that month, with the memorial letter written by Miss Bonney, the central thought of which was the binding obligation of treaties. It said, "We would express that when a treaty is changed or modified the free consent of both parties is necessary"; and it urged faithfulness in the case, "because we are strong and the Indians are weak." Both the petition and letter were placed upon the records of Congress. Another petition and various leaflets

---

* See also the "Sketch and Plans" of The Indian Treaty-keeping and Protective Association, July, 1881, and "The Official Record" of The National Indian Association for 1882.

† The petition was as follows:

To the President of the United States, and to the Senate and House of Representatives:

We, the undersigned men and women of the United States, resident in or near ———, do most respectfully but most earnestly request the President and the Houses of Congress to take all needful steps to prevent the encroachments of white settlers upon the Indian Territory, and to guard the Indians in the enjoyment of all the rights which have been guaranteed them on the faith of the nation.

were prepared and circulated the next year, Miss Bonney at first meeting all expenses, her gifts to the cause during the first two years being nearly $500, while those of all others,—and all were at her solicitation,—were less than $200, and during the first four years amounting to nearly $1400, while those from all other sources were less than $2000. In May, 1880, at her suggestion, two other ladies, Mrs. Boardman and Mrs. Chase, were added by the missionary circle to the volunteer committee of two, the four being then appointed, as its minutes say, "a committee of ways and means to act in the distribution of the petitions and tracts." At the first formal meeting of this committee,—this was in December, 1880,—its members, and the society indorsing them, having approved the plea of the writer that this work should be unsectarian and national, four other ladies of different denominations were invited to join it, and it became thenceforth undenominational and independent. At this first meeting, at Miss Bonney's request, Mrs. Chase was made chairman, retaining the office for three months, Mrs. Boardman was elected treasurer, and the writer, secretary, reporting her work and the publications from May 1879. This previous work, according to the minutes of that date, "included the circulation of the petitions of 1879 and of the present year [1880]; the preparation and circulation of the literature published to accompany these petitions; the presentation of the aims and work of the committee in missionary and other meetings; at anniversaries, associations, and pastors' conferences, in this and other States; the securing promises for two popular meetings and the presentation in them of our petition, with the general subject of Indian wrongs, and the preparing articles for the press, with other writing, traveling, and visiting in aid of some or all of these lines of work."

The eight ladies of this committee were Miss Bonney, Mrs. Boardman, Mrs. Chase, Miss Fanny Lea, Mrs. Mary C. Jones, Mrs. Margaretta Sheppard, Mrs. Edward Cope, and the writer.

The second popular petition,* then already gathered from

---

* This was as follows:

To the Senate and House of Representatives in Congress Assembled:

We, the undersigned men and women of these United States, resident in or near ———, do most respectfully, but most earnestly pray the Houses of Congress to take all needful steps to prevent the encroachments of white settlers upon the Indian Territory, and upon *all* Indian reservations; also to keep all treaties with the Indians until they are changed by the mutual and free consent of both parties, and to guard them in the enjoyment of *all* the rights which have been guaranteed them upon the faith of the nation.

all the States and several of the Territories of the Union, and representing fifty thousand citizens, was carried the next month, January, 1881, by the chairman and secretary of the committee to Washington, where, with the memorial letter prepared by the secretary,* it was presented by the Honorable H. L. Dawes, United States Senator, to the Senate on the 27th of that month, and on the 31st, by the Honorable Gilbert De La Matyr, to the House of Representatives, all being placed upon the records of Congress, and the proceedings, with the speech of Senator Dawes being widely published.

In March, 1881, at the fourth meeting, Mrs. Chase resigning connection with the committee, Miss Mary L. Bonney, "the originator and most generous patron of the work, was," as the minutes state, "unanimously elected chairman." In June, 1881, with five addional members, the committee adopted its first written constitution and changed its name to "The Indian

---

* MEMORIAL LETTER.

ACCOMPANYING THE INDIAN PETITION OF 1881.

To the Senate and House of Representatives in Congress Assembled:

The men and women of this nation herewith present their second petition to your Honorable Body for the faithful fulfillment of treaties and other guarantees given by our government to the different tribes of Indians within our borders. Your petitioners do not suggest any political policy to be pursued, leaving such matters to wise statesmanship. They come with but one thought, conviction, prayer. The thought recognizes the *moral obligation* of nations, as of individuals, to keep compacts. The conviction is that recognized moral obligation should result in the *fulfillment* of such obligation. The prayer is for such fulfillment as being ever, we believe, the *highest political wisdom*, the truest national safety.

An objection has been made by some to treaty-keeping with Indians, on the ground that the Indian tribes among us were never "nations," and that, therefore, so-called "treaties" with them were never *real* treaties. Your petitioners, with deep feeling recall the fact that *our government* has for a hundred years recognized these tribes as "nations," in its hundreds of compacts with them calling the latter "treaties," and has, by Acts of Congress, bound itself faithfully to observe all such made in the past, though deciding to make no new treaties with Indians. Your petitioners, therefore, pray, for the sake of national honor, which demands honest dealing with all men, that the terms "nation" and "treaty" may be kept to the heart as they have hitherto been made and explained to the ear.

Again it has been urged that the law of *eminent domain* nullifies these treaties, and requires our government to take legal jurisdiction of Indian lands, to divide the same in severalty, and to open the remainder for white settlement. Your petitioners are deeply impressed that for any government to apply the law of eminent domain to the property of others than its own citizens, is to necessitate, if there be resistance, a war of conquest,—a measure wholly opposed to the fundamental principles of this government,—and that Indians, with few exceptions, are not citizens of the United States, but

Treaty-keeping and Protective Association." Adding other representative ladies, the work of organization, as foreshadowed and provided for in the constitution, went forward. The association was to be composed of this central executive committee and of consenting "Associate Committees" in the various States and Territories, and the writer, thenceforth designated the general secretary, with a *carte blanche* as always in lieu of instructions other than those suggested by herself, began her pilgrimage beyond State limits, seeking and finding individual and groups of workers, with editorial and ecclesiastical helpers for the cause, organizing thirteen associate committees in five different States before the year ended,—those in the ten great cities of the country having the rank of State committees,—addressing meetings large and small at Chautau-

---

are under their own legislative and executive authority, as in the Indian Territory, and this by the terms of our sales of territory to them, and their titles to the same.

Your petitioners therefore present their memorial to your honorable body, feeling that the plea for treaty-keeping is a protest against any enactment of Congress which would extend legal jurisdiction over territory not under the control of this government, and which would do this, as for example the Oklahoma Bill proposes, contrary to explicit treaty stipulations.

Finally, your petitioners would express the earnest conviction that the nation, which has spent five hundred millions of dollars on Indian wars growing out of the *violation* of treaties, can best afford to make it to the interest of the Indian tribes among us *voluntarily* to become citizens of the United States, and not by the coercion of Acts of our Congress.

Our petition of last year was from fifteen States ; that of the present year represents every State of the Union and several of the Territories ; and has many more than double the number of last year's signatures. The work of circulating the petition, and accompanying pamphlets, has been done by few persons, and chiefly by Christian women already busy in benevolent work ; yet the roll contains the names of people of all occupations and in all ranks of society ; of great business firms and manufacturers ; of distinguished men and officials ; of judges, governors, and ambassadors to foreign courts ; of authors and editors ; of the faculties and students of not a few of our most noted collegiate and theological institutions, and of literary and art associations. Besides all these, the roll includes the signatures of women's mission boards, Christian associations, and other benevolent societies ; the names of pastors and bishops of the churches ; also the records of the indorsement of a rising vote from various church-meetings of different denominations ; of meetings held specially to consider the Indian question ; of minister's unions in different towns and cities, and of various other bodies. All these and many other evidences reveal the fact that the *moral sentiment* of those classes who largely make and control public opinion already requires governmental faithfulness to our Indian treaties. For this your petitioners most earnestly and respectfully pray.

AMELIA S. QUINTON.
Secretary of Indian Treaty-Keeping Committee.

qua, Ocean Grove, and other centers, where leaders for work in various places were found, corresponding with these and with government officers regarding the interests of Indians, publishing reports, appeals, and circulars, and closing the year with importunate requests for committees on editorial, financial, publication, and State work. At the opening of 1882, under the revised constitution, the associate committees were reorganized by the general secretary as permanent auxiliaries, and new ones were added in other States. The third annual petition,* representing more than one hundred thousand citizens, was, with the memorial letter, presented to

---

* This said:

To the President of the United States, and to the Senate and House of Representatives in Congress Assembled:

We, the undersigned men and women of these United States, do most respectfully but most earnestly pray our President and your honorable body:

1. To maintain all treaties with Indians with scrupulous fidelity until these compacts are modified or abrogated by the free and well-considered consent of the Indian tribes who were also parties to these treaties.

2. That since the number of Indian children within the limits of the United States does not probably exceed sixty thousand, or one-third the number of children in the public schools of some of our larger cities; and since treaties with many tribes already bind our government to provide a teacher for every thirty Indian children among these tribes: therefore we pray that a number of common schools, sufficient for the education of every child of every tribe, may be provided upon their reservations, and that industrial schools also may be established among them.

3. We pray that a title in fee-simple to at least one hundred and sixty acres of land may be granted to any Indian within the reservation occupied by his tribe, when he desires to hold land in severalty, and that said land shall be inalienable for twenty years.

4. We also earnestly pray for the recognition of Indian personalty and rights under the law, giving to Indians the protection of the law of the United States for their persons and property, and holding them strictly amenable to these laws; also giving them increased encouragements to industry, and opportunity to trade, and securing to them full religious liberty.

MEMORIAL LETTER OF THE INDIAN TREATY-KEEPING AND PROTECTIVE ASSOCIATION, PRESENTED WITH THEIR PETITION FOR 1882.

To the Senate and House of Representatives in Congress Assembled:

Again the women of a national Indian association beg leave to present to your honorable body the petition they have circulated and received again from the people of the United States. Their roll represents, at a low estimate, considerably more than a hundred thousand citizens,—instead of thirteen thousand as did their first, three years ago,—and is an earnest plea for a righteous, speedy, and permanent settlement of the Indian question.

Among the petitioners are many hundreds of churches, which have adopted the petition by a unanimous rising vote, this often having been taken at a regular Sabbath service; various popular meetings have also here presented

President Arthur, at the White House, by Mrs. Hawley, the devoted and lamented president of the Washington Auxiliary and wife of the Connecticut Senator; Mrs. Keifer, wife of the Speaker of the House, and the secretary of the association, the chairman of the committee. This was on February 21, 1882, and Senator Dawes introduced the petition and letter in the Senate on the same day, both being presented to the House of Representatives on the 25th, and the proceedings and debate on these occasions occupied several pages of the *Congressional Record.* The discussion of Senators, hotly expressing on the one hand Western impatience with Indians, and antagonism to Eastern sympathy, and on the other hand the moral sense of Christian men and women of many States, was closed by Senator Dawes in a brilliant speech of thrilling

---

their plea, similarly expressed ; while the roll contains names of members of legislative bodies, of governors, judges, and lawyers ; names of bishops and of many hundreds of the clergy—among the latter the entire ministry of three denominations in the city of Philadelphia and numbering nearly three hundred; names of the professors and students of theological seminaries like those at Hartford, Cambridge, Rochester, and Upland ; colleges and universities like Yale, Harvard, Brown, Cornell, Rochester, Washington, and Lee ; names of editors of leading periodicals ; the boards of hundreds of missionary and other benevolent societies, not a few of these being national ones ; with names of art, literary, and social clubs. Besides all these, the roll contains the signatures of hundreds of business and manufacturing firms, who control capital to the amount of many millions of dollars, and who employ many thousand operatives—all showing that not only has there been a rapid growth of sentiment among the religious and intellectual leaders of the community, demanding legislation which shall end oppression of Indians and secure to them full opportunity for industrial, mental, and religious development, but that the commerical interests of our land also are fast coming to demand a just and speedy settlement of the Indian question.

Permit an expression from the association who to-day present to your honorable body their third annual petition,—an association having sixteen State committees and one in each of the larger cities, with helpers in every State, all these committees being composed of patriotic Christian women ; permit these to say that into their ears and hearts comes the cry of suffering, undefended, ever-endangered, Indian women and children, and that this cry is our appeal to you to secure for them legal protection ; that the plea of Indian women for the sacred shield of law is the plea of the sisters, wives, and mothers of this nation for them, the plea of all womanhood, indeed, on their behalf to you as legislators and as men. Permit us also to say, that in laboring by every means in our power to fill our land with a knowledge of the present condition of Indians, and of our national obligations to them, we most deeply feel, that while justice demands the recognition of Indian personalty before the law, thus most surely and simply, it seems to us, securing to Indians protection and fostering care, we yet feel that legislation securing this recognition will be an honor to the present Congress and to our beloved country. For this legislation we most earnestly and respectfully pray.

eloquence, giving telling facts of outrages upon Indians by the Government and white settlers, and the speech was received with prolonged applause. Later, the ladies of the committee were introduced to the speakers in the Marble Room, and the subject was there continued in an animated conversation representing both sets of speakers. Enthusiastic popular meetings in various cities were next secured, and the organization, already of national proportions, received many testimonies to and proofs of its power, and that it had really influenced legislation. Before the close of the year the name of the society was changed to "The National Indian Association," and its intention soon to begin educational and missionary work among unprovided Indian tribes was announced.

At the end of 1883 the word "Women's" was introduced into the name of the association in recognition of and compliment to the new "Indian Rights Association" of gentlemen, the amended constitution, substantially as it still remains, was adopted, and preparation was made for the new work of missions. An extract from the annual report of that year indicates the growth of the organization to that date: "During this history twenty-six auxiliaries have been gained, while we have still vice-presidents and helpers in States not organized. Besides circulating and presenting the three petitions named, a million pages of information and appeal have been circulated, many great and small societies, ministerial conferences, assemblies, and anniversaries have been visited and have responded, indorsing our work and appeals to Government, while hundreds of articles concerning our objects have been secured in the secular and religious press, and hundreds of meetings have been addressed by your secretary and others regarding justice to Indians." The kind of work done by auxiliaries will be more fully seen by referring to the report of that year.*

* One paragraph will perhaps be an encouragement to those organizing similar women's movements hereafter: "Under the head of 'Meetings Held,' the New Hampshire branch reports twelve ladies' meetings and a crowded mass-meeting; the Massachusetts Association reports eleven ladies' meetings and a very successful mass-meeting in Tremont Temple; Connecticut reports fourteen ladies' meetings and two mass-meetings; New York City has had various ladies' meetings and a mass-meeting in Rev. Dr. Hall's church; Brooklyn has had thirteen ladies' meetings and two mass-meetings; Philadelphia, including local auxiliaries and meetings of the National Executive Board, has had about forty ladies' meetings and five mass-meetings; Baltimore has had eight ladies' meetings and two mass-meetings, and Washington sixteen ladies' meetings and four mass-meetings. Regarding the dis-

Miss Bonney's presidency over the association closed November, 1884, but her ardent interest still remains, and she has continued to be largely the financial provider for the department of organization. Her noble character, broad spirit, wise counsels, generous gifts, wide reputation, and devotion to this as to all redemptive work, made her a constant power for the cause and association, and though her more active share in its labors ceased with her official duties, she is still its beloved honorary president.

The second chairman of the society was the accomplished and well-known writer, Mrs. Mary Lowe Dickinson, who, upon a unanimous election, accepted the presidency November, 1884, and for three years discharged the duties of her office with great ability. Possessing rare literary talents and culture, being a natural and enthusiastic leader and a charming speaker, and having a wide circle of friends, she brought much to the aid of the enterprise. Her thoughtful addresses, her strong articles in magazine and journal, her poems replete with deep religious feeling, her graceful presiding, her wise suggestions, tact, and, above all, her earnest interest in the cause of Indian emancipation and elevation constituted her a leader of unusual value, and it was with great regret that the association was forced, because of her then impaired health, to accept her resignation, October, 1887.

Upon the retirement of Mrs. Dickinson, the writer, who had continued to do the work of general secretary until that date, was, by the executive board, made president, receiving the unanimous election of the association at its following annual meeting, November, 1887; an office which she still holds, having been four times re-elected.

The later growth of the association is revealed in the following facts: The annual report of 1885 reported fifty-six branches in twenty-seven States, and $3880 raised for the cause; that of 1886 registered eighty-three branches, showing much advance for a yet unpopular cause, and that $6793 were expended. In the report of 1887 the collections had grown to $10,690; in 1888 to $11,336; in 1889 to $16,300, and in 1890 to

---

tribution of leaflets, New Hampshire reports 5500 sent out, with 401 petitions; Connecticut 5000 leaflets, and petitions sent to all her towns; Maryland has sent leaflets to fifty towns and secured petitions representing 21,000 citizens. Of articles in the press, New Hampshire has sent sixty, and Philadelphia over a hundred. Brooklyn has raised $325; New York, $405; Boston, $724, and, naturally, being the home of the movement, Philadelphia has raised more than these and all other auxiliaries combined."

$16,500. During one year the Connecticut auxiliary raised over $4000, and the Massachusetts association put into the treasury of the national association $3000, a third of which was designated for missionary purposes and the rest for loans for Indian Home Building, and gifts for educational and legal work. These two are the strongest auxiliaries, though there are now branches and helpers or officers in thirty-four States and Territories of the Union.

Nor has the advance of ideas been less marked than the increase of the numbers and receipts of the association. The first impulse of the first partnership of means and work, which began the active movement, resulting in the organization of a national society, was an impulse of protection for Indians and their lands from the robberies and horrors of enforced removals, and it voiced itself in pleas for treaty-keeping and the honest observance of all compacts with the Indians until their real consent to changes should be justly won. The impulse was one of common humanity, and recognized the manhood and womanhood of Indians, and their claims in common with all men because human beings. The facts gained from the first investigations, given in the first leaflets, and sent forth into many States, laid hold upon the minds of free white men and women by revealing to their consciences the responsibility of silence while our native Indians were still the victims of wholesale robbery by military ejectment from their own territory, often to be sent to unwholesome, non-supporting lands, into utter helplessness, or out of perishing need into wars for mere subsistence. The facts popularly made known that Indians were practically under the supreme control of the United States agent over them; that they could not sue or be sued,* make contracts, sell their lumber, or work their mines; that they had no law; that it was legally not a crime to kill an Indian; that Indian women and girls could be and often were appropriated to become mothers of agricultural slaves to till their master's soil,—all these facts, startling to republican minds, thrilling to humane hearts, and thundering out appeals to Christian consciences, led to this impulse of protection. But soon the question of "How most wisely to protect" led to still more thoughtful study of the situation, and to the rapidly grown

* See "Protection of Law for Indians," by General J. B. Leake; "The Indian before the Law," by H. S. Pancoast, Esq.; "Our Indian Wards," by Col. George Manypenny, and "Our Wild Indians," by Col. Richard J. Dodge; "The Indian Question," by G. W. Owen, pages 90–97 and 639–650.

conviction that only law, education, and citizenship could be the real cure of such oppressions. This conviction was embodied in petitions for law, land in severalty, education, and citizenship, while yet the popular idea was that Indians could not be civilized and were not worth civilizing, and while even some so-called Christian ministers still counseled treating them as Israel of old felt commanded to treat the Canaanites. That the quiet but far-reaching work of the association, as has often been said by those publicly and conspicuously devoted to Indian welfare, has probably done more than the work of any other one organization for Indian liberation and elevation, no one familiar with its quality and quantity can well doubt. Its members recall the many testimonies to this effect, and, with grateful pride, that the Honorable H. L. Dawes, Chairman of the Indian Committee of the United States Senate, author of the long-needed Severalty Bill which became law in March, 1887, and ever the faithful friend of the women's work, stated in a public speech that the "new Indian policy," to-day everywhere approved, was "born of and nursed by the women of this association." And, indeed, all the features of the new policy are found in the early petitions * and literature of the society. That the Indian Rights Association, the evening that it was organized, just as the women's associa-

---

* That of January, 1883, said :

We, the undersigned citizens of the United States, resident in or near ———, viewing the results of our past national Indian policy ; viewing also the present positions and relations of the white and Indian races within our borders, and being convinced by many considerations, both moral and political, that only that Indian policy is just, and therefore wise, which has for its ultimate aim citizenship for Indians, through the abolition of the reservation, system by granting to all Indians, not now under the Indian Government of the Indian Territory, lands in severalty, with the same titles, law protection, property rights, common school education, and religious liberty enjoyed by other races among us :

Now, therefore, we do respectfully but most earnestly pray that such a policy as above suggested may be adopted and in future pursued, having due regard to the principles of equity and justice involved in past treaties with Indians, yet granting to them upon their present reservations as fast as individuals so desire (and we pray that our Government will generously allure them to this desire).

FIRST : Lands in severalty, with fee-simple titles, inalienable for thirty years.

SECOND : The same law-protection, legal personalty and citizenship that white men and black men enjoy.

THIRD : Adequate common-school and industrial education upon their present reservations, and,

FOURTH : Full religious liberty.

tion, was ready to present its fourth annual petition, crystallized its plans of work, after reading the constitution of the women's society, and adopted its lines and methods of work ; that the Boston Indian Citizenship Committee, and that the new Commissioner of Indian Affairs and the present administration have but done and are doing, what the association's literature and petitions have for years advocated is a sufficient testimony to the principles and aims of the association. That its leaders have been divinely led many humbly and gratefully feel, for, as said the venerable Bishop Whipple, " The women have builded better than they knew ;" and as said Hannah Whitall Smith, now of London, England, well known on two continents as an uplifting writer and speaker on religious subjects, one of the early treasurers and still a patron of the association, " This Indian work is but the Christian motherhood of the nation obeying its instincts toward our native heathen." It would require a portly volume to mention the names and deeds of the earnest and eminent women who have had share in this work for the aborigines of our country. Among its honorary officers and members, as seen in its annual reports and those of its auxiliaries, are names distinguished in the world of letters and in political and social circles, as well as those known in philanthropic and Christian work, while many in its corps of active officers and in its executive board are widely known and honored. But the temptation to catalogue these in this chapter, must manifestly be resisted or restricted to incumbents of the leading offices and to the chairmen of departments. Among those most active in State work, Mrs. Sara Thomson Kinney, president of the Connecticut auxiliary, and now first vice-president of the national association, has given very largely of time, thought, and labor, has compactly organized her State with branches in its leading towns, has inaugurated in her association a variety of important work and brought it to its present standard of excellence. Under Miss Fletcher's inspiration she introduced Indian Home Building by loan funds and is chairman of that department in the national association, forty or fifty Indian homes having, under her management, been built or remodeled in civilized fashion, and among ten or fifteen tribes. Many smaller loans she has also made, enabling individual Indians to adopt civilized and self-supporting industries. Mrs. Elizabeth Elliot Bullard, president of the Massachusetts auxiliary, and chairman of the new national Committee on Special Education of bright individual Indians brought to her association influence and new friends, and has, with the aid of a corps of eminent women, achieved large results, having in her society more branches than are to be found in any other State, her association having been also the largest and most enthusiastic supporter of the Missionary Department. In New York City an admirable board of officers, led by the accomplished Mrs. Theodore Irving and Mrs. Edward Elliott, are supporting a new station of the Ramona Missions, and are meeting with other new successes, as is the Brooklyn association, which, under the leadership of Mrs. Lyman Abbott, assisted by the former president of that society, Mrs. Jerome Plummer, inaugurated the Kiowa Mission and is preparing to open a station among the Piegans of Montana. Miss Sarah M. Taylor, of Philadelphia, a devoted and far-seeing worker and generous giver, is now chairman of the Missionary Department which, in six years, has planted directly or indirectly, missions in twenty different tribes, building four missionary cottages and four chapels in these, transferring them, one after another, when well established, to the care of the permanent denominational societies. Miss Kate Foote, president of the auxiliary at the national capital, whose bright letters from that city and whose charming magazine articles are so widely enjoyed, is chairman of the Department of Indian Legislation, her racy reports of laws secured, and notices of the more numerous ones needed, having both a popular and legislative value, while her prescient watchfulness is constantly achieving other and important help for Indians. The supplemental work for Indian civilization at Crow Creek Agency, Dakota, for furnishing on the reservation, to returned Indian students, civilized employments and continued religious nurture, thus making them self-supporting and an aid to their entire tribes, led to the election of Miss Grace Howard, of New York, who originated, successfully inaugurated, and continues it, as chairman of the association's department of Indian Civilization Work. The Young People's Department has for chairman Miss Marie E. Ives, of New Haven, whose first effort so inspired a quartet of young girls in New York City that their first entertainment placed $327 in the treasury for the association's new Seminole Mission, and, naturally, awakened large hope for the success of this important division of work. The chairman of the committee on Indian Libraries, Miss Frances C. Sparhawk, of Massachusetts, originated and is vigorously serving her own department, while the latest committee, that on hospital work, is led by Miss Laura E. Tileston, of Virginia, though the first hospital, for which funds are already in hand, will soon be built by the National Missionary Committee for the Omahas. The devotion of our corresponding secretary, Miss Helen R. Foote; of our late recording secretary, Mrs. Rachel N. Taylor; the generous service of our recent treasurer, Mrs. Harriet L. Wilbur, and of the present one, Miss Anna Bennett, and the labors of other workers in different sections of the country come up in remembrance, and it would be a pleasure to record the names of all these did space permit. Many women have wrought well during and since the inauguration of the new Indian policy, by the influence of which already more than one third of the forty-eight thousand Indian pupils are in the various government and other schools, and under which the people of more than twenty tribes are receiving lands in severalty. By the success of this policy, developed with the aid of all officials, individuals, and organizations friendly to them, the quarter of a million Indians of our country are, by taking individual farms or by adopting civilized avocations, at last really passing out of barbarism into civilization, and from the oppressions, disabilities, and helplessness of the reservation system into the freedom, protection, and development of United States citizenship. The work of the association for these ends has been pressed with all the vigor which its numbers and means permitted, and it has given its whole thought to the accomplishment of its purposes. Not contemplating a permanent existence, it has given small though adequate attention to mere form. One of its members, a poet, Indian educator, an able writer on Indian topics, and now a government superintendent of Indian schools, Miss Elaine Goodale, says: "This association stretches out sympathetic hands and loses itself in all other good work for the Indians so that the measure of its influence may not be expressed in any rows of figures however significant, or set down in any report however complete. The striking and hopeful feature, after all, of this Women's National Indian Association is, as its president constantly reminds us, that it is not intended as a permanent organization. The women have undertaken to meet a particular crisis, to bridge a dangerous gap. As fast as the regular missionary societies are ready to accept its independent missions, these are placed entirely in their hands. As soon as our rich and powerful Government comprehends and faithfully discharges its duty to the Indians the women will cease to urge their needs and their rights, and the association will cease to exist. Its work will have been done. Its demand is not for its own honor or extension but that the object for which alone it lives may speedily be accomplished."

Until this object is gained, The Women's National Indian Association will not sound retreat nor its great company of consecrated workers disband. It is possible that its best and longest record may be made in the future and its work be finished by wholly new laborers. God grant that this may be so if the work, political, educational, industrial, and religious, still so imperatively demanded by justice for our native Indian Americans, cannot otherwise be done.

XVI.

WORK OF ANTI-SLAVERY WOMEN.

BY

LILLIE B. CHACE WYMAN.

PRUDENCE CRANDALL, a Quaker school teacher in Canterbury, Conn., was the woman whose name we encounter in the earliest records of anti-slavery labor in this country. She took counsel with Mr. Garrison in 1833, and opened a school for colored pupils, which she bravely maintained for over a year, although she was subjected therefore to a great amount of persecution. She was arrested, and even thrown temporarily into jail, and her house and its inmates were made the mark for every species of insult and outrage which her neighbors dared to perpetrate. She married the Rev. Calvin Philleo, and still survives him, living in Kansas. The Legislature of Connecticut, a few years ago, granted her a pension in atonement for the wrongs she formerly suffered in that State.

Hatred of slavery was the motive which first called women in this country into public life. Sarah and Angelina Grimké were two sisters belonging to a prominent slaveholding family in South Carolina. As a child, Sarah was shocked by the cruelties practised upon the slaves around her, but her first deep interest in early life was in religious questions. The family were Episcopalians, and she remained for many years of the same faith. She made a visit to the North, came under Quaker influences, and finally joined the Society of Friends, and this led to her going to live in Philadelphia, in 1821. Angelina, who was twelve years younger than Sarah, remained in Charleston. She manifested, like Sarah, a tendency to extreme asceticism in dress and manner, and she became a Presbyterian. She detested the evils of slavery, but she does not seem to have thought slave-holding sinful in itself, till after she had visited Philadelphia in 1828, when she was twenty-three years old. After that, she grew to feel more and more keenly that she was living amid a great wrong, and she suffered intensely at the participation in it of her family. She entreated and argued, begged her brother to be merciful to his slaves, besought her mother and sisters to feel as she did. In May, 1829, she wrote in her diary, "May it not be laid down as an axiom, that that system must be radically wrong, which can only be supported by transgressing the laws of God." A little later, she determined to leave her home, because of her inability to do any good there in regard to the slaves, and she writes, "I cannot but be pained at the thought of leaving mother. . . . I do not think, dear sister, I will ever see her again until she is willing to give up slavery." In the autumn of 1829 she left Charleston and her mother, whom she never saw again.

She went to Philadelphia and joined the Society of Friends. After some years of comparatively quiet life, Angelina wrote in 1835 a sympathetic letter to Wm. Lloyd Garrison, which he published in *The Liberator*. She wrote next "An Appeal to the Christian Women of the South," a pamphlet which "produced," says Mrs. Birney, "the most profound sensation wherever it was read." Not long afterward "the city authorities of Charleston learned," writes Mr. Theodore D. Weld, "that Miss Grimké was intending to visit her mother and sisters, and pass the winter with them. Thereupon the mayor called upon Mrs. Grimké and desired her to inform her daughter that the police had been instructed to prevent her landing while the steamer remained in port, and to see to it that she should not communicate, by letter or otherwise, with any persons in the city; and further, that if she should elude their vigilance and go on shore, she would be arrested and imprisoned until the return of the vessel." Threats of personal violence were also made, should she come.

A year later Sarah published "An Epistle to the Clergy of the Southern States," and the sisters began to address meetings of women on the subject of slavery. They proposed at first to hold parlor meetings, but found it necessary at once to engage the session room of a Baptist Church in New York. The gathering there was "the first assembly of women, not Quakers, in a public place in America, addressed by American women." Two clergymen performed the opening ceremonies, offered prayer and made an address of welcome, and then left, so that none but women should hear women speak. Similar assemblies were held afterward, and in a letter dated "second month, 4th, 1837," Angelina writes, that one man had got into the last meeting, and people thought he must be a Southern spy. She says, "somehow, I did not feel his presence embarrassing at all, and went on just as though he had not been there."

After this, the sisters went to New England to pursue their labors. In Dorchester two or three men "slyly slid" into the back seats of the hall and listened to the speakers, and one of them "afterward took great pains to prove that it was unscriptural for a woman to speak in public." From this time a few men were generally present at the gatherings, and on the 21st of July, 1837, Angelina wrote, "In the evening of the same day addressed our first *mixed* audience. Over one thousand present." "The opposers of abolitionism, and especially the clergy, began to be alarmed," says Mrs. Birney. The sisters were denounced, halls were refused them, the Society of Friends condemned their course, aud violence was threatened; but Sarah writes, "They think to frighten us from the field of duty; but they do not move us." Even some of the Abolitionists doubted the propriety of their labors, and the question of Womans' Rights was fairly launched on the tide of the anti-slavery movement.

The General Association of Congregational Ministers of Massachusetts passed a resolution censuring the sisters, and issued a pastoral letter, containing "a tirade against female preachers."

Sarah next published letters on "The Province of Woman."

In February, 1838, Angelina addressed a committee of the Massachusetts Legislature on the subject of slavery. She wrote of this memorable occasion, "My heart never quailed before, but it almost died within me at that hour." She was given two hearings, and she says "We abolition women are turning the world upside down, for during the whole meeting there was sister seated up in the speaker's chair of State."

Angelina was the more eloquent of the two sisters, and although Sarah spoke, she preferred to serve the cause by writing.

In May, 1838, Angelina married Theodore D. Weld, who was an earnest and eloquent abolition orator. After this marriage she spoke once again, and then was obliged to relinquish all public work on account of her health, while Mr. Weld's loss of voice, prevented him from continuing his lecturing service. They never faltered, however, or relaxed in their principles. They were all three engaged in schoolwork and received colored pupils as readily as white ones. When the war came, and slavery was abolished, some peculiar family trials fell to the lot of the Grimké sisters, and old wounds were re-opened. They bore these renewed sufferings with fortitude, and with patient and loving spirits. They succored their impoverished kindred, who had long been alienated from them, and they fulfilled some difficult and delicate duties which grew out of the old ties which their Southern relatives had discarded.

Lucretia Mott was a Quakeress, and a very beautiful woman. She exercised a singular power over people with whom she came in contact, influencing and inspiring them to all high and holy purposes. She became an Abolitionist in early life, and was sent as a delegate to the World's Anti-Slavery Convention, held in London, in 1840.* Like the other women who were delegates, she was refused admission to the body, and attended its sessions only as an outsider.

She was an eloquent and persuasive speaker in anti-slavery and religious meetings. She, with other Philadelphia women, used to attend the courts whenever a fugitive slave case was tried, in the hope that the silent protest of their presence, would have some effect on judges and juries, who were inclined to be subservient to the slave power. On one occasion, she and her companions sat all night in the court-room, the commissioner deferring his sentence, thinking that the women would be tired out, and would leave and, finally, unable to get rid of them, he availed himself of a legal quibble, and ordered the fugitive to be set free. Years later, when the Civil War came, the lawyer who acted in this affair on behalf of the slave-holder, and who had been an ardent supporter of the interests of slavery, wheeled around, and gave in his allegiance to the Union party. Some one asked him how he dared thus oppose all his former friends, and he replied that the man who had endured to sit all night before Lucretia Mott and knew what she was thinking of him all the time, would fear nothing else on earth.

She was herself brave, and once, when an old colored woman was refused a seat in a horse-car, and forced to ride on the front platform, exposed to a pelting winter storm, she went out and stood by her side, and rode for nearly an hour, in all the bitter weather.

She was very charming, and she retained her great personal beauty to the last, dying finally in 1880, at the age of eighty-seven.

---

* See chapter Woman in the State.—Ed.

Abby Kelley was a New England girl, a Quaker, and a school-teacher. She began her anti-slavery work by giving half of all she earned to the cause. Afterward she decided that it was her duty to lecture and talk to people about slavery. She received no salary from the anti-slavery societies for her labor, but went from town to town, staying with friends when it was possible, going by private conveyance if she could, getting up meetings, and everywhere, in season and out, pleading for the slave. When her clothes were worn out, she went to a sister's and did house-work, till she had earned enough money to get what she needed, and then she started again on her mission. She encountered great opposition from press and pulpit. Every epithet was hurled at her which was most calculated to wound the spirit of a sensitive woman. Nothing overcame her. The cry of the slave mother sounded in her ears and drowned the clamor about herself. She pursued her way, fighting, as it were, for every inch of the ground she traversed.

It is no exaggeration to say that what she did and suffered, has made the path easier for every woman, since her day, who has sought to work in any public manner in America. The Grimké sisters retired early from the field, and Abby Kelley bore the brunt of a long and painful contest with prejudice and opposition, which were directed not only against the anti-slavery cause, but against her personally, for doing what women had not till then done.

Abby Kelley married Stephen S. Foster, an Abolitionist, so resolute, unflinching and uncompromising as to be a fit mate for her. They established a home, but both of them often went from it on anti-slavery lecturing trips, until she had entirely worn out her voice, and was obliged to refrain from using it in public. Once in a while, however, in later life, she addressed some convention for a few minutes at a time, when the impulse to speak in behalf of something she thought right, proved too strong to be resisted. A hoarse whisper was all that remained to her from the young voice, with which she had once challenged the scorn of men and the timid contempt of women, but her listeners almost hushed their hearts to hear these faint breathings, remembering reverently all the sacrifice and pain she had endured.

Mrs. Foster lived in all respects a conscientious life. She was a careful housekeeper and a devoted wife and mother. She and her husband were ardent Woman Suffragists and they protested against the payment of taxes to a government which allowed her no representation. Their home was in Worcester, Mass., and they both lived to see slavery abolished. She survived him for several years, without abating her interest in the general principles to which their lives had been consecrated.

Sallie Holley was one of the later anti-slavery speakers. She was generally accompanied in her lecturing trips by a friend, Miss Caroline F. Putnam, and after the war the two went to Virginia to live and work among the freed people.

Lucy Stone and Susan B. Anthony were also anti-slavery speakers before the Civil War. Anna Dickinson made a few speeches in her very early girlhood as agent of one of the anti-slavery societies. There were also women employed by the societies as workers in other ways, such as circulating petitions, raising money, distributing tracts, and talking with people in private ways.

Miss Mary Grew, of Philadelphia, occasionally addressed meetings. Miss Grew was one of a large number of women all over the North, who gave all their energies to anti-slavery work. These women helped fugitive slaves, cared for Abolition speakers, raised money, arranged meetings, distributed papers and pamphlets, corresponded, wrote articles for newspapers, sewed for fairs, went without luxuries and even necessities so as to be able to give to the cause, and spent themselves in body and brain without stint, and without asking any reward but the achievement of the end they sought. Mrs. Sidney Lewis, of Philadelphia, kept the anti-slavery office in that city. It would be impossible to name the half of these silent workers.

Lydia Maria Child * was one of the foremost literary women of her day, when she avowed herself to be an Abolitionist, and her popularity was greatly injured thereby. She edited the *Anti-Slavery Standard* for two years, and did noble work. During the war there was a last outbreak of pro-slavery fury in Northern cities, and mobs assaulted Wendell Phillips in Boston. One night, after an anti-slavery meeting, the crowd threatened to kill him, and she took his arm and walked serenely by his side through the raging multitude, and it was considered that her presence with him awed them to such an extent that she really saved his life.

Harriet Beecher Stowe wrote "Uncle Tom's Cabin," † when public sentiment was beginning to turn against slavery, and the book went all over the world, and was translated into many

---

* See chapter Woman in Literature.—ED.

† See chapter Woman in Literature.—ED.

tongues, to make all men feel the wickedness of an institution which needed that the Fugitive Slave Law should be enacted and enforced for its support. The effect of the book was incalculable.

Maria Weston Chapman and her sisters brought grace, beauty, and wit, in social circles, to the aid of the Abolitionists in the very first years of the long moral warfare. They became so unpopular in Boston, in consequence of their course, that Mrs. Chapman told a friend that she feared to walk alone on Washington Street, because the very clerks in the stores would insult her as she passed. She was very energetic in getting up anti-slavery fairs on a scale which seemed large in those days, and she enlisted the sympathy of people in England, and secured large contributions from them.

Ann Green Phillips, the wife of Wendell Phillips, was a life-long invalid, but she first converted him to anti-slavery opinions, and then inspired and sustained him, and from her sick bed sent him forth to do the work she could not do.

Helen E. Garrison, the wife of Wm. Lloyd Garrison, the shyest and most modest of women, encouraged her husband, and by her unselfish devotion at home, made it possible for him to use his time and strength combating the system which he held to be "the sum of all villainies." When the mob dragged him through the streets of Boston, in 1835, and word was brought to this beautiful young woman, who was then a recent bride, that his life was in danger, her spirit rose at the tidings, and she proudly said, "I do not believe my husband will be untrue to his principles."

XVII.

WORK OF THE W. C. T. U.

BY

FRANCES E. WILLARD.

LET me try to set forth the sequel of that modern Pentecost called the "Woman's Crusade." That women should thus dare was the wonder after they had so long endured, while the manner of their doing left us who looked on bewildered between laughter and tears. Woman-like, they took their knitting, their zephyr work, or their embroidery, and simply swarmed into the drink-shops, seated themselves, and watched the proceedings. Usually they came in a long procession from their rendezvous at some church where they had held morning prayer-meeting, entered the saloon with kind faces, and the sweet songs of church and home upon their lips, while some Madonna-like leader with the Gospel in her looks, took her stand beside the bar, and gently asked if she might read God's word and offer prayer.

Women gave of their best during the two months of that wonderful uprising. All other engagements were laid aside; elegant women of society walked beside quiet women of home, school, and shop, in the strange processions that soon lined the chief streets, not only of nearly every town and village in the State that was its birth place,* but of leading cities there and elsewhere; and voices trained in Paris and Berlin sang "Rock of Ages, cleft for me," in the malodorous air of liquor-rooms and beer-halls. Meanwhile, where were the men who patronized these places? Thousands of them signed the pledge these women brought, and accepted their invitation to go back with them to the churches, whose doors, for once, stood open all day long; others slunk out of sight, and a few cursed the women openly; but even of these it might be said,

---

* Ohio.—Ed.

that those who came to curse remained to pray. Soon the saloon-keepers surrendered in large numbers, the statement being made by a well-known observer that the liquor traffic was temporarily driven out of two hundred and fifty towns and villages in Ohio and the adjoining States, to which the Temperance Crusade extended. There are photographs extant representing the stirring scenes when, amid the ringing of church bells, the contents of every barrel, cask, and bottle in a saloon were sent gurgling into the gutter, the owner insisting that women's hands alone should do this work, perhaps with some dim thought in his muddled head of the poetic justice due to the Nemesis he thus invoked. And so it came about that soft and often jeweled hands grasped axe and hammer, while the whole town assembled to rejoice in this new fashion of exorcising the evil spirits. In Cincinnati, a city long dominated by the liquor trade, a procession of women, including the wives of leading pastors, were arrested and locked up in jail; in Cleveland dogs were set on the Crusaders, and in a single instance a blunderbuss was pointed at them, while in several places they were smoked out, or had the hose turned on them. But the arrested women marched through the streets singing, and held a temperance meeting in the prison; the one assailed by dogs laid her hands upon their heads and prayed; and the group menaced by a gun marched up to its mouth singing, "Never be afraid to work for Jesus." The annals of heroism have few pages so bright as the annals of that strange crusade, spreading as if by magic through all the Northern States, across the sea, and to the Orient itself. Everywhere it went, the attendance at church increased incalculably, and the crime record was in like manner shortened. Men say there was a spirit in the air such as they never knew before; a sense of God and human brotherhood.

But after fifty days or more, all this seemed to pass away. The women could not keep up such work; it took them too much from their homes; saloons reopened; men gathered as before behind their sheltering screens, and swore "those silly women had done more harm than good," while with ribald words they drank the health of "the defunct crusade."

Perhaps the most significant outcome of this movement was the knowledge of their own power gained by the conservative women of the churchse. They had never seen a "woman's rights convention," and had been held aloof from the "suffragists" by fears as to their orthodoxy; but now there were women, prominent in all church cares and duties, eager to clasp hands for a more agressive work than such women had ever before dreamed of undertaking.

Nothing is more suggestive in all the national gatherings of the Women's Christian Temperance Union, that sober second thought of the crusade, than the wide difference between these meetings and any held by men. The beauty of decoration is specially noticeable ; banners of silk, satin and velvet, usually made by the women themselves, adorn the wall ; the handsome shields of States ; the great vases bearing aloft grains, fruits and flowers ; the moss-covered well with its old bucket ; or the setting of a platform to present an interior as cozy and delightful as a parlor could afford, are features of the pleasant scene. The rapidity of movement with which business is conducted, the spontaneity of manner, the originality of plan, the perpetual freshness and ingenuity of the convention, its thousand unexpectednesses, its quips and turns, its wit and pathos, its impromptu eloquence and its perpetual good nature—all these elements, brought into condensed view in the National Convention, are an object lesson of the new force and the unique method that womanhood has contributed to the consideration of the greatest reform in Christendom. It is really the crusade over again ; the home going forth into the world. Its manner is not that of the street, the court, the mart, or the office ; it is the manner of the home. Men take one line, and travel onward to success ; with them discursiveness is at a discount. But women in the home must be mistresses as well as maids of all work ; they have learned well the lesson of unity in diversity ; hence, by inheritance and by environment, women are varied in their methods ; they are born to be "branchers-out." Men have been in the organized temperance work not less than eighty years—women not quite fifteen. Men pursued it at first along the line of temperance, then total abstinence ; license, then prohibition ; while women have already over forty distinct departments of work, classified under the heads of preventive, educational, evangelistic, social, and legal. Women think in the concrete. The crusade showed them the drinking man, and they began upon him directly to get him to sign the pledge and "seek the Lord behind the pledge." The crusade showed them the selling man, and they prayed over him, and persuaded him to give up his bad business, often buying him out, and setting him up in the better occupation of baker, grocer, or keeper of the reading-room, into which they converted his saloon after converting him from the error of his ways.

But oftentimes the drinking man went back to his cups, and the selling man fell from his grace ; the first one declaring, "I can't break the habit I formed when a boy;" and the last averring, "Somebody's bound to sell, and I might as well make the profit." Upon this the women, still with their concrete ways of thinking, said, "To be sure, we must train our boys; and not only ours but everybody's ; what institution reaches all ?—the public schools." Under the leadership of Mrs. Mary H. Hunt they have secured laws requiring scientific temperance instruction in the public school system of thirty States.

To the inane excuse of the seller that he might as well do it since somebody would, the quick and practical reply was, "To be sure ; but suppose the people could be persuaded not to let anybody sell ? why, then that would be God's answer to our crusade prayers." So they began with petitions to municipalities, to legislatures, and to Congress, laboriously gathering up, doubtless, not fewer than ten million names in the great aggregate, and through fourteen years. Thus the Woman's Christian Temperance Union stands as the strongest bulwark of Prohibition, State and national, by constitutional amendment and by statute. Meanwhile, it was inevitable that their motherly hearts should devise other methods for the protection of their homes. Knowing the terrors and the blessings of inheritance, they set about the systematic study of heredity, founding a journal for that purpose. Learning the relation of diet to the drink habit, they arranged to study hygiene also; desiring children to know that the Bible is on the side of total abstinence, they induced the International Sunday School Convention to prepare a plan for lessons on this subject ; perceiving the limitless power of the Press, they did their best to subsidize it by sending out their bulletins of temperance facts and news items, thick as the leaves of Vallambrosa, and incorporated a publishing company of women.

It is curious to watch the development of the women who entered the saloons in 1874 as a gentle, well-dressed, and altogether peaceable mob. They have become an army, drilled and disciplined. They have a method of organization, the simplest yet the most substantial known to temperance annals. It is the same for the smallest local union as for the national society with its ten thousand auxiliaries. Committees have been abolished, except the executive, made up of the general officers, and "superintendencies" substituted, making each woman responsible for a single line of work in the local,

State, and national society. This puts a premium upon personality, develops a negative into a positive with the least loss of time, and increases beyond all computation the aggregate of work accomplished. Women with specialties have thus been multiplied by tens of thousands, and the temperance reform introduced into strongholds of power hitherto neglected or unthought of. Is an exposition to be held, or a State or county fair? there is a woman in the locality who knows that it is her business to see that the W. C. T. U. has an attractive booth with temperance literature and temperance drinks; and that, besides all this, it is her duty to secure laws and by-laws requiring the teetotal absence of intoxicants from grounds and buildings. Is there an institution for the dependent or delinquent classes? there is a woman in the locality who knows that it is her duty to see that temperance literature is circulated, temperance talking and singing done, and that flowers with appropriate sentiments attached are sent to the inmates by young ladies banded for that purpose. Is there a convocation of ministers, doctors, teachers, editors, voters, or any other class of opinion-manufacturers announced to meet in any town or city? there is a woman thereabouts who knows it is her business to secure, through some one of the delegates to these influential gatherings, a resolution favoring the temperance movement and pledging it support along the line of work then and there represented. Is there a legislature anywhere about to meet, or is Congress in session? there is a woman near at hand who knows it is her business to make the air heavy with the white, hovering wings of prohibition for the better protection of women and girls, for the preventing of the sale of tobacco to minors, for the enforcement of the Sabbath or for the enfranchisement of women. Thus have the manifold relationships of the mighty temperance movement been studied out by women in the training-school afforded by the real work and daily object-lessons of the W. C. T. U. Its aim is everywhere to bring women and temperance in contact with the problem of humanity's heart-break and sin, to protect the home by prohibiting the saloon; and to police the State with men and women voters committed to the enforcement of righteous law. The women saw, as years passed on, that not one, but three curses were pronounced upon their sons by the nineteenth century civilization; the curse of the narcotic poisons, alcohol and nicotine; the curse of gambling; the curse of social sin, deadlier than all; and that these three are part and parcel of each other. And so, "distinct like the billows, but one like the sea," is their unwearied warfare against each and all. They have learned, by the logic of defeat, that the mother-heart must be enthroned in all places of power before its edicts will be heeded. For this reason they have been educated up to the level of the equal suffrage movement. For the first time in history the women of the South have clasped hands with their Northern sisters in faith and fealty wearing the white ribbon emblem of patriotism, purity and peace, and inscribing on their banners the motto of the organized crusade, "For God and Home and Native Land."

"No sectarianism in religion," "no sectionalism in politics," "no sex in citizenship,"—these are the battle cries of this relentless but peaceful warfare. We believe that woman will bless and brighten every place she enters, and that she will enter every place on the round earth. We believe in prohibition by law, prohibition by politics, and prohibition by woman's ballot. After ten years' experience, the women of the crusade became convinced that until the people of this country divide at the ballot box, on the foregoing issue, America can never be nationally delivered from the dram-shop. They therefore publicly announced their devotion to the Prohibition party, and promised to lend it their influence, which, with the exception of a very small minority, they have since most sedulously done. Since then they have not ceased beseeching voters to cast their ballots first of all to help elect an issue rather than a man. For this they have been vilified as if it were a crime; but they have gone on their way kindly as sunshine, steadfast as gravitation, and persistent as a hero's faith. While their enemy has brewed beer, they have brewed public opinion; while he distilled whisky, they distilled sentiment; while he rectified spirits, they rectified the spirit that is in man. They have had good words of cheer alike for North and South, for Catholic and Protestant, for home and foreign born, for white and black, but gave words of criticism for the liquor traffic and the parties that it dominates as its servants and allies.

While the specific aims of the white ribbon women everywhere are directed against the manufacture, sale, and use of alcoholic beverages, it is sufficiently apparent that the indirect line of their progress is, perhaps, equally rapid, and involves social, governmental and ecclesiastical equality between women and men. By this is meant such financial independence on the part of women as will enable them to hold men to the same high standards of personal purity in the habitudes of life as they have required of women such a participation in the affairs of government as shall renovate politics and make home questions the paramount issue of the State, and such equality in all church relations as shall fulfill the gospel declaration, "There is neither male nor female, but ye are all one in Christ Jesus."

The cultivation of specialties, and the development of *esprit de corps* among women, all predict the day, when, through this might-conserving force of motherhood introduced into every department of human activity, the common weal shall be the individual care; war shall rank among the lost arts; nationality shall mean what Edward Bellamy's wonderful book, entitled "Looking Backward," sets before us as the fulfillment of man's highest earthly dream; and Brotherhood shall become the talismanic word and realized estate of all humanity.

In concluding this portion of my article I cannot better express my view of what we are, and what we may be, than by the following quotation from my address before the Woman's Congress at its meeting in Des Moines, Ia., 1885:

Humanly speaking, such success as we have attained has resulted from the following policy and methods:

1. The simplicity and unity of the organization. The local union is a miniature of the national, having similar officiary and plan of work. It is a military company carefully mustered, officered, and drilled. The county union is but an aggregation of the locals and the district of the counties, while each State is a regiment, and the national itself is womanhood's "Grand Army of the Republic."

2. Individual responsibility is everywhere urged. "Committees are obsolete to us, and each distinct line of work has one person, called a superintendent, who is responsible for its success in the local, and another in the State, and a third in the National union. She may secure such lieutenants as she likes, but the union looks to her for results, and holds her accountable for failures.

3. The quick and cordial recognition of talent is another secret of W. C. T. U. success. Women, young or old, who can speak, write, conduct meetings, organize, keep accounts, interest children, talk with the drinking man, get up entertainments, or carry flowers to the sick or imprisoned, are all pressed into the service. There has been also in our work an immense amount of digging in the earth to find one's own buried talent, to rub off the rust and to put it out at interest. Perhaps that is, after all, its most significant feature, considered as a movement.

4. Subordination of the financial phase has helped, not hindered us. Lack of funds has not barred out even the poorest from our sisterhood. A penny per week is our basis of membership; of which a fraction goes to the State, and ten cents to the National W. C. T. U. Money has been, and I hope may be, a consideration altogether secondary. Of wealth we have had incomputable stores; indeed, I question if America has a richer corporation to-day than ours; wealth of faith, of enthusiasm, of experience, of brain, of speech, of common sense—this is a capital stock that can never depreciate, needs no insurance, requires no combination lock or bonded custodian, and puts us under no temptation to tack our course or trim our sails.

5. Nothing has helped us more than the entire freedom of our society from the influence or dictation of capitalists, politicians, or corporations of any sort whatever. This cannot be too strongly emphasized as one of the best elements of power. Indeed, it may be truly said that this vast and systematic work has been in no wise guided, molded, or controlled by men. "It has not even occurred to them to offer advice until within a year, and to accept advise has never occurred to us, and I hope never will. While a great many noble men are 'honorary members,' and in one or two sporadic instances men have acted temporarily as presidents of local unions at the South, I am confident our grand constituency of temperance brothers rejoice almost as much as we do in the fact that we women have from the beginning gone our own gait and acted according to our own sweet will. They would bear witness, I am sure, to the fact that we have never done this flippantly, or in a spirit of bravado, but with great seriousness, asking the help of God. I can say personally what I believe our leaders would also state as their experience, that so strongly do good men seem to be impressed that the call to Christian women in the Crusade was of God, and not of man, that in the eleven years of my almost uninterrupted connection with the National W. C. T. U. I have hardly received a letter of advice or a verbal exhortation from minister or layman, and I would mildly but firmly say that I have not sought their counsel." The hierarchies of the land will be ransacked in vain for the letter-heads of the W. C. T. U. We have sought, it is true, the help of almost every influential society in the nation, both religious and secular; we have realized how greatly this help was needed by us, and grandly has it been accorded; but what we asked for was an indorsement of plans already made and work

already done. Thus may we always be a society "of the women, by the women," but for humanity.

6. The freedom from red-tape and the keeping out of ruts is another element of power. We practice a certain amount of parliamentary usage, and strongly urge the study of it as a part of the routine of local unions. We have good, strong "constitutions," and by-laws to match; blanks for reports; rolls for membership; pledges in various styles of art; badges, ribbons, and banners, and hand-books of our work, are all to be had at "national headquarters," but we will not come under a yoke of bondage to the paraphernalia of the movement. We are always moving on. "Time cannot dull nor custom stale our infinite variety." We are exceedingly apt to break out in a new phase. Here we lop off an old department, and there we add two new ones. Our "new departures" are frequent and oftentimes most unexpected. Indeed, we exhibit the characteristics of an army on the march rather than an army in camp or hospital.

The marked *esprit de corps* is to be included among the secrets of success. The W. C. T. U. has invented a phrase to express this, and it is "comradeship among women." So generous and so cherished has this comradeship become that ours is often called a "mutual admiration society." We believe in each other, stand by each other, and have plenty of emulaion without envy. Sometimes a State or an individual says to another, "The laurels of Miltiades will not suffer me to sleep;" but there is no staying awake to belittle success; we do not detract from any worker's rightful meed of praise. So much for the "hidings of power" in the W. C. T. U.

There are two indirect results of this organized work among women, concerning which I wish to speak.

First. It is a strong nationalizing influence. Its method and spirit differ very little, whether you study them on the border of Puget Sound or the Gulf of Mexico. In San Francisco and Baltimore white ribbon women speak the same vernacular, tell of their gospel meetings and petitions, discuss the *Union Signal* editorials, and wonder "what will be the action of our next annual convention."

Almost all other groups of women workers that dot the continent are circumscribed by denominational lines, and act largely under the advice of ecclesiastical leaders. The W. C. T. U. feels no such limitation. North and South are strictly separate in the women's missionary work of the churches, but Mississippi and Maine, Texas and Oregon, Massachusetts and Georgia, sit side by side around the yearly camp-fires of the W. C. T. U. The Southern women have learned to love us of the North, and our hearts are true to them; while to us all who fight in peaceful ranks unbroken, "For God and Home and Native Land," the Nation is a sacred name.

Second. Our W. C. T. U. is a school, not founded in that thought or for that purpose, but sure to fit us for the sacred duties of patriots in the realm that lies just beyond the horizon of the coming century.

Here we try our wings that yonder our flight may be strong and steady. Here we prove our capacity for great deeds; there we shall perform them. Here we make our experience and pass our novitiate that yonder we may calmly take our places and prove to the world that what is needed most was "two heads in counsel" as well as "two beside the hearth." When that day comes the nation shall no longer miss, as now, the influence of half its wisdom more than half its purity, and nearly all its gentleness, in courts of justice and halls of legislation. Then shall one code of morals—and that the highest—govern both men and women; then shall the Sabbath be respected, the rights of the poor be recognized, the liquor traffic banished, and the home protected from all its foes.

Born of such a visitation of God's spirit as the world has not known since tongues of fire sat upon the wondering group at Pentecost, cradled in a faith high as the hope of a saint, and deep as the depths of a drunkard's despair, and baptized in the beauty of holiness, the Crusade determined the ultimate goal of its teachable child, the W. C. T. U., which has one steadfast aim, and that none other than the regnancy of Christ, not in form but in fact; not in substance but in essence; not ecclesiastically, but truly in the hearts of men. To this end its methods are varied, changing, manifold; but its unwavering faith these words express: "Not by might, nor by power, but by my spirit, saith the Lord of Hosts."

The Woman's National Christian Temperance Union has a publishing house in Chicago that in 1889 sent out 130,000,000 pages of temperance literature; employs 146 men and women, mostly women; pays a dividend of seven per cent. on money invested; is the proprietor of its own presses and of its machinery, including an electrotyping department. It publishes the *Union Signal*, organ of the World's and National W. C. T. U., with a weekly circulation of 85,000 copies; also four other papers for the young people, children, and Germans; and has connected with it a large job office for general printing. The directors of this great establishment are all women, and the editors women. No one can hold stock except a white ribbon woman that is a member of the W.C.T.U. This enterprise constantly enlarges because it has a sure foundation in the ten thousand local unions of the W. C. T. U.

The National W. C. T. U. has also founded a woman's temperance hospital in Chicago, conducted throughout by women, its object being to prove experimentally that alcoholics have no necessary place in medicine.

A woman's temperance temple, to cost over a million of dollars, was projected by Mrs. Matilda B. Carse, president of the W. C. T. U., of Chicago, and is now in course of erection. While the national society is in no wise responsible for this movement, it has done much to help it forward, and hopes in the course of time to have headquarters here for its publishing department, etc., a large hall for public meetings, a kindergarten, restaurant, and all the paraphernalia of a great temperance headquarters. Besides this it expects to realize from the rentals, as the building is located in the heart of the city, a large annual endowment for its various lines of work.

A Woman's Lecture Bureau has been established in Chicago, which is constantly sending out speakers to all parts of the United States and Canada. These speakers may be men or women, but the management is in the hands of white ribboners.

Some local unions do as much work as a whole State society: for instance, the Chicago Union, which last year sheltered 60,000 friendless men in its great lodging house; which maintains a temperance restaurant, an anchorage for degraded men and women, where 5,000 were cared for last year, a kindergarten, daily gospel meetings, and many other forms of Christian philanthropy.

In 1883, on the suggestion of the National President of the W. C. T. U., a World's Union was projected, and Mrs. Mary Clement Leavitt, of Boston, started out to organize all civilized countries. She has now (1890) been seven years absent, and is reaching a greater variety of nationalities than any woman who ever lived. She has thus far traveled over fifty thousand miles; held over a thousand meetings; more than eleven thousand pages have been written; she has spoken, through interpreters, to people in twenty-three languages. Other missionaries are constantly being sent to follow Mrs. Leavitt, and the white ribbon is acclimated in every country in the world. Its methods are the universal circulation of a pledge against the legalizing of the sale of brain poisons, including of course, and chiefly, alcoholics and opium. This is to be presented to all governments by a deputation of women to which the petition will be entrusted when the number of signatures reaches two millions, and they will carry it round the world. The methods of the National W. C. T. U. have been universally adopted, of which the principal ones are total abstinence for the individual, and the effort to secure total prohibition for the State. The noon hour of prayer is everywhere observed, asking God's blessing on the work and workers. The white ribbon—emblem of purity, prohibition, patriotism, and philanthropy—is the badge worn, and the motto, "For God and Home and Every Land."

The first president of the World's W. C. T. U. was Mrs. Margaret Bright Lucas, sister of John Bright, and president of the Woman's Temperance Association of Great Britain. The second and present president is Frances E. Willard.

Australia is organized, also Japan, China, Ceylon, Madagascar, the civilized portions of Africa, Scandinavia, Great Britain, Canada, and the United States. In continental Europe the progress is slow, as drinking habits are well nigh universal; but much progress has been made in Switzerland, also in Berlin. In the former country through the efforts of Miss Charlotte Gray, in the latter city through Mrs. Mary Bannister Willard, of the Home School for Girls.

A World's W. C. T. U. convention is to be held in connection with the World's Fair in Chicago, in 1893.

Wherever white ribboners are found, will be found friends of woman's complete enfranchisement and admission to all professions and trades, on the ground that no artificial barrier should be thrown in her way, but that she should be freely permitted and welcomed to enter every place where she has capacity to succeed. Perhaps no motto of the W. C. T. U. is more frequently quoted than the following: "Woman will bless and brighten every place she enters, and she will enter every place."

XVIII.

THE ORIGIN AND APPLICATION OF THE RED CROSS.

BY

CLARA BARTON.

In no way, perhaps, is more clearly proven the just necessity for some explanation concerning the subject of the Red Cross than by the fact that I am asked to make these explanations as a contribution to woman's work, when, in fact, every original idea of the humanities sought to be organized, and the methods of relief ordained, were, like the terrible and needless cruelties which led to them, the work of men, and have largely continued to be such.*

It would scarcely be conceded that, because many women have found a place to work, and work well, in the United States Treasury, Patent, and Pension Bureaus, that these de-

---

* I have steadily refrained from adding biographical notes on the authors of the chapters of this book, notwithstanding the fact that they themselves, in having accomplished so very much on the very lines of progress which they have set about to describe, have deprived us of much that could have been gracefully added, had they been less fully identified with their subjects. Between the lines, however, much may be gleaned; and to relate the lives of such women is to presume ignorance on the part of the reader; a presumption of which a discreet editor would never be guilty.

But when, through excess of modesty, the ignorance of the editor of this book is delicately held up as a proof of the lamentably universal ignorance on the subject of the Red Cross, the awful dignity of the editor is aroused! Without the following explanation or extenuation, moreover, I do not see how the chapter in question could have any place in the book. "Woman's Work in America" can hardly be made up of histories of work which is emphasized as "*the work of men*," no matter how gracefully apologized for. Therefore the following little sketch of a *woman's* work in the direction of originating and applying the methods of the Red Cross in this country, written by one connected officially with the society is presented, with the editor's apologies to the modesty of the President of the Red Cross: "It is with great pleasure I am permitted to add a few words of explanation to Miss Barton's story of the Red Cross, and in as brief a space as possible

partments themselves should be exclusively classed as woman's work.

If, in our rapid march of progress over newly acquired territory, we should be found appropriating to ourselves some of the old landmarks and strongholds, a philosophical solution may perhaps be found in the familiar principles of the angles of incidence and reflection. It might be added that, presumably, the circumstance of the leadership (if so presumptuous a term may be allowed) of the Red Cross in this country having incidentally fallen to a woman's hands has had a tendency to mislead in this direction.

Considering how very little has yet been definitely comprehended of the characteristics of this young child of their adoption, the tones of parental kindness and good feeling in which it is spoken by the people of the entire country, is touching to us who watch its course and destiny. Their very natural endeavors to square its habits and methods by those of ordinary charitable organizations, are not unfrequently perplexing to them and embarrassing to us; and their consternation at times, when this strange duckling suddenly takes to the water, is suggestive of other scenes.

The mass of correspondence constantly pouring in, asking how one shall become a member of the "order," or proposing to organize a "chapter," or a "branch," or "corps," or "sec-

---

present the colossal magnitude of this remarkable woman's work on Battlefield, in Hospital, amid Cyclone, Fire, and Flood; Standing '*alone*' among women even as a Napoleon or a Lincoln does among men.

"Endowed by nature with a dual being, as it were; possessing the strong, reasoning, powerful brain of a leader and the gentle, tender, loving heart of the most delicate of women, Clara Barton stands before us a symbol of what woman might be when she bursts the bonds that dictate to her 'woman's work.'

"Confined in this note to the relation of Miss Barton with the 'Red Cross work,' I still consider it fitting to suggest that the services rendered by her in the war for the Union, in organizing, conducting, and leading the service of field nurses upon actual battle-fields, in directing hospital organization, in managing other details of field relief, and, more than all, in conceiving and carrying out the great work of tracing and recording the fate of many thousands of missing soldiers, were naturally and necessarily a proper prelude to the great service she has since rendered in European combat, in presenting the Geneva Treaty to her own government, and in so broadening its field of service as to include that of help in great natural and national calamities.

"Miss Barton has herself explained the object of the Geneva International Committee; and has given an account of the long-delayed acceptance of the Treaty by the United States.

"In 1870 Miss Barton joined the Red Cross workers in the Franco-Prus-

tion," independent, for special use, calling for copies of the constitution and by-laws of the national to aid in forming their own, so they can go on by *themselves*, reveals a vagueness of ideas concerning the subject which a few words might serve to render more clear and definite. First, the Red Cross is not an "order," and has no tendency in that direction any more than the medical department of an army, which it was instituted to assist, is an "order"; or the great movement toward the general peace of mankind through arbitration and kindly fellowship, to which it is both an advance guard and a stepping-stone, is an "order." It is not a "secret society" any more than is the Association of Charities and Correction, Adams Express, the Western Union Telegraph, a railroad corporation or a fire company, all of which the nature of its work at times assimilates. While societies, as usually existing, seek the advancement of ideas and the general progress of the world intellectually, morally, or religiously, mainly by expression of thought and opinions analogous to their subject, the Red Cross, by its relation, must deal in *active* ways, mentally and physically, with people direct, and become responsible for their welfare as for funds and material for their use; and while it may properly have been designated as the culmination of the best humanities of the warring agencies of the past, finding possible expression in the latter half of the nineteenth century, it still needs to be explained that this medium of expression was the Treaty of Geneva of 1864 for the relief of the wounded

---

sian War. We see her leading in beneficence in Strassburg; working day and night organizing the frightened and bewildered women and children; not doling out charities, but vitalizing and making them self-reliant by work; presenting the truest of all ways of helping themselves by helping others. In sober words, Miss Barton's work in Strassburg was the founding of workshops and the employment of women and others to labor therein. So successful was she that when Metz passed into German hands, with loaded cars, bearing clothes and food, she entered that city again to help the stricken inhabitants; afterward in Paris, at that awful hour when the 'Commune fell,' and the streets were black with fire and red with blood, we see this American woman reaching the stricken city with her train of garments, ready for the naked; hope and comfort following in her path; healing and binding wounded bodies and minds. She was called on by Monsieur Thiers himself, and honored as few men are. The cross of the Legion of Honor should be among her rewards, but the law governing its bestowal is that it be formally solicited by the one by whom it might be received.

"Clara Barton has never sought it. In 1873, invalided and entirely prostrated, Miss Barton returned to America, promising to use her influence with the government to open the Red Cross treaty. Her health entirely failing her, it was 1877 when she was able to call for the documents lying unused in

and sick of armies. The Red Cross *means*, then, the people's help for suffering through military necessities (a help hitherto mainly ignored), and it *is* the result and the direct outgrowth of an international treaty, entered into by the civilized nations of the world for the mitigation of the sufferings from war, by first eliminating from its code all needless cruelties and old-time barbarities ; and, secondly, by rendering neutral and exempt from capture all disabled soldiers requiring aid, all appliances, all material, and all personnel designed for them.

It is to be borne in mind, and not for an instant lost sight of, that while other methods leading up to these points have been always the outgrowth of the grandest human sentiments of mankind, they still remained *sentiments*, usually individual, and, beyond this, binding on no one ; or, if organized for the moment, were lost as soon ; while the Red Cross, embodying all these humanities, organizes and pledges the entire world, through its governments, to the one purpose and effort, and binds the whole by the stern sacredness of an international treaty, which no government will ever be found reckless and indecent enough to violate. The non-fellowship of the world would follow such an act. Indeed, no nation has a treaty it would hold so sacred in time of need.

Following a preliminary conference of 1863, a convention, composed of delegates appointed by and representing the heads of all the governments of the world, was held at Geneva, Switzerland, for the purpose of considering some method for mitigating the horrors of war, if wars must be.

---

our State Department ; the communications were all in foreign languages, and they seemed almost incomprehensible to the American mind.

"From the year 1877 to 1881, we see Miss Barton in a new rôle. She translated, wrote, published, and lectured, all at her own expense, trying to educate some minds into the work of the Red Cross. In constant communication with the heads of foreign governments, with the eyes of all of them watching and waiting for the success of this patient, earnest, pleading woman with her stubborn nation, ready to publish the least progress in her task, it was not until 1881, at the commencement of President Garfield's administration, that her labors had any success. President Garfield and his Cabinet listened, comprehended, and approved.

"President Arthur faithfully carried out his noble predecessor's idea. After one year's consideration, during which Miss Barton personally explained, before the Senate and House Committees on Foreign Affairs and Relations, the work of the Red Cross, the United States unanimously acceded to the Treaty of Geneva.

"Since the adhesion of the United States to this treaty, there have been two International Conferences, to which Congress appointed Miss Barton as chief delegate to represent the United States. The conferences were com-

And however disdainfully we at the present moment may curl our lips over the uselessness of such a consideration in the light of better methods, however scorn every thought of any effort in behalf of the woes of those who consent to deluge the world in blood, it is to be remembered that we ourselves at *that* moment were not altogether exempt from the perplexing problem of war, and did not, as now, present to the world the grand and beautiful "Christian example" of arbitration and peace, of which we are at present the most advisory and conspicuous of advocates. Indeed, whoever will take down from the shelves one of the volumes of decisions of our then Minister of State, Mr. Seward, will find there recorded that the reason given for the United States having declined official representation in the Convention of Geneva was *not* on the ground of high moral elevation, advanced views and consequent disapproval, but rather in this wise, that we were *ourselves* in the midst of a cruel and relentless war, which did not admit of time for considerations of that kind. This decision was the first block over which a woman ungracefully stumbled, when, thirteen years later, an attempt was made to officially call the attention of our government to the knowledge even of the existence of such a treaty among other nations.

This convention, which occupied several days, discussed as never before the great question of an international agreement for the neutralizing of certain departments of all fields of bat-

---

posed of delegates sent by the heads of the nations adhering to the treaty. The first conference met in Paris, the second in Berlin, the third in Geneva, the fourth in Carlsruhe. Miss Barton was present at the two latter.

"The legal application of the Red Cross to great national calamities, already referred to as the American Amendment to the Red Cross, is the work of Clara Barton.

"The practical demonstrations of the administrations of the American Amendment, which Miss Barton has had to lead in and carry on, are: First, in the relief work of the Michigan forest fires; second, in the overflow of the Mississippi River in 1882; third, in the cyclone of Lousiana in 1883, and the floods of the Ohio River in the same year; fifth, in the overflow of the Ohio and Mississippi Rivers in 1884. In the drought of Texas in 1886. In the Mount Vernon cyclone, Ill., in 1887. In the yellow fever pestilence of Florida. And in 1889, when the world received the shock of the Johnstown horror, we see this wonderful being, like some subtle, silent, force, appearing noiselessly on a scene of such horrors as a Dante never conceived, and by the power of her will and a remarkable endurance, as if by the hand of an enchantress, work order out of horror and chaos, restoring life and comfort where all was before desolation and death!

"These feeble words are all I can now say in this brief way of the work of Clara Barton—*The Woman* in the Red Cross!"

tle, and the protection of all the personnel and material designed for them.

The establishment, as it were, of a goal in the midst of the most relentless field of animosity and strife, where those who could no longer run could touch and be safe ; as if, in the midst of the wildest storm at sea, a haven could be established in mid-ocean where the disabled ships might find a harbor and rest.

The councils of this convention resulted in the formulation of a code of ten articles, which, upon solemn acceptance by the heads of each government, became the treaty of Geneva. These articles were as follows :

ARTICLE 1. Ambulances (field hospitals) and military hospitals shall be acknowledged to be neutral, and as such shall be protected and respected by belligerents so long as any sick or wounded may be therein. Such neutrality shall cease if the ambulances or hospitals should be held by a military force.

ARTICLE 2. Persons employed in hospitals and ambulances, comprising the staff for superintendence, medical service, administration, transport of wounded, as well as chaplains, shall participate in the benefit of neutrality while so employed, and so long as there remain any to bring in or to succor.

ARTICLE 3. The persons designated in the preceding article may, even after occupation by the enemy, continue to fulfill their duties in the hospital or ambulance which they may have, or may withdraw in order to regain the corps to which they belong. Under such circumstances, when the persons shall cease from their functions, they shall be delivered by the occupying army to the outposts of the enemy. They shall have specially the right of sending a representative to the headquarters of their respective armies.

ARTICLE 4. As the equipment of military hospitals remains subject to the laws of war, persons attached to such hospitals cannot, on withdrawing, carry away any articles but such as are their private property. Under the same circumstances an ambulance shall, on the contrary, retain its equipment.

ARTICLE 5. Inhabitants of the country who may bring help to the wounded shall be respected and shall remain free. The generals of the belligerent powers shall make it their care to inform the inhabitants of the appeal addressed to their humanity, and of the neutrality which will be the consequence of it. Any wounded man, entertained and taken care of in a house, shall be considered as a protection thereto. Any inhabitant, who shall have entertained wounded men in his house, shall be exempted from the quartering of troops as well as from a part of the contributions of war which may be imposed.

ARTICLE 6. Wounded or sick soldiers shall be entertained and taken care of to whatever nation they may belong. Commanders-in-chief shall have the power to deliver immediately to the outposts of the enemy soldiers who have been wounded in an engagement, when circumstances permit this to be done, and with the consent of both parties. Those who are recognized, after they are healed, as incapable of serving, shall be sent back to their country. The others may also be sent back on condition of not again bearing arms during the continuance of the war. Evacuations, together with the persons under whose directions they take place, shall be protected by an absolute neutrality.

ARTICLE 7. A distinctive and uniform flag shall be adopted for hospitals, ambulances, and evacuations. It must on every occasion be accompanied by the national flag. An arm badge [*brassard*] shall also be allowed for individuals neutralized, but the delivery thereof shall be left to military authority. The flag and arm badge shall bear a red cross on a white ground.

ARTICLE 8. The details of execution of the present convention shall be regulated by the commanders-in-chief of belligerent armies, according to the instructions of their respective government and in conformity with the general principles laid down in this convention.

ARTICLE 9. The high contracting powers have agreed to communicate the present convention to those governments which have not found it convenient to send plenipotentiaries to the international convention at Geneva, with an invitation to accede thereto ; the protocol is, for that purpose, left open.

ARTICLE 10. The present convention shall be ratified, and the ratification shall be exchanged at Berne, in four months, or sooner if possible.

The nations adopting the Treaty are:

France, September 22, 1864.
Belgium, October 14, 1864.
Italy, December 4, 1864.
Sweden and Norway, Dec. 13, 1864.
Baden, December 16, 1864.
Great Britain, February 18, 1865.
Prussia, June 22, 1865.
Wurtemberg, June 2, 1866.
Bavaria, June 30, 1866.
Portugal, August 9, 1866.
Russia, May 22, 1867.
Roumania, November 30, 1874.
San Salvador, December 30, 1874.
Servia, March 24, 1876.
Chili, November 15, 1879.
Peru, April 22, 1880.
Bulgaria, March 1, 1884.
Luxembourg, October 5, 1888.
Switzerland, October 1, 1864.
Netherlands, November 29, 1864.
Spain, December 5, 1864.
Denmark, December 15, 1864.
Greece, January 17, 1865.
Mecklenburg-Schwerin, Mar. 9, 1865.
Turkey, July 5, 1865.
Hesse Darmstadt, June 22, 1866.
Austria, July 21, 1866.
Saxony, October 25, 1866.
Pontifical States, May 9, 1868.
Persia, December 5, 1874.
Montenegro, November 29, 1875.
Bolivia, October 16, 1879.
Argentine Republic, Nov. 25, 1879.
United States, March 1, 1882.
Japan, June 5, 1886.

The United States of America was the thirty-second in order. This treaty has changed not only the methods of procedure of the medical and hospital departments of all armies, but their insignia, flags, etc. There is but one military hospital flag in the world to-day. The commander who knows his own, knows that of the enemy, and he breaks an international treaty if he knowingly turns even a gun or a stray shot upon it. The convoy of prisoners under escort bearing that sign is safe ; no officer can fire upon that unarmed and defenseless body of men by "mistake" ; no "mistake" can be made nor pretend to be made. No captured men can longer suffer for lack of food ; the *world* is pledged to supply this want, and the way is opened to do it. No fields nor hospitals can lack attendance, nursing, nor the necessaries of life ; to this relief the way is opened. No wounded men can lie unattended upon a field, and no attendant upon them can be captured. No distinction can be made in the care of the sick and wounded. By the articles of the treaty, all are non-combatants, all neutrals, and hence one common relation for all.

At the conclusion of the convention, the body of gentlemen of Switzerland who had convened it were designated by choice of the governments as the international head by whom all general intercourse between nations upon the subject of war-relief should be directed, and through whom all communications should be made. This is the "International Committee of Geneva."

The first action of a country after the adoption of the treaty, is to form a National Society, or committee, through which the International Committee may communicate with the government of that country. To this National Society is committed the care of all communications from the International Committee to the government of a country, whether relating to the work of war relief in other nations, or to their methods of advancement, *e.g.* to observe if the provisions of the treaty are duly regarded by its military departments; if the suitable orders are given for the spread of such knowledge among the troops at the field; if the appropriate insignia is worn by them; the arrangement for attendance upon international conferences in which the government is represented, and reports to foreign powers on such occasions. Naturally, but one National Society or body of administration in a country is, or can be, recognized, either by the government at home, or the international authorities abroad, on the same principle that but one Department of War, or State, could be recognized. To this body is submitted the direction of such aid as shall be rendered by its country for the relief of suffering from the calamities of war in other countries, such aid always passing through the neutral hands of the "International Committee" for application; thus wisely avoiding national jealousies. The best inventions and most improved machinery and methods for the convenient handling, nursing, and treatment of disabled persons from whatever cause, in either military or civil life, for the last twenty-five years, are directly traceable to the thought and endeavors of the Red Cross, through its wise encouragement thereof, and the necessities revealed upon the fields of war which it sought to relieve.

To turn now to the little part taken by our government and people in this world-wide humanity, we shall find ourselves subjects for the adage of the "short horse soon curried." As previously remarked, it was thirteen years, namely, from 1863 to 1877, before the attention of our government was awakened to the existence of such a treaty among nations, and its adhesion seriously recommended. Our great commissions, sanitary and Christian, had died and passed into history, and it was not realized that their embalmed memory would not be sufficient for all future exigencies,—old Egypt, relying upon its catacombs, great, but silent and past! It required five other years, namely, from 1877 to 1882, to bring the government to a clear comprehension of the subject, when, by a unanimous vote of both Houses of Congress, the Treaty of Geneva of 1864 was adopted and became a law, immediately receiving the signature of President Arthur, fully carrying out the decision of his lamented predecessor, Garfield, who had recommended it in his first message to Congress. The treaty was next sent to the Congress of Berne, Switzerland, which, by consent of all governments, is made the ratifying power for the treaties of the nations as they adhere. When ratified, it was proclaimed by the President of the United States, and directions duly given to the departments of the government to take the necessary steps for conforming to its provisions.

It is this which has changed all military hospital flags in our country to a red cross on a white ground; the same for ambulances, supplies, and attendants, and has instituted this insignia throughout the medical departments of the regular army, and gives the present impetus to the movement of the National Guard in that direction as well. Previous to the actual adoption of the treaty by the United States, but in view of it, our National Society had been founded at the instance of President Garfield, and the honor of its presidency unanimously tendered to him. This courtesy was declined by him in favor of its present president, who, without change of original officers, and with their concurrence, has conducted the affairs of the society from that time, July, 1881. In forming the constitution of the National Society of the United States, it was decided by the framers, in view of our liability to great national calamities, and non-liability to the exigencies of war, to ask of the ratifying powers of the treaty to accept the National Society of America, with power to extend its scope to the relief of great national calamities other than war. This was granted, constituting the only national society under the treaty having such privilege, and known among other nations as the "American Amendment to the Red Cross." It is under this provision, or grant, alone, that the work of the Red Cross in national calamities in this country during the last nine years has been done. Within that time it has afforded relief at twelve fields of national distress. And while these scenes of active labor constitute mainly all that appears to the public eye as the work of the society, they are in reality the smaller and by far the less difficult and painstaking. The over-laden desks, translations from all languages, international correspondence, advices sought, and decisions to be wisely and delicately rendered, tell a different tale to the thought-burdened, weary officers at Red Cross headquarters.

In the early days, a few societies were allowed (but never invited) to form as auxiliaries, more for the purpose of familiarizing the people with the subject than for aid really expected; for after all, it is the entire people whom the Red Cross is designed to serve; they have direct and individual access to it; it is their servant at the moment of woe, which falls on all alike. With a National Red Cross on a field, the way is open to all; no special avenues are needed; and the capable personages as individual aids the country over, which it is constantly gathering to itself, ready for instant response to any call, leave no lack of help even for a day. However well auxiliary societies might do, and some have done grandly, it was the people at large, over the entire country, who solicited the Red Cross to become the almoner of their bounties in Johnstown. The great manufacturing companies which asked of it to put their tens of thousands of dollars worth of new furniture into the homes which had not one article left, were not Red Cross societies. The great lumber companies, shipping the material thousands of miles to construct new homes almost before the old ones had reached the bottom of the stream which bore them away, were not Red Cross societies nor ever sought to be. They wished to serve humanity, wanted their gifts to reach the needy in some direct and practical way, and chose their avenue. In this same spirit of self-forgetfulness, the Red Cross accepted and applied, faithfully we know, and acceptably we hope, with the only desire, under heaven, of safely and wisely transmitting those substantial tokens of sympathy and love from a pitying world to a homeless, bereaved, and terror-stricken people as a present help in time of trouble. It went to them in the same spirit, with the same regulations, and under the same discipline as if those thousands had fallen in human rather than elemental conflict. It found the military at the field, and reported for duty the same as at a field of battle. The relations thus at once established were incalculable in their benefits. Every courtesy from headquarters was extended ; as by *right*, not favor ; all passes, countersigns, and facilities of movement of any kind were given without asking. The character of the work was from the first understood to be in accord with the government and discipline of the field, and not a separate dynasty set up in its individual or ambitious and unskilled effort, to be guarded against, lest it commit some egotistical indiscretion which could not be tolerated. The same advantages over unrecognized aid were realized here as are enjoyed by the Red Cross on a field of battle. The work of the Red Cross in this country has thus far been rather a test than otherwise of its efficiency, usefulness, and possibilities ; and so fully has it met, and even surpassed, all early expectations, that any limited description like the present seems rather an annoyance, leaving the subject where its best interests should commence ; and although in our land we may never have need of its protecting arm on the fields of human warfare, it is enough for us to know that we *have* needed it as no words can tell. Only the low lonely graves, the desolate homes speak more eloquently than words.

APPENDICES.

APPENDIX A.

Historical Memoranda for Reference to Article II., on Education in the Eastern States.

CO-EDUCATIONAL COLLEGES.

State.	Name.	Locality.	Denomination.	Admitted Women.	No. of Students, Regular Collegiate.	No. of Students, Total.
Maine	Bates College	Lewiston	Baptist	(When opened), 1863	33	33
	Colby University	Waterville	Baptist	1871	18	18
Vermont	University of Vermont	Burlington	Non-sectarian	1871	20	20
	Middlebury College	Middlebury	Non-sectarian	....	8	8
Massachusetts	Boston University	Boston	Methodist	(When opened), 1869	163	207
	Mass. Inst. Technology	Boston	Non-sectarian	1883	33	33
Connecticut	Wesleyan College	Middletown	Meth. Epis	1872	15	16
New York	Cornell University	Ithaca	Non-sectarian	(When opened), 1862	109	139
	Syracuse University	Syracuse	Meth. Epis	(When opened), 1870	63	244
Pennsylvania	Swarthmore	Swarthmore	Society Friends	(When opened), 1869	55	79

COLLEGES FOR WOMEN.

State.	Name.	Locality.	Denomination.	Admitted Women.	No. of Students, Regular Collegiate.	No. of Students, Total.
Massachusetts	Mount Holyoke	So. Hadley	Non-sectarian	Founded 1836	85	188
	Smith College	Northampt'n	Non-sectarian	Founded 1871	448	551
	Wellesley	Wellesley	Non-sectarian	Founded 1875	595	694
New York	Vassar College	Po'keepsie	Baptist	Founded 1865	227	326
Pennsylvania	Bryn Mawr	Bryn Mawr	Society Friends	Founded 1880	142	169

AFFILIATED COLLEGES.

State.	Name.	Locality.	Denomination.	Admitted Women.	No. of Students, Regular Collegiate.	No. of Students, Total.
Massachusetts	Harvard Annex	Cambridge	Non-sectarian	Founded 1879	71	168
New Jersey	Evelyn College	Princeton	Presbyterian	Founded 1888	7	25
New York	Barnard College	New York	Non-sectarian	Founded 1889	24	45

APPENDIX B.—TABLE I.

Historical Memoranda for Reference to Article III., on Education in West.

OHIO.—Incorporated in the Northwest Territory in 1787. Admitted as the State of Ohio in 1802.

INDIANA.—Incorporated in the Northwest Territory in 1787. Territory of Indiana in 1800. State of Indiana in 1816.

ILLINOIS.—Incorporated in Northwest Territory in 1787. Territory of Indiana in 1800. Territory of Illinois in 1809. State of Illinois in 1818.

MISSOURI.—Territory of Missouri 1812. Admitted as a State in 1821. (French Cession.)

MICHIGAN.—Incorporated in Northwest Territory in 1787. Territory of Indiana in 1800. Territory of Michigan in 1805. State of Michigan 1837.

IOWA.—Territory of Michigan 1834. Territory of Wisconsin 1836. Territory of Iowa 1838. State of Iowa 1846. (French Cession.)

WISCONSIN.—Incorporated in the Northwest Territory 1787. Territory of Indiana 1800. Territory of Illinois 1809. Territory of Michigan 1818. Territory of Wisconsin 1836. State of Wisconsin 1848.

CALIFORNIA.—Ceded by Mexico 1848. Admitted as State 1850.

MINNESOTA.—Territory of Michigan 1834. Territory of Wisconsin 1836. Territory of Iowa 1838. Territory of Minnesota 1849. State of Minnesota 1858. (French Cession.)

OREGON.—Territory of Oregon 1848. State of Oregon 1859.

KANSAS.—Territory of Kansas 1854. State of Kansas 1861. (French Cession.)

NEVADA.—Ceded by Mexico 1848. Territory of Utah 1850. Territory of Nevada 1861. State of Nevada 1864.

NEBRASKA.—Territory of Nebraska 1854. State of Nebraska 1867. (French Cession.)

COLORADO.—Territory of Colorado 1861. State of Colorado 1876. (French and Mexican Cessions.)

NORTH DAKOTA.—Territory of Michigan 1834. Territory of Wisconsin 1836. Territory of Iowa 1838. Territory of Minnesota 1849. Territory of Dakota 1861. State of North Dakota 1889. (French Cession.)

SOUTH DAKOTA.—Same as North Dakota.

MONTANA.—Territory of Nebraska 1854. Territory of Dakota 1861. Territory of Idaho 1863. Territory of Montana 1864. State of Montana 1889. (French Cession.)

WASHINGTON.—Territory of Oregon 1848. Territory of Washington 1853. State of Washington 1889.

IDAHO.—Territory of Oregon 1848. Territory of Washington 1853. Territory of Idaho 1863. State of Idaho 1890.

WYOMING.—After several transfers Territory of Wyoming 1868. State of Wyoming 1890. (French Cession mainly.)

UTAH.—Ceded by Mexico 1848. Territory of Utah 1850.

APPENDIX B.—TABLE II.

Location.	Name.	Denomination.	Number of Female Students.		Opened.	Opened to Women.
			Collegiate.	Total.		
Ohio—						
Akron	Buchtel College	Universalist	44	112	1872	....
Alliance	Mount Union College	M. E.	21	205	1858	1858
Ashland	Ashland College *	Brethren	..	13	1879	....
Athens	Ohio University	Non-sectarian	20	50	1809	1871
Berea	Baldwin University *	M. E.	28	73	1846	1846
Berea	German Wallace College	M. E.	2	16	1864	1864
Cincinnati	University of Cincinnati	Non-sectarian	35	36	1874	1874
Cleveland	Adelbert College of Western Reserve University	Non-sectarian	6	59	1888	1888
Cleveland	Calvin College	Reformed	8	37	1883	1883
College Hill	Belmont College *	Non-sectarian	6	41	1846	....
Columbus	Ohio State University	Non-sectarian	29	47	1873	1873
Delaware	Ohio Wesleyan University	M. E.	176	372	1844	1876
Findlay	Findlay College	Church of God	8	159	1886	....
Germantown	Twin Valley College	Non-sectarian	..	18	1886	1886
Granville	Denison University	Baptist	..	44	1831	. ..
Hiram	Hiram College	Christian	15	97	1850	1850
New Athens	Franklin College	Non-sectarian	..	40	1825	1856
New Concord	Muskingum College	Un. Presb.	12	29	1837	1854
Oberlin	Oberlin College	Non-sectarian	353	821	1833	1833
Oxford	Miami University	Non-sectarian	2	2	1816	....
Richmond	Richmond College	Non-sectarian	1	42	1843	1843

Rio Grande	Rio Grande College	Baptist	5	38	1876	1876
Scio	Scio College	M. E.	108	144	1866	1866
Springfield	Wittenberg College	Lutheran	..	..	1845	....
Tiffin	Heidelberg College*	Reformed	19	96	1850	1850
Urbana	Urbana University	New Church	1	15	1851	1851
Westerville	Otterbein University	U. B.	16	122	1847	1847
Wilberforce	Wilberforce University	....	..	..	1856	1856
Wilmington	Wilmington College*	Friends	15	15	1871	1871
Wooster	University of Wooster	Presbyterian	42	201	1870	1870
Yellow Springs	Antioch College	Non-sectarian	15	106	1852	1852
Indiana—						
Bloomington	Indiana University	Non-sectarian	82	131	1824	1867
Franklin	Franklin College	Baptist	40	113	1837	1866
Greencastle	De Pauw University	M. E.	..	..	1837	1867
Hanover	Hanover College	Presbyterian	25	39	1828	1880
Hartsville	Hartsville College	U. B.	12	34	1849	1849
Irvington	Butler University	Christian	20	49	1855	1855
Merom	Union Christian College*	Christian	..	46	1859	1859
La Fayette	Purdue University	Non-sectarian	58	114	1874	1874
Moore's Hill	Moore's Hill College	M. E.	12	55	1854	1854
Richmond	Earlham College	Friends	66	114	1859	1859
Ridgeville	Ridgeville College	Baptist	1	39	1867	1867
Illinois—						
Abingdon	Hedding College	M. E.	10	50	1855	1855
Bloomington	Illinois Wesleyan University	M. E.	37	225	1853	1870
Carlinville	Blackburn University	....	..	..	....	....
Carthage	Carthage College	Lutheran	10	39	1869	....
Champaign	University of Illinois	Non-sectarian	57	72	1868	1871
Eureka	Eureka College	Christian	25	86	1849	1849

* Statistics of 1887–88.

APPENDIX B.—TABLE II.—(*Continued.*)

LOCATION.	NAME.	DENOMINATION.	NUMBER OF FEMALE STUDENTS.		OPENED.	OPENED TO WOMEN.
			Collegiate.	Total.		
Illinois (continued)—						
Evanston	North-Western University	M. E.	119	340	1855	1869
Ewing	Ewing College	Baptist	11	34	1867	1867
Galena	German-English College	M. E.	7	30	1868	1868
Galesburgh	Knox College *	Non-sectarian	55	123	1841	1872
Galesburgh	Lombard University	Universalist	24	55	1852	....
Lake Forest	Lake Forest University	Presbyterian	..	90	1876	1876
Lebanon	McKendree College	M. E.	9	31	1828	1869
Lincoln	Lincoln University	Cumb. Presb	15	74	1866	1866
Monmouth	Monmouth College	Un. Presb	61	187	1856	1856
Naperville	North-Western College	Ev. Association	19	62	1861	1861
Quincy	Chaddock College	M. E.	10	74	1876	1876
Rock Island	Augustana College	Lutheran	1	32	1860	1883
Upper Alton	Shurtleff College	Baptist	15	72	1827	1867
Westfield	Westfield College	U. B.	21	76	1865	....
Wheaton	Wheaton College	Congregational	..	..	1860	1860
Michigan—						
Adrian	Adrian College	Meth. Prot.	11	77	1859	1859
Albion	Albion College	M. E.	39	229	1861	1861
Ann Arbor	University of Michigan	Non-sectarian	194	207	1841	1870
Agricultural College	Michigan Agricultural College	Non-sectarian	16	16	1857	1870
Battle Creek	Battle Creek College *	7th Day Adven.	..	165	1874	1874

Benzonia	Grand Traverse College *	Congregational	..	24	1863	....
Hillsdale	Hillsdale College	Baptist	37	139	1855	1855
Holland	Hope College	Reformed	2	103	1865	1878
Kalamazoo	Kalamazoo College *	Baptist	18	55	1833	....
Olivet	Olivet College *	Cong. and Presb.	42	117	1859	1859
Wisconsin—						
Appleton	Lawrence University	M. E.	24	94	1849	....
Galesville	Galesville University *	Presbyterian	1	21	1859	1859
Madison	University of Wisconsin	Non-sectarian	139	140	1850	1871
Milton	Milton College	Baptist	33	110	1867	1867
Ripon	Ripon College	Congregational	16	129	1863	1863
Minnesota—						
Hamline	Hamline University *	M. E.	26	126	1854	1854
Macalester	Macalester College *	Presbyterian	0	3	1884	....
Minneapolis	University of Minnesota	Non-sectarian	67	155	1868	1868
Northfield	Carleton College	Congregational	32	178	1867	1867
Northfield	St. Olaf College	Lutheran	0	23	1875	1875
Iowa—						
Ames	Iowa State Agricultural College	Non-sectarian	83	83	1869	1869
Cedar Rapids	Coe College	Presbyterian	8	48	1881	1881
College Springs	Amity College	Non-sectarian	17	139	1871	1871
Davenport	Griswold College	Prot. Epis	0	98	1859	....
Des Moines	Drake University *	Christian	26	186	1882	1882
Des Moines	Des Moines College	Baptist	6	28	1865	1865
Fairfield	Parsons College	Presbyterian	40	80	1875	1875
Fayette	Upper Iowa University	M. E.	24	164	1857	1857
Grinnell	Iowa College	Congregational	130	..	1847	....
Hopkinton	Lenox College	Presbyterian	42	74	1859	1859

* Statistics of 1887–88.

APPENDIX B.—TABLE II.—(*Continued.*)

LOCATION.	NAME.	DENOMINATION.	NUMBER OF FEMALE STUDENTS.		OPENED.	OPENED TO WOMEN.
			Collegiate.	Total.		
Iowa (continued)—						
Indianola	Simpson College	M. E	29	169	1867	1867
Iowa City	State University of Iowa	Non-sectarian	87	87	1860	1860
Mt. Pleasant	German College	M. E.	2	52	1873	1873
Mt. Pleasant	Iowa Wesleyan University	M. E.	28	161	1855	1855
Mt. Vernon	Cornell College	M. E.	66	272	1857	1857
Oskaloosa	Oskaloosa College	Christian	27	78	1863	1863
Oskaloosa	Penn College	Friends	33	77	1872	1872
Pella	Central University of Iowa	Baptist	8	50	1854	1854
Tabor	Tabor College	Congregational	31	82	1866	1866
Toledo	Western College	U. B.	23	59	1856	1856
Dakota—						
Brookings	Dakota Agricultural College	Non-sectarian	..	..	1884	1884
East Pierre	Pierre University	Presbyterian	9	25	1883	1883
Fargo	Fargo College	Congregational	1	85	1887	1887
Grand Forks	University of North Dakota	Non-sectarian	7	83	1884	1884
Mitchell	Dakota University	M. E.	..	50	1885	1885
Rapid City	Dakota School of Mines	Non-sectarian	8	9	1887	1887
Vermillion	University of Dakota	Non-sectarian	14	201	1883	1883
Yankton	Yankton College	Non-sectarian	..	102	1882	1882

Nebraska—						
Bellevue	Bellevue College	Presbyterian	2	25	1883	1883
Central City	Nebraska Central College *	Non-sectarian	40	53	1885	....
Crete	Doane College	Congregational	13	97	1872	....
Lincoln	University of Nebraska	Non-sectarian	73	206	1871	1871
Neligh	Gates College	Congregational	3	54	1882	1882
Kansas—						
Atchison	Midland College	Lutheran	8	23	1887	1887
Baldwin	Baker University	M. E.	40	177	1858	1858
Emporia	College of Emporia	Presbyterian	7	59	1882	1882
Highland	Highland University *	Presbyterian	9	47	1867	1867
Holton	Campbell University	Non-sectarian	..	268	1882	1882
Lawrence	University of Kansas	Non-sectarian	35	168	1866	1866
Lecompton	Lane University	U. B.	12	..	1862	....
Lindsborg	Bethany College	Lutheran	2	76	1882	1882
Manhattan	Kansas State Agricultural College	Non-sectarian	176	177	1863	1863
Ottawa	Ottawa University	Baptist	15	140	1869	1869
Salina	Kansas Wesleyan University	M. E	2	65	1886	....
Sterling	Cooper Memorial College	Un. Presb.	..	59	1887	....
Topeka	Washburn College *	Congregational	12	103	1865	....
Wichita	Garfield University	Christian	17	356	1887	1887
Montana—						
Deer Lodge	College of Montana	Presbyterian	17	72	1883	1883
Colorado—						
Boulder	University of Colorado	Non-sectarian	13	49	1877	1877
Colorado Springs	Colorado College	Non-sectarian	20	20	1875	1875
Denver	University of Denver	M. E.	3	199	1880	1880
Fort Collins	State Agricultural College	Non-sectarian	29	41	1879	1879

* Statistics of 1887–88.

APPENDIX B.—TABLE II.—(*Concluded.*)

Location.	Name.	Denomination.	Number of Female Students.		Opened.	Opened to Women.
			Collegiate.	Total.		
Utah—						
Salt Lake City	University of Deseret	Non-sectarian	..	129	1850	1850
Nevada—						
Reno	State University of Nevada	Non-sectarian	18	77	1874	1874
Washington—						
Seattle	University of Washington	Non-sectarian	18	112	1862	....
Walla Walla	Whitman College	Congregational	62	110	1882	1882
Oregon—						
Corvallis	Oregon State Agricultural College	Non-sectarian	23	33	1888	1888
Eugene City	University of Oregon	Non-sectarian	62	62	1876	....
Forest Grove	Pacific University *	Congregational	5	41	1854	1854
McMinnville	McMinnville College	Baptist	2	42	1860	1860
Salem	Willamette University	M. E.	7	98	1844	1844
California—						
Berkeley	University of California	Non-sectarian	72	72	1869	1869
College City	Pierce Christian College *	Christian	22	44	1874	1874
Los Angeles	University of Southern California	M. E.	8	161	1880	....
Napa City	Napa College	M. E	1	87	1872	1872
Oakland	California College	Baptist	26	50	1887	1887

College Park	University of the Pacific	M. E.	47	226	1852	....
Santa Rosa	Pacific Methodist College	M. E., South	30	46	1861	1868
Woodbridge	San Joaquin Valley College	U. B.	11	41	1879	1879
Woodland	Hesperian College	Christian	25	120	1860	1860
Missouri—						
Avalon	Avalon College	United Brethren	11	70	1873	1873
Bolivar	Southwest Baptist College	Baptist	..	..	1879	1879
Canton	Christian University	Christian	36	39	1857	1867
Columbia	University of Missouri	Non-sectarian	..	125	1843	1870
Edinburg	Grand River College	Baptist	30	50	1850	1850
Glasgow	Lewis College (*b*)	M. E.	19	24	1867	....
Glasgow	Pritchett School Institute	Non-sectarian	26	26	1866	1866
La Grange	La Grange College	Baptist	..	51	1866	....
St. Louis	Washington University	Non-sectarian	9	9	1858	1870
Springfield	Drury College	Congregational	11	73	1873	1873
Tarkio	Tarkio College *	United Presb.	4	38	1884	1884
Warrenton	Central Wesleyan College	Ger. M. E.	4	47	1864	1864
Neosho	Scarritt Collegiate Institute	M. E., South	..	80	1878	1878

* Statistics of 1887–88. (*b*) Statistics of 1886–87.

APPENDIX C.—Table I.

To Article IV.—Education in the Southern States.

CO-EDUCATIONAL COLLEGES IN THE SOUTHERN STATES.

Location.	Name.	Denomination.	Number of Women Students.	
			Collegiate.	Total.
Alabama—				
Greensborough	Southern University	M. E., South	1	1
Selma	Selma University * (*a*)	Baptist	3	225
Arkansas—				
Batesville	Arkansas College	Presbyterian	..	25
Boonsborough	Cane Hill College	Presbyterian	3	63
Little Rock	Little Rock University (*a*)	Meth. Epis.	8	69
Little Rock	Philander Smith College (*a*)	Meth. Epis.	5	75
Fayetteville	Arkansas Industrial University	Non-sectarian	22	164
District of Columbia—				
Washington	National Deaf-Mute College	Non-sectarian	3	8
Washington	Howard University (*a*)	Non-sectarian	0	58
Washington	Columbian University	Baptist	25	25

Florida—				
De Land	John B. Stetson University	Baptist	1	62
Orange City	St. John's River Conference College	Meth. Epis.	0	45
Leesburg	Florida Conference College	M. E., South	20	49
Winter Park	Rollins College	Congregational	4	39
Georgia—				
Atlanta	Atlanta University (*a*).	Non-sectarian	1	252
Atlanta	Clark University (*a*)	Meth. Epis.	2	30
Bowdon	Bowdon College *	Non-sectarian	30	52
Macon	Mercer University	....	....	....
Kentucky—				
Berea	Berea College (*b*)	Non-sectarian	7	147
Eminence	Eminence College	Christian	56	71
Hopkinsville	South Kentucky College	Christian	52	60
Murray	Murray Male and Female Institute	Non-sectarian	....	81
New Liberty	Concord College	....	....	....
North Middletown	Kentucky Classical and Business College *	Christian	44	57
Lexington	Agricultural and Mechanical College of Kentucky	Non-sectarian	24	44
Louisiana—				
Keachie	Keachie College	Baptist	34	84
New Orleans	Leland University (*a*)	Baptist	....	....
New Orleans	New Orleans University (*a*)	Meth. Epis.	3	156
New Orleans	Southern University (*a*)	Non-sectarian	4	242
New Orleans	Straight University (*a*)	Non-sectarian	10	260
New Orleans	Tulane University	Non-sectarian	77	282

* Statistics of 1887–88. (*a*) Colored. (*b*) Majority of the pupils are colored.

APPENDIX C.—TABLE I.—(*Continued.*)

LOCATION.	NAME.	DENOMINATION.	NUMBER OF WOMEN STUDENTS.	
			Collegiate.	Total.
Maryland—				
New Windsor	New Windsor College*	Presbyterian	25	51
Westminster	Western Maryland College	Meth. Prot	52	71
Mississippi—				
Holly Springs	Rust University * (*a*)	Meth. Epis	....	182
Holmesville	Kavanaugh College	Non-sectarian	37	57
University	University of Mississippi	Non-sectarian	11	11
Rodney	Alcorn A. and M. College (*a*)	Non-sectarian	3	10
North Carolina—				
Raleigh	Shaw University * (*a*)	Baptist	7	146
Rutherford	Rutherford College	Non-sectarian	53	53
Salisbury	Livingstone College (*a*)	A. M. E. Zion	2	111
South Carolina—				
Clinton	Presbyterian College of South Carolina	Presbyterian	10	40
Columbia	Allen University (*a*)	Meth. Epis.	0	140
Orangeburg	Claflin University (*a*)	....	2	379

Tennessee—				
Athens, Chattanooga,	U. S. Grant University	Meth. Epis.	....	169
McKenzie	Bethel College	Cumb. Presb.	....	134
Maryville	Maryville College	Presbyterian	34	109
Milligan	Milligan College	Christian	16	41
Mossy Creek	Carson and Newman College	Baptist	28	147
Nashville	Central Tennessee College (*a*)	Meth. Epis.	1	264
Nashville	Fisk University (*a*)	Congregational	5	268
Nashville	Roger Williams University (*a*)	Baptist	3	130
Tusculum	Greenville and Tusculum College	Presbyterian	10	46
Texas—				
Austin	University of Texas	Non-sectarian	40	40
Fort Worth	Fort Worth University	Meth. Epis.	20	125
Georgetown	Southwestern University	M. E., South	70	138
Italy	Hope Institute	Christian	40	67
Marshall	Wiley University	Meth. Epis.	....	123
Salado	Salado College *	Non-sectarian	11	44
Tehuacana	Trinity University *	Cumb. Pres.	40	112
Waco	Baylor University	Baptist.	175	267
West Virginia—				
Bethany	Bethany College	Christian	32	32
Flemington	West Virginia College	F. W. Baptist	1	12

* Statistics of 1887–88. (*a*) Colored.

APPENDIX C—TABLE II.

THE SEMI-COLLEGES.

Alabama—
Marion, Judson Institute.

Georgia—
Athens, Lucy Cobb Institute.
Covington, Methodist Female College.
Lagrange, Female College.
Macon, Wesleyan Female College.
Marietta, Harwood Seminary.
Rome, Shorter College.

Kentucky—
Bowling Green, Pleasant J. Potter College.
Cedar Bluff, Female College.
Georgetown, Female Seminary.
Hopkinsville, Bethel Female College.
Millersburg, Female College.

Louisiana—
Clinton, Silliman Collegiate Institute.

Maryland—
Frederick, Female Seminary.

Mississippi—
Starkville, Female Institute.
Oxford, Union Female College.

North Carolina—
Greensborough, Female College.

South Carolina—
Anderson, Female College.

Tennessee—
Nashville, College for Young Ladies.
Winchester, Mary Sharp College.

West Virginia—
Wheeling, Female College.

APPENDIX C.—Table III.

The Schools for Superior Instruction.

States.	Number of Schools.	Denominations.									Number of Students in Collegiate Department, including Resident Graduates.	Number Authorized by Law to Confer Degrees.	Income.
		Meth. Episcopal.	Presbyterian.	Baptist.	Christian.	Roman Catholic.	Lutheran.	Cumb. Presb.	Prot. Episcopal.	Non-sectarian.			
Alabama	10	3	2	2	..	..	..	..	..	3	543	6	$43,952
Georgia	13	5	..	4	..	..	..	..	..	4	1,055	9	11,404
Kentucky	19	3	3	3	1	1	..	..	..	8	1,127	15	45,044
Louisiana	3	1	1	..	..	..	..	..	..	1	186	2	5,000
Maryland	5	..	..	..	..	1	1	..	..	3	363	3	16,100
Mississippi	13	3	1	4	..	..	..	1	..	4	904	8	42,822
Missouri	14	1	4	2	2	1	..	..	..	4	588	9	44,400
North Carolina	12	3	3	3	..	..	..	..	1	2	850	5	22,848
South Carolina	4	1	..	1	..	..	..	..	..	2	416	3	8,700
Tennessee	13	4	..	2	..	1	..	1	..	5	860	11	35,380
Texas	4	2	..	..	..	1	..	..	..	1	217	2	14,855
Virginia	14	3	..	3	..	..	2	..	1	5	727	12	42,785
West Virginia	3	..	..	1	..	..	..	..	..	2	78	3	2,000
	127	29	14	25	3	5	3	2	2	44	7,914	88	$335,290

APPENDIX C.—TABLE IV.—*Secondary Instruction for* 1886–87.

States.	Public Schools.					Partly Public Schools.					Private Schools.				
	Number of Schools.	Number of Students.		No. of Female Students preparing for College.		Number of Schools.	Number of Students.		No. of Female Students preparing for College.		Number of Schools.	Number of Students.		No. of Female Students preparing for College.	
		Male.	Female.	Classical.	Scientific.		Male.	Female.	Classical.	Scientific.		Male.	Female.	Classical.	Scientific.
Alabama	..	....	...	..	..	6	436	333	69	10	20	753	880	..	..
Arkansas	2	57	91	..	..	4	220	218	14	15	5	371	412	..	..
District of Columbia	1	302	506	20	7	..	....	....	..	..	10	(20) 458	328	..	6
Florida	2	40	60	..	..	..	....	...	..	..	8	(70) 280	671	..	..
Georgia	4	319	512	160	50	35	1,821	1,715	50	5	39	2,238	2,703	..	..
Kentucky	3	139	613	2	2	5	342	352	13	14	31	(810) 950	1,829	..	..
Louisiana	1	146	344	..	..	1	53	....	..	..	10	652	373	..	..
Maryland	4	46	769	..	..	2	144	....	1	..	23	1,115	588	..	..
Mississippi	2	85	85	..	..	7	222	388	6	..	10	(271) 638	562	..	..
North Carolina	2	80	79	..	..	6	238	248	5	..	54	(127) 2,692	1,859	..	..
South Carolina	1	40	27	2	..	3	163	140	10	..	10	(135) 834	782	7	..
Tennessee	6	339	449	11	20	7	549	439	7	..	25	1,191	1,523	20	50
Texas	6	140	368	1	..	6	462	482	5	..	16	(200) 1,055	1,236	..	..
Virginia	6	400	806	23	..	..	...	....	..	..	22	(225) 978	553	5	6
West Virginia	1	80	95	..	..	..	....	....	..	..	5	(113) 81	162	..	..
	41	2,163	4,806	219	79	82	4,650	4,315	180	44	288	14,286	14,561	32	62

APPENDIX D.

To Article VII.—Woman in Medicine.

LIST OF MEDICAL ESSAYS AND COMMUNICATIONS WRITTEN BY WOMEN PHYSICIANS BETWEEN 1872 AND 1890.

A.

Abdominal section, a case of. Anita Tyng.
Æsthesiometry, with new instrument. Grace Peckham.—*N. Y. Med. Record*, 1885.
Alexander's operation, two cases —*N. Y. Med. Record*, 1888.
Amyl Nitrite in dysmenorrhœa. Mary Putnam Jacobi.—*Record*, 1875.
Anal occlusion, an unusual case. Susan Dimock.—*Record*, 1875.
Anencephalous monster. Mary Putnam.—*Archives* Brown-Sequard, 1872.
Antagonism of medicines. *Ibid.*—*Archives of Medicine*, 1881.
Aphasia, with special loss of nouns. *Ibid.*—*Journal Mental and Nervous Dis.*, 1886.
Apoplexia neonatorum. Sarah McNutt.—*Am. Jour. Obstet.*, 1885.
Apostoli's clinic, report of. Mary Hobart.—*Boston Med. and Surg. Jour.*, 1889.
Apostoli's clinic, report of. Alice T. Beall.—*Am. Jour. Obstet.*, 1889.
Atropine, lecture on. Mary Putnam Jacobi.—*Record*, 1873.

B.

Blood, is it a living fluid? Frances Emily White.—*Record*, 1883.
Botanical notes. Mary K. Curran.—*Proceedings California Academy of Sciences*, 1889.
Basilar kyphosis, its relations to certain cerebral deformities. Sara A. Post.—*Record*, 1889.
Bacteria, their rôle in fermentation and putrefaction. Emma Sutro Merritt. *Trans. Med. Soc. California*, 1890.
Biology, practical study in. Mary Putnam Jacobi, address at Massachusetts State Med. Soc.—*Boston Med. and Surg. Journal*, 1889.
Brain tumor. *Ibid.*—*Wood's Reference Handbook Medical Sciences.*

C.

Catamenial decidua, microscopic examination of. Jeannette Greene.—*Am. Jour. Obstet.*, 1882.
Cerebrum, multiple tumors of, case of in a child. Sarah J. McNutt.—*Trans. Am. Neurological Ass'n.*
Cirrhosis liver with splenic tumor in a child. Mary Putnam Jacobi.—*Archives Pediat.*, 1889.
Cold pack and massage in treatment of anæmia. Mary Putnam Jacobi and Victoria White.—*Archives of Medicine*, 1880.
Colpo-hysterectomy for cancer. Sara A. Post.—*Am. Jour. Med. Sciences*, 1886.

Conjunctivitis, new method of treating. Elizabeth Sargent.—*Trans. Med. Soc. of California*, 1890.
Cutaneous irritation and effect on pulse. Sara A. Post.—*N. Y. Med. Record*, 1883.
Chlorine in diphtheria. Caroline Conkey.—*Record*, 1884.
Camphor, case of fatal poisoning by. Mary J. Finley.—*Record*, 1887.
Cerebro-spinal meningitis, case of. Mary Putnam Jacobi.—*Record*, 1877.
Cocculus indicus, an experimental study. *Ibid.*—*N. Y. Med. Jour.*, 1887.

D.

Deformities, brain and cord. Sara A. Post.—*Keating's Cyclopædia Children's Diseases.*
Dermoid cysts, two cases aspiration followed by inflammation. Mary Putnam Jacobi.—*Am. Jour. Obstet.*, 1883.
Diphtheria and croup, comparison. *Ibid.*—*Record*, 1877.
Digestibility as test of food value. Sara A. Post.—*Diet Gazette*, 1888.
Diseases of children, classification by development. Mary Putnam Jacobi.—*Boston Med. and Surg. Jour.*, 1881.

E.

Endometritis, studies in. Mary Putnam Jacobi.—*Am. Jour. Obstet.*, 1885.
Empyema, a case of, with new device for measuring chest by plaster casts. *Ibid.*—*Med. News*, 1890.
Electricity in obstetrics. Mary W. Moody.—*Trans. Med. Soc. California*, 1888.
Episiotomy, a plea for. Anna Broomall.—*Am. Jour. Obstet.*, 1878.
Epithelioma vulva, following long-standing pruritus, operative cure. Elizabeth Cushier.—*Record*, 1879.
Exercise for women, as illustrated by a study of circus riders. Sara A. Post.—*Record*, 1884.

F.

Fibroid tumor of uterus removed by Thomas's scoop. Mary Putnam Jacobi.—*Am. Jour. Med. Sciences*, 1880.
Fibroid tumor successfully treated by electricity. *Ibid.*—*Am. Jour. Obstet.*, 1888.
Fatty degeneration of new-born children (Buhl's disease). *Ibid.*—*Am. Jour. Obstet.*, 1878.

H.

Hernia of diaphragm, congenital. Anna Broomall.—*Am. Jour. Obstet.*, 1879.
Hot and cold drinks. Sara A. Post.—*Record*, 1888.
Hysterectomies, recent, for cancer. *Ibid.*—*Am. Jour. Obstet.*, 1888.
Hydrocele in a female. Ellen A. Ingersol.—*Am. Jour. Obstet.*, 1882.
Hydro-nephrosis, fatal case in a parturient woman. Helen Bissell.—*Record*, 1887.
Hysteria, some considerations on. Mary Putnam Jacobi. 1888.
Hysteria, post-epileptic. *Ibid.*—*Journal Nervous and Ment. Disease*, 1888.
Hysterical locomotor ataxia. *Ibid.*—*Archives of Medicine*, 1883.
Hysterical fever. *Ibid.*—*Journal Nervous and Mental Diseases*, 1890.
Hygiene as basis of morals. Francis Emily White.—*Popular Science Monthly*, 1889.
Hysterical coma, case. Elizabeth Peck.—*N. Y. Med. Record*, 1888.
Heart, anomalous malformation of. Mary Putnam.—*Record*, 1872.
Hæmatocele, anterior, case. Fanny Berlin.—*Am. Jour. Obstet.*, 1888.

I.

Influence of city life on health and development. Grace Peckham.—*Journal Social Science Assoc.*
Infancy in the city.—*Popular Science Monthly*, 1886.
Inflated ring pessary. Sara A. Post.—*Med. Record*, 1887.
Instruments for electro-massage. *Ibid.*—*Record*, 1880.
Iodoform in diabetes. *Ibid.*—*Archives of Medicine*, 1884
Intra-cranial hæmorrhage. Sarah J. McNutt.—*Quarterly Bulletin Post-Graduate Clinical Society*, August, 1884.
Infantile paralysis, pathogeny of. Mary Putnam Jacobi.—*Am. Jour. Obstet.*, 1874.
Infantile paralysis. *Ibid.*—*Pepper's Archives of Medicine*, Philadelphia, 1885.
Intra-uterine therapeutics. *Ibid.*—*Am. Jour. Obstet.*, 1889.
Inversion uterus, acute spontaneous. Araminta V. Scott.—*Am. Jour. Obstet.*, 1880.
Intestinal obstruction, rare case of. Mary Putnam.—*Record*, 1872.

K.

Kinesio neuroses of childhood. Grace Peckham.—*Journal Mental and Nervous Dis.*, 1884.
Knee-chest position. Mary S. Whelstone.—*Am. Jour. Obst.*, 1886.

L.

Language study, physiological place for, in curriculum education. Mary Putnam Jacobi.—*Journal Psychology*, 1888.
Local reflex symptoms in uterine disease (analysis 2000 cases) Grace Peckham.—*Record*, 1888.
Lupus or esthiomene of the vulva, a case. *Ibid.*—*Am. Jour. Obstet.*, 1887.
Loco weed, its toxicity. Mary G. Day.—*N. Y. Med. Jour.*, 1889.

M.

Mania, acute, after operations. Mary Putnam Jacobi.—*Record*, 1889.
Macerated fœtus as complication of labor. Sara A. Post.—*Record*, 1889.
Mastitis. Julia A. Post.—*Record*, 1885.
Matter and mind. Frances Emily White.—*Popular Science Monthly*, 1887.
Muscle and mind. *Ibid.*—*Ibid.*, 1889.
Morals, evolution of. *Ibid.*—*Open Court*, 1889.
Moner to man. *Ibid.*—*Popular Science Monthly*, 1884.
Mechanical restraint of the insane. Alice Bennett.—*Medico-Legal Journal*, 1883.
Meningocele, rare case of. Sarah J. McNutt.—*Quarterly Bulletin Post-Graduate Clinical Society*, 1887.
Menstrual subinvolution or metritis of non-parturient uterus. Mary Putnam Jacobi.—*Am. Jour. Obstet.*, 1885.
Metritis, chronic, and parturient subinvolution. *Ibid.*—*Ibid.* August, 1885.
Menstruation, new theory of. *Ibid.*—*Ibid.*, June, 1885.
Menstruation, question of rest in. Theory. Boylston prize essay, 1876.—*Ibid.*
Miliary tuberculosis and endometritis, case of. *Ibid.*—*Record*, 1875.
Microcephalus, case of. *Ibid.*—*Record.*
Menstrual bodies, anomalous in oöphoritis. Mary Dixon Jones.—*N. Y. Med. Jour.*, 1890.

Metallo-therapy. Grace Peckham.—*Archives of Medicine*, 1883.
Mirror writing. *Ibid.*—*Record*, 1886.
Mineral water in diseases of children. Isabel Lowry.—*N. Y. Med. Record*, 1888.
Midwifery cases, analysis of 187 in private practice. Marie Zakrzewska.—*Boston Med. and Surg. Journal*, Dec., 1889.
Myoma, uterine, 13 lbs., removal. Mary Dixon Jones.—*Am. Jour. Obstet.*
Myxœdema, case of, with microscopic examination of cord. Elizabeth Cushier.—*Archives Med.*, 1882.

N.

Nephritis, acute diffuse, following intestinal catarrh. Sarah J. McNutt.—*Archives Pediatrics*, 1885.
Nervousness of Americans. Grace Peckham.—*Journal Social Science.*
Negative pulse of veins. Sara A. Post.—*Record*, 1883.

O.

Ovarian complications of endometritis. Mary Putnam Jacobi.—*Am. Jour. Obstet.*, 1886.
Ovaries, hemorrhage into. *Ibid.*—*Record*, 1872.
Ovariotomy for double ovarian tumor with tubercular peritonitis. Mary S. Whelstone.—*Am. Jour. Obstet.*, 1886.
Ovaries and tubes, support in treatment of. Sara A. Post.—*N. Y. Med. Jour.*, 1887.

P.

Paquelin cautery, value of. Sarah A. Dolley.—*Trans. Monroe Co. Med. Soc.*, 1879.
Paralysis in puerperal state, two cases. Imogene Bassett.—*Jour. Nerv. Dis.*, 1880.
Parovarian cyst with twisted pedicle attended by persistent uterine hemorrhage. Elizabeth Cushier.—*N. Y. Med. Jour.*, 1884.
Pemphigus neonatorum, epidemic of. Eleanor Kilham.—*Am. Jour. Obstet.*, 1889.
Pericarditis in a child. Mary Putnam Jacobi.—*Record*, 1873.
Perineo-rectal laceration, extensive, of 32 years' standing, cure by operation. Victoria A. Scott.—*Am. Jour. Obstet.*, 1883.
Pontine tumor, or diffuse brain sclerosis? Mary Putnam Jacobi.—*Jour. Nerv. Dis.*, 1889.
Placenta, waxy degeneration of. Jeannette Greene.—*Am. Jour. Obstet.*, 1880.
Placenta, hyaline degeneration. Sara A. Post.—*Trans. Am. Gyn. Assoc.*, 1888.
Poisoning by sulphate of iron, case. Lucy M. Hall.—*N. Y. Med. Jour.*, 1883.
Prolapsus, complete, and Lefort's operation, three cases. Fanny Berlin.—*Am. Jour. Obstet.*, 1881.
Prophylaxis of insanity. Mary Putnam Jacobi.—*Archives Med.*, 1881.
Pseudo-muscular hypertrophy. *Ibid.*—*Pepper's Archives.*
Pseudo-negative sphygmographic trace. Sara A. Post.—*Archives of Medicine*, 1884.
Persistence in individual consciousness. Frances Emily White.—*Penn Monthly*, 1878.
Protoplasm. *Ibid.*—*Popular Science Monthly*, 1881.

Pulse tracing, showing cardiac inhibition during sudden pain. Mary Putnam Jacobi.—*Archives Medicine*, 1879.
Psychical Society, English; critical digest of proceeding. Grace Peckham. —*Jour. Ment. Dis.*, 1888.
Periodical insanity among women. Alice Bennett.—*Medico-Legal Jour.*, 1883.
Primary Education. Mary Putnam Jacobi.—*Popular Science Monthly*, 1886.

Q.

Quinine, effect of, on cerebral circulation. Mary Putnam Jacobi.—*Archives of Medicine*, 1879.
Quinine, indications for, in pneumonia. *Ibid.*—*N. Y. Med. Jour.*, 1887.

R.

Relations of the sexes. Frances Emily White.—*Westminster Review*, 1879.
Restiform body, section of. Mary Putnam Jacobi.—*Record*, 1873.
Rhythmical myoclonus. Grace Peckham.—*Archives Med.*, 1883.
Rotary spasm, nocturnal, a case. Mary Putnam Jacobi.—*Jour. Ment. Dis.*, 1880.

S.

Salpingitis, etiology and treatment of. Marie Mergler.—*Trans. Illinois State Med. Soc.*, 1888.
Septicæmia and pyæmia. Mary Putnam.—*Record*, 1872.
Sternum, trephining, case of. *Ibid.*—*Am. Jour. Obstet.*, 1881.
Specialism in medicine. *Ibid.*—*Archives of Medicine*, 1882.
Spinal myelitis and meningitis in children. *Ibid.*—*Keating's Cyclopædia*, 1890.
Spastic double hemiplegia of cerebral origin. Sarah J. McNutt.—*Am. Jour. Med. Science*, 1885.
Surgical notes in hospital for women and children. Charlotte Blake Brown.—*Pacific Med. Jour.*, 1889.
Syphilitic brain disease, a case, with autopsy. Lucy M. Hall.—*N. Y. Med. Jour.*, 1884.

T.

Therapeutics children's diseases. Sarah J. McNutt.—*Quarterly Bulletin Post-grad. Clin. Soc.*, 1884.
Typhoid fever, two peculiar cases. Mary Putnam Jacobi.—*Archives Med.*, 1884.

U.

Urethra, rare case of absence of. Sara A. Post.—*Am. Jour. Obstet.*, 1885.
Uterus, rudimentary, two cases of. Susan Dimock.—*Record*, 1874.
Uterine appendages, removal of, five cases. Mary Dixon Jones.—*Am. Jour. Obstet.*, 1888.
do. *Ibid.*—*Record*, 1885–1886.

W.

Woman's place in nature. Francis Emily White.—*Pop. Science Monthly*, 1875.
Women in professions. *Ibid.*—*Penn Monthly.*
Wormian bones, their effect in childbirth. Grace Peckham.—*Record*, 1888.
do. *Ibid.*—*Wood's Handbook Medical Sciences.*

APPENDIX E.

To Article X.—Woman in the State.

THE CIVIL RIGHTS OF WOMEN.

Women born or naturalized in the United States, and subject to the jurisdiction thereof, are citizens of the United States and of the State wherein they reside. The right of suffrage is regulated in each State by its own law, subject to Article XV. of the Amendments to the constitution of the United States. When the right to vote is denied to any of the male inhabitants of a State, being twenty-one years of age and citizens of the United States, except for participation in rebellion or crime, the representation of such State in Congress is proportionately reduced; but there is no penalty attached to the denial of the right of suffrage to women. The constitutions of all the States, except Wyoming, specify that the elective franchise is confined to males. This relates to the right of voting for the federal electors and the State legislature and executive, and statutes permitting women to vote in local elections are deemed to be constitutional. In many States women may vote at the election of school officers or upon any measure relating to schools. In Wyoming and in the Territory of Utah women vote in all respects like men. Woman suffrage also existed in the Territory of Washington, but was rejected at the election for the adoption of the constitution, when Washington became a State. The right of women to vote is by the constitution of South Dakota to be submitted by the legislature to the electors at the first general election after the admission of the State. The constitutions of Colorado, Wisconsin, and North Dakota provide that the legislature may at any time extend the right of suffrage to women, such enactment to take effect, if approved by a majority of the electors, at a general election.

In the absence of special statute or of the necessity for special license, it would seem that there is nothing to prevent an unmarried woman from engaging in any occupation she may choose. In Georgia and Louisiana, however, the statute declares that women cannot hold any civil office or perform any civil functions, unless specially authorized by law. The constitution of California provides that no person shall on account of sex be disqualified from entering upon or pursuing any lawful business, vocation, or profession; and in Illinois there is a law that no person shall be debarred or precluded from any occupation, employment, or profession (except military) on account of sex. But this does not extend or modify the right of women to hold office, nor does it enable or require them to serve on juries or to labor in the streets. Military, jury, police, patrol, and road duties are generally specifically confined to males. The constitution of Missouri specifies that the Governor and members of the legislature must be male, and in other States such a restriction follows from the requirement that office-holders shall be chosen from among electors. Certain offices, such as that of recorder of deeds, notary public, etc., may in many States be held by women, and in many States women may hold any office under the school law. In Massachusetts, the office of overseer of the poor may be held by a woman.

At common law, a married woman, however, had in general no capacity to contract, and hence could not engage in business or follow an independent vocation ; but the common law disabilities, imposed upon married women, have been very generally removed by statutes. In Louisiana and North Carolina, however, the contracts of a married woman are declared to be generally void, and so says a statute of Georgia, which seems, however, to be overruled by constitutional provision, as judicially construed. In Alabama and New Mexico a married woman may contract, provided she have her husband's assent, and in certain cases this is allowed in Louisiana. In Illinois a wife may make all kinds of contracts, except that she may not enter into a partnership without her husband's consent, and in South Carolina it is held that the law does not empower a married woman to enter into a partnership. But in most of the States, a married woman may as a general rule make all kinds of contracts as if she were unmarried. In Mississippi, Oregon, and Washington, all the civil disabilities peculiar to married women, except as to voting and holding office, have been expressly swept away. In about a dozen States there is a certain process, such as recording a certificate, etc., by which a married woman can become a " sole trader," or carry on business in her own name ; but in as many other States she can do this without any formalities. In all the States, the real property of a woman, and in most of the States her personal property, upon her marriage, remain her separate property ; and so generally remains all property acquired by the wife after marriage ; and over this separate property a married woman has now, in nearly all the States, more or less complete control. Louisiana, however, is peculiarly conservative in this respect, and in Texas, Florida, and Idaho, the husband has the management and control of all the wife's separate property. The property claimed by married women must, by the laws of several States, be specially registered. In many States a married woman can convey her own real estate, without her husband joining in the conveyance ; but in a narrow majority of the States the husband must, as a rule, join with the wife to make a valid transfer. In most of the States a married woman may prosecute or defend suits concerning her own property, as if unmarried ; and in about half of the States she may in all cases sue and be sued without joining the husband. As a prevailing rule, the husband is not liable for the debts of the wife, except those incurred for necessaries for herself or the family, nor is he now liable for her torts ; neither is the wife's property liable for the debts of the husband, but her own debts may be enforced against her own property. In many States contracts between husband and wife are now valid, though in some States they are still void at law.

Married women have, as a rule, the same right to dispose of their property by last will and testament as they have to convey it during their life-time ; but in some States, as Maryland, their right so to do is restricted in certain respects. In many States a wife cannot by her will deprive her husband of a certain share of her property. The laws of descent and of intestate succession vary diversely in the several States. In Tennessee it is expressly provided that absolute equality shall be observed in the division of estates of deceased persons dying intestate, and no difference of sex is known in the laws of succession in North Carolina and Louisiana. In many States the distributive shares of husband and widow, and their respective rights of curtesy and dower, are similar ; but in other States there are complicated differences ; in New York, for instance, the husband being favored with respect to personal property, and the wife being better protected with regard to real estate. In Louisiana women are declared incapable of being witnesses to wills.

The laws of California, the Dakotas, Georgia, New Mexico, Ohio, and Idaho expressly enact that the husband is the head of the family, and that the wife is subject to him. The constitution of Kansas, however, declares that the legislature shall provide for women equal rights with the husband in the possession of their children. Such equality is also provided by the laws of Washington. In Maine, California, the Dakotas, and Georgia, the father is declared to have the right to the custody of his minor child. In Louisiana, in case of difference between the parents, the authority of the father prevails. The common law authority of the husband and father is, with modifications, upheld in most of the States, at least until abandonment, separation, or divorce.

The duty of the husband at common law to support the wife finds further statutory recognition in acts making the husband's failure to support the wife cause for absolute or limited divorce. Alimony is usually granted to the wife on a divorce for the husband's fault. In North Carolina, Kentucky, and Texas, divorce is granted for adultery only when committed by the wife, unless the husband abandon the wife and live in adultery with another woman.

While women, and particularly married women, still in the world of activity, often labor under disabilities imposed upon them by law for their protection and benefit—"so great a favorite is the female sex of the laws of England"—it must be admitted that in the course of a century woman has made a great advance in the direction of personal freedom. When Blackstone wrote, the husband became entitled by marriage to all the personal property of the wife, and to the rents and profits of her lands, and the very being or legal existence of the woman was suspended during marriage, or at least was incorporated and consolidated into that of the husband, under whose wing, protection, and *cover* she performed everything. The emancipation of married women has been gradually, silently, successfully accomplished.—ED.

APPENDIX F.—Bibliography.

The following works will be found useful by those who wish to pursue further the subjects treated in the foregoing chapters.

ADAMS, OSCAR FAY
Handbook of American Authors. Boston, 1884.

BOONE, RICHARD G.
Education in the United States. New York, 1889.

BRACKETT, ANNA C. AND OTHERS
Education of American Girls. New York, 1886.

CAMPBELL, HELEN
Prisoners of Poverty. Boston, 1887.
Anne Bradstreet. Boston, 1891.

CLARKE, E. H.
Sex in Education. Boston, 1873.

DALL, CAROLINE H.
Life of Dr. Marie Zakrzewska; a Practical Illustration of Woman's Right to Labor. Boston.

DODGE, COLONEL RICHARD IRVING
Our Wild Indians. Hartford, 1882.

ELLET, E. F.
Women of the American Revolution. Philadelphia, 1853.

ENGLES, FREDERICK
Condition of the Working Classes in England in 1844. Translated by Florence Kelly Wischnewetsky. New York, 1887.

GREELEY, HORACE
Recollections of a Busy Life. New York, 1867.

GRISWOLD, R. W.
Female Poets of America. New York, 1849.

D'HERICOURT, MME.
La Femme Affranchie. Paris.

HIGGINSON, THOMAS WENTWORTH
Common Sense about Women. Boston, 1882.
Women and Men. New York, 1887.

HOWE, JULIA WARD AND OTHERS
Sex and Education. Boston, 1874.

JACKSON, HELEN HUNT ("H. H.")
A Century of Dishonor. New York, 1881.

JACKSON, SHELDON, D.D.
Alaska. New York, 1880.

LARCOM, LUCY
The Story of a New England Girlhood. Boston, 1889.

LEAKE, GENERAL G. B.
Protection of Law for Indians.

LIVERMORE, MARY A.
My Story of the War. Hartford, 1888.

LOWELL OFFERING

MANYPENNY, COLONEL GEORGE
Our Indian Wards. Cincinnati, 1880.

MARTINEAU, HARRIET
Society in America. New York, 1837.

MILL, JOHN STUART
Subjection of Women. New York, 1870.

OWEN, G. W.
The Indian Question.

PANCOAST, HENRY S.
The Indian before the Law.

PENNY, VIRGINIA
Think and Act: Men and Women: Work and Wages. Philadelphia, 1868.

REPORT OF INTERNATIONAL COUNCIL OF WOMEN HELD IN WASHINGTON, D. C., 1888. Washington, 1888.

RIGGS, REV. STEPHEN R., D.D.
Mary and I. Chicago, 1880.

ROBINSON, H. H.
Massachusetts in Woman Suffrage Movement. Boston, 1881.

SEDGWICK, C. M.
Letters from Abroad to Kindred at Home. New York, 1841.

SIMS, MARION
Story of My Life. New York, 1884.

STANTON, THEODORE
The Woman Question in Europe. New York, 1884.

STEDMAN, E. C.
Poets of America. Boston, 1885.

STEDMAN, E. C. AND HUTCHINSON, E. M.
Library of American Literature. New York, 1887–1890.

TIFFANY, REV.
Life of Dorothea Dix. Boston, 1889.

WILLARD, FRANCES E.
Autobiography.

WOLLSTONECRAFT
The Rights of Women. Boston, 1890.

INDEX.

American Women: Images and Realities

An Arno Press Collection

[Adams, Charles F., editor]. **Correspondence between John Adams and Mercy Warren Relating to Her "History of the American Revolution," July-August, 1807.** With a new appendix of specimen pages from the **"History."** 1878.

[Arling], Emanie Sachs. **"The Terrible Siren": Victoria Woodhull, (1838-1927).** 1928.

Beard, Mary Ritter. **Woman's Work in Municipalities.** 1915.

Blanc, Madame [Marie Therese de Solms]. **The Condition of Woman in the United States.** 1895.

Bradford, Gamaliel. **Wives.** 1925.

Branagan, Thomas. **The Excellency of the Female Character Vindicated.** 1808.

Breckinridge, Sophonisba P. **Women in the Twentieth Century.** 1933.

Campbell, Helen. **Women Wage-Earners.** 1893.

Coolidge, Mary Roberts. **Why Women Are So.** 1912.

Dall, Caroline H. **The College, the Market, and the Court.** 1867.

[D'Arusmont], Frances Wright. **Life, Letters and Lectures: 1834, 1844.** 1972.

Davis, Almond H. **The Female Preacher, or Memoir of Salome Lincoln.** 1843.

Ellington, George. **The Women of New York.** 1869.

Farnham, Eliza W[oodson]. **Life in Prairie Land.** 1846.

Gage, Matilda Joslyn. **Woman, Church and State.** [1900].

Gilman, Charlotte Perkins. **The Living of Charlotte Perkins Gilman.** 1935.

Groves, Ernest R. **The American Woman.** 1944.

Hale, [Sarah J .] **Manners; or, Happy Homes and Good Society All the Year Round.** 1868.

Higginson, Thomas Wentworth. **Women and the Alphabet.** 1900.

Howe, Julia Ward, editor. **Sex and Education.** 1874.

La Follette, Suzanne. **Concerning Women.** 1926.

Leslie, Eliza . **Miss Leslie's Behaviour Book: A Guide and Manual for Ladies.** 1859.

Livermore, Mary A. **My Story of the War.** 1889.

Logan, Mrs. John A. (Mary S.) **The Part Taken By Women in American History.** 1912.

McGuire, Judith W. (A Lady of Virginia). **Diary of a Southern Refugee, During the War.** 1867.

Mann, Herman . **The Female Review: Life of Deborah Sampson.** 1866.

Meyer, Annie Nathan, editor. **Woman's Work in America.** 1891.

Myerson, Abraham. **The Nervous Housewife.** 1927.

Parsons, Elsie Clews. **The Old-Fashioned Woman.** 1913.

Porter, Sarah Harvey. **The Life and Times of Anne Royall.** 1909.

Pruette, Lorine. **Women and Leisure: A Study of Social Waste.** 1924.

Salmon, Lucy Maynard. **Domestic Service.** 1897.

Sanger, William W. **The History of Prostitution.** 1859.

Smith, Julia E. **Abby Smith and Her Cows.** 1877.

Spencer, Anna Garlin. **Woman's Share in Social Culture.** 1913.

Sprague, William Forrest. **Women and the West.** 1940.

Stanton, Elizabeth Cady. **The Woman's Bible** Parts I and II. 1895/1898.

Stewart, Mrs. Eliza Daniel . **Memories of the Crusade.** 1889.

Todd, John. **Woman's Rights.** 1867. [Dodge, Mary A .] (Gail Hamilton, pseud.) **Woman's Wrongs.** 1868.

Van Rensselaer, Mrs. John King. **The Goede Vrouw of Mana-ha-ta.** 1898.

Velazquez, Loreta Janeta. **The Woman in Battle.** 1876.

Vietor, Agnes C., editor. **A Woman's Quest: The Life of Marie E. Zakrzewska, M.D.** 1924.

Woodbury , Helen L. Sumner. **Equal Suffrage.** 1909.

Young, Ann Eliza. **Wife No. 19.** 1875.